THE PUNIC WARS

THE PUNIC WARS

Brian Caven

Senior Lecturer in Classics and Ancient History,
Birkbeck College, University of London

BOOK CLUB ASSOCIATES
LONDON

This edition published 1980 by
Book Club Associates
by arrangement with Weidenfeld and Nicolson

© 1980 by Brian Caven

George Weidenfeld and Nicolson Ltd
91 Clapham High Street   London SW4

Printed in Great Britain by
Butler & Tanner Ltd, Frome and London

CONTENTS

CONTENTS

PLATES

The Dioscuri (Castor and Pollux) on a silver *denarius* (*reproduced by courtesy of the Trustees of the British Museum*)

The ruins of Euryalus, Syracuse (*by courtesy of ENIT, Rome*)

Scipio Africanus on a New Carthage coin (*reproduced by courtesy of the Trustees of the British Museum*)

Hasdrubal Barca on a coin (*reproduced by courtesy of the Trustees of the British Museum*)

Contour model of the site of the battle of Baecula (*Thames and Hudson Ltd*)

Site of the battle of Metaurus

Head of Nike (Victory) on a Bruttian coin (*reproduced by courtesy of the Trustees of the British Museum*)

Poseidon (Neptune) on a Bruttian coin (*reproduced by courtesy of the Trustees of the British Museum*)

King Masinissa on a Numidian coin (*reproduced by courtesy of the Trustees of the British Museum*)

King Syphax on a Numidian coin (*reproduced by courtesy of the Trustees of the British Museum*)

Numidian horseman on a coin (*reproduced by courtesy of the Trustees of the British Museum*)

Carthage, looking towards the harbour (*courtesy of the Kelsey Museum of Archaeology, University of Michigan*)

Carthage, from the Byrsa (*courtesy of the Kelsey Museum of Archaeology, University of Michigan*)

Head of Tanit on a late Carthaginian coin (*reproduced by courtesy of the Trustees of the British Museum*)

Horse on a late Carthaginian coin (*reproduced by courtesy of the Trustees of the British Museum*)

MAPS AND BATTLE PLANS

FOREWORD

This book is intended to offer to the general reader who has a taste for history a detailed narrative of the conflict between Rome and Carthage that opened in the summer of 264 BC and closed with the destruction of the latter city, one hundred and eighteen years later. The narrative, in annalistic form, confines itself to military matters, and the reader who wishes to know more about the political and social history of the times must turn to the general histories of Rome, such as the *Cambridge Ancient History*, the Methuen *History of the Roman World*, the *History of the Roman World* by Cary and Scullard and the *History of Rome* by Michael Grant, and to such special studies as those by Toynbee, Brunt and Scullard listed in the Select Bibliography.

Ancient history is a field in which almost every other statement and interpretation is debatable and in which conjecture plays a larger rôle than one could wish. The writer of a work intended primarily for the general reader has to choose between encumbering his pages with a mass of notes (the seriousness of a scholar's work is regularly judged by the volume of his footnotes) and appendices, in which he argues and defends his opinions; or presenting his reader with his views without comment or explanation.

By doing the latter he not only lays himself open to the charge of dogmatizing but also offends against the unwritten rule, that indebtedness to other writers should always be acknowledged. Nonetheless I have decided to dispense entirely with notes, and in their place to make a species of General Confession. The narrative is based primarily on the ancient authorities: Polybius, Nepos, Diodorus Siculus, Livy, Plutarch, Appian and Zonaras. Modern historians, whose opinions I have adopted – or rejected – without individual acknowledgement are listed in a Select Bibliography, and my indebtedness to them will be at once apparent to any student of ancient history. In particular, a person who uses Polybius as a source is dependent upon Walbank, one who writes about Scipio Africanus must follow Scullard, and anyone who touches on naval matters must study Thiel. At the personal level I wish to thank Professor R. Browning for his encouragement, Professor Walbank and Professor Scullard for giving me helpful answers to certain specific questions, Dr Carson and Dr Price of the British Museum for their great helpfulness in the selection of coins to illustrate the book and colleagues and friends at Birkbeck College and in the Map Library of University College, London, for advice and assistance.

In addition to the Select Bibliography, a very brief account of the Roman constitution is given in an appendix, for the benefit of those who are not completely familiar with the matter, and a short glossary of certain terms which might be unfamiliar to the general reader and which it would be cumbersome to explain in the body of the text.

INTRODUCTION

Carthage and her empire.

Although the oldest of the great powers of the western Mediterranean, Carthage was the New Town (Kart Hadasht); younger than her near neighbour Utica, perhaps younger than Gades on the southern coast of Spain. She was founded (according to tradition) in 814 BC by Dido, the daughter of a King of Tyre, on the seaward end of a peninsula (the Phoenicians had a predilection for peninsula and island sites), at the point of division of the eastern and western basins, and she formed one link in a chain of Phoenician settlements on the ancient trade-route between Asia Minor and the kingdom of Tartessus (Tarshish) in Spain from which silver came, 'the El Dorado of the ancient world' (F. Decret). Her people like the Phoenicians generally were traders, and militarily unaggressive. Into the western basin, from the middle of the eighth century, came Greeks hungry for land and trade. Unaggressiveness was not one of their salient national characteristics and the Phoenician communities of Spain, western Sicily and north Africa (the latter also vulnerable to attack from the warlike nomads of the interior) began to see their only hope of survival in unity under the leadership of Carthage, already the strongest city amongst them.

Thus arose the Carthaginian empire, an armed trading-association whose purpose was to create and preserve a monopoly of the trade of Spain and western north Africa. Some of its members, like Utica and Gades, were sovereign allies of Carthage, the rest were subordinate allies, autonomous but paying tribute and harbour dues to their overlord. By the end of the sixth century BC the Greek 'invasion' had been checked and thrown back and only Massilia and a few of her colonies survived west of Corsica and Sardinia. The western basin had become a *mare clausum*, whose trade was strictly regulated by Carthage in her treaties with 'friendly' powers, such as the Etruscan cities and Rome.

In the fifth century the rulers of Carthage, having established a footing on the fertile island of Sardinia and failed disastrously in an attempt to subjugate the Greeks of Sicily, turned their attention to the conquest of their own hinterland (hitherto they had been content to pay a rent to the native Libyans for the site of their City) and under leaders of the

Magonid dynasty Carthage became a continental power, acquiring a territory of some nine and a half thousand square miles of what is today northern and central Tunisia; and the aristocracy, from being a purely commercial class, joined the ranks of the world's landed proprietors. However the fifth century was also a century of great colonial and commercial expansion, which made Carthage the overseer and chief beneficiary of a trading connection that stretched from the frontiers of Cyrenaica to beyond the Pillars of Heracles and from the Niger and Sierra Leone to Spain and Brittany.

Unfortunately for the peace of the western Mediterranean, the Sicilian Greeks found it impossible to live in harmony either with each other or with their 'barbarian' neighbours. Towards the end of the fifth century the Carthaginians were drawn into their quarrels and by the middle of the fourth century they had come to be regarded as a threat to Greek liberty and the Greeks were talking of the desirability of expelling them from the island. Greek resistance centred on the great city of Syracuse and in the closing decades of the century the tyrant Agathocles invaded Africa and threatened Carthage herself. On his death in 289 BC the Carthaginians, who had by now come to regard Syracuse as a threat to *their* interests, attempted to gain control of the city. The Syracusans, in political disarray (their normal condition), called on King Pyrrhus of Epirus to rescue Hellenism from the barbarians. Pyrrhus, who was campaigning at the time in southern Italy against the Romans on behalf of the Greek city of Taras, brought a professional army and war elephants to Sicily; but he failed to complete the undertaking – as he failed to complete every undertaking of his ambitious, restless career – and when he departed the Carthaginians quickly recovered their lost ground and pushed the frontier of their province up to the borders of the kingdom of Syracuse at the eastern end of the island.

The constitution of Carthage at the end of the fourth century BC bore a superficial resemblance to that of Rome. Originally ruled by kings, Carthage evolved, by way of a form of elective kingship, an oligarchic republican régime based on an annually elective dual magistracy, that of the *shofets*, the judges (in Latin, *suffetes*); a Grand Council with an inner permanent committee of thirty elders (usually referred to as the *Gerousia*); a high court of 104 judges selected for life by a college of pentarchs; and a popular Assembly comprising all the citizens. All offices were reserved to the aristocracy, membership of which was determined by wealth so that it was recruited from the ranks of successful merchants. By the third century this aristocracy was landowning as well as mercantile and owned the most fertile areas around the City which they farmed intensively for profit. The rulers of Carthage expected to make a handsome profit out of office-holding too, and pluralism was normal and corruption widespread. Nevertheless they were careful to ensure that a good part of the immense wealth of the City, derived from the public revenues and from trade, found its way into the purses of the ordinary people, so that all acquiesced in a régime from which everyone benefited. Overpopulation and consequent hardship (the bane of ancient societies) were obviated by a policy of despatching colonists to reinforce existing colonies and dependencies – a policy which served at the same time to strengthen the bonds of empire. Since any political impasse arising between the suffetes and the Council had to be resolved by the submission of the question to the popular Assembly whose decisions on all matters were sovereign, the popular element of the constitution gradually gained strength; and when the Assembly acquired the power of electing the suffetes and the generals electoral corruption became open and flagrant.

The Carthaginian empire was held together by common interests and alliances and the element of coercion was supplied by the Carthaginian navy, which also and more importantly ensured that outsiders did not intrude into the closed trading area which Carthage shared with her Libyphoenician allies and her colonies. The free population of Carthage consisted not of peasant farmers but of tradesmen and seamen (including fishermen), who manufactured, imported and exported the goods which the city bartered with the inhabitants of 'underdeveloped areas' in return for raw materials, base and precious metals and luxury goods. As early as the end of the sixth century BC the rulers of Carthage had come to realize that their citizen population was too small, and too valuable economically, to supply the defence requirements of the empire; and in the fifth century, when they began to undertake large-scale military operations in Sicily and in Africa, they had recourse to mercenaries, and the citizen militia (a feature of the city state elsewhere in the Mediterranean) disappeared, apart from the Sacred Corps of 2,500 knights. The suffetes ceased to command armies and a separate military command was instituted. Generals and admirals were appointed, and later elected by the Assembly, for specific wars or tasks, normally being retained in command for as long as they continued to enjoy the confidence of the government.

Their own experience and that of their Greek (and particularly their Sicilian) neighbours had shown that militarism endangers an oligarchy, as it is likely to give rise to tyranny if reliance is placed on mercenaries, and to democracy if the citizens are armed. In 308, at the height of the struggle with Agathocles, a general named Bomilcar had tried to make himself tyrant by a military coup. The ruling class therefore eschewed militarism – which was likely, anyway, to interfere with commerce – and when they went to war it was usually for an essentially defensive purpose, which did not of course exclude the pre-emptive war. They regarded the successful generals with almost as little favour as the unsuccessful. Those who failed were regularly crucified; less, it is to be supposed, *pour encourager* than *pour décourager les autres*, and to assert the superiority of the civil over the military power. The court of 104 judges had as part of its responsibility for internal security the task of ensuring that generals did not fall short of the City's expectations and as, from the end of the fifth century, involvement in war became the normal instead of the exceptional condition of the City, so this court acquired a predominant position in the state. In the third century BC, the Carthaginians began to make extensive use of Numidian cavalry, provided by allied chieftains, and after Pyrrhus had shown them the war elephant they replaced the traditional Tyrian war chariot with this new weapon, supplied by their Numidian allies from the forests of the interior.

The Carthaginians and the Romans were by no means strangers to each other when they came into conflict in 264 BC. They had enjoyed diplomatic relations at least as early as the first years of the Republic and probably before that, in the time of the kings at Rome, when she was already the *hegemon* of a section of the Latins. The earliest known treaties, those of 509 and 348, had been negotiated by Carthage solely for her own advantage, in order to secure recognition of her commercial monopoly of the western basin. They are evidence not only for Carthage's all-absorbing interest in trade but also for Rome's complete indifference to overseas commerce. The third treaty was negotiated at a time when, with the advance of Rome's hegemony into southern Italy, a delimitation of spheres of interest (a Hellenistic concept, better understood at Carthage than at Rome) became a matter of importance, although not yet one of urgency. When Pyrrhus was invited by the Syracusans to 'liberate' Sicily from the Carthaginians Carthage negotiated an alliance with Rome whose purpose was rather to ensure that neither party assisted Pyrrhus against the other than to cement an active war agreement, each side being perfectly content to see Pyrrhus thoroughly involved in hostilities with the other. However that may be, the relationship between Rome and Carthage in 264 was, if only in the stock language of diplomacy, a friendly one. A Punic fleet that appeared off Taras while the Romans were besieging the city after the retirement of Pyrrhus probably represented nothing more sinister than a reconnaissance – if not actually an offer of assistance to the Romans – rather than the hostile act which later Roman propaganda made of it.

CHAPTER I

280-263 BC

The Mamertine incident and the outbreak of war.

The Punic Wars are three in number: the First, the Second and the Third, so named by Cicero. Yet although the First is separated from the Second by twenty-three years and the Third from the Second by fifty-two years, they should still be thought of as a single struggle; a contest in three rounds in which the two greatest city states of the Hellenistic world fought each other, first for the suzerainty of Sicily, then for the hegemony of the western Mediterranean, and lastly – with the result a foregone conclusion – for the survival or extinction of the weaker contestant. They mark one of the turning-points of western history. Not only are they the last great wars between city states in antiquity but the outcome of the First and Second Wars was that Rome was set firmly upon the road that led her to the overlordship of the *oecumene*, the civilized world. It is fortunate for us that their significance had already been appreciated by Polybius of Megalopolis; a man of integrity and ability who was in a position to discuss the Second War with some of those who had played leading parts in it and who was an eye-witness of the final catastrophe. Polybius saw himself as a historian in the tradition of Thucydides (although he was not of his stature), playing an active rôle in the affairs of Greece before beginning the synoptic history that he undertook in order to explain to educated Greeks how and why Rome, in the space of only fifty-three years, succeeded in acquiring the world empire that (as he saw it) Fate had willed her to enjoy.

The connected narrative of Polybius has survived only down to the year of Cannae, after which time it appears only in fragments or incorporated in the writings of later historians such as Appian (second century AD), our principal authority for the Third War. For the First War, however, we possess it virtually complete and this is the more fortunate because our other principal sources, Livy and Diodorus Siculus, here fail us to a large extent. The fragments of Diodorus (which date from the second half of the first century BC) preserve a good pro-Carthaginian tradition, which is also drawn on extensively by Polybius himself; and this is often useful as a corrective of Polybius in his more pro-Roman moods. Livy's history, our main source of information about the Second

War, which owes a great deal both to Polybius and to Polybius' sources as well as to the native Roman tradition, has come down to us only in the form of an epitome for the periods covering the First and Third Wars.

The attempt to understand the causes as well as the course of the First Punic War is not made easier by the fact that Polybius himself chose to regard it merely in the light of a curtain-raiser, as it were, to his drama of the imperial progress of Rome. As a result his account of the causes of the war, as well as of the events leading up to the actual outbreak of hostilities, is so condensed and at the same time so ill-balanced that a certain measure of uncertainty must always surround them.

Livy's power of judgement has often been criticized but even Polybius' warmest admirers are compelled to admit that the latter does not appear to have resolved a confusion that existed in his mind between a deterministic view of history according to which Fate (Tyche) ordered world history towards one end, namely the achievement of Rome's domination of the *oecumene*, and a rationalistic approach which explained Rome's intervention in Sicilian affairs – her first overseas military adventure – in terms of a calculated reaction by her government to circumstances and events. According to this explanation, the Romans, having embarked deliberately upon a career of aggrandizement after the liberation of their city from the Celts in 386 BC, had by the third century come to regard Italy as belonging to them by right. Following the defeat in 275 of King Pyrrhus, they acquired the hegemony of the south Italian Greeks (Magna Graecia), with all its responsibilities; and in 264 they intervened in the quarrels of the Sicilian powers out of fear that Carthage, after overthrowing the kingdom of Syracuse and so becoming mistress of the whole of Sicily, would constitute a threat to the security of southern Italy and hence of Rome herself.

Modern historians in general, taking their cue from Polybius, look for the cause of the First Punic War in a policy of 'defensive imperialism' on the part of Rome. Rome (they say) forestalled a Carthaginian takeover of eastern Sicily (something that had come very close to realization on more than one occasion, the most recent being in 280) by means of diplomacy backed by military force, in order to make sure of at least the northeast corner of the island which constitutes the most convenient bridgehead for an invasion of Italy from Sicily. This explanation requires us to assume, first, that in 265/4 BC Carthage was in the same aggressive mood that she had been in some sixteen years earlier; secondly, that the Roman Senate, influenced by certain powerful families who were particularly interested in southern Italy, recognized that a serious threat was developing to the security of Rome's allies there and was ready to take measures to counter it; and thirdly that Rome's actions in 265/4 were undertaken primarily with Carthage in mind.

This interpretation of Rome's foreign policy would appear to be borne out by the subsequent course of events, but it need not necessarily be the true one. It is indisputable that Carthage, ever since the early fifth century, had periodically launched an offensive designed to gain for her the suzerainty of the whole of Sicily. What is less evident is that she was planning to do so in 265/4. Essentially unaggressive militarily, the Carthaginians normally took the offensive only in response to aggressiveness on the part of their neighbours and at this time their relations with the kingdom of Syracuse, their ancient rival for the control of the island, appear to have been formally friendly if not actually cordial. As regards the Romans, there must of course have been some senators who now felt that the finest military machine in Italy might profitably be employed in reaping glory for its leaders and booty for all in a war of conquest in Sicily. But there is nothing except Polybius' opinion to support the view either that the Romans felt themselves threatened by Carthage, or that either the Senate as a whole or the people – for Polybius' narrative seems to be designed to shift the burden of war guilt from the former onto the latter – was in an imperialistic frame of mind and aimed at the acquisition of Sicily. Finally, even the confusing testimony of Polybius himself suggests that Rome's foreign policy in 265/4 was directed primarily against Syracuse and not the Carthaginians.

If the series of incidents that led up to the outbreak of hostilities and beyond is examined without reference to the subsequent unfolding of events, what appears to emerge is a classic example of an incident that got out of hand – of what in today's jargon is usually described as escalation. It has been said that almost every war is avoidable, and it is easy to believe that if a little trouble had been taken the First Punic War could have been prevented from occurring as and when it did. This is not to deny that in the long run Rome would almost certainly have come into conflict with Carthage and would have had to fight her for possession of Sicily, always provided that her career was not checked elsewhere in the meantime. However, such a war would probably have been entered into deliberately and in the furtherance of a calculated policy; for the attitude of ancient societies to war was in general frankly Clausewitzian, and they undertook wars in order to gain – or to deny to others – specific advantages. Yet it looks very much as if in 265/4 the Romans neither appreciated that they were involving themselves in a situation out of which a major war might develop nor realized that they were going to come into collision with Carthage; and when in fact the two great powers did become embroiled with one another a little well-timed diplomacy might yet have limited the conflict to the north-east corner of Sicily.

If the war of 264–41 began as an 'incident' it is all the more to be regretted that the accounts that we have of the events that led up to the outbreak of hostilities should be either so fragmentary or so condensed as to be seriously misleading. Because contemporary and near-contemporary writers were anxious to place the responsibility for beginning a war that took such an appalling toll of life, particularly on the Roman side, upon the shoulders of one party or the other, they made their selections of these events with this purpose in mind; and in the case of Q. Fabius Pictor, senator during the Hannibalic War, whose history probably forms the basis at this point of Polybius' narrative, the matter is further complicated by his manifest desire to exculpate the Roman Senate from all blame, at the expense of the popular Assembly.

Polybius prided himself on his impartiality, and he tried to appear objective in his apportionment of war guilt between Rome and Carthage. Unfortunately, however, he decided to allot less than three-quarters of one book, out of a total of forty, to the war as a whole, and consequently treated the preliminaries with a parsimony of detail and a compression that produce a narrative that is partly incomprehensible and largely misleading. On the other hand, the narrative of Diodorus, which probably derives from Philinus of Acragas (who is believed to have written a contemporary monograph on the First Punic War from the Carthaginian standpoint), breaks off at precisely the point at which it is most needed in order to supplement and correct the work of Polybius. Discouraging as this may appear, it is nonetheless possible to arrive at a coherent and reasonably plausible picture of the train of events that produced the catastrophe; and while it is quite impossible to establish their exact chronology, their order, a much more important matter, can be deduced with some degree of probability.

If war had not resulted the affair would probably be known as the Mamertine incident. The trouble all began in the city of Messana, which stood – and under its later name, Messina, still stands, rebuilt after being devastated by an earthquake in 1908 – on the western shore of the straits to which it has given its name. Its position and its good harbour make it important strategically, especially if it is held in conjunction with Rhegium (today, Reggio) on the Italian side. These two cities constitute the ferry terminals – or, if one is thinking militarily, the bridgeheads – between Sicily and Italy.

Even by 265 Messana had had a stormy history. Founded under the name of Zancle in the second half of the eighth century by pirates from Cumae (the oldest city of Magna Graecia), it was seized in the early fifth century by a tyrant of Rhegium of Messenian descent who partly repeopled it with his compatriots and renamed it (in the Dorian dialect) Messana. Destroyed and rebuilt in the early fourth century in the course of the wars between the Syracusans and the Carthaginians, it was captured by Agathocles, the lord of Syracuse, towards the end of the century and again incorporated in the Syracusan kingdom.

To the gates of this small city, one fateful day in the early eighties of the third century BC, came a small army of desperados. They were unemployed mercenary soldiers hailing originally from Campania; Oscan (Italic) speakers of Samnite stock, hard, ruthless professional fighting men. They worshipped Mamers, the god of battles whom an even harder people, some distance to the north, venerated under the name of Mavors or Mars. Until very recently they had been in the pay of Agathocles, who had settled them at Syracuse. After his death in 289, being shut out of the city they gave their support to a pretender to his throne who also had the assistance of the Carthaginians, and the townspeople were finally compelled to readmit them, without, however, giving them citizen rights. It soon became apparent that civil life in harmony with their neighbours was little to their taste and they were prevailed upon to sell up their possessions and depart from Syracuse and from Sicily.

So this jovial band marched north to Messana, a town on whose amenities they had already cast covetous eyes. Welcomed as friends and allies by the people, they were taken by the better off into their homes. This trust and hospitality they repaid by falling upon their hosts in the dead of night, cutting the throats of those who did not escape into exile and seizing the town. They divided among themselves the wives and properties of their victims and became the new citizens of Messana, styling themselves Mamertines (Martians) on the coinage that their Greek moneyers struck for them.

About this time Syracuse fell under the rule of a new tyrant, Hicetas, who became involved in a mutually destructive war with Phintias, the master of Acragas and the ally of the Carthaginians, who heavily defeated Hicetas when he became embroiled with them. As a result, the Mamertines, who had lost none of their warlike propensities when they became burghers, were able to take advantage of the confused state of Sicily, whose cities were divided between contending Greek tyrannies and the watchful power of Carthage. They plundered the cities of Camarina and Gela (Gela was later demolished by Phintias and its inhabitants transplanted to the new foundation which bore his name) and they consolidated their position in the north-eastern part of the island.

On the death of Hicetas, Syracuse again became the prey of rival claimants to the tyranny and the Carthaginians, who had been provoked by Hicetas, saw once more an opportunity to gain control of the principal Greek city and so of the whole of Sicily, and laid siege to Syracuse. Finally the Syracusans, aroused at last to the danger that threatened the liberty of them all, called upon King Pyrrhus, who was then (280 BC) campaigning

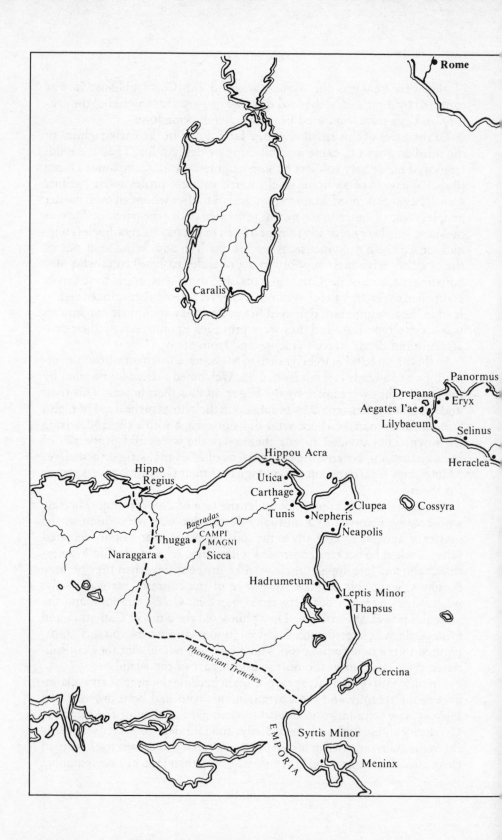

Rome

Caralis

Panormus

Drepana · Eryx
Aegates I'ae
Lilybaeum
Selinus

Heraclea

Hippou Acra

Hippo
Regius
Utica
Carthage
Tunis · Nepheris
Clupea
Cossyra

Bagradas
CAMPI
MAGNI
Thugga ·
Naraggara ·
Sicca

Neapolis

Hadrumetum

Leptis Minor
Thapsus

Phoenician Trenches

Cercina

EMPORIA

Syrtis Minor

Meninx

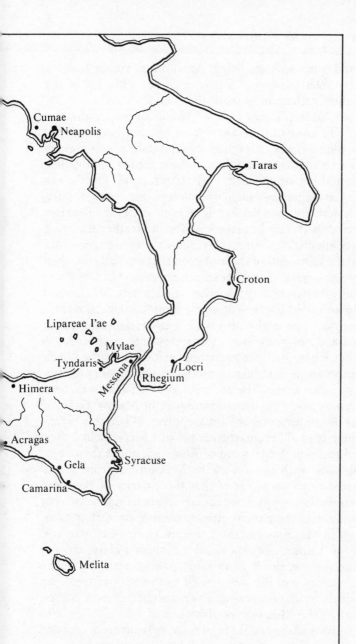

Cumae
Neapolis

Taras

Croton

Lipareae I'ae
Mylae
Tyndaris
Messana
Locri
Rhegium
Himera

Acragas
Gela
Syracuse
Camarina

Melita

The First Punic War:
Southern Italy, Sicily and North Africa

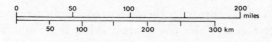

0   50   100   200
                                           ┘ miles
    50   100   200   300 km

in southern Italy and very willing, being Agathocles' son-in-law, to assert his claim to the overlordship of Sicily, to come to the aid of the Hellenes and drive the Carthaginians from the island.

A conclusive victory for the Greeks in Sicily would have spelt disaster for the Mamertines. The equivocal manner in which they had acquired Messana (one of the oldest Greek cities in Sicily) and their aggressiveness towards their Greek neighbours caused them to be regarded as brigands, barbarian vermin, mouthing an uncouth, barbarian tongue. The Greeks as a whole found the Carthaginians much more acceptable as neighbours. The latter, when not actually engaged in one of their periodic offensives against them, appeared as civilized businessmen with a rather flattering taste nowadays for Hellenistic culture. If Syracuse, with the assistance of Pyrrhus, achieved the fulfilment of the ambition that she had cherished for almost a century and a quarter and became the *hegemon* of the whole of Sicily, she would give short shrift to the Mamertines, who could scarcely expect to be accorded the benefit of the more humane and civilized rules of war that were generally observed in the Hellenistic world.

However the Mamertines were not utterly destitute of friends. A couple of years earlier Rome had put garrisons into some of the Greek towns of southern Italy to protect them against the more predatory of their Italian neighbours and also against the ambition of the Tarantines, then bestirring themselves to assert their predominance in Magna Graecia, threatened as it was by the advance of Roman power. When the Tarantines summoned Pyrrhus to aid them, the people of Locri expelled their Roman garrison; whereupon the garrison of Rhegium, under their commander Decius Vibellius, with the aid of the Mamertines from across the straits, anticipated any similar move that the citizens of Rhegium might have been contemplating by seizing the city, massacring the citizens or expelling them and establishing themselves as the new owners, in emulation of their friends in Messana. For these men were also Campanians, being inhabitants of Capua, incorporated as second-class citizens (citizens without the vote) in the Roman body politic, and they spoke the same language and came of the same stock as the Mamertines with whom they established an alliance cemented by bonds of common interest and mutual sympathy. The Mamertines also entered into alliance with the Carthaginians and did all they could to prevent Pyrrhus from crossing over into Sicily. When the king abandoned his Sicilian enterprise in 275 BC and returned to Italy, he left Carthage to extend her dominion over an even larger area of Sicily than before, and the Mamertines made themselves masters of quite a respectable little empire of their own in the northeast.

In 270, however, a serious threat to their security began to develop from the direction of Syracuse. Some five years previously an ambitious and energetic young officer named Hiero, who had made a reputation for himself against the Carthaginians, took the lead in an army coup which resulted in his being elected general, that is to say, president and commander-in-chief. In order to make his position secure when absent from the city on campaign he formed an alliance with the leader of the popular faction. He is said to have given assistance to the Romans when at last, in 270, they took action against the revolted garrison of Rhegium, which had by now degenerated into a mere robber band, whose depredations were highly damaging to Rome's credit and prestige as the overlord of peninsular Italy. Whether or not Hiero in fact sent help to the Romans, he certainly began to pay attention to the Mamertines about this time. He had excellent reasons for doing so. Messana was (in his eyes) a part of the Syracusan dominion to be recovered. Then again the Mamertines held a number of Greek cities in subjection to themselves, and by freeing these and extirpating the 'brigands', he would appear as the champion of Hellenism against the barbarian and so strengthen his claim, as the ruler of Syracuse, to the hegemony of the Sicilian Greeks.

Rhegium fell, the surviving mutineers were taken to Rome for execution, and the town was restored to its former owners. This left the Mamertines almost wholly isolated, for Hiero had established a *modus vivendi* with the Carthaginians who, after the excitement of the eighties and seventies, had once more withdrawn into their habitual path of peaceful commercial relations with their Greek neighbours. It is quite impossible to recover the chronology of Hiero's campaigns against the Mamertines, but it looks as if he first marched against them by the inland route to the west of Mount Etna, to liberate their southernmost possessions; and on the River Cyamosorus (Salso), in the neighbourhood of Centuripa, suffered a severe defeat at their hands, in which his mercenary troops (which his apologists later said were proving unreliable and were therefore deliberately sacrificed by him) were annihilated.

Hiero seems to have taken further measures on his return, discomfited, to Syracuse in order to strengthen his political position and began to make serious preparations for a decisive war against the 'barbarians'. He enlisted fresh mercenaries and trained the citizen militia and then, in the middle sixties, took the field once more. This time the Mamertines did not venture out to defend their more remote possessions and Hiero took town after town, sometimes adding their garrisons to his own force. Finally, when the Mamertines, now confined to the north-eastern triangle of the island, offered battle with inferior forces on the Longanus (or Loitanus) River in the territory of Mylae, they were defeated disastrously and it seemed that nothing could save Messana from capture. Indeed, the first reaction of the Mamertines, perhaps at the instigation of the elders, was to throw themselves upon the mercy of the victor.

At this point Hannibal son of Gisgo, the commander of the Carthaginian naval force stationed at Lipara, decided to take a hand in the game. That Carthage should have gone to the expense of keeping ships at Lipara is probably attributable less to her interest in Italy than to her anxiety over Hiero's triumphant progress in north-eastern Sicily. However friendly the relations between Syracuse and herself may have been, she can hardly have been anything but disquieted by the prospect of the elimination of the sole remaining unaligned power in Sicily. The fall of Messana would leave Hiero free to turn his attention to the 'liberation' of those other Greek cities still under the suzerainty of the 'barbarians' and he might very well turn out to be yet another tyrant in the tradition of Dionysius I, Agathocles and Hicetas.

Hannibal the diplomat acted with greater promptitude and skill than he was later to display as military commander. As soon as he heard the news of the battle (it is a reasonable conjecture that he had observers there), he sailed directly to Hiero's camp to offer his congratulations. We are told that he 'deceived' the victorious general into delaying his march on Messana; perhaps he told him that Messana was already an ally of Carthage. At all events, Hiero remained where he was and Hannibal went at once to Messana and persuaded the occupants – that is to say, the elders, the survivors of Agathocles' old warriors, scarcely subtle diplomats – to admit a small Punic force into the citadel, so that Messana became in effect a Carthaginian protectorate. It is probable that this took place in the late summer or autumn of 265 BC. Hiero was clearly nonplussed by the course events had taken. He was wholly unprepared, mentally as well as militarily, for war with Carthage, which might well ensue if he proceeded to extremes against Messana. Moreover the fact that the end of the campaigning season was at hand permitted him to retire without loss of face. Swallowing his resentment therefore for the present, he returned to Syracuse where, according to Polybius, he was universally acclaimed king.

The Mamertines were now at liberty to think a little more deeply about the future. Hannibal's action had saved them for the moment, but they had no guarantee that if Hiero decided to return in the spring Carthage either would or could give them effective protection. Her power was notoriously slow to move and Hiero might give adequate assurances of his peaceful intentions towards her. She had no field army in Sicily, and Messana, its walls undermanned as a result of the Longanus disaster, might well fall before Punic reinforcements could arrive. The Mamertines decided to look further afield for protection. Ever since the fall of Rhegium, if not before, they must have given consideration to the question, what their relations should be with the new overlords of Rhegium and of the whole peninsula across the straits. With their survival still in jeopardy, they began to think that Rome might offer them a better long-term security than Carthage.

They were well aware that the Romans made a practice of admitting free peoples to their alliance and protecting them against their enemies. It was in this way that they had acquired the suzerainty of Campania and Magna Graecia. Hitherto this policy had been confined to Italy, but the Mamertines felt that they could appeal to them as fellow Italians, speaking a language closely related to theirs, worshipping the god from whom the Romans, Greek-taught, claimed descent as a people. The Romans could hardly fail to see the advantage of having a foothold in Sicily and so controlling both the bridgeheads between that island and Italy. In the nineties Agathocles had taken an army into Bruttium. Syracuse had subsequently been the ally of King Pyrrhus (the Mamertines had been on the same side as Rome in that struggle) and had close and friendly relations with Taras; Syracuse was now ruled by a man who might well prove another Agathocles. The Mamertines decided to approach Rome and ask for her protection, and no doubt their embassy put forward these and other arguments. It is most unlikely that they anticipated any violent reaction on the part of the Carthaginians, who were still, if only nominally, allies of the Romans; for their decision to join the Roman alliance was not directed against Carthage but against Syracuse. So much is clear even from the garbled account given by Polybius.

Accordingly the Mamertines placed themselves under the protection (*dederunt se in fidem*) of the Roman people and were probably (although not certainly) granted a formal treaty of alliance. Polybius, who has telescoped two Mamertine embassies separated by several months, would have us believe that the Roman Senate was unable to reach a decision on the matter; but probability, supported by the epitome (book sixteen) of Livy, suggests that it was the question not of granting the treaty but of implementing it later that gave rise to a serious disagreement in the Senate. After all, since the Mamertines were seeking protection against Syracuse, a city whose total field force was smaller than a single consular army, the Senate need have had no serious misgivings over the risk involved. As for the possibility that offence might be taken by Carthage, that would appear no great matter at Rome. The terms of the alliance of 280 against Pyrrhus reflect the almost complete lack of interest taken at that time by the Romans in Sicily and by the Carthaginians in Italy; each party was quite content to have the intruder comfortably embroiled in the dominions of the other.

More important to the question of Rome's good faith towards Carthage in accepting Messana into her alliance is the so-called Treaty of Philinus, whose authenticity is vouched for by Philinus of Acragas and scornfully rejected by Polybius; and the controversy about it continues among historians today.

There are, however, good reasons for believing that the treaty existed and that it belongs to the year 306. And if we assume that in fact it excluded the Romans from interference only in those parts of Sicily that were then subject to Carthage, and Carthage from interference in those parts of Italy that were subject to Rome, and that Philinus was wrong when he said that it referred to the whole of Sicily and the whole of Italy, many of the problems connected with it disappear. The tradition preserved by Servius in the fourth century AD supports this conjecture and adds, for good measure, the wholly plausible stipulation that Corsica should be regarded as common ground to both parties. Thus Carthage could regard herself as a party wronged, inasmuch as Messana had put itself under her protection, while the Romans could feel innocent of giving offence, since Messana was a free sovereign state and not a part of Carthage's province.

Armed with their treaty the Mamertines in some unexplained way finessed Hanno, the Punic garrison commander, into withdrawing his troops from their citadel. He was, of course, in a very difficult position. He must have been perfectly aware of the value, political and ultimately strategic, of Messana to Carthage. But his was not an occupying force; nor, it seems, was his presence the result of any formal treaty between his City and Messana, and he had no moral or legal right to remain in the citadel after being ordered by the citizens to depart. His force was evidently a small one – essentially a token force, much too small to enable him to gain control of the town or its port – nor, apparently, had he received any instructions how to act in such a contingency as the present. He was no doubt ruefully aware that whatever course he adopted would prove to be the wrong one, and his worst forebodings turned out to be well founded. He was judged by his own people to have acted supinely and crucified; whether by Hannibal, disgusted at the reversal of his coup, or, more likely, by the home government, is not certain.

Hiero must have been exasperated at the grant of a fresh lease of life to the Mamertines. Carthage might have kept them in order or been prevailed upon, by timely concessions, to hand them over to himself. Rome could not be expected to do either: she was not responsible for their conduct as she had been for that of her mutinous citizens at Rhegium. He can scarcely have been blind to the undesirability of allowing Rome to obtain a foothold in the island, for to a Hellenistic Greek Carthage would appear less barbarous than Rome. The Sicilians knew where they stood with Carthage, whereas the Romans must have seemed merely a more remote, although undoubtedly more formidable, species of Mamertine, an essentially primitive nation unversed in the rules that governed the intercourse of civilized peoples.

Therefore Hiero made an alliance with Carthage during the winter of 265/4, the object of which was to provide a 'final solution' of the Mamertine problem. We may reasonably conjecture that it was agreed that Messana should be razed (a not uncommon fate for Sicilian cities), the non-Greek elements sold and the Greek incorporated into the Syracusan citizen body. The Carthaginians entered into this alliance partly no doubt out of pique but mainly out of anxiety to preserve the balance of power in Sicily, for if Hiero, acting on his own, were to capture Messana Carthage would have suffered a setback. On the other hand if Rome came to the help of her ally and either defeated Hiero decisively or forced him to join her alliance Carthage would find her Sicilian province menaced by a more formidable power than Syracuse. It is safe to say that neither Hiero nor Syracuse wanted – or anticipated – war to the knife with Rome. They probably hoped to finish off Messana before Rome was ready to intervene; and if they failed to do so the Carthaginians, who must have known that Rome had no effective navy, should have been able to prevent a Roman army from landing in Sicily. In fact Carthage had, over the past century and a half, repulsed so many attacks by land powers upon her Sicilian province that she probably took the threat, at that time still fairly remote, of Roman invasion far more lightly than she should. With Messana destroyed no good reason for going to war would remain, and peaceful relations could be resumed with Rome.

That Carthage did not envisage a major war seems to be demonstrated by the fact that the general whom she sent to Sicily in the spring of 264 BC, Hanno son of Hannibal, had at his disposal only the garrisons of the cities of the province. He concentrated these at Lilybaeum and then persuaded the people of Acragas, allies of Carthage in the eighties, to throw in their lot with Carthage. Returning to Lilybaeum he was met by envoys from Hiero, and a common war strategy was agreed upon, in accordance with which the Carthaginian fleet positioned itself near Cape Pelorias (Capo di Faro) and their land forces attacked Messana from the north, while Hiero, coming up with his army from Syracuse, invested it from the south. Even after the heavy losses of the Longanus battle there were evidently enough Mamertines left to deter the allies from making a naval assault upon the harbour.

No doubt as soon as the full extent of their danger became apparent to them the Mamertines sent an embassy to Rome to ask for assistance. This was evidently in the summer of 264, certainly not earlier than 1 May, the date when the new consuls came into office, and perhaps much later. A lengthy debate in the Senate ensued, for there could now be no avoiding the fact that Rome, by helping Messana, would be risking almost certain war not only with Syracuse but also with Carthage, which was something that she had not bargained for when she accepted Messana into her alliance. On the other hand Rome attached great importance to the sanctity of her fides, her guarantee of protection, and she could not afford to let it be thought that those to whom she gave it could not rely upon its implementation. And the risk involved in helping Messana would not have seemed so very serious. It is unlikely that Hiero had in front of the city much more than the 11,500 men that he had commanded in the Longanus battle, and the Punic land forces were probably less numerous. Pyrrhus had had no difficulty in driving the Carthaginians from the open field – and Rome had conquered Pyrrhus. It was true that only one consul, Ap. Claudius Caudex, was available for Sicily; his colleague, M. Fulvius Flaccus, was at Volsinii in Etruria, assisting the lords of the city to crush a revolt of their serfs. Claudius, however, was anxious to go, and the opportunity of winning booty was already beginning to make war attractive to the rank and file. A single consular army – about twenty thousand men – should be sufficient, it was felt, to raise the siege of Messana and teach its assailants a salutary lesson, not to attack an ally of Rome.

Modern historians have been much exercised by the problem of the declaration of war: who declared war on whom and when? This has led to ingenious reconstructions of the course of events prior to the opening of hostilities and even to the suggestion that Carthage sent an embassy to Rome and declared war on her. It is difficult to believe, however, that such an embassy could have been lost sight of by our sources, since partisans of each side could have made good use of it in order to fasten the 'war guilt' upon the other. It is best to suppose that the people sent Claudius to Sicily specifically to relieve Messana, by force of arms if necessary, and that it was left to him to issue the *rerum repetitio*: that is, the ultimatum whose rejection automatically involved war already provisionally authorized by the Roman people.

Claudius' difficulties began when he arrived with his army at Rhegium. Messana lies somewhat to the north of Rhegium and the prevailing winds in the straits blow from the north, so that the Punic ships at Pelorias, probably still under the command of Hannibal, could sail down upon his invasion fleet almost at will. Moreover although he evidently possessed a few warships, borrowed from the Greek allies, his escort was no match for the Carthaginians, and it was getting late in the year, when storms might be expected in those waters. Indeed, an attempt to throw an advance force into Messana under the military tribune C. Claudius was frustrated by the Carthaginians. However, the latter were so anxious to avoid open war with Rome that they returned the trireme and the prisoners that they had captured to the consul, protesting at the same time at Rome's unjustifiable conduct in moving out of her own sphere of influence and crossing water to invade theirs. In fact regular negotiations followed between the consul, desirous in view of the difficulties that faced him of securing the safety of Messana without further fighting, and Hiero and Hanno, who were equally anxious to prevent a complete rupture but resolute in their determination to destroy the Mamertines. It was improper of Rome, declared Hiero, to commit her fides to the protection of godless men and her actions laid her open to the suspicion of using it as a cloak for deep imperialistic designs.

Fleets of galleys such as the Carthaginians and their allies possessed (although we hear nothing of Hiero's ships in this campaign) could not maintain a blockade except by occupying a land station in the immediate vicinity of the locality to be blockaded. Claudius got his army on board a makeshift fleet and slipped across the straits by night and entered Messana, from which he again and for the last time endeavoured in vain to persuade the allies to raise the siege and so avoid war with Rome. It was presumably at this stage that he made the formal declarations of war.

It is impossible, because of the contradictory nature of the ancient accounts, to arrive at any degree of certainty concerning Claudius' military operations, beyond the basic fact that when he left Sicily in the summer of 263 Messana was still in Roman hands. It is a reasonable assumption, since Claudius, a member of one of Rome's most powerful clans, was not accorded a triumph on his return, that he did not win the victories so confidently attributed to him by Polybius over first the Syracusans and then the Carthaginians, causing both to retire in disorder to their own parts of Sicily. A reasonably competent general should perhaps have been able to do so, since the Roman army, almost certainly much larger than that of either of the besiegers, lay between them and was in a position to destroy them in turn. Perhaps the most plausible account is that of Philinus, with such modifications as may be required in order to correct his pro-Carthaginian bias. According to this, Hiero – who had once already been tricked by the Carthaginians and knew that Hanno had been in communication with Claudius – believed that they had betrayed him again and had deliberately allowed the Romans to land in Sicily. He therefore abandoned his camp, perhaps after an indecisive engagement with the Romans, and retired into winter quarters in Syracuse. Claudius then attacked the Carthaginians. Hanno no doubt kept his men within their fieldworks but aware that he was heavily outnumbered and finding himself deserted by his ally withdrew in turn into the Carthaginian province and dispersed his soldiers among their various garrisons.

Claudius is then credited with an advance south and an unsuccessful and costly attempt upon the town of Echetla, which, if true, involved his bypassing a number of more important places. The Roman tradition credited him with an attack upon Syracuse itself, but this is generally, and rightly, rejected by modern historians.

As far as Rome and Carthage were concerned the fighting might have ended there. The siege of Messana had been raised, while Carthage had no strong reason to desire the destruction of the Mamertines. The story that they had devastated her territory is unlikely to be true; it may have its origin in their former plundering of Gela, which later, together with Phintias, passed under her control. Hiero, on the other hand, could not accept his setback. His security as ruler of Syracuse rested largely upon his military prestige and he had committed himself and his régime firmly to the extirpation of the 'barbarians'. Emboldened by their escape and by the knowledge that they had Rome behind them, there was no telling what acts of aggression they might not commit against Syracusan territory. So no propitiatory embassy arrived at Rome during the winter from Hiero, and it was clearly necessary for Rome to reduce him to a properly compliant frame of mind before she could think of withdrawing her forces from Sicily. The consuls elected for 263 BC were no friends of Claudius; one of them, Manius Otacilius Crassus, was a new man of Campanian descent, a political ally of the Fabian clan, perhaps accustomed to think in terms of south Italian politics. The situation in Sicily seemed to offer the opportunity of a quick and easy victory for the two consular armies that could now be employed in Sicily, since Volsinii was pacified. Accordingly the patrician Manius Valerius Maximus crossed over unhindered into Sicily, probably late in June, and was joined by his colleague in September.

This account of the military operations of 264/3 is consistent with the accounts given by our sources. It would however be unwise, in view of certain historical problems that remain unsolved, to dismiss out of hand the possibility that Claudius did not cross over into Sicily until the early spring of 263, that he failed to drive Hiero and Hanno from their siege-works, and that it was M.' Valerius, arriving in June of the same year, who finally raised the siege of Messana and chased Hiero back into the shelter of his own city walls. Certainly Valerius took the name Messalla, and exhibited on an outside wall of the Senate House a painting representing his defeat of the Carthaginians and Hiero. Neither of these circumstances, however, necessarily proves that the initial half-success attributed by Philinus and Fabius Pictor to Claudius should be translated into full-blooded victories for Valerius. The Mamertines themselves may well have offered him the title Messalla, since it was certainly he that forced Hiero out of the war and so ensured the survival and future prosperity of Messana; while the famous picture, intended no doubt to discomfort Claudius as well as to exalt Valerius, need not have been more than a symbolic representation of Valerius' triumphant progress through eastern Sicily.

It seems more probable, then, that Valerius found no armies prepared to encounter him in the field and advanced south by the inland route into the kingdom of Syracuse, the Sicel and Greek cities going over to him one after another. He was probably joined by his colleague Otacilius for the siege of Syracuse, so that about forty thousand Romans encamped in front of the city. Hiero, who felt that he had been deserted by his ally – who sent a naval force under Hannibal into Syracusan waters too late for it to play any part in the war – and who was aware that his political position had become insecure, lost no time in asking for peace.

No doubt Valerius was anxious to end the war with Hiero before the close of the campaigning season, for it seems most improbable that he could have taken the city or forced it to capitulate before the arrival of his successor, who would then have reaped the glory of making a victorious peace. Rome herself had no serious quarrel with Hiero, nor had she suffered any military disaster that must be avenged. Her sole purpose in invading Sicily had been to vindicate her fides by helping Messana and impressing upon Hiero and his ally the inadvisability of giving her any further trouble. This purpose was most wisely achieved, as far as concerned Hiero, by making a peace that not only left him unresentful but converted him from being an unwilling enemy into a loyal and devoted friend of Rome.

Under the terms of this peace, subsequently ratified by the Roman people, he gave up the prisoners of war that he had taken from Claudius (and, presumably, the captured Mamertines as well) and agreed to pay an indemnity of a hundred talents, perhaps making a down-payment of twenty-five talents and paying the remainder in smaller instalments; at all events, there appears to have been an amount still outstanding fifteen years later. This was, however, a small price to pay for the ending of a war that he could not hope to win and for the granting to him by Rome of a treaty of friendship and alliance that not only left him independent and in possession of a large part of his kingdom, but also, while obliging him to assist Rome on demand, assured him of Rome's protection and support. Although forced to abandon any dreams that he might have cherished of rebuilding the evanescent Sicilian empires of Dionysius and Agathocles, he could at all events feel that his own position was now secure and that Carthage could hold no terrors for him. As well as being a lifelong friend to Rome he proved a wise and enlightened ruler of his kingdom and a great upholder of Hellenism everywhere.

CHAPTER II

262-255 BC

The war in Sicily and at sea. The invasion of Africa.

In Sicily a state of affairs had been reached by the winter of 263/2 which might have allowed hostilities there to be brought to an end. Messana's independence was assured and Syracuse had been transformed from an enemy of Rome into an ally and friend. That left only the Carthaginians, and Rome had no real quarrel with Carthage, whose fleet had played no effective part in the campaign of 263 and who had no field army in Sicily. Indeed it seems likely that Carthage had deliberately sought to avoid a clash with Rome and so far nothing had been done by either party to inflame resentment or outrage national feelings. No doubt Valerius' easily won success (he triumphed in March 262) fired the ambition of many Roman nobles to emulate or surpass his achievement: Carthage had never shown herself a very terrible enemy in the field. Again, by assuming the protectorate of eastern Sicily, Rome must, in Greek eyes, have seemed to have succeeded to the rôle of defender of the Greeks against the barbarians. The Greeks had always been past masters of the art of flattery, and the Romans, just beginning to be conscious of their cultural deficiencies when brought into contact with the centres of Hellenistic civilization, may have been pleased with the idea of heading a crusade of the civilized peoples against barbarism. Roman policy, in the winter and spring of 263/2, was balanced on a knife's edge. On the one side was adherence to the conservative and unadventurous ways of an agricultural people aggressive only when threatened or attacked; on the other, a yielding to the first stirrings of imperialism, militarism and greed. Yet conservatism was still, and was to remain, very strong; and military glory and booty apart, Rome had nothing to gain from a continuance of the war or from the conquest of Sicily. There is no good reason to suppose that a conciliatory embassy from Carthage would not have decided the Romans in favour of peace.

The Carthaginians, however, although anxious to localize the war, were in no frame of mind to propitiate the aggressor. Some of her subject cities had apparently gone over to Rome, although it is difficult to believe that, at this juncture, they included her old ally Segesta and Halicyae in the far west of the island, as Diodorus suggests. Moreover, she had suffered at least a reverse militarily before Messana. No imperial power can afford to allow her subjects to revolt with impunity and the close alliance concluded between Rome and Syracuse aroused all her fears for the security of her province. The aristocratic businessmen who governed Carthage were certainly shrewd enough to realize that Rome was likely to prove a very different proposition from the military adventurers who, over the centuries, had tried to expel them from Sicily. They had watched the inexorable advance of Roman power in Italy since the retirement to Gaul of Brennus. On the other hand, for all their shrewdness, they mis-judged the ruthless determination of the Romans and underestimated their almost limitless resources, human and economic. They believed that with the command of the sea secure in their own hands they could wear Rome down in the end and force her to withdraw into what, with Hellen-istic and good business logic, they were prepared to recognize as her legiti-mate sphere of influence. For the Carthaginian nobles were not imperial-istic, they were unmoved by the prospect of the glory that military con-quest bestows, and they thought in terms of profit and loss, as befitted businessmen. As a result they failed to appreciate that their Roman counterparts, uninterested in commerce and unversed in its rules, might be prepared to go on fighting for something that was going to bring them little quantifiable profit; and that the political stability of Roman society and the cohesion of her confederacy were such that both her citizens and her allies would continue to follow and support her rulers, long after a man with any business sense would have cut his losses and abandoned the struggle.

So the Carthaginian government sent recruiting agents to Liguria, Gaul and Spain to hire mercenaries, and in the spring of 262 they put a strong advance force under Hannibal son of Gisgo into Acragas, the second city of the island, which Hanno, the commander-in-chief in Sicily, had forti-fied as a precautionary measure in 264. They also sent strong naval forces to Sardinia, to carry out diversionary attacks from there upon the west coast of Italy. It seems to have been the intention of the Roman Senate to send only one consul to Sicily that year, perhaps because they expected the Carthaginians to make overtures for peace. However, the new troops sent to Acragas, and the activities of the Punic navy, as well as the reports which no doubt reached them of the very much larger army that Carthage was putting together in Africa, destined for Sicily, decided them not to relax their efforts; and accordingly both the consuls, L. Postumius Megellus and Q. Mamilius Vitulus, were sent to the island with their armies.

The strongest-held as well as one of the more forward of Carthage's strongpoints in Sicily was Acragas and upon this city the consuls marched immediately, and camped about a mile from its walls. Acragas, situated

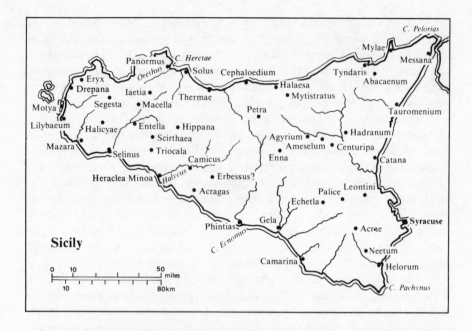

Sicily

in the triangle formed by the junction of the River Hypsas and its tributary the Acragas, was built in 582 BC by colonists from Gela on rising ground about two and a half miles from the sea, between the terrace on the south side that is today known as the Valley of the Temples and the heights, precipitous on their northern side, at whose highest point was the citadel. The immense circuit of the walls enclosed some nine hundred acres. The harbour lay below the town at the mouth of the Hypsas. It was mid-June by now and the corn was ripe; so the Roman soldiers, with the prospect of a long, hard siege before them, scattered to gather in the harvest. If Hannibal had been a better general and had kept his men together the sortie that he loosed upon them might well have inflicted a major defeat. As it was, although the foragers were put to flight, only a part of his men attacked the Roman covering force and these, after a fierce fight with heavy losses on both sides, were routed. The Romans then fell upon the rest of the mercenaries, who had attacked the Roman camp, where the booty was to be gained, surrounded them and finally drove the badly depleted enemy back into the city.

Both sides resigned themselves to the rigours of a siege. The Romans fortified two camps, one to the south or east of the city, we cannot be sure which, the other to the west, and constructed regular siege-works that totally encompassed it. They established their supply base at Erbessus, which their allies kept well stocked, and for some five months maintained a blockade of the fifty thousand people within the city. By the end of November Hannibal was in serious difficulties and had been sending frequent appeals to Carthage for assistance. By now Carthage had at last got together a force large enough to challenge the two consular armies in Sicily and despite the lateness of the season she shipped it across to Lilybaeum. Hanno son of Hannibal concentrated all the forces at his disposal at Heraclea Minoa: 50,000 foot, 6,000 horse and 60 elephants, according to Philinus. Here he had a piece of good fortune: an offer to betray Erbessus to him. The loss of their supply base was a serious blow to the Romans, who now found themselves in a position scarcely better than that of the Acragantines, and but for the efforts of Hiero to throw supplies into their camps they would probably have been forced to raise the siege.

As things were, shortage of food and disease were hitting the besiegers so hard that Hanno decided to press them more closely still and advancing from Heraclea he first routed the Roman horse which, inferior in numbers and quality to the enemy, allowed itself to be provoked into giving battle and then established himself on high ground a little over a mile to the west of the city. Matters remained in this state for two further months, during which Hannibal's condition became desperate and that of the Romans almost as bad. Finally, in response to the appeals of the former, Hanno decided to stake everything on a set-piece battle, believing that his men were in better shape than the enemy. He appears to have held his elephants in reserve, perhaps in order to deliver the *coup de grâce*; it must be remembered, however, that this was probably the first occasion on which the Carthaginians employed elephants for military purposes and they had not yet learnt how to use them effectively: nor was Hanno himself a military genius. The rout after desperate fighting, of his first line, which was thrown back upon the rest, led to the disorderly withdrawal of the whole army. His total losses, both in this battle and in its predecessor, would seem to have amounted to 3,000 infantry and 200 cavalry killed, 4,000 (presumably infantry) taken prisoner, and the disablement of the greater part of his elephant corps.

The Romans captured Hanno's camp, but were, not surprisingly, too exhausted, and perhaps, after their recent privations, too bloated with food and drink, to pay attention to Hannibal, who succeeded in effecting a break-out after nightfall with his soldiers and was almost beyond pursuit by first light. The Romans skirmished with his rearguard and then entered the undefended city which, in accordance with Roman custom but contrary to the more civilized practice of the Hellenistic age, was comprehensively sacked and the population sold. That fifty years later Acragas was once more a flourishing and prosperous city is probably to be accounted for by the charity of the other Greek communities of Sicily and of Hiero, who purchased their unhappy neighbours and restored them to freedom. It is impossible to assess the Roman losses incurred in the siege; the figure given by Carthaginian sources, over thirty thousand out of a total of perhaps forty-five thousand, is clearly much too high. They must, however, have been very heavy, since despite the capture of the city and the defeat of Hanno in the field neither consul was awarded a triumph.

Both sides were now too heavily involved in the struggle to be able to withdraw. Rome could not evacuate Sicily leaving a Carthaginian field army of about fifty thousand men billeted for the winter in the west of the island. Moreover Italy had been raided from Sardinia and Rome had been compelled to take measures to defend the coastal areas. On the other hand, apart from one or two strongholds such as Tyndaris on the north coast of Sicily and Mytistratus, the Punic province was now reduced to the area west of a line drawn from Cephaloedium to Heraclea Minoa and even within this area there were defectors such as Segesta and Halicyae – unless (as seems more likely) these defected to Rome in 261. With the Romans wintering at Messana and showing no signs of leaving the island, Carthage knew that the war and the whittling away of her possessions were to continue.

In the summer of 261, L. Valerius Flaccus and T. Otacilius Crassus, the brother of the consul of 263, arrived in Sicily. On the Carthaginian side Hanno was recalled and, as was customary with the Carthaginians, severely punished. No doubt only the facts that Hannibal had managed to escape with his soldiers from Acragas and that the Romans had lost many more men during the campaign than themselves prevented them from crucifying him. In his place an able soldier, Hamilcar, was sent to take command in Sicily and against him, supported as he was by the Carthaginian navy, the Romans were unable to make any real headway. Certainly many inland communities went over to them and they ambushed and destroyed a force of four thousand Gallic mercenaries, who may or may not have been intentionally sacrificed, being mutinous, by Hamilcar himself. But these gains were more than offset by the desertion to the Carthaginians of even more coastal towns: many of them, no doubt, out of disgust at the barbarous treatment of Acragas by its 'liberators'. Moreover, Hannibal, who had been reinstated in his old command of the fleet, raided Italy again.

The chief result of this year's campaign was to impress on the Roman Senate first that the 'liberation' of Sicily was to be no quick and easy matter, and secondly that if the Carthaginians were to be driven out of Sicily, Rome would have to challenge her command of the sea which enabled her to hold out indefinitely in the maritime cities of western Sicily that formed at once the nucleus of her province and the springboard from which she could launch fresh offensives in order to recover the whole, when her enemy at last wearied of the hopeless task of besieging them.

Up till now the Romans had taken little interest in the sea. They were an agricultural people and they farmed in order to subsist and not for profit. Their wars had hitherto been fought only against Italian powers (or invaders of Italy) and they had dealt with such of these as had naval pretensions (the Antiates in the fourth century and Taras in the third) by defeating them on land. However by the end of the fourth century they began to feel the need of at least a coastguard force, and in 311 they formed a fleet of twenty ships (triremes) under two officials styled *duoviri navales*. This fleet fared badly in the war with Taras and appears to have fallen into disuse, the Romans in the third century relying upon the naval forces of their allies – Carthage in the war against Pyrrhus, and the ship-owning towns of their confederacy later – to supply their naval requirements. Four new officials, the *quaestores classici*, were instituted in 267 to supervise the working of this system and to keep the maritime allies (*socii navales*) up to the mark. It was in ships supplied by their allies (Polybius specifically mentions the Tarantines, Locrians, Eleans and Neapolitans) that Claudius, and presumably his successors, shipped their troops across to Sicily.

Adequate though this arrangement may have been for the protection of Italian waters and coasts against piracy, it was wholly unequal to the task of providing a battle fleet that could challenge the Carthaginians. They had, indeed, remained unchallenged for so long that they had come to regard the command of the sea as theirs by prescriptive right; yet the same anti-militarist and commercialist attitudes of mind that tended to make them dilatory in their reaction to military threats also led them to spend no more on their navy – upon whose efficiency their whole commercial empire outside of Africa ultimately rested – than was absolutely necessary. Even so, they now had over a hundred ships in commission and these were mostly 'fivers' (*pentereis*), far superior in power as well as in the tactical proficiency of their officers and the training and efficiency of their rowers, to anything that Italy could produce. If Rome was to fight Carthage at sea she must build a fleet from scratch with which to do it. The fatal error which was to lose Carthage the war was the failure of her government to realize until too late that the Romans were capable not only of rising to but also of sustaining such a challenge.

Therefore in the winter of 261/0 the Roman Senate decided to build a fleet of a hundred fivers (*quinqueremes*), a class of vessel that Rome had never possessed, as well as twenty triremes – a curious example of Roman conservatism. Among the strongest proponents of this policy were Messalla, who must have been fully aware of the difficulties that he would have met with if he had been forced to besiege Syracuse without naval support, the men who expected to be elected to the consulship of 260 and, we may assume, the consuls of 261, who had been the first to feel fully the lack of a fleet.

It is often assumed that while the Roman government paid for the construction of these ships many or all of them were actually built by the experienced maritime allies in their own yards. The Roman tradition, however, as preserved by Polybius, insists, I believe rightly, that the fleet was Roman-built. It would appear to be a simpler and certainly a more satisfactory arrangement for the Romans to mobilize the resources of Italy in shipwrights and raw materials and concentrate them on the beach at Ostia, where Roman magistrates and officials could supervise the work and keep it to its schedule, rather than to rely upon the efforts of local town councils and shipyards.

Again, while it is probable that Polybius' assertion that fivers had never formed part of Italian navies is a patriotic invention designed to enhance the Roman achievement, there is no need to reject (as certain historians do) the statement that the Romans used a Carthaginian fiver that had run ashore during the skirmishing in the Straits of Messana in 264, and so fallen into their hands, as the prototype of their new fleet. Equally to be accepted is the story that they gave the rowers, recruited from the maritime allies, their initial training on stagings set up on dry land; for however many good seamen Italy might be able to provide, she certainly could not muster some thirty-three thousand rowers on demand.

The ships were all built within sixty days – a remarkable enough but not an unparalleled achievement – and while the bulk of the fleet indulged in a brief period of sea training, the consul appointed to the command, Cn. Cornelius Scipio, went on ahead to Messana with seventeen ships to get things ready there for the reception of the rest of the fleet. His colleague C. Duilius crossed to Sicily, where, in this year of naval effort, a single consular army was to operate. While Scipio was at Messana a proposal was made to him to betray to the Romans Carthage's useful advanced naval station at Lipara, a town which, although in Punic hands for at least a decade, had formerly been friendly towards Rome. Unfortunately the betrayal was itself betrayed to Hannibal at Panormus, and he sent off Boödes, a member of the Carthaginian Inner Council, with twenty ships to frustrate the attempt. Scipio arrived first, but Boödes sailed in during the night and at daybreak caught the Roman ships beached and unmanned and captured the whole squadron and its commander – an ill-omened opening to Rome's first major naval campaign which apparently earned for the luckless Scipio the soubriquet Asina (Ass). A few days later the main body of the Roman fleet arrived at Messana after a brush, possibly off Cape Vaticano, with a strong Punic reconnaissance force under Hannibal himself.

The fleet that assembled at Messana had not inspired any great measure of optimism in its commanders on its passage south from Ostia. The crews were inexperienced and only half-trained, the ships slow and un-handy. Who the person was who suggested fitting these clumsy vessels with the corvus we do not know. The 'someone' of Polybius' narrative probably conceals the name of an ingenious Greek, perhaps a Syracusan – there was a long tradition of military ingenuity at Syracuse. It has even been suggested that it was the great mathematician Archimedes, whom Polybius' Roman source was unwilling to credit with this war-winning invention.

The corvus (raven) was a movable boarding-bridge, thirteen feet in length overall, which could be rotated about a stump-mast twenty-four feet high stepped in the bows of the galley. Its outer end, beneath which was a kind of spike, could be raised by means of a rope passing through a pulley set on the top of the stump-mast. When a hostile vessel came within its reach it was dropped upon her deck which the spike penetrated and so held her fast alongside and enabled the soldiers who packed the Roman ship's deck to board and take the enemy. Its vigorous pecking motion when in action gave it its whimsical name. It was hoped that the corvus would provide an answer to the favourite tactics of the well-drilled galley fleet, the so-called *diecplus*, by which better-handled ships rowed rapidly through the gaps in the enemy's line – ancient fleets normally advanced towards one another in line abreast – and then, turning quickly, rammed their opponents from behind. A further refinement was to use the ram as they went past, to cripple the oarage on one side of the enemy.

C. Duilius had already opened his campaign on land, where fighting was taking place in the region around Segesta in western Sicily. Segesta, a town of the non-Greek Elymi, had long been friendly towards Carthage because of her ancient enmity with Selinus; but she had now gone over to Rome, claiming sisterhood on the grounds of her legendary foundation by Aeneas. Segesta was besieged by Hamilcar, while Duilius attacked neighbouring Macella. When the patrician Scipio was captured Duilius succeeded to the command of the fleet and leaving his troops in the keep-ing of the military tribunes went back to Messana.

Hannibal had concentrated 130 ships, not all of them fivers, at Panormus; and now, in the late summer of 260, he sailed along the north coast of Sicily and attacked Mylae (Milazzo), no doubt with the purpose of drawing the ill-trained and inexperienced Roman fleet out to battle. Duilius at once accepted the challenge; whether or not he put on board each of his ships more than the forty infantrymen, drawn from the lowest Roman class (the *proletarii*), that was to become the standard comple-ment we do not know. On the approach of the Roman fleet the Cartha-ginians put to sea, Hannibal commanding from a great seven-er captured from King Pyrrhus, and attacked so over-confidently that they completely lost formation. Seldom in the history of war can a secret weapon have been more devastatingly successful than the corvus. The thirty leading Punic ships, including the flagship, were grappled, boarded and taken, Hannibal himself escaping in the longboat. The Carthaginian attack broke up, and after vainly trying to use their superior manœuvrability in order to avoid the pecking of the corvus they broke off the engagement and fled, with a total loss of fifty ships. A centuries-old command of the western Mediterranean and a myth of invincibility were destroyed in a single day.

Duilius did not attempt to follow up his victory by an attack from the sea on the Punic strongholds in western Sicily. Hannibal still had about eighty ships fit for service and the Roman land army had run into trouble and been defeated, under C. Caecilius, a military tribune, by Hamilcar, who had reduced Segesta to dire straits. Duilius therefore landed his marines, probably in the Gulf of Termini, and marched to rejoin his army and to raise the siege. He also captured Macella. After these successes Duilius sailed back to Italy, early in 259, to celebrate Rome's first naval triumph. A column decorated with the beaks of captured vessels was erected in the Forum and from the spoils of his campaign he built in the vegetable market a temple to Janus, who from his connection with gates and beginnings was a proper object of gratitude for a campaign success- fully accomplished. It is a strange fact that although Duilius is known to have been still alive nearly thirty years later he was never given another command.

In spite of Duilius' unprecedented triumph, however, the consular year 260/59 did not end on a triumphant note for Rome. Hamilcar learnt that owing to a quarrel between the Romans and their Sicilian allies the latter had established an entirely separate camp, in the coastal plain to the east of Thermae (Termini). As the result of either treachery or first-rate mili- tary intelligence Hamilcar surprised them in the act of breaking camp and killed several thousands of them, Diodorus says six thousand, Poly- bius four thousand. He then captured the town of Mazara.

That the operations of the Punic navy against the Italian coast had as much to do with Rome's decision to challenge Carthage's command of the sea as the desire to drive her out of Sicily seems to be indicated by the fact that in 259 the Roman fleet under L. Cornelius Scipio (the brother of Asina) attacked Carthage's most highly prized overseas posses- sion, Sardinia, and with it Corsica. Scipio appears to have gained some successes, capturing Aleria, the chief city of Corsica and winning over some of the native tribes.

However in the early spring of 258, Hannibal, who must have possessed considerable influence at Carthage to have not only escaped punishment for losing the battle of Mylae but also been reinstated in his command of the fleet, crossed over from Carthage into Sardinian waters. Whereupon Scipio, with his tenure of office approaching its end, withdrew to celebrate a somewhat cheap triumph in March of that year and to dedicate a temple to the Tempestates (gales) who had been propitious to him in the off-season for sailing. On land in Sicily his colleague C. Aquillius Florus made no headway against the able Hamilcar, who retook Enna and Camarina and at the close of the year transferred the Elymian population of Eryx, whose loyalty was perhaps suspect following the secession to Rome of Segesta, to nearby Drepana, which he fortified against the now inevitable Roman attack. Indeed, things had been going so well for the Carthaginians that Florus was ordered to winter in Sicily, his *imperium* being prorogued after 1 May, 258 BC.

In June he was joined by the consul A. Atilius Caiatinus, whose appointment suggests a recrudescence at Rome of the influence of the great Fabian clan, of which the Atilii, whose origins lay in Campania, were political adherents. Caiatinus and the proconsul Florus advanced first to Panormus (Palermo), but the Carthaginians prudently declined to come out and fight the two armies, which then moved away south to capture Hippana and east to take the strong city of Mytistratum, which had already withstood two Roman sieges. Enna and Camarina were also recovered, as well as Camicus and Erbessus, in the territory of Acragas. However an attempt on Lipara was frustrated with loss to the Romans by Hamilcar.

At sea the second consul C. Sulpicius Paterculus was sent to challenge Hannibal in Sardinian waters. He tricked the Carthaginian admiral into believing that he intended to attack Africa and having the advantage in numbers decisively defeated him off Sulci when he put out to sea. Hannibal himself was killed by his mutinous crews, but an officer named Hanno, who took over the command, defeated the Romans when they made a landing. Nevertheless Sulpicius' exploits by sea and land earned him a triumph on his return to Rome.

Although the Romans had won the battle of Mylae the Carthaginians had not as yet admitted defeat at sea. They had offered a vigorous challenge in Sardinian waters and they now set themselves to build a fleet which should put an end to Roman pretensions. For their part the Romans probably also began preparations in 257 for a decisive effort which, in emulation of Agathocles' strategy but improving upon it, would first clear the seas of the Carthaginians and then bring the war to an end by striking at Carthage herself. This was to be no mere retaliatory raid upon the coast of Africa but an invasion carried out as a combined operation by the army and the navy, for the purpose of compelling Carthage to evacuate Sicily. The military force that Rome could put into the field in such a campaign was limited more by the native conservatism of the Roman people and the narrowness of her politico-military system of command than by available resources of manpower. The crews of the ships involved were to amount to between seventy-five and a hundred thousand men; yet because the war was an overseas war and the security of Rome and Italy was not directly threatened the Senate could not dispose of more than two consular armies, each of no more than two legions, of which one would have to be left in Sicily where Hamilcar commanded what was left out of an army of fifty thousand men after battle, sickness and desertion had taken their toll.

As a result of this change of policy the two Roman armies in Sicily in 257 – that of Caiatinus, who was continued in his command (either as proconsul or as praetor) and that of the consul Cn. Cornelius Blasio – were content to hold on to what had been won without attempting to make any further gains. But the commander of the fleet, C. Atilius Regulus, after raiding Melita (Malta), was preparing to make yet another attempt upon Lipara from Tyndaris when Hamilcar's ships appeared in the offing, intending to forestall him. The Romans, who attacked in disorder and lost nine ships, ultimately restored the day, the Carthaginians losing eighteen. However Hamilcar made good his escape to Lipara.

The consuls of 256 were L. Manlius Vulso Longus and Q. Caedicius. The latter, however, died before the opening of the campaign and M. Atilius Regulus, the father of the consul of 257, who had already been consul and had triumphed over the Sallentini (in the heel of Italy) in 267, was elected as his replacement (*consul suffectus*). The Romans had prepared a fleet so powerful that it seemed to them either that the Carthaginians would not dare to engage it in battle or, if they did, that they would be brushed aside or destroyed with the minimum amount of trouble. According to our most reliable sources this fleet consisted of 330 quinqueremes. However the majority of modern historians take the view that this total of 330 is inclusive of transports, and that the battleships numbered only 230. If the higher total is accepted, as I believe it should be, some adjustment has to be made to the figures given us by Polybius for the number of troops embarked, both in gross and in detail. The Roman plan was simple and straightforward. The two consuls were to concentrate the fleet at Messana and from there sail down the east coast of Sicily, double Cape Pachynus (Passero) and then make for Phintias under Mount Ecnomus, where the army had been assembled. There were four legions in Sicily; two had probably wintered there under Blasio while the other two, replacing Caiatinus' army, perhaps proceeded to the island in the spring of this year. From these four legions four brigades of picked men, probably to the number of about half the total force, were to be formed for the invasion of Africa, and the fleet was to be divided into four squadrons to correspond.

All went according to plan. The invasion army embarked upon the fighting ships and the fleet moved off, the two consuls leading in six-ers, perhaps procured from Syracuse, where ships of this type had been built by Agathocles. The formation adopted by the Romans was that of a vast wedge, the two sides being composed of the second and first squadrons, proceeding in double-quarter line, an inverted V, to port and starboard respectively of the two flagships, the third squadron, which had the numerous horse transports under tow, forming the base of the wedge, while the rear of the whole formation was covered by the fourth squadron – dubbed the *triarii*, or reserve – moving, like the third squadron, in line abreast, but with its wings overlapping the base of the wedge. It looks very much as if the consuls expected to encounter an enemy greatly inferior in numbers, whose line, if they ventured on an engagement, would be broken and its centre destroyed by the impact of the great mass of Roman ships, which would then proceed relentlessly on their way to Africa, leaving the Carthaginian fleet too shaken and demoralized to interfere further. The formation adopted would also serve to protect the fleet and its vulnerable transports from attack from flank or rear. Doubts raised by modern historians about the ability of the Roman ships to keep such a formation need not be taken too seriously. The executive officers and steersmen of the Roman vessels were drawn from the Italian and Sicilian maritime communities and as long as the weather remained fair no great difficulty should have been experienced in keeping station.

If the Romans went into action with 330 ships in the expectation of not encountering more than 220 Punic vessels at the outside, they were sadly disappointed. Whatever the numbers engaged in the battle of Ecnomus the Carthaginian fleet, if indeed it was (as some modern historians believe) outnumbered by the Romans, was certainly not outnumbered by more than about 30 ships. On the other hand, the ancient authorities give it some 20 ships more than the enemy, that is to say 350 quinqueremes against Rome's 330. For although up till that time the Carthaginians never seem to have commissioned more than about 200 ships at a time (and usually not more than about 130), and their ship houses had accommodation for only 220, they can scarcely have been ignorant of the intense activity that had prevailed in the Roman shipyards during the preceding months. With their centuries-long maritime traditions of naval construction, and with highly developed techniques which appear to have included a form of prefabrication, they would have had no difficulty in out-building the Romans on this occasion, given their immense resources in manpower and raw material, if they once came to the conclusion that the urgency of the threat to their own security, estates and prosperity justified an extraordinary expenditure of effort and money.

The Punic fleet sailed from Carthage in the summer of 256, first to Lilybaeum and from there to Heraclea Minoa, a little over forty miles by sea from Phintias. It was under the command of Hamilcar and of the Hanno who had been defeated (but had managed to save the bulk of his army) before Acragas in 262. It is clear that they established a system of patrols, by land or sea, in order to keep them informed of the movements and apparent intentions of the enemy. Therefore when the Romans put out to sea and headed slowly westward along the coast they found the huge Punic fleet lying squarely across their course. Probably because their patrols had been able to observe the Romans on manœuvres – for they must have practised their wedge formation before embarking their troops and sailing for Africa – the Carthaginian admirals had been able to devise a plan for dealing with them.

They placed their ships in line abreast, considerably outflanking the Romans at both ends of the line, which was still further extended on the left flank by a division amounting to a quarter of the total force, thrown forward at an angle to the rest of the line, owing to the proximity of the land. Hamilcar, who seems to have been in overall command, was counting for victory on what the Roman generals had overlooked, accustomed as they were to the movements of maniples and legions: namely that when the two fleets clashed the Roman ships would no longer be able to maintain their formation. Hamilcar, flying his flag in the centre of his line, had given orders for the centre to fall back before the Roman charge, thus inevitably causing the disintegration of the wedge and exposing the rear of the Roman first and second divisions to an enveloping movement by his wings, the advanced left-flank division being perhaps intended to hold off the triarii until victory had been achieved in the main action.

However Hamilcar himself was to discover that it is one thing to make a battle plan and quite another to get it carried out – especially at sea. The Carthaginian centre retired according to plan before the Roman attack, and when the wedge had been thoroughly dislocated they rallied at a signal from the flagship and vigorously counter-attacked the Roman first and second divisions. But Hanno, commanding the crack right-flank division, instead of falling on the rear of the Roman advanced divisions and so ensuring their annihilation, attacked the triarii and speedily had them in trouble, while the left-wing outflanking division fell upon the Roman third line and the horse transports. Tow-lines were at once cast off and the third of three quite distinct and widely separated battles commenced.

Once again the corvus proved its worth. The Carthaginian centre was routed and took to flight, leaving Regulus to hasten to the help of the hard-pressed triarii, while Vulso secured the prizes. Hanno was driven out of the battle and both consuls rowed to the rescue of the Roman third division, which was in imminent danger of being driven ashore by the greatly superior Carthaginian left wing; indeed, only the wholesome respect in which the enemy held the corvus had saved it from destruction or capture. The tables were at once turned by the arrival of the consuls, and the majority of the Punic vessels were taken. Altogether Hamilcar lost over thirty ships sunk and sixty-four taken; Roman losses amounted to twenty-four galleys sunk.

The battle of Ecnomus could – and should – have been the decisive battle of the war. Carthage had made the greatest naval effort in her long history and her navy had been decisively defeated. When the Romans had repaired and manned the vessels taken as prizes – even if, as is probable, they were forced by shortage of rowers to underman them – they would have an immense superiority in numbers. Moreover the morale of the Carthaginian navy, after its rout and flight, must have been very low. Hanno withdrew from Sicilian waters with the fleet and established himself where he could cover the sea approaches to Carthage, while Hamilcar remained with the army in Sicily. The consuls put back after the battle, possibly to Messana, and renewed their preparations for the invasion of Africa. It is not impossible that the Carthaginians put out 'peace feelers' at this juncture; if so, they were certainly rejected. Finally, towards the end of the summer, the fleet set out once more, and arrived at Cape Hermaeum (Cape Bon) without interference from the Carthaginians. From there they proceeded south to the town of Aspis, later (and more familiarly) called Clupea. Here they landed, fortified a naval camp, and took the town by siege, still without interference from the enemy, who had concentrated all his forces at Carthage for its defence.

Clupea supplied the Romans with a firm base, from which they could cut the Carthaginians off from some of their richest and most valuable possessions in the eastern coastal regions of what is today Tunisia, as well as plunder the estates of the rich on the Cape Hermaeum peninsula. The booty included twenty thousand slaves, among whom, it is said, were numerous Roman deserters and prisoners of war.

When they first established themselves at Clupea the consuls wrote a full report home to the Senate and asked for further instructions. The reply came back that one consul should return to Rome with the fleet leaving his colleague with the bulk of the land forces to maintain the pressure upon the Carthaginians until the following summer. This was, on the face of things, a sensible decision, since there were no facilities at Clupea for servicing a huge mass of ships, and the fleet, whose crews numbered at least seventy-five thousand at the lowest estimate and about a hundred thousand at the highest and would have to be fed by foraging, would merely have been an encumbrance on the army during the off sailing season. Nor would the popularity of naval service among Rome's Italian allies have been enhanced by keeping them away from their homes during the whole of the autumn, winter and spring.

It was therefore decided that M. Atilius Regulus should remain behind with fifteen thousand infantry and five hundred cavalry and, so that he should not feel totally cut off from home, forty ships. This was not of course an army with which to attack the massive walls of Carthage, but it was one which, given the superiority of Roman troops over the Libyan levies, would make a competent general master of the open country and so encourage widespread revolt both among the oppressed Libyan subjects of Carthage and her Numidian allies, whose dynastic and domestic conflicts might be exploited by a 'liberator' possessed of any diplomatic ability. Agathocles had had considerable success in this direction during his invasion of Africa in 310. By raising the whole country against Carthage, Regulus might very well have frightened the enemy into evacuating Sicily and so achieving Rome's war aim. He would at least have been in a position to cooperate in a total blockade of Carthage by land and sea when the Roman fleet returned with reinforcements in the following summer.

Agathocles, however, with all his shortcomings, was a cleverer man than Regulus, who was that most unfortunate thing, a mediocrity – a man without imagination or versatility – placed in a situation that demanded a touch of genius. He failed completely to appreciate the importance of winning over the Libyan towns and the Numidian princes to his side – a failure the more serious even from the narrowly military point of view because the latter could have supplied him with what he was seriously short of for the purpose of scouring the country, namely cavalry.

On the departure from Clupea of the fleet (which reached home safely, Vulso triumphing for his part in the naval victory), Regulus began to advance towards Carthage, taking and plundering the towns and villages in his path. The Carthaginians now realized that they did not have to deal with a mere raiding force (as they had at first supposed) but with a full-scale invasion. Accordingly they recalled Hamilcar from Sicily and ordered him to assume the command against Regulus, together with Hasdrubal the son of Hanno and Bostar. Hamilcar brought with him five thousand veteran infantry and five hundred horse, and these, added to the forces already available in the city, encouraged the Carthaginians to take the field against the enemy, who was by now besieging the town of Adys (perhaps Oudna, about fifteen miles south of Tunis).

The Carthaginians were strong in cavalry and had a number of elephants; but the elephant was a new arm and they were not yet proficient in its use (against Agathocles they had been still using the ancient Phoenician war chariot). Hamilcar had learnt to hold the Roman legion in profound respect, and so because they did not venture to face the Roman infantry on the level plain they made the mistake of occupying high ground in the neighbourhood of the town, where their elephants and cavalry could not be used to advantage, and Regulus knew enough about war to perceive and to seize his opportunity. He attacked the enemy camp at first light from two sides and although a vigorous counter-attack by Hamilcar's mercenaries forced one legion to give way the other legion came up behind them, and the whole Punic army was forced to abandon its position and make good its retreat to Carthage. Having taken Adys, Regulus advanced to Tunis, which he captured, making it a base from which to raid the countryside around and also his winter quarters.

Carthaginian morale sank to its lowest point. They had been defeated at sea despite the magnitude of their efforts, and now on land, and the victorious enemy was at liberty to plunder their territory at will. More serious still was the revolt of the Numidians, released by Regulus' victory from their age-old fear of Carthage. Although they did not actually co-operate with the Romans, they did even more damage to Carthage's economy by their raids. The city was full of refugees from the countryside, and famine conditions prevailed. In these circumstances it is not surprising that the Carthaginians, acting on a hint conveyed to them from the Roman camp to the effect that Regulus would listen sympathetically to a request for terms, sent a deputation headed by Hanno son of Hamilcar to negotiate.

Although Regulus had suggested peace talks (it would have been a personal triumph for him if he could have been the one to dictate the peace and bring the war to a successful close) and although the Carthaginians had responded eagerly to his suggestion, it at once became apparent that terms of peace acceptable to both parties were not going to be agreed upon. It would be unwise to assume that Carthage would not, at this juncture, have given up Sicily. Sicily was indeed the most illustrious of her provinces, for possession of it gave her the hegemony over Greek cities and kept her in contact with Hellenistic trade and culture, but it was perhaps not the most profitable or the most highly prized. It also involved her in constant and expensive military operations and there was probably an influential body of opinion in the Council which would not have been sorry, especially since the growth of Roman power in southern Italy, to see Sicily go. On the other hand, even if we do not accept the details given us by late Roman writers, it is quite clear that Regulus went beyond the mere evacuation of Sicily in his demands. Polybius and Diodorus (both probably following Philinus) agree that acceptance by Carthage of his conditions would have been tantamount to acceptance of

Roman suzerainty, and the merchant aristocrats of Carthage did not as yet feel so militarily bankrupt that they could accept that. They decided, therefore, to continue fighting.

Among the Greek mercenaries who arrived at Carthage about this time, hired by one of the City's recruiting officers, was a Spartan adventurer named Xanthippus, a member of a military caste whose standing in the Hellenistic world was roughly comparable to that of a Prussian Junker three-quarters of a century or so ago. His outspoken comments on the inadequacy of Punic generalship led to his being given the rôle of military adviser to the commanders of the army, and after a short time spent in training the Carthaginians took the field again, probably in early May 255, with their morale completely restored by the conviction that a real professional was now in effective command. The numbers given by our authorities for the Punic army are surprisingly low considering that this was in the nature of an all-out offensive designed to destroy Regulus before reinforcements could reach him from Italy in late May or early June. Twelve thousand infantry and four thousand cavalry seem a poor levy-in-mass for a city the size of Carthage, especially as she had a fair number of mercenaries still at her disposal. It has been suggested that the Carthaginian numbers have been doctored by Philinus to the greater glory of a fellow-Greek, Xanthippus. However even if their infantry was substantially less numerous than the Roman, they were greatly superior in cavalry, and they brought with them nearly a hundred elephants, and (what was even more important) a soldier of experience who had studied how to employ them.

The Carthaginians advanced across the plain, showing that this time they did not intend to avoid the set-piece battle, and pitched their last camp a little over a mile from the Roman position. Regulus, who had beaten them once and probably felt that another victory would clinch the whole business, accepted the challenge. He has been censured by modern historians for not playing safe and waiting at Tunis for the re-inforcements that were due to arrive within a month. To do so, however, would have been to surrender the countryside to the enemy, to endanger his own food supply, to throw away the moral advantage that he had gained in 256, and to present to his successor as commander-in-chief the glory of winning the war. For although his own imperium had been prorogued, the consul who was coming to Africa would be his superior. Regulus himself, brave, stubborn, and an aristocrat, saw no reason why a once-beaten collection of shopkeepers and mercenaries should not be beaten again.

On Xanthippus' advice the Carthaginian generals drew up their army with the Carthaginian levies forming the centre and left wing and the heavy-armed mercenaries on the right wing. Before each wing they posted

a mixed force of horsemen and light-armed mercenaries, and they stationed their elephants in line covering their whole front. Regulus placed
his small force of cavalry on the wings, and to meet the menace of the
elephants – the training of a Roman nobleman did not equip him to deal
with elephants – he deepened (and thus shortened) his line and put his
skirmishers out in front of the heavy infantry.

When the Punic army advanced the Romans came forward to meet
them. The African cavalry in front of the wings soon chased the Roman
horse off the field and then wheeled inwards to encircle the legions. On
the extreme left of the Roman line their infantry apparently avoided the
elephants, broke the mercenaries opposed to them, and pursued them
as far as the camp; but the bulk of their forces, halted and trampled underfoot by the elephants in front and then charged on flanks and rear by
the victorious cavalry, were soon in desperate trouble. The foremost
maniples fought their way past the elephants, who were probably supported by the Punic light infantry, and then, coming face-to-face with
the unbroken citizen phalanx, were annihilated. The rest either fell where
they stood or, taking to flight, were ridden down by the horsemen and
the elephants. A mere handful – some five hundred – together with the
proconsul cut their way out of the shambles, but were overtaken and
forced to surrender. Only the infantry of the left wing, about two thousand in number, and no doubt some of the cavalry also, made good their
escape to Clupea, where in conjunction with the garrison and the ships'
crews they succeeded in defending themselves against a brief siege by the
jubilant Carthaginians. They perhaps rejected an offer to let them depart
freely in their ships in return for laying down their arms and evacuating
the town. It is generally agreed that the legend of Regulus' journey to
Rome and back to a cruel death at Carthage ('Well though he knew what
the savage torturer had in store for him' [Kipling]) is a late invention.
An invention, too, although a much older one, is the story that the Carthaginians attempted, out of spite and jealousy, to drown Xanthippus on
his return voyage to Greece. In fact, he left Carthage's service after the
victory (he had, no doubt, made many enemies there – Spartans were
not noted for their diplomacy) and may have served Ptolemy III of Egypt
almost a decade later.

The news of the disaster apparently reached Rome – the journey could
be done in three days – before the relief expedition set sail. There was
no question of trying to restore the military situation in Africa. Indeed
Roman public opinion had probably all along been equivocal with regard
to the African adventure and to the despatch of tens of thousands of
citizens and allies to another continent in a war which it now required
a certain degree of casuistry to represent as a war in defence of an ally.
There is even a suggestion that there was some vocal opposition at Rome

to the sending of the fleet to pick up the heroes of Clupea. Yet Rome did not make any move towards a negotiated peace nor could she pull her forces out of Sicily, leaving the Carthaginians in triumphant possession of their western strongholds. In fact the war seemed already to be approaching a stage with which the Carthaginians were quite familiar from past experience: a position of stalemate from which the aggressor withdrew, leaving Carthage to reimpose her hegemony upon the greater part of the island. There was, however, one important factor that had been missing from earlier deadlocks: Rome still held the command of the sea. But Carthage was already hard at work, fitting out the ships that she had and building new ones; and if the Romans could only be driven off the sea she believed that this crisis, too, would have been surmounted.

The consuls of 255, Marcus Aemilius Paullus and Servius Fulvius Paetinus Nobilior, set sail probably in June. Again, as in the case of the previous year, there can be no certainty as to the size of their fleet; but since I am inclined to accept the figure of 330 ships for 256 BC, I am also in favour of accepting Polybius' 350 ships for the relief expedition. They were carried out of their course by a storm to Cossyra (Pantelleria), which they garrisoned (the Carthaginians recovered it, the following year); and from there they sailed to Cape Hermaeum, where the Carthaginians engaged them with two hundred ships. Polybius, dismissing in twelve words what would, if they were true, be the greatest Roman naval victory of the war, says that the consuls captured 114 of the enemy vessels. Diodorus, no doubt following Philinus, says 24, and this figure is more likely to be the correct one. Polybius himself describes this victory as 'easy', and we hear of no Roman losses from him, although Orosius mentions 9. On balance it appears much more probable that the Carthaginians, finding themselves heavily outnumbered, broke off what was clearly a hopeless action after a comparatively small number of their ships had been taken.

The fleet arrived at Clupea and prepared to evacuate the troops and rowers numbering perhaps 15,600 that the town contained. As at the lowest computation there must now have been about 100,000 men assembled at Clupea, 13,600 of them infantrymen, it is likely that some extensive foraging took place, but the purpose of the expedition was to cover the withdrawal of Regulus' 40 ships and their complements and this was accomplished by mid-July. Fate now struck the Romans a more serious blow than ever before in her history; nor is it at all clear, despite the strictures levelled against the obstinacy of the Roman admirals by Polybius, that anything – short of not putting to sea at all – could have been done by them to avoid it. When not in a hurry ancient warships preferred, because of the cramped conditions in which their rowers worked, to keep close to the shore and put in at nightfall in order to rest the crews; the western end of Sicily was in enemy hands; and so the armada had no option but to coast along the southern rim of the island on its way back to Italy. Off Camarina it was caught on a lee shore by a westerly or north-westerly gale and only eighty of its hundreds of quinqueremes and transports escaped. Of the loss of lives involved it can only be said with certainty that the survivors must have numbered not less than twenty-seven thousand. These struggled on to Syracuse, where King Hiero fed, clothed and rested them. They then moved to Messana to winter.

CHAPTER III

254-248 BC

Panormus, Lilybaeum and Drepana. Carthage rules the waves.

Although 255 BC must be reckoned one of the blackest years in Roman military history the Senate's resolution did not falter. Aware that Carthage was preparing a fleet of two hundred ships for next year's campaign they undertook an immense building programme themselves and within three months had completed 220 new vessels. Much more remarkable, in view of the Camarina disaster, is the fact that they found crews to man them. With the survivors of the previous year's fleet they now had a total of three hundred vessels, which gave them an ample margin over the Carthaginian fleet. The latter, however, never appeared at sea. Faced as a result of Regulus' initial successes by extensive revolts on the part of their Libyan subjects and their Numidian and even Moroccan allies, the Carthaginian government now bent all its available resources to defeating the more vital threat to the security and prosperity of the nation, and the Sicilians were left to look after themselves.

The consuls of 254 were men who had commanded in this war already. Under pressure of misfortune the Roman nobility was prepared to waive, at least to some extent, the prescriptive right to the consulship of those of its members that had not yet held it, in the interest of securing war leaders of experience. One of them was the Cn. Scipio Asina who had been captured at Lipara in 260 and subsequently exchanged; the other was A. Caiatinus, who had triumphed for his modest successes on land in 258. They had at their disposal two consular armies – four legions. Nobilior and Paullus, to whom their compatriots, at all events, attached no blame for the loss of the fleet, had their imperium prorogued, and when they returned to Rome they were accorded a triumph for their capture of Cossyra and the victory off Cape Hermaeum.

One at least of the Punic commanders in Sicily, Carthalo, was a soldier of enterprise and ability. Either in the autumn of 255 or, more likely, early in 254, he besieged and took Acragas and razed its walls. When in the summer of 254 the consuls, picking up the forces that had wintered at Messana, proceeded along the north coast of Sicily, taking Cephaloedium (Cefalu) as a result of treason within and attacked

Drepana in the extreme west of the island, Carthalo marched to its relief and raised the siege. The Romans then moved against Panormus (Palermo), the largest and most populous city and also the richest of the Carthaginian province. The fleet, commanded by the proconsuls, was beached close to the city so as to blockade it from the seaward side; and while Scipio threw up a circumvallation round the two 'cities' – the Old and the New – of which Panormus was composed and assaulted the weaker New City with two legions, his colleague operated at large with the other two to hold Carthalo in check. Scipio stormed the New City, whereupon the inhabitants of the Old City, to which the refugees from the New had fled, negotiated its surrender; fourteen thousand of the more wealthy purchasing their freedom at the rate of two hundred drachmas a head. The rest of the population, some thirteen thousand, and the contents of the city were taken as booty and sold by the victors. It is possible that some of the transports taking the booty home to Italy were captured by Carthaginian cruisers. Panormus received a garrison and later, when Sicily came to be organized as a Roman province, was given the status of a free, and tax-free, city. Solus and Tyndaris on the north coast and three inland towns now went over to the Romans. Caiatinus returned to Italy with the fleet and one consular army, while Scipio remained in Sicily with the other. His imperium was prorogued in 253 and Cn. Servilius Caepio and C. Sempronius Blaesus were elected consuls.

In spite of the capture of Panormus, which might have been expected to spur on the Romans to make a greater effort to reduce, by combined operations, the remaining Punic strongholds in Sicily, the Senate reverted in 253 to the policy of loosening Carthage's grip upon western Sicily by striking at Africa, where the natives were still in revolt. A late source speaks of an unsuccessful attempt upon – perhaps an attempt to surprise – Lilybaeum, and then Blaesus took the fleet and a part of his army, including cavalry, and sailed south to raid the coast of Africa between Hermaeum and Meninx (Djerba), some of Carthage's richest territory. Through ignorance of the peculiarities of the tides in the Syrtis Minor he put his ships on the sands and had to jettison everything of any weight in order to get them off. However, although such raids could not alter the course of the war, he probably succeeded in inflicting serious damage upon Carthage's economy. But Neptune had not done with him yet. He took the shorter, western route home, putting in to Panormus and then heading directly across the open sea for Italy but was caught by a storm and lost 150 warships and all his transports. Yet once again the Romans showed magnanimity in not blaming their admiral for the vagaries of the elements, and Blaesus was awarded a triumph for his raid on Africa, while Scipio triumphed, as proconsul, for his capture of Panormus.

No doubt this disaster, like that of 255, was attributed – at all events in the popular mind – to the malevolence of the gods. For the year 252 there could be no question of attempting to raise the tens of thousands of rowers required for a fleet that could influence decisively the course of the war. Superstitious fears apart, the maritime allies would not have submitted to such an imposition for a war which was only remotely their business and from which, in fact, many coastal communities must have been suffering economically on account of the disruption of trade, including the grain trade, with Sicily and Carthage. However the Romans recognized only one possible ending to a war to which they had fully committed themselves, and they determined to give Italy a breathing-space before demanding another war-winning effort on the part of their allies. They sent the consuls, C. Aurelius Cotta and P. Servilius Geminus, with their armies to Sicily and commissioned just enough ships – probably sixty – to retain command of the waters between that island and Italy. The consuls showed some enterprise, however, and although they failed in a combined siege of Heircte to the north-west of Panormus they succeeded in capturing the isolated coastal town of Thermae to the east; and Cotta, borrowing additional ships from King Hiero, sailed across to the Liparian Islands and besieged and took the chief city, Lipara, which had been Carthage's one remaining possession to the east of Panormus. It was no doubt mainly on account of this achievement that he was awarded a triumph on his return to Rome.

Carthage herself was still engaged in restoring her shaken suzerainty over the revolted Libyans and Numidians. She had, however, made sufficient progress to be able to afford, either late in 252 or in the spring of 251, to send to Sicily Hasdrubal son of Hanno (one of the trio of generals who had defeated Regulus) with fresh troops and no fewer than 140 elephants. The soldiers may have been mainly Libyans, for it would seem that Carthage now raised the status of her African subjects from what had been virtually helotry to that of tributary free cultivators. As a result they became suitable for recruitment as mercenaries, and by recruiting them Carthage might hope to remove from Libyan soil the most pugnacious, and therefore the most dangerous, of her subjects. The survivors of Regulus' disaster had brought back with them horrific tales of the overwhelming nature of an elephant attack and the consequence was that although the consuls of 251, L. Caecilius Metellus and C. Furius Pacilus, marched and countermarched between the territories of Lilybaeum and Selinus in the far west of the island they did not venture to come down off the high ground and engage Hasdrubal's army on the flat; while Hasdrubal, with inferior numbers, could not risk abandoning the good elephant country in order to attack the legions on their own ground. Neither side, therefore, made any gains during the campaigning season of 251, and towards the close of the consular year Pacilus returned to Rome with his army.

It was now plain to the Roman Senate that another major effort by land and sea would have to be made if the war in Sicily was to be won. Therefore it ordered the construction of fifty new ships so as to bring the fleet up to a strength of two hundred ships for the consuls of 250, who were to be two of Rome's most experienced, successful and well-omened generals: C. Atilius Regulus, the victor in the sea fight of Tyndaris in 257, and L. Manlius Vulso, who had commanded, with the elder Regulus, in the battle of Ecnomus and the landing in Africa. Metellus in Sicily had his imperium prorogued.

Before the new consuls arrived in Sicily, however, the military situation had been dramatically altered in Rome's favour. Heartened by the timorousness displayed by the legions in the face of his elephants and learning that there was now only one consular army in the island, and probably also learning of the extensive preparations being made in Italy for the coming season, Hasdrubal had decided to strike a decisive blow before the balance of strength tipped against him once more. He led his army, whose morale was high, up from Lilybaeum by way of Iaetia (San Giuseppe) into the territory of Panormus, which Metellus had occupied in order to afford protection against Punic marauders to the harvest of Rome's western allies. It was June when Hasdrubal marched into the valley of the Orethus (Oreto) and began to ravage systematically the ripening crops in his advance towards the city, within which he probably expected to find sympathizers who might even betray the place to him.

Metellus, keeping his legions within the walls, allowed Hasdrubal to cross the river, which flows into the sea just south of the city, without interference. He then employed some of his light infantry to harass the enemy and force him to deploy, and stationed others in front of the city ditch, with orders to provoke the elephant corps into attacking them, and so by retreating to draw the enemy close up to the wall which was lined with javelin throwers. When he saw that his plan was succeeding he reinforced the men on the lip of the ditch, and the elephants, halted by the ditch and showered with missiles, stampeded into their own infantry and threw it into confusion. At the tactical moment Metellus made a sally with his infantry against the left wing of the Punic army and drove it from the field in headlong flight. Then and subsequently all the surviving elephants were captured; they were later shipped to Rome, to be slaughtered in the Circus to grace Metellus' triumph on his return to Rome in September. It is impossible to say whether or not there is anything in the annalistic account of the arrival of the Punic fleet at the very moment of the rout. If the story is true it seems likely that a combined attack on Panormus had been planned whose timing went wrong (as was so often the case with complicated plans in classical times).

News of the victory, which left Carthage without a field army in Sicily that could challenge even one consular army, greatly raised the spirits and morale of the expedition then making ready for a decisive blow at Lilybaeum, the Punic headquarters in the island. Lilybaeum (Marsala) was a relatively new city, having been founded only in 396 to replace the ancient stronghold of Motya which had been destroyed by Dionysius of Syracuse. Like most Phoenician settlements it occupied a peninsula, the most westerly one of the island. It was defended by strong walls and by a moat ninety feet wide and sixty feet deep. The harbour, which faced north, was protected by a mole, and entrance to it – indeed, all approach to the town by water – was made dangerous for the uninitiate by shoals, the 'pitiless Lilybaean shoals' of Vergil. The city had successfully resisted Pyrrhus in 276. In order to prevent the dispersal of their forces, and also to defend more effectively the population of a loyal ally, the Carthaginians razed the city of Selinus and transferred the inhabitants to Lilybaeum, where there was an ample store of provisions. The size of the garrison presents yet another of those historical problems that cannot be solved with certainty. It seems fairly safe to assume, however, that at the commencement of the siege the town commander Himilco had seven thousand infantry and seven hundred cavalry – Greek and Celtic mercenaries, presumably the survivals of Hasdrubal's débâcle – in addition to the citizen levies.

Both consuls arrived with their fleet of two hundred ships in the territory of Lilybaeum in the late summer and when their legions, which had come by the overland route, had been concentrated before the town they commenced vigorous operations against it, cutting it off from the hinterland by siege-works and attacking the south wall and its towers. Himilco responded as vigorously, and with heavy and costly fighting continuing night and day the progress of the Romans was slow – although an attempt to betray the town into their hands by certain of the mercenary captains was only narrowly averted by the loyalty of one of them. However the morale of the besieged was greatly raised and that of the Romans proportionately depressed by the arrival in the harbour of a powerful relief force from Carthage under Hannibal, son of the Hamilcar who had been defeated at Ecnomus and before Adys but who was now playing a leading part in the restoration of Carthaginian suzerainty in Africa. The fleet of fifty ships carrying provisions, money and either four thousand fresh troops, according to Diodorus or, more probably, ten thousand, according to Polybius, sailed from Carthage under Adherbal to the Aegates Islands, which lie north-west of Lilybaeum. From there Adherbal proceeded to Drepana, entrusting the blockade run to his friend and lieutenant Hannibal. The latter waited for a fresh following wind and then ran in under the noses of the Romans, who were deterred from interfering by ignorance of the waters and fear of being blown into the harbour.

Himilco at once made use of this reinforcement of both the numbers and spirits of his men to make an all-out assault upon the Roman works, throwing twenty thousand men into a dawn attack which the Romans met with equal determination and superior forces; and when Himilco sounded the retreat the Romans were left in secure possession of their lines. Following the failure of this attempt to raise the siege Hannibal slipped out of Lilybaeum by night with his fleet and rejoined his commander Adherbal at Drepana. One effect of Hannibal's double exploit was to indicate that Rome's two hundred ships were quite unable to prevent ships from entering and leaving the harbour almost at will. Thus Himilco was able to ship his horsemen – wasted as wall fighters – to Drepana, where they could be used with advantage for raiding the Roman supply lines and ravaging the countryside. At Carthage a bold and enterprising sea captain, Hannibal the Rhodian, undertook to run the blockade and did so with such audacity and frequency that many others followed his example, despite Roman attempts to close the harbour with booms and other obstructions. Finally an end was put to his career when the Romans, having captured a particularly fast quadrireme which had grounded on a man-made shoal, used it to capture his galley as it attempted to break out into the open sea. After this, with two especially fast vessels in their possession, the Romans were able to put an end to the operation of the blockade runners.

At the end of the campaigning season one of the consuls returned to Italy with his army, but already by then the Romans had been obliged to abandon the idea of taking the city by storm and had fallen back upon the plan of reducing it by blockade and circumvallation. But the Greek mercenaries took advantage of gale-force winds blowing towards the Roman camp and made a sortie, firing the siege-engines and siege-works at three points, and the flames spread with such violence through the tinder-dry woodwork that the whole was destroyed or irreparably damaged. Pestilence and famine further harassed the besiegers, and for this reason one army was withdrawn. The loyalty to the Roman cause of King Hiero, who sent them quantities of provisions, was an important factor in encouraging the Romans to continue the siege.

Not the least serious problem was the partial immobilization of the fleet owing to the losses sustained in the fighting, and no doubt also as the result of disease, by the maritime allies – the rowers and seamen of the galleys – who had been employed ashore to work the siege-engines and as sappers and light infantry. When exaggerated reports of their casualties reached Rome, the Senate in the early summer of 249 managed

– with what difficulty and in the face of much local resentment, we can well imagine – to recruit ten thousand fresh rowers. These may have included both Roman proletarii and slaves, and they were despatched overland to the camp. The new consuls were P. Claudius Pulcher and L. Iunius Pullus. Of these the former went immediately to Lilybaeum to take over the army and fleet there, while his colleague gathered a huge supply convoy and prepared to join him later in the season.

The Claudii have been handled unkindly by Roman historians. Publius may have been hot-headed and arrogant as they say; but the anecdotes told by annalistic sources to illustrate 'the innate arrogance of his family' may equally well have been fabricated, to provide an explanation for the inexplicable: namely the desertion of Rome's cause by her gods and a major Roman defeat. Claudius may well have had specific instructions from the Senate to strike at the Carthaginian naval base of Drepana, from which Adherbal had been raiding the coast of Italy with his hundred ships, and as soon as his ten thousand newly enlisted rowers arrived he proceeded to carry out the operation, probably in May of 249. It has been plausibly suggested that he had learnt that seventy ships were being got ready at Carthage to reinforce Adherbal and that he was anxious to destroy the latter before their arrival. He discussed his plan with his War Council and got their enthusiastic approval (no evidence of arrogance here) and put picked volunteer legionaries on board the galleys. There is no possibility of knowing for certain how many ships he manned. Polybius says that he manned all he had, but as he does not tell us how many that is we are little better off, and Diodorus' figure of 210 (not impossible in itself) is difficult to reconcile with both his own and Polybius' numbers of casualties and survivors. It is however likely that the Romans had more vessels lying on the beach before Lilybaeum than they could fully man with the resources available to them.

It looks on the whole as if Claudius had about 150 ships when he put to sea at midnight for the eighteen-mile row to Drepana. He expected to arrive there around daybreak and to catch the Punic vessels unmanned and the mercenaries dispersed in their billets; for Adherbal, informed of the Roman losses but not of the recent reinforcements, would not be expecting an attack from the direction of the sea. It could hardly be expected that the ships of Claudius' unpractised fleet would be able to keep perfect station and avoid straggling during the night, and as a result he would have had to heave to at first light and re-form his line before making his approach to the harbour. This allowed time for Adherbal to be informed of his arrival, man his own ships with rowers and fighting men and get under way before the Roman galleys entered the port. Like a good seaman, he preferred to take his chance at sea rather than try to fight the Roman legionaries on the beach or permit the enemy to shut

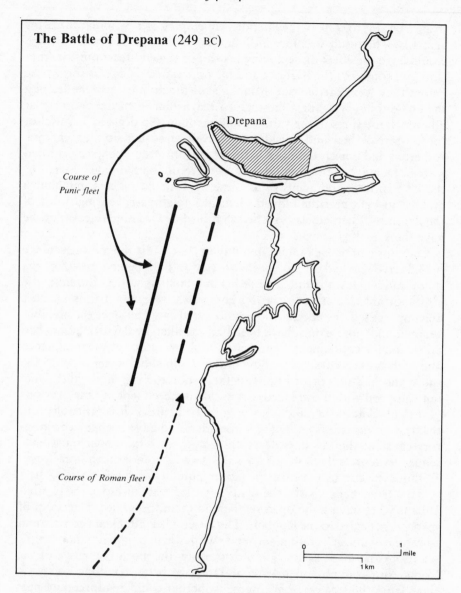

The Battle of Drepana (249 BC)

Drepana

Course of
Punic fleet

Course of Roman fleet

0   1 mile

1 km

him up in Drepana and thus perhaps seal the fate both of that city and of Lilybaeum.

Therefore as the Roman galleys began to crowd into the narrow harbour from the south they saw the Punic vessels with Adherbal in the van racing for the open sea by the north exit, beyond the island of Colombaia. Claudius' line can hardly have been less than three miles long, and he was at the rear of it, having positioned himself there, quite correctly,

so as to be able to control the intended enveloping attack upon the Carthaginians. The result was that although he at once issued orders which
would have the effect of deploying his ships in line-abreast outside (that
is to say, south of) the harbour and facing westwards, it was some time
before they were carried out. It looks as if the military tribune leading
the line did not wait for a message to reach him from the flagship; at
all events, the ships in the van, turning through 180 degrees, fell foul of
those astern of them and considerable confusion ensued. In the meantime
Adherbal had got clear of the harbour and into the open sea and had
hove to facing, but to the south of and therefore outflanking, the tail of
the Roman line; and as his ships came up his staff officers, moving to
and fro in light craft, stationed them in line-abreast, bearing north of
the flagship. When he was satisfied that his line was in perfect order, he
gave the signal to attack.

Claudius had the advantage in numbers, but it was the only advantage
he did have. He had already been worsted in the opening moves of the
battle and had lost the initiative to his opponent as well as forfeiting the
all-important element of surprise. His crews were new to the benches
and unpractised, the fleet had not manœuvred as a fleet since the previous
summer and morale must have been badly shaken by the turn events had
taken and the consequent confusion. The ships – some of them damaged
and with broken oars – were now drawn up in shoal water close to the
shore and had no sea room. Most fatal shortcoming of all, they were
not equipped with the dreaded corvus, having been sent out the previous
year to blockade a city and not to fight naval battles. It is probable, too,
that the corvus had been – or was considered to have been – a contributory cause of the disasters of 253 and 255, since its weight must have
tended to depress the bows of the galleys and to render them top-heavy.
Without the corvus the superior fighting quality of the Roman soldiers
was rendered ineffective by the vastly superior seamanship of the Carthaginians who, having the open sea behind them, possessed a freedom of
manœuvre denied to the Romans. The latter when attacked had no room
to retreat without running aground, while their opponents had ample
sea room and made skilful use of it to draw the more aggressive of the
Roman ships out into open water and then, by better handling, to attack
them from the side or from astern. Adherbal could reinforce any part
of his line that he wished; Claudius' ships had to fight where they lay.
Many – perhaps twenty-four – Roman galleys were sunk, and ninety-
three were taken, of which some had been deliberately run ashore in order
to enable the crews to escape and make their way overland back to the
Roman camp, while others had gone aground inadvertently. Claudius
himself, with about thirty ships from the left wing, escaped along the
coast into open water and got away to the camp before Lilybaeum.

The Carthaginians were now masters of the waters around western Sicily, and they followed up their victory energetically. Hannibal was sent to make a descent upon Panormus with thirty ships; he captured the Roman supplies and shipped them to Lilybaeum, thus ending the food shortage. An experienced officer, Carthalo, arriving from the metropolis with a fleet of seventy warships and as many transports, brought Adherbal's total strength up to at least 170 galleys. Adherbal seems to have kept seventy of these under his own command, probably in order to watch and close to the Romans the direct, north-coast sea route to western Sicily; the rest he entrusted to Carthalo, to make a dawn raid on the Roman naval station outside Lilybaeum. The action was a sharp one, as Himilco launched a vigorous sortie in support of the fleet, and Carthalo succeeded in capturing or destroying a few of the Roman galleys. Then, after a short stay in Lilybaeum, he received intelligence of the movements of Claudius' colleague and brought his ships, apparently reinforced by twenty from Drepana, down the coast to the vicinity of Heraclea Minoa to wait for him.

L. Iunius Pullus had set out from Ostia with a huge convoy of transports and sixty warships – a figure that may be accounted for by supposing that they had returned to Italy with the consular army withdrawn from before Lilybaeum during the previous winter. He sailed to Messana and there added a further sixty galleys to his fleet. These sixty ships have given some modern historians a lot of trouble, but this is largely because they reject Diodorus' figure of 240 ships for the consular fleets of 250 BC. Thirty ships had escaped with Claudius from the battle, and it is probable that at least as many had been left behind at Lilybaeum, some if not all of which would subsequently have been manned by those crews that had returned to the camp on foot after running their ships ashore outside Drepana. Claudius was recalled to Rome by an irate Senate (he was later to be tried on a charge of high treason (*perduellio*), saved from conviction by a portent, but condemned and heavily fined on some lesser charge). If we suppose that he sent or took to Messana, as Polybius' narrative suggests, all the ships that he had manned at Lilybaeum, and if we take into account scattered vessels acting as guard-ships at Messana itself and other Sicilian ports, as well as borrowings from King Hiero, it is not difficult to see how the total may have been made up.

At Messana Pullus probably heard of the arrival in Sicily of Carthalo's ships – their number perhaps inflated by rumour – and fearing that a victorious fleet greatly outnumbering his own would fall upon him if he attempted to sail directly to either Panormus or Lilybaeum (in the latter case actually having to sail past Drepana), he decided to make for Lilybaeum by the southerly route, along a coast which, with the exception of Heraclea Minoa, was in friendly hands. When he arrived at Syracuse

Pullus made the fatal decision to split his immense convoy, which had straggled badly during the passage down the east coast of Sicily, and to send the quaestors on in advance to Lilybaeum with half the merchantmen (no less than four hundred sail) and part of the war fleet. He himself would remain behind to round up the strays and to raise additional supplies from Rome's allies.

Any account of the events that followed must, once again, be to some extent conjectural. Of our two principal authorities Diodorus, in many respects the more reliable here, bases his narrative on that of the pro-Carthaginian Philinus, while Polybius' is a contamination of Philinus' with that of the highly partisan Roman Fabius Pictor, whose aim it is to present his countrymen in a less unfavourable light than the facts seem to warrant. Now unless we are to ascribe to Pullus a degree of foolhardiness unusual even in Roman commanders of the First Punic War we must assume that he did not expect to encounter the Carthaginian navy between Syracuse and Lilybaeum. It is therefore probable that Polybius is correct is saying that he gave only 'some' of his warships to the quaestors, whereas Diodorus' account implies that they had by far the greater part of the fleet. On the other hand most of Diodorus' details have the ring of authenticity and it seems likely, in view of what he tells us about the course of the action, that the quaestors had at least thirty warships – a sufficiently large squadron to deter an attack by enemy cruisers or small raiding forces.

The Roman convoy rounded Cape Pachynus (Passero) and proceeded along the south coast with light craft scouting ahead. Carthalo, who had been informed of the Romans' departure from Syracuse and had decided to waylay them off the inhospitable coast between Acragas and Camarina where they would find it difficult to beach their ships and rely for their defence upon their formidable infantrymen, now moved his fleet further down the coast. He too had his scouts out – perhaps horsemen as well as light galleys – and when he learnt of the enemy's approach he put to sea and rowed towards them. The quaestors, aghast at their scouts' report that the whole Punic navy was bearing down on them, took refuge in a roadstead off the small fortress town of Phintias, which provided a fairly sheltered anchorage but no port and only very inadequate beaching facilities, and set up artillery taken from the fortress to cover their ships. Carthalo sailed in and a fierce engagement ensued, in which the Carthaginians sank 17 of the Roman quinqueremes and disabled 13. They also damaged 50 of the transports and captured a few others. Carthalo who had suffered some damage and casualties and knew enough about the meteorology of the central Mediterranean area not to wish to linger off a harbourless coast then broke off the engagement and returned to his base near Heraclea, where he still lay between the Romans and their objective.

The winds were still easterly, so that the quaestors were unable, had they so wished, to fall back on the consular fleet. Nor, apparently, did they take steps to inform their general of what had happened. It was only when he arrived off Phintias that Pullus learnt of the presence of the Punic fleet somewhere to the west, and Carthalo, whose intelligence and reconnaissance services seem to have been exceptionally good, appeared shortly afterwards in the offing. With perhaps less than ninety warships at his disposal and a huge fleet of unwieldy transports to protect Pullus did not venture to offer battle. Moreover the wind had changed direction and was now blowing strongly from the west or north-west and offered a chance, however slight, of escaping before it from the enemy. He therefore collected the whole convoy, burnt the crippled vessels, and made off to the south-east. Hampered as he was by the transports he had little hope of outrunning the galleys of Carthalo, who overtook him when he was off the treacherous coast of Camarina – the very stretch on which the consular fleets had come to grief in 255. But Carthalo was no longer thinking of fighting. He, like his enemy, was now running before a rising gale, and so he kept to the open sea. He stood on past the Roman convoy, weathered Cape Scaramia and finally rounded the promontory of Pachynus and found safety under its lee.

Pullus was less fortunate, or rather, very much less skilful. In his flight from Phintias he had kept close inshore, intending to take refuge on the beach – on a lee shore – if Carthalo brought him to action. Now he found himself hopelessly embayed in the Gulf of Gela and the entire convoy, all but two galleys, one of which was the flagship, was pounded to pieces on the rocks and cliffs. Polybius speaks only of the complete destruction of the ships. Diodorus tells us that most of the crews were also lost, but as he is giving the Carthaginian version of the disaster it may be better to assume that the loss of life was rather less serious than in the calamity of 255.

Yet the loss must have been very heavy, and the Roman Senate would not dare to ask the maritime communities to supply the crews for another great fleet until their memory of the series of disasters suffered by the Roman navy since 256 had become somewhat less vivid. Nor could the national economy support the cost of another large shipbuilding programme. Rome did not have at her disposal the silver mines of Spain and the gold of Senegal, and there was a limit to the amount of tax (*tributum*) that could be extracted from what was still essentially a community of subsistence farmers. Moreover it must have been by now apparent to all that the gods were ill-disposed towards Roman ventures on the sea. The Romans found it difficult to accept the fact that the Carthaginians could decisively beat a numerically superior Roman fleet like that of Claudius, or that they could so intimidate a second consular fleet that it preferred self-immolation upon the rocks of Sicily to meeting the enemy in battle. It is no wonder that rumours spread the report that both consuls had disregarded the auspices, and that Claudius, his nature being what it was, had even gone so far as to drown the sacred chickens when they refused him a favourable omen. It is easy to credit the statement of Cicero, that the unhappy and conscience-stricken Pullus subsequently committed suicide.

For the present, however, and in the best tradition of Roman fortitude he took the survivors of the disaster to Lilybaeum and did what he could to improve the military situation in western Sicily. Without the cooperation of strong naval forces he could not hope to achieve anything against either Lilybaeum or Drepana: two consular armies had failed to make much impression on the fortifications of the former. On the other hand without a field army the Carthaginians could not re-take Panormus. However Pullus saw an opportunity of surprising the Punic positions on Mount Eryx (Monte San Giuliano) to the east of Drepana, and he captured both the abandoned Elymian city and the great temple of Aphrodite upon the summit. He garrisoned the latter and also fortified a strongpoint at Aegithallus (Pizzo Argenteria, or Sant'Anna), which covered the approach from the direction of Drepana. Carthalo, who had returned to Drepana and probably now commanded there, since Adherbal had returned to Carthage, landed a force by night from his ships which recovered Aegithallus (although only temporarily, it would appear), and according to the annalistic tradition took Pullus himself prisoner. The luckless consul was probably exchanged a couple of years later.

Claudius, the surviving consul, was directed to nominate a dictator to take command of the army in Sicily during the remaining months of the consular year, and after showing his resentment of his treatment by the Senate by nominating a dependant of his own, a scribe and therefore a person ineligible for any magistracy, he nominated A. Atinius Caiatinus, who as consul and praetor had soldiered without disgrace in Sicily in 258, 257 and 254. The Romans do not appear to have lost any further ground under him, the first dictator to command an army outside Italy. The consuls elected for 248 were experienced and successful men, C. Aurelius Cotta and P. Servilius Geminus, who had held office in 252. However they were not given the naval forces, without which they could not hope to take Lilybaeum or Drepana or even to make any serious impression upon their defences.

CHAPTER IV

247-243 BC

Hamilcar Barca. Stalemate in Sicily.

From the Carthaginian point of view, the situation in Sicily was now such that the war should logically have come to an end. Rome was too close to bankruptcy and the maritime communities of Italy were too exhausted for her to be able to mount the large-scale combined operation that alone could finish off the war in her favour. The census returns preserved in the epitome of Livy show a fall in the citizen population of over 50,500 between the start of the war and 247. Even allowing for the likelihood that the figure for 247 does not include the soldiers serving in Sicily, the loss of life over a period of less than two decades is still very heavy, and the allies had suffered even more severely. The Cathaginians must have found it quite inexplicable that Rome did not pocket her losses, as so many other would-be conquerors of Sicily had done, and withdraw, leaving to Carthage the ancient nucleus of her province, from which, when freed from her military entanglement in Africa, she could once again advance her dominion to the Himera and beyond. Indeed the Carthaginians behaved as if an eventual Roman withdrawal were a matter of course. They reinforced neither their fleet nor their army in Sicily, although it is hard to believe that if the victorious Carthalo had been supported by twenty thousand fresh mercenaries and a force of elephants he might not have inflicted enough damage on the Romans to cause them, dispirited as they undoubtedly were, to abandon the struggle, at all events in western Sicily. Carthalo employed his ships to raid the coast of Italy but did not succeed in frightening the Senate into withdrawing the legions from the island; and by the end of the year his own soldiers were in a state of mutiny because they had not received their pay.

The truth of the matter is that the eyes of the rulers of Carthage were most often turned to Africa, where Hanno the Great, the leading proponent of the 'continental empire' policy, was re-establishing his city's suzerainty, capturing the rebel city of Hecatompylus and beginning a seven-year military governorship that made him the uncrowned King of Libya. There was to be no large-scale withdrawal of forces from Africa – and to reinforce Sicily with an army composed of freshly levied troops that would be capable of taking on two consular armies would be to impose a strain upon the economy which, in view of Rome's anticipated withdrawal, could not be countenanced by astute businessmen. Moreover Carthage herself was by now short of money. The war in Africa and the extraordinary demands being made upon her merchant marine must have interfered seriously with her vital trade for precious metals to the west. About this time she tried in vain to negotiate a loan of two thousand talents from Ptolemy II of Egypt, and at the end of the war she was unable to find the money to pay her soldiery. Indeed after 248 part of the fleet was apparently withdrawn from Sicily, as there was no enemy at sea for it to fight, in order to lessen the burden on both the treasury and the maritime population of Africa – citizen, allied and subject – upon which the imperial City depended for her prosperity and hence for her power.

Carthage had usually been opposed by military potentates who had been obliged, to a greater or less extent, to husband the submissiveness of their peoples and the loyalty of their mercenary armies. Her rulers, for all their shrewdness, do not appear to have appreciated the difference between a Dionysius or a Pyrrhus and the Roman Republic, the tenacity of whose aristocracy was matched alike by the obedience of the free people to their duty and by the fidelity of her allies. Indeed King Hiero now renewed his treaty with Rome, although on more favourable terms; his claim to certain additional cities was recognized and he was released from whatever portion of his war indemnity was still outstanding. Nonetheless he had demonstrated his faith in Rome's eventual victory, and this was a valuable and heartening gesture at this juncture, quite apart from the immense material importance to Rome of the alliance.

In the spring of 247 Carthalo was recalled and replaced as admiral by Hamilcar Barca (*Baraq*, perhaps meaning lightning). One of the most serious gaps in our understanding of the First Punic War results from our almost complete lack of information about the details of Carthage's domestic politics, which were superficially so like those of Rome and yet so different in essentials. We know nothing about the rivalries of the great families, the intrigues, the political and dynastic alliances – some lasting, others ephemeral – or the interplay of oligarchy and democracy which was so significant in times of stress. We cannot tell why a Hannibal or a Hamilcar was reappointed to the generalship after a defeat while another man was crucified for mere ineptitude, or why successful generals like Adherbal and Carthalo quickly disappear from history while others, like Hanno the Great and Hamilcar Barca, remained in office for years on end. We know that later the Barcas were prepared to ally themselves with the popular leaders, and perhaps popular support helps to explain the earlier, as it does the subsequent, career of Hamilcar Barca. Be that as it may the appearance on the scene of Hamilcar Barca has a significance beyond the purely military. It marks the re-emergence of individualism in the Carthaginian ruling class; the emergence of a man of war whose patriotism was an extension not of his subordination and loyalty to his class (for class loyalty is the cohesive force of oligarchy) but of loyalty to his own genius and to his house. In this as in other respects he foreshadows the great proconsuls who brought about the downfall of the Roman Republic.

He is described by Nepos as a young man at this time and it is surely not fanciful to suppose that he first saw action in the campaign against Regulus under Xanthippus, and that he then perceived how effective a professional army might be in which, without derogation of military discipline, a close personal relationship was achieved between a permanent commander and his soldiers, and perceived also that the devotion of the latter to their leader, based on their complete confidence in his ability and in his loyalty to them, could take the place of patriotism and loyalty to a state which was no more than their paymaster. Hamilcar's first task was to suppress the mutiny that had broken out among the mercenaries under Carthalo, and this he did with the ruthless severity that the sternness of his character and the circumstances alike dictated. The degree of success with which he imposed his own authority upon these tough and disaffected fighting men is shown by the loyalty with which they followed him for the remaining six years of the war.

By the summer, when the consuls L. Caecilius Metellus (the victor of Panormus) and N. Fabius Buteo arrived in Sicily, their appointment illustrating the recovery of the influence in the Senate of the great Fabian clan, Hamilcar had restored discipline in his command and was ready to begin operations against the enemy. He had under his authority a number of ships (how many we do not know) and the remnants of Carthage's field army in Sicily, plus whatever volunteers may have joined him from the populations of the three loyal cities, Roman deserters and perhaps some Greek and Sicel adventurers. However it seems quite impossible to arrive at even an approximation of the number of troops at Hamilcar's disposal, since the rowers of the ships, after a little training and experience in the field, would be as effective as regular infantrymen in the guerilla warfare to which he committed himself.

Hamilcar's first move was by sea, striking at Rome's maritime allies in the toe of Italy as Carthalo had done; no doubt in the twin hopes of forcing the Romans to keep one consular army at least for home defence and encouraging their allies to revolt. This was a policy which was to become at once central and ultimately fatal to Barcid strategic thinking, and it may have been suggested by Carthage's experience in the case of her own very differently constituted empire. The Romans replied by founding citizen colonies – essentially military coastal strongpoints – at Alsium (Palo) and later, in response to further raids, at Fregenae in Etruria, while a Latin colony was established at Brundisium (Brindisi). Moreover the Carthaginians did not have it all their own way at sea. A group of Roman privateers raided Hippou Acra, burnt the shipping in the harbour and many buildings and got away with their plunder. Of the consuls, Metellus occupied himself with the siege of Lilybaeum while Buteo, who was operating against Drepana, captured the island of Pelias at the mouth of the harbour and held it against attempts by Hamilcar (on his return from Bruttium) to recover it.

Hamilcar countered the threat to Drepana by moving his army by sea into the territory of Panormus and occupying a strong position, usually referred to as Heircte, on an abrupt hill, plausibly identified as Monte Castellacio, about six miles north-west of the city, whose summit offered a fertile plateau about eleven and a half miles in circumference, the possession of which enabled him at once to command the pass between the hill and Monte Gallo near the coast and to beach his ships conveniently at Isola delle Femmine. From this position, which although isolated in the midst of enemy country was open to the sea and defensible against attack by any of the three difficult approaches, Hamilcar maintained for three years a war of raids by sea against the Italian coast as far north as Cumae and of guerilla activity on land against the consular army which the Romans were obliged to keep between him and Panormus. His position was too strong for the Romans to force it and without a fleet they could not starve him out, while he for his part did not have the troops to encounter the Roman heavy infantry in a pitched battle.

It is easy enough from this distance in time to see that the only possible result of this strategy – forced upon Hamilcar by the comparative paucity of the resources allotted to him by his government – was to prolong the war, the Roman people being what they were. It is true that the Roman army and its essentially amateur commanders were quite unsuited to this kind of guerilla warfare. In the six months during which a consul commanded his two legions in the field he had no time to learn a new trade of war; and the Roman and Italian conscripted peasants who composed the maniples must have suffered more, psychologically if not physically, than Hamilcar's mercenaries from the seemingly endless and apparently purposeless skirmishing under a Sicilian sun. Yet Rome's prestige and hence the security of her hegemony of Italy, as well as her fides and the honour of her aristocracy, were committed to the defeat of Carthage; and if Hamilcar was to drive the Romans from Sicily it could only be by destroying their two armies there to the last man. For it is very doubtful if even Roman fortitude could have survived another military or naval débâcle.

In fact it was Hamilcar who first wearied of this inconclusive warfare, which was perhaps proving less effective in relieving the pressure upon Drepana than he had hoped. In the summer of 244 he flitted by night from Heircte to Drepana, disembarked his men and led them against the abandoned town of Eryx and put the Roman garrison to the sword. He then established himself at Eryx, thus isolating the Roman forces stationed in the temple of Aphrodite on the summit of the mountain and putting them in a state of siege and also neutralizing the Roman strongpoint below the town at Aegithallus, from which they had been threatening Drepana and severing its communications with the surrounding countryside. We hear of no further raids on the Italian coast; indeed his ships must by now have been in very poor condition (perhaps this was one of the factors that induced him to move from his totally isolated ground at Heircte to the proximity of friendly Drepana), and they were now sent back to Africa and laid up there, apart from the few that he kept in service in order to provision his army.

He reopened the guerilla warfare from his new positions. For two more years consuls and their armies came and went. They failed to dislodge Hamilcar from the heights of Eryx or to relieve the garrison in the temple precinct of Aphrodite, and they made no impression on the walls of Lilybaeum. Yet Hamilcar could neither give battle to the consuls nor overpower the Romans in the temple; and for all his skill in preserving his army from destruction and in keeping the loyalty of the majority of his men, his achievements between 247 and 243 could have no bearing on the outcome of the war. The continuation of hostilities was costing Carthage nothing except the mounting arrears of her mercenaries' pay, while it was burdensome to Rome in terms of lives and money expended to no useful purpose, conveying a sense of futility. Yet Rome, with her vast resources of manpower, could continue such a war almost indefinitely, whereas Hamilcar's forces, unless he were heavily reinforced from Carthage, must in the long run become too attenuated to defend their essentially precarious position. Indeed a thousand of his Gauls – always an unreliable breed – attempted to betray Eryx to the enemy, to whom they then deserted. They subsequently compensated themselves for their disappointment by plundering the temple of Aphrodite. In effect the Hamilcaric interlude in the large-scale fighting gave Italy the opportunity of recovering from the appalling maritime disasters of 255–249 and made it possible for the Roman Senate, by the end of 243, to ask the people and the allies to make one more mighty effort to break the deadlock in western Sicily and bring the war to an end.

CHAPTER V

242-241 BC

Roman victory at sea. The Peace of Catulus.

The Roman treasury was in fact exhausted, but once the decision to build another fleet had been taken moral pressure was exerted upon the wealthiest members of society to put up the money for the new ships and to undertake the construction – either individually or in groups of two or three, of two hundred quinqueremes (an arrangement similar to the Athenian system of *symmories*). They were to be reimbursed out of the war indemnity that would be extorted from a defeated Carthage, and modern cynicism should not be allowed to belittle this expression of patriotism in view of Rome's more recent performance at sea. The new ships were built to the pattern of Hannibal the Rhodian's blockade runner – lighter, faster and more manœuvrable than the older design. There was no corvus. The consuls for 242 BC were C. Lutatius Catulus and A. Postumius Albinus. However the latter was also *flamen martialis*, responsible for the cult of no less a deity than the god of war, and his office was one of especial sanctity. The *pontifex maximus*, L. Caecilius Metellus, accordingly forbade him to leave the city; we can only conjecture what considerations apart from the religious ones led him to take this step. The command of the expedition was therefore entrusted to C. Lutatius Catulus, who was probably one of the chief proponents of the resumed naval policy. In the absence of the second consul the city praetor, Q. Valerius Falto, accompanied him, and this arrangement ensured that the overall command would be firmly in the hands of a single senior magistrate.

Catulus set sail with his enormous convoy – it included seven hundred transports according to the annalistic account – in May or early June 242, and descended on the coast between Drepana and Lilybaeum. He seized the port of Drepana and the roadstead of Lilybaeum and having thus cut both places off from the sea made an attempt to take Drepana by assault which failed. He then proceeded to besiege the city, which like Lilybaeum and like Hamilcar's positions on Mount Eryx would inevitably fall in the long run to starvation unless relief were sent from Carthage. Hamilcar has been criticized for sending his fleet home, but we are wholly ignorant of the circumstances in which he did so. Apart from the

60

considerations that the ships were probably in a bad state, that he may have needed the rowers for use ashore as light infantry and that he may have been ordered by the Council to send them home in order to reduce the cost of the war, the ships that he had at his disposal when he first assumed command could hardly have been numerous enough, even if they had still been at Drepana, to do more than present the Roman navy with an easy initial victory. On the other hand Carthaginian intelligence, deprived of reconnaissance and scouting vessels, had been taken wholly unawares by the arrival of Catulus' armada.

Carthage awoke belatedly to her danger. The policy of attrition had failed. Rome was not going to abandon the attack on her last strongholds in Sicily and make a peace that would eventually enable her to recover the lost ground. She at once set herself to prepare a fleet that would be able to break the Roman blockade and recover the command of the sea. Presumably a large number of new vessels had to be built, seventy-five thousand rowers had to be enlisted, and many, perhaps the majority of them, had to be trained. This was a far greater task than Carthage, habitually slow in such matters, could accomplish before the end of the sailing season of 242. Thus not only did the Carthaginian position in Sicily greatly deteriorate during 242 but Catulus was able, by daily exercise of his crews and continual manœuvres, to train his fleet to a far higher pitch of efficiency than any Roman fleet had previously attained, in preparation for the struggle at sea which would decide the outcome of the war. Indeed when the two fleets met the customary relationship between them was to be reversed, and a skilful and practised Roman fleet, relying for victory on seamanship and rapidity of manœuvre, would encounter an inexperienced and only part-trained enemy who intended to place much, if not all, his trust in the fighting quality of Hamilcar's mercenaries.

It was March 241 BC – the very beginning of the new sailing season – before the Carthaginians were ready to attempt the relief of their beleaguered towns and army. There is no good reason to suppose that they did not know approximately how many Roman ships they would have to fight, or that they did not prepare what they believed to be an adequate fleet. It is therefore probably best to ignore modern estimates of its size and to accept the 250 ships that Diodorus gives us, drawing on the pro-Carthaginian Philinus. The commander was a Hanno (not to be identified with Hanno the Great and probably not with the Hanno who had failed before Acragas and off Ecnomus in 262 and 256), and his ships were laden with stores which it was his intention to land, presumably north of Eryx since Drepana was being closely besieged. He would then take on board Hamilcar and the pick of his soldiers, before engaging the Roman fleet in the decisive battle.

Hanno, with his convoy of warships and transports, sailed first to

Hiera, an outer island of the Aegates group (Egadi) lying some thirty miles west of Drepana, and waited there for a wind that would enable him to run straight in to his destination before the Romans could intercept him. Catulus had his scouts out and learning of Hanno's arrival at Hiera put picked legionaries on board his galleys and rowed to the island of Aegusa, thus putting himself between Hanno and both Lilybaeum and Drepana. Daybreak of 10 March saw a stiff westerly breeze blowing with heavy seas running – perfect conditions for Hanno's blockade run. Catulus, however, had come to Sicily to end the war, and he must have realized that he might never again be offered by the gods so favourable an opportunity of doing so, notwithstanding contrary winds and seas and the fact that he himself, probably as a result of a wound received in the assult on Drepana, was partially disabled and had to fight the ensuing battle from his litter. When the Punic fleet was sighted heading for Sicily under sail he put to sea and laid his fleet in line of battle across the enemy's path, the arduous training to which he had earlier subjected his crews now paying a handsome dividend. Hanno had no option but to accept battle, and so he struck his masts and engaged the enemy. The battle, in which the tactical command was probably exercised by the praetor Falto, was a short one, the Carthaginian defeat was decisive, and it is probable that it was only the complete shift of the wind that saved Hanno's fleet from total destruction, for it enabled those ships that had broken off the action to raise their masts and escape to the west under sail (the Romans had no doubt left their sailing gear on shore). As it was, fifty Punic ships were sunk and seventy taken, with nearly ten thousand prisoners. The Roman losses (in spite of what Philinus says) probably amounted to only twelve ships. Catulus and Falto sailed back to Lilybaeum and the principal Roman camp, fully confident that the war was won.

Catulus and Falto were right. Even if the Carthaginian government had been prepared to make another effort to relieve its cities and army in western Sicily it is difficult to believe that it could have mounted another expedition, building at least 120 new ships and raising thirty-six thousand fresh rowers in order merely to achieve parity with the Romans, before the end of the summer. And by that time Lilybaeum and the other strongholds would inevitably have succumbed to famine or treason. The Roman annalistic tradition asserts that the Carthaginians crucified the luckless Hanno for the crime of failing to carry out a task which the dilatoriness of his own people had made immensely more difficult.

The Carthaginian government, unwilling to shoulder the responsibility of abandoning Sicily, gave Hamilcar plenipotentiary power to decide what course should be adopted and to negotiate a peace if he felt further resistance to be useless. Hamilcar was a realist. He knew that so far from there being nothing to gain by delay it was actually to his own and his country's advantage to make peace at once. The longer he waited the more serious would become the food situation in his camp and in the cities. Morale would deteriorate, the likelihood of treachery increase, and his own unbeaten army begin to appear less formidable in the eyes of the confident Romans. Moreover he was doubtless aware that Catulus was as anxious as anyone for peace to be concluded swiftly. The consular year was almost at an end and if 1 May found the war still in progress, the new consuls A. Manlius Torquatus (who had failed, three years earlier, to make any impression on Hamilcar's position at Eryx) and Catulus' brother Quintus would be sent to Sicily, to reap the glory of concluding a war which Gaius had won. Until the end of April then, Hamilcar possessed an important bargaining counter, apart from the un-defeated condition of his army.

Hamilcar was anxious to save as much as he could of his own prestige and credit, as well as his army. He appears, very astutely, to have opened negotiations with Catulus through Gisgo, who had replaced Himilco as military governor of Lilybaeum and who perhaps belonged to the faction in the Council that was opposed to himself. Catulus quite naturally demanded that Hamilcar should lay down his arms and hand over all deserters, who were probably pretty numerous; but Hamilcar was already thinking of the future and of the importance of preserving un-blemished his 'image' as the undefeated general. So he rejected these con-ditions which Catulus had no alternative but to waive, if he was to have the glory of concluding the peace. The peace terms which Hamilcar accepted were that the Carthaginians should evacuate Sicily completely and that they should not make war upon Hiero or upon the Syracusans if Hiero ceased to be king, or upon his allies (thus recognizing the indepen-dence and legitimacy of Hiero's greater kingdom), or upon the other allies of Rome. The Romans for their part undertook not to molest Carthage's allies. In addition the Carthaginians agreed to give up all Italian prisoners of war without ransom (they would have to ransom their own) and to pay an indemnity of 2,200 Euboeic talents (over 125,000 pounds of silver) in twenty annual instalments, thus rendering Carthage to all intents and purposes a tributary state for almost a generation.

On Hamilcar's agreeing to these terms, he was granted an armistice and was allowed to send envoys to Rome to secure the necessary ratifica-tion of the treaty by the sovereign people in centuriate assembly. How-ever, when the consul laid the terms of the treaty, which must have received the prior approval of the Senate, before the centuries they refused to accept them. They did not care very greatly whether or not C. Catulus had the distinction of ending the war; they only knew that Carthage was beaten and that having cost Rome and Italy so many tens of thousands of lives and so much treasure she should be made to pay more heavily for the peace. So the Senate, perhaps as the result of a bill passed in the plebeian Assembly by a tribune, since the centuriate Assembly did not have the power to initiate proposals or to amend those laid before it, sent ten commissioners to Sicily to look into the matter. In spite of the unpacific attitude of the Roman people, the commissioners made no fresh demands upon Carthage which might harden her resolution to continue the war. They raised the indemnity by a thousand talents and shortened the period of repayment to ten years, thus releasing her the sooner from her obligation. They also required the evacuation of the Lipari and Aegates Islands (Lipara was already in Roman hands) and perhaps added the clauses that certainly appeared in the final treaty, forbidding Carthage to recruit mercenaries in Italy or Sicily or to send her warships into Italian or Sicilian waters. Hamilcar, true to his policy of dissociating himself from a defeat in which he did not feel that he shared, was not one of those who swore to this treaty, which in its revised form was accepted by the centuriate Assembly. The extra thousand talents no doubt seemed a grand sum to the Roman farmers, who would thus have their tributum repaid, and the shortened time for payment of the whole indemnity would have satisfied their natural wish both to see their money more quickly and to grind their enemy a little in the process.

So ended the first and longest of the three Punic Wars; or, if viewed from a more romantic standpoint, the first act of a three-act tragedy, the tragedy of the destruction not only of Carthage but also of old Rome – of Rome the city state. Perhaps the most astonishing thing about this first war is the tenaciousness with which the Romans prosecuted it. The nobility was as yet uncorrupted by greed for material gain, and to its members the consulship, and with it the command of a consular army, was an end in itself, the attainment of a triumph was the crown of a successful career, and fides was a concept fundamental to the solidarity not only of the Italian confederation but also of the uniquely Roman aristo-democratic régime. That the nobility should have been prepared to fight on to the bitter end in order to vindicate the fides of the city with which, corporately and individually, they identified themselves is not so surprising. Moreover the war scarcely touched them as a class economically, and many individuals did very well, quite legitimately, out of the distribution, sale and shrewd re-purchase of booty. Nor is it surprising that the nascent capitalist class – the businessmen and contractors, before long to be identified socially and politically as the Equestrian Order – favoured the continuation of a war which, if it interfered with trade, enabled fortunes to be made out of senatorial contracts.

What is at first sight astonishing is that in an age when the democratic

impetus was by no means spent and when the Republic might, at a superficial viewing, seem to be slipping down the road that, two hundred years
earlier, the Athenians had followed towards a genuinely popular régime,
the Roman people should have been prepared to pour out their blood
and their scanty money, neglecting the agriculture which was the business
of life of most of them, in order to fight abroad mainly under inexpert
generals in a war which seems to us to have been remote from their interests. Yet the burden of the war upon the peasantry probably did not
appear as heavy to them as it does to the retrospective eye of history.
Rome's citizen body had increased in size during the by no means peaceful
quarter of a century that preceded the outbreak of the war by seven per
cent and was probably in danger of becoming larger than Rome's territory could well support. The annual levy of four legions, at the most
twenty thousand citizens, was well within the capacity of an adult male
population of 292,000 to supply and the practice of keeping one or both
armies in Sicily for longer than a single campaign meant that the full levy
was not held every year. It is true that the heaviest losses, such as those
suffered at sea between 256 and 249, were so great that no community
of that size could sustain many repetitions of them. Yet in most years
of the war the loss of life must have been relatively slight, and the citizen
body was dispersed over such a wide area that the impact upon the morale
of Roman society even of such a disaster as the loss of the fleet off
Camarina was probably less damaging than would have been the case
with a more compact community, such as the Carthaginian. It is worth
noting that even in the years immediately following such disasters, Rome
was able to maintain two consular armies in the field, that we do not
hear of popular or tribunician opposition to the levies or to the war, and
that the generals who commanded the fleets wrecked in 255 and 253 were
awarded triumphs for earlier successes. Indeed the only tribunician
activity we hear of is the attack in 248 upon P. Claudius Pulcher and
that upon his sister Claudia two years later: attacks not upon the war
as such but upon the *superbia*, the arrogance, of the Claudii. The only
occasion on which we hear of the people rejecting the policy of the Senate
was that on which they turned down the moderate terms of peace.

Sicily, westward of the borders of Hiero's kingdom and of the sovereign
allied states of Messana and Tauromenium, became Rome's first overseas
possession. There were probably at this time more than five free cities,
and of these Panormus was and remained the most important. The
remaining Sicilian communities became Roman subjects and paid tithes
to the Roman treasury in accordance with the system familiar to many
of them from the rule of the Kings of Syracuse (the *Lex Hieronica*), and
all communities in the province were liable to indirect taxation such as
harbour dues. Sicily became one of Rome's principal suppliers of grain,

especially in time of war. The Republic was at first represented in the island by a quaestor stationed at Lilybaeum, but it was found by experience that a magistrate with imperium was needed to act as chief judge and military governor, and so in 227 two new praetorships were created, one for Sicily and one for Sardinia and Corsica. The territory supervised by the praetor constituted his province (*provincia*), and thus the word came to acquire the significance with which we are familiar, that of an extra-Italian territorial possession of the Roman people.

CHAPTER VI

241-237 BC

The Libyan war and the rape of Sardinia.

The great war – in Polybius' opinion, the greatest war in history down to that time – was over, and to mark its ending the Romans ceremoniously closed the temple of Janus. Carthage, however, had immediately to face the consequences of her ill-timed parsimony in a new war that brought her much closer to destruction than ever the Romans had succeeded in doing. Hamilcar Barca had not accepted his command in Sicily in order to preside over the dissolution of the Carthaginian empire. Moreover that command came to an end with the ending of the war and there is really no need to suppose, as some historians do, that he was forced to resign by his political opponents. At all events he brought his men down to Lilybaeum and at once retired into private life, leaving to Gisgo, the governor of the town, the onerous and invidious task of shipping back to Africa for paying off the twenty thousand mercenaries who composed the garrisons of Lilybaeum, Drepana and perhaps Heraclea Minoa, and the field force from Eryx. They consisted of Iberians, Celts, Balearic islanders, Ligurians, Phoenicians, half-breed Greeks (mostly runaway slaves) and Libyans, these last being the largest ethnic group. Gisgo, who understood the men that he was dealing with, took the wise precaution of sending them to Carthage by instalments so that the City should not be encumbered with a horde of barbarians no longer subject to the restraints of military discipline and should be able to pay them off and send them home piecemeal as they arrived.

Funds were low in the public treasury as a result of the expense of fitting out Hanno's fatal expedition and paying the first instalment of the war indemnity to Rome, coming on top of twenty-three years of costly warfare by land and sea, and the magnates were always averse to dipping very deeply into their own pockets, as long as any alternative could be found. Moreover no businessman likes having to find the money to pay for a speculation that has already failed. So instead of doing as Gisgo expected the government waited until the whole body of mercenaries was assembled in Carthage and then, because they were proving troublesome in the City, persuaded them to withdraw, bag and baggage, to the more permissive environment of Sicca, a little over a hundred miles to the south-west of Carthage. There it informed them through the mouth of Hanno, the military governor of Africa and the chief of the anti-Barcine party in the Council, that because of the burden of the cost of the late war and of the war indemnity the Republic was unable to meet their demands. Indeed, the latter had in the interval become enormously inflated as the soldiers recalled the length and harshness of their service and the lavish promises of reward that their generals, particularly Hamilcar, had held out to them.

Once again, as so often in the past, the rulers of Carthage had been betrayed by their commercializing habit of thinking. In business a creditor who is himself in difficulties will often agree to compound a debt rather than wait indefinitely for the whole amount, but the heterogeneous mob of fighting men at Sicca were not imbued with business principles. Their ignorance of the Punic language, except in basic military matters, defeated the eloquence and sweet reasonableness of Hanno, and they understood only that Carthage was proposing to bilk them of their hard-earned pay. Nor was it really tactful of the Republic to have sent to them as its negotiator a man whom most if not all of them regarded, rightly or wrongly, as one of the causes of their having been left for so many years to fight the Romans unaided. Their response to Hanno's arguments was to march to Tunis, a little over thirteen miles from Carthage, and to back their demands – which steadily became more and more outrageous as the frightened citizens gave way on every point – with a show of force. Finally, they agreed, since Gisgo had earned their trust by his handling of the evacuation of Sicily, to accept him as paymaster and arbitrator. Hamilcar, who would seem to have been the obvious choice for the rôle, apart from being at odds with the oligarchy was also suspect in the eyes of the mercenaries, who considered, not perhaps without justification, that he had abandoned them just when his leadership and advocacy were most needed and had sacrificed their interests to his own.

However it did not at all suit the most desperate and turbulent men among them that the mutiny should end so tamely. They worked upon the easily aroused fears and suspicions of their fellow soldiers, particularly of the largest and most vulnerable group, that of the native Libyans. Those who were for settling the matter peaceably, such as the officers, were stoned and the Libyan Matho, who had made himself a marked man by his violent conduct, and a Campanian deserter named Spendius, a man without a country, who had been chiefly responsible for bringing about the breakdown of the agreed settlement, were elected as the mercenaries' generals. They seized and imprisoned Gisgo and his staff and bound their followers by oath to wage war, without respect for the generally accepted rules, against Carthage.

So began the Truceless War, which Polybius calls the Libyan War because almost all Carthage's Libyan subjects embraced the cause of the mercenaries out of resentment at the harshness of Punic rule and the grinding weight of Punic taxation. Hanno, the military governor of Africa and the principal architect of Carthaginian oppression, who had made his reputation by the suppression of the Libyan and Numidian revolts that had followed the expedition of Regulus, was naturally given the command against the rebels. An administrator rather than a fighting soldier he gained an initial victory before Utica with his massive elephant corps and then allowed his army to be surprised and routed by a counter-stroke delivered by the veterans of Mount Eryx. Indeed he mishandled the campaign so consistently that Carthage turned to the man with a reputation for invincibility and sent Hamilcar out with ten thousand men and seventy elephants to retrieve the situation. Apart from the odium that attached to him most unfairly as the man who had negotiated the surrender of Sicily, Hamilcar had more recently been blamed for the mutiny of his former troops on the grounds that the lavishness of his promises to them when general was responsible for their present rapacity and intransigence. Politically isolated, he had allied himself with the leader of the popular party, Hasdrubal, who was to become his son-in-law, and the intervention of the people – formidable when they did take a hand in affairs – got him out of trouble and procured him his command.

Hamilcar quickly improved Carthage's military position, defeating both Matho and Spendius; but the latter were still able to keep the field and Hamilcar was powerless to prevent the revolt of the Sardinian garrison and the massacre not only of the Carthaginians already there but also of the officers of a relieving force that went over to the mutineers. In Libya the rebels also butchered the hapless Gisgo and their other Punic captives and this atrocity, in conjunction with a deliberate 'policy of frightfulness' adopted by the mutineers, forced Hamilcar to abandon his own policy of mildness and conciliation towards his former comrades-in-arms and to meet atrocity and treachery with the same. No two generals who hated each other as Hanno and Hamilcar did could possibly have cooperated effectively, and this failure was reflected by the revolt of the traditionally loyal cities of Utica and Hippou Acra and the appearance of the rebel army before the walls of Carthage, to which it laid regular siege. Hanno was now relieved of his command, on the vote of the soldiers themselves, and this left Hamilcar free to cut the mercenaries off from the hinterland and from their supplies and to raise the siege. In this operation he had the assistance of another son-in-law-to-be, a Numidian chief named Naravas. A war of movement in the open country began again, with Hamilcar always having the advantage, which culminated in the annihilation, possibly by treachery, of Spendius and his force of perhaps twenty thousand men at a place called the Saw. Even so the war was not over, for Matho not only held out in Tunis but succeeded in defeating and killing Hamilcar's lieutenant, Hannibal, and in forcing Hamilcar himself to relinquish his control of the open country. Following this setback the thirty members of the Gerousia waited on Hamilcar in his camp and persuaded him to become formally reconciled with Hanno, who had now been reinstated in his command. Working together in rare harmony, the two generals quickly forced Matho to abandon Tunis and withdraw to the east coast, to the region about Leptis Minor, where they brought him to battle. His defeat and capture were followed at once by the submission of those Libyans still in revolt, apart from the cities of Utica and Hippou Acra which were besieged and forced to capitulate. Carthage was now more secure in her domination of Libya than ever, following the defeat in the field of those Libyans who had taken up arms against her and the exemplary punishment of Matho, the inspiration and leader of the revolt. Moreover the victories won, in part with citizen soldiers, by Hamilcar and Hanno over the veterans of the Sicilian war, and the recovery of Utica, the oldest Phoenician city in north Africa, must have gone a long way towards restoring the confidence and spirit of the Carthaginians, which had been so badly shaken by the war with Rome and its terrible aftermath.

Throughout the war, which lasted from the summer of 240 probably until the early summer of 237, the Romans had pursued a scrupulously correct – even a friendly – line of conduct towards Carthage. A diplomatic incident involving some five hundred Italian traders seized at sea whilst engaged in running supplies to the rebels and now held prisoner at Carthage was settled amicably. Rome not only laid a strict embargo on trade with the insurgents but also encouraged her nationals to trade with Carthage, and when the City was besieged an important part was played in its resistance by the supplies sent in from Italy and from Syracuse, whose astute ruler saw in the survival of Carthage an essential counter-balance to the preponderance of Rome. Moreover the Romans as a gesture of good will released all the prisoners of war whom they still held unransomed, and when the mutinous garrison of Sardinia invited them to take the island over they very properly refused, subsequently rejecting a similar proposal on the part of the citizens of Utica.

However when the war in Africa came to an end the triumphant Carthaginians found themselves confronted by what they – although not necessarily the Romans – could only regard as a fundamental change of Roman attitude and policy. When in the second year of the war the Senate had refused to intervene in Sardinia, it had done so for several very good reasons. In the first place the Treaty of Catulus expressly forbade any such action and adherence to the terms of the treaty involved not only Rome's fides but also that of Catulus himself, whose views must still have carried great weight in the Senate. Again, although the war had been a long and costly one it had involved very little damage to Italian property and so had left no legacy of bitterness and hatred such as might influence a nation of farmers to break their faith; nor is it good policy for one imperial power to encourage the revolt of another's subjects in time of peace. But above all the Senate was not yet thinking in 'Mediterranean' terms. The war just ended had been fought for control of Sicily, regarded as a geographical and therefore a political extension of Italy, not for domination of the western Mediterranean, and after a couple of half-hearted campaigns against Sardinia the Romans had ignored the island completely, and the terms of Catulus' treaty had implicitly confirmed Carthage in possession of it.

The mutineers in Sardinia, having gained control of the whole province, before very long fell out with the natives, were driven out by them and fled to Italy. On their arrival they once more approached the Senate, no doubt hoping to be employed by Rome in the reconquest and garrisoning of the island. From Rome's point of view the circumstances were now quite different from those of 239. Then the mercenaries, albeit in a state of mutiny, had represented a Carthaginian presence in Sardinia. That presence had now been removed, the natives by expelling their garrison could be considered to have renounced their alliances with Carthage, and Sardinia itself could be regarded as unoccupied territory which Rome might legitimately occupy.

It is not necessary to assume that the Senate had undergone a radical change of outlook and was taking a conscious step in the direction of ultimate control of the Mediterranean and thus of world empire. No doubt at the earlier date voices had been raised to point out that a Punic Sardinia not only posed a permanent threat to the coastlands of Etruria, Latium and Campania but also left Carthage in a position to close the sea routes between Italy and Spain, as she had already done for centuries; something not to be tolerated by the power that had wrested from her the command of the sea. Moreover if Sicily, being an extension of Italy geographically, was to be regarded as an extension politically, it could be argued that the same was true of Sardinia and Corsica. It is likely that the second debate took place before Carthage's final victory over the mercenaries but when the outcome of the war seemed no longer in doubt. It was evident that Carthage would emerge from her present straits more completely in control of Libya and so more formidable, once she had restored her financial position, than before the Truceless War. Rome (it was argued) should therefore seize the opportunity offered by the Carthaginian evacuation of Sardinia to take over the island and ensure the security of the Italian seaboard from attack in the event of a future war with Rome's dangerous maritime neighbour, while Carthage still had her hands tied by the war in Africa. It was decided accordingly that Rome should forestall a Punic reconquest of Sardinia by occupying the island herself, and the consul Tiberius Sempronius Gracchus crossed over and took formal possession of it.

When the Carthaginians learnt of Rome's action they were naturally indignant and protested against this seizure of part of their empire contrary to the Treaty of Catulus. They also began to prepare an expedition to the island for the purpose of re-establishing their authority over it. But however morally justifiable the action of Carthage may have been, the Romans – unless they were prepared to renounce their claim to Sardinia and to appear in the eyes of the world to have done so out of fear of Carthage – were bound to regard such an expedition as being directed against themselves. Accordingly the Senate secured a vote of the Assembly in favour of war 'unless . . .', and sent an ultimatum to the Carthaginians which, as the Romans refused to discuss the matter, they had no choice in the circumstances but to accept. Two further clauses were appended to the treaty, by which Carthage gave up Sardinia and agreed to pay an additional 1,200 talents indemnity in order to buy off the threat of war.

This action was dictated rather by expediency and a certain nervousness about the future than by any deep-seated hostility towards Carthage, much less by any long-term plan for the dismemberment of her empire. Nonetheless it was fatal to any hope of re-establishing good relations between the two powers. From the strictly legalistic standpoint – which was how the Roman Senate regarded the matter – Rome had a case. That she refused, however, to argue it shows how close to the legal wind she was conscious of sailing. Nor was there any getting around the fact that her action was both an unfriendly one and a shabby one in taking advantage of a friendly power's embarrassment in this way. That the Romans were aware that they came out of the matter badly is shown by the attempts made by their historians and apologists to justify the seizure of Sardinia by claiming that it was formally ceded to Rome, either as compensation for Carthage's arrest of the Italian traders or even under the terms of the Treaty of Catulus. It is a human trait, says Tacitus, to hate those whom you have injured. Certainly only the very insensitive can avoid being suspicious of those they have injured. The Romans must have been well aware that they had done Carthage an unforgiveable injury and that henceforth the mistress of Africa must be considered as a potential enemy and that a second Punic War – a war of revenge – was a possibility that must always be taken into account.

CHAPTER VII

237-219 BC

First interlude. The Barcas in Spain. Rome, the Gauls and the Illyrians.

Sardinia had been Carthage's most treasured overseas possession; more valuable to her, although less illustrious, than Sicily which throughout its history had involved her in costly and ultimately disastrous wars with her Greek neighbours. Many prominent Carthaginians may in their hearts have been relieved to see Sicily go, and to be rid of a liability; but the loss of Sardinia, and especially the manner of its loss, were things deeply felt and resented. This, then, was what was meant by the faith of the Roman people. Those members of the ruling class who, like Hanno, saw the future in terms of the consolidation and expansion of Carthage's economic empire in Africa and the western Mediterranean in friendship with Rome – or at least avoiding the occasions of conflict with her – now found it harder to rebut the assertion of Hamilcar and his faction that Rome was to be regarded as the City's implacable enemy, determined to injure her whenever the occasion offered and ultimately to strip her of the empire upon whose exploitation her prosperity and power depended.

It was indeed time for the Carthaginian governing class to take fresh stock of their position as masters of an empire, now that for the first time since the sixth century their monopoly of the trade of the western Mediterranean might seem to be in jeopardy. The Carthaginian empire was overtly parasitical and exploitative, being maintained, irrespective of the benefits that it might confer incidentally upon its subject peoples, solely for the benefit of the Carthaginian people in general and of the ruling aristocracy in particular. However, it had always been a matter of policy with the aristocracy to keep to a minimum the burdens imposed upon their City by the demands of imperial defence and administration. In time of peace they maintained no military establishment, for to arm and train a citizen militia would inevitably be to increase the political influence of the popular Assembly, while to keep a standing army of mercenaries would be unacceptably expensive. They spent no more than they had to upon the navy; and they allowed the subject peoples the free management of their own affairs and discouraged them from revolting

73

against their economic bondage by the threat of harsh reprisals when at length the City should bestir herself to act.

It could be argued that the traditional methods were no longer effectual. The late war with Rome had shown that the City was at a serious disadvantage when confronted by a great military power whose rulers were able to persuade their people that the national interest coincided with their own pursuit of honour and glory. Her own leaders, accustomed to think in terms of profit and loss, had been quite unable to assess accurately the policies of such an adversary. If it was the case that Rome must henceforward be regarded not as a potential trade rival but as an enemy, some way had to be found of counterbalancing her apparently limitless resources in manpower and raw materials, and some improvement had to be made to the defences of the empire so as to enable Carthage to respond quickly and effectively to any military threat that might develop from the direction of Rome. In short, the government had to face up to the necessity of providing the empire with a permanent military establishment and with sinews of war to match those of the Roman confederation.

As has been said already, the militarization of the people was out of the question, for political, social and economic reasons. If Carthage was to have a standing army it must consist of mercenaries, and there was not likely to be any shortage of these. The City's recruiting agents were familiar figures to the warlike tribes of Iberia, the Balearic Islands, Gaul and Liguria, and she had also the large native populations of Libya and Numidia to draw on. A policy of reliance upon a mercenary standing army, however, posed several serious problems. The first and most essential was that of finding the money with which to pay it. Next, a way must be found of keeping it regularly and profitably occupied, for an unemployed army soon becomes demoralized and mutinous. Thirdly, long-term commanders had to be found, men capable of winning from professional soldiers drawn from half a dozen or more races a personal devotion to match the deeply rooted loyalty which the Roman conscript gave to his fatherland and to his elected leaders. And lastly the rulers of Carthage had to ensure that the commander and his devoted army were not drawn into domestic politics, with the result that the former came to dominate or overthrow the régime, as Hiero had done at Syracuse.

The problem of finding a commander might be regarded as almost resolved, provided solutions could be found to the remaining problems. Hamilcar Barca had been undefeated in the war with Rome and had played the leading part in crushing the mutineers and their African allies. Moreover, by his conduct of the campaigns of Heircte and Mount Eryx he had shown that he possessed the gift of inspiring mercenary soldiers with a loyalty and devotion that far transcended the demands of a merely contractual obligation. Yet Hamilcar's own loyalty to the oligarchy of which he was a member was not thought to be above suspicion.

As has been already noted, it was the traditional policy of the governing class to ensure that the odium of defeat was borne not by the régime but by the individual immediately involved. Hamilcar had been left to cope with the Romans for nearly six years virtually unsupported, while the resources of the City were employed by Hanno in reconquering Libya. It would be remarkable if he had not become embittered against the oligarchs. However, he had refused to be defeated in the field by the Romans and he had refused also to be made the scapegoat for the surrender of Sicily – even though the onus of negotiating this had been passed on to him by the Council. He had refused to sign the treaty and had handed over to Gisgo the inglorious task of shipping home the troops who had failed to win the war. He probably hoped to keep himself unmarked by the stigma of a defeat in which he did not feel that he himself shared, but if this was so his subtlety rebounded upon him; for he not only forfeited the respect of his veterans but also gave his enemies in the Council the opportunity of laying upon him part at least of the odium of the mutiny. Moreover if he and not first Hanno and then the honest Gisgo had been the one to negotiate with the mutineers and try to mollify them, the situation might well not have got out of hand.

However by his astuteness in making a political ally of the leader of the people and by his resounding successes in the field he had more than recovered the ground he had lost, and at the end of the Truceless War his prestige and his political influence stood higher than ever. The question now was, what was to become of him. War was his occupation, as another nobleman's might be politics or commerce or the management of his estates. For him victory in the terrible game of war was its own reward. Even in less critical circumstances such a man would have been an embarrassment to his City, for it is difficult to see how he could have reconciled himself to the inaction and boredom of peace. Such men sometimes became soldiers of fortune, and there was usually a ready market for their talents in the great kingdoms of the eastern Mediterranean. Hamilcar, however, was at once the most popular and influential man in Carthage and a virtual outcast from his own class. He must have appeared to constitute a real threat to the security of a régime that depended above all for its survival upon the loyalty and solidarity of its members.

Like a democracy, a 'constitutional' oligarchy (what Thucydides calls *isonomia*) is secure only as long as its members are agreed on fundamental issues. Political struggles, the war of conflicting political ambitions, are a matter of shifting alliances within the framework of the oligarchical system. Even where – as at Rome and to a modified degree at Carthage – the people enjoy an arbitral rôle, the system is not endangered, since no individual member, or minority group of members, will go to lengths which might lead to the undermining of the authority of the ruling class. When, however, there is disagreement over fundamentals there is the danger that the minority will look for allies outside the ruling class. It may turn to the people, considered as the antithesis of oligarchy, which may lead to the establishment of democracy, as happened at Athens between 508 and 462 BC; to the army, which may produce a military dictatorship; or even to a foreign power.

There is good reason to suppose that by the middle of the third century the Carthaginian ruling class was divided over a fundamental issue and that matters were brought to a head by the outcome of the Roman war and in particular by the loss of Sardinia. The dispute was between those who, like Hanno, had adopted the habits of mind of a landed aristocracy and believed that Carthage should concentrate her efforts upon preserving and extending her dominion over Libya and that she should concern herself less with the acquisition of overseas possessions which were likely to bring her into conflict with her Greek and Italian neighbours, and those who still considered that Carthage's destiny lay upon the sea. The loss of Sicily by itself would very probably have decided the issue in favour of the continentalists. However the rape of Sardinia, and the evidence which it appeared to provide of Rome's unrelenting hostility, reopened the debate, for it revealed the military and economic vulnerability of the empire and pointed to the necessity of making a fresh appraisal of the situation.

Not the least significant factors in this situation were the personality and attitude of Hamilcar himself. Barca was still in the prime of life, and he lived for the day when he could renew – only this time on terms more favourable to himself – the struggle with Rome, which from his own point of view had been brought to an inconclusive halt by the culpable failure of his own government to wrest the command of the sea from Rome. Rome's bad faith in seizing Sardinia played into his hands, for it reinflamed the resentment of the nation, which Rome's earlier friendly behaviour had appeased, and provided a cogent argument bearing upon the national interest for embarking at once upon an energetic programme of overseas conquest which suited exactly both his own ambitions and the interests of his ally, the people. For the loss of Sardinia, following hard on that of Sicily, had not only struck a serious blow at the revenues of the state and the prosperity of the commercial class but also jeopardized the very livelihood of at least a part of that large section of the people which made its living as craftsmen, industrial workers and seamen.

Even these immediate hardships, however, were less grave than those which would inevitably follow a failure to appreciate the seriousness of the strategic aspect of the matter. Sardinia and Corsica had formed a military and also a psychological barrier between the Romans on the one hand and their allies the Massiliots and Spain on the other, and it was this, more perhaps than any other factor, that had turned the western Mediterranean into a Punic *mare clausum*. Apart from an extensive trade in other commodities Spain provided Carthage with the silver which she required in order to pay her mercenaries and rowers and – what was now a matter of immediate urgency – to discharge her heavy indemnities to the Romans. Her foothold, never very secure, in southern Spain had been weakened during the recent wars, and with Sardinia and Corsica lost to her the Massiliots might well feel encouraged to try to put an end to Carthage's centuries-old monopoly of the Iberian trade in precious metals and raw materials. Morever, Spain might very well prove to be Rome's next objective after Sardinia. It was imperative not merely for Carthage's continuing prosperity but for her very safety that she forestalled both Greeks and Italians and made herself absolute mistress of the wealth and resources of Spain.

Accordingly an agreement was reached between the majority party in the Council and Hamilcar and his friends that promised a solution of all, or most, of Carthage's immediate problems. Hamilcar was given a command, the precise definition of which cannot be recovered with certainty from our scanty sources. He may, as Diodorus says, have been appointed military governor (*strategos*) of Libya in the first instance; or perhaps he was simply appointed commander of the mercenaries (*xenagos*), but for an indefinite period. Certainly – as appears from his own subsequent action and that of his son, Hannibal – he was responsible, as commander of Carthage's standing army, for the defence and internal security of Carthage's African dominions. But his immediate task was the subjugation of Spain, of which he was to be military governor, at least during the period when it was actually being reduced by force of arms. In all probability the army that he took with him from Carthage was composed largely of Libyans, and in this way the most adventurous – and therefore potentially the most dangerous – native Africans will have been removed from the recently rebellious province. Once firmly established in Spain he would be able to recruit the natives of the Peninsula. Spain was to be opened up to Carthaginian trade and its resources exploited for the benefit of Carthage. The country would of course bear the cost of its own subjugation and subsequent military occupation.

In this way the threat to the security of the régime arising from the alliance of popular military hero and people – a classic prelude to tyranny – was obviated. Hamilcar as well as his son-in-law were removed from the arena of domestic politics with the result that the people were left leaderless. However with the restoration, and indeed the expansion, of national prosperity the people would be prepared to acquiesce once more in the quasi-paternalistic rule of the oligarchs, who would, of course, be themselves the principal beneficiaries, and the augmented war indemnity could be easily and painlessly paid off. Libya would be drained of its most restless elements and profitable occupation would be found, at a safe distance from the city's frontiers, for the predatory horsemen of Numidia. The military position would be immeasurably improved, for the empire would from then on be protected and secured by a formidable professional standing army, which was unlikely to pose any threat to the régime as long as its commanders enjoyed what may be described as a palatinate position in Spain. Moreover this army was to cost the City and its rulers nothing. Indeed once the conquest of Spain was achieved, Carthage could economize with impunity on the navy, always the most expensive arm, since the vital trade-routes lay along a coast the whole of which was under her control and there were no longer any island provinces to protect. And perhaps one day, when Rome had suffered disaster at the hands of some other victim of her aggressiveness – the Gauls or the Macedonians – Carthage would be in a position to seize the opportunity offered by the gods to recover Sardinia and maybe even Sicily.

Hamilcar sailed to Gades, Carthage's ancient ally, in the summer of 237 BC, with what Polybius describes merely as a force adequate for the conquest of Spain. It included no fewer than a hundred elephants – an engine of war that Hamilcar had used with devastating effect in Libya. With him went his son-in-law Hasdrubal as admiral, and also his nine-year-old son Hannibal, who had volunteered to accompany his father and had been sworn by him on the altar of Baal Hammon to undying hostility to the Romans, as he was to reveal to King Antiochus in later life.

In the winter of 229, while besieging with only a part of his army the town of Helice (probably identical with Ilici, nowadays Elche, a few miles south-west of Alicante), Hamilcar was defeated as the result of treachery on the part of the King of the Oretani and was drowned in a swollen river while recovering the retreat of his scattered forces and his sons. At the time of his death (if he was a 'young man' in 247, he was no more than middle-aged when he died) he had, partly by diplomacy but more by force of arms, re-established and strengthened Carthaginian domination in southern Spain as far north as his new foundation of Acra Leuce (Lucentum, today Alicante). His career of conquest – or, as he preferred to regard it, re-conquest – had been interrupted by a revolt of some of Carthage's Numidian allies, which he was obliged to detach forces under Hasdrubal to suppress. The revolted Numidians were reduced to tributary status.

It is reasonable to assume that the arrival and triumphant progress of Hamilcar in southern Spain had been a grave disappointment to the Massiliots, who will have made it their business to keep alive the embers of suspicion at Rome. Accordingly in 231 the Romans sent a fact-finding mission to southern Spain, which came away satisfied that Rome had nothing to fear from that direction and indeed that it was in Rome's interest, if she wished to see the indemnity paid, for Carthage to recover her former control of the trade in silver.

On the death of Hamilcar, Hasdrubal was acclaimed as his successor by the army and the command was confirmed by the government; who, whatever its real feelings in the matter, could not go against the wish of the army and the people. Hasdrubal had at his disposal no less than 50,000 foot, 6,000 horse and 200 elephants, and his first concern was to crush the Oretani, avenging the death of Hamilcar and at the same time conveying a warning to other tribes. Hasdrubal was a statesman rather than a soldier, preferring to get his way by diplomacy rather than by war; and it seems probable that in the nine years of his governorship he brought all or most of Iberia south of the Ebro River into the sphere of Carthaginian hegemony either by military conquest or – and this must have accounted for most of the country – by treaty.

In the latter case the personal element will have been all-important, and the permanence of such treaties and hence the stability and security of Carthaginian sovereignty will have depended on the stature and prestige of the governor himself, the personal loyalty and trustworthiness of the native princes, the degree to which they could control the unruliness of their own subjects and the vicissitudes which tend to accompany changes, especially violent changes, in tribal chieftaincy.

On the site of Mastia he founded a city to which he gave the name of his birthplace: Kart Hadasht, New Town, generally known by its Roman name, Carthago Nova (today Cartagena). Here, in a city that possesses one of the best harbours in the world, he established his fine palace and administrative centre, and he emphasized both the permanent character and the Iberian rather than African character of his régime by marrying an Iberian princess – as did his brother-in-law Hannibal also. According to Diodorus he was recognized by the Spanish chieftains as military governor with plenipotentiary power (*strategos autokrator*), but it is more likely that what they called him was king.

It was in fact under Hasdrubal that the 'palatinate' position of the Barcids in Spain was firmly established, and on a more solid footing than that of any Persian or Macedonian satrap, in that they controlled the whole of Carthage's military strength. Nothing shows this more clearly than the manner of Hasdrubal's succession to the command, foreshadowing the day when Roman armies would choose the rulers of the empire.

On the other hand the Carthaginian empire was more secure than it had ever been, and as the Carthaginians could now undertake the direct exploitation of Spain's mineral wealth the City's prosperity rapidly recovered and increased. Moreover large numbers of the people will have found new homes and affluence in the New Town and elsewhere in Spain.

There is no reason to suppose that either Hamilcar or Hasdrubal regarded himself as anything other than a loyal son of Carthage. Yet as long as they retained the personal loyalty and devotion of the army they were absolute masters of Punic Spain and could neither be recalled nor dismissed against their inclinations; and conducting as they did a foreign policy in Spain quite independently of the home government they were in a position to commit Carthage to policies or to courses of action which might go beyond what the oligarchy would regard as desirable in the interests of the City. Carthage had, indeed, less cause for anxiety in Hasdrubal's independence of domestic control than in that of others of his clan. He was not a militarist and, not being a Barca, he was unaffected by the Barcine feud with Rome which was the mainspring of Hamilcar's career and the careers of his sons.

Since the end of the struggle with Carthage the Romans had been involved each year in military operations either to subjugate the Sardinians and Corsicans or as a result of trouble with the Ligurians and the tribes of Gallia Cisalpina. In 229 they campaigned in the Adriatic with a huge fleet as well as a consular army against Queen Teuta, in order to curb the aggressiveness of the Illyrians; a campaign which led to the establishment of a Roman protectorate covering about 120 miles of the Adriatic coast from Lissus to Epirus, which excluded Macedonia from those waters. As a result the Romans were admitted to the Isthmian Games, as friends of the Hellenes, and thus to the family of civilized peoples. In 232, under the terms of the highly controversial agrarian law of the popular tribune C. Flaminius, the Ager Gallicus, which formed the north-eastern march between Italy and Cisalpine Gaul and which had been neglected by Rome since the defeat of the Senones in 284, was settled in family allotments following the expulsion of its former owners. Whether or not this action was, as the Romans later believed, a factor in bringing to a head the hostility of the Gauls, the Cisalpine tribes subsequently formed the most dangerous coalition against Rome that the Republic had so far been called upon to face, and in 226 a massive Gallic invasion of Italy was imminent.

In this crisis it was natural that the Senate should once again seek a reassurance of the pacific intentions of Carthage; especially if the unsleeping resentment of the Massiliots, which had intensified as Hasdrubal's power reached towards their own sphere of influence in northern Spain, was working on the suspicions and fears of the Romans and suggesting to them that the Gauls would be much more formidable if their invasion was spearheaded by Hasdrubal's disciplined, professional army and his elephants. Moreover there was continuing unrest in Sardinia and Corsica (one of the consuls was actually campaigning in Sardinia when the Gauls invaded Italy in 225), and some senators will have attributed the fact to the intrigues of Carthage.

There was probably nothing further from Hasdrubal's thoughts than the idea of an alliance with the Gauls. He was a statesman, essentially a man of peace. He had no quarrel with the Romans, whose interests, as matters stood at present and as he was quite content that they should continue to stand, nowhere conflicted with his own as ruler of Spain or with those of Carthage (unless in one minor sphere: see pages 88–9); and we may be sure that the Carthaginian government would not have sanctioned an attack upon Rome at this juncture. But even if he had desired to pursue his late father-in-law's vendetta Hasdrubal was not in a position to do so. Much the greater part of Spain, although largely acquiescent in his suzerainty, was militarily unconquered. A great deal of fighting had yet to be done before the road was open for an army to march to the foot of the Pyrenees, and he did not have enough ships to transport his army by sea to southern Gaul or Liguria, and Carthage would certainly not have found them for him. He therefore willingly gave Rome the assurance she asked for in the form of a formal unilateral undertaking not to cross the Ebro River in arms. It is probable that the Ebro line, regarded as the *ne plus ultra* of Carthaginian military expansion in the Iberian peninsula, represented a concession by the Romans, thinking in purely military terms, to Hasdrubal's Hellenistic conception of spheres of influence. Carthaginian arms at this time had probably nowhere reached, or even approached, the Ebro, and we may be sure that Massilia (and perhaps also Saguntum) pressed for a Punic boundary much further south. The choice of the Ebro rather than Spain's natural frontier, the Pyrenees, was dictated by Rome's concern for the interests and security of her ally Massilia and of her colonies in Catalonia, as well as by the wish to leave a sizeable stretch of neutral territory between the Punic province and the land of the Gauls.

This undertaking given by Hasdrubal – the so-called Ebro Treaty – provided the Romans with an indicator of Carthage's intentions towards them. On one side of the Ebro stood peace, on the other war. The treaty was to acquire an inflated importance when the history of the times came to be written, owing to the fact that the apologists of both parties were to adduce it in support of their respective moral positions. In fact it had no bearing, as will be seen, on the subsequent outbreak of hostilities between Rome and Carthage, and its real historical importance lies rather in the evidence it supplies of Hasdrubal's desire to enjoy good relations with Rome, and also of his diplomatic ability in securing such a satisfactory boundary.

The Ebro Treaty – unlike the Treaty of Philinus – was not a reciprocal agreement. If the Romans (an unsubtle people) had intended to recognize Spain as a Cathaginian province they would have done so explicitly. The implied concession on Rome's part was not 'Rome will not intrude south of the Ebro', but 'Rome will not send an expeditionary force to Spain, when she has finished with the Gauls, and drive you out of the Peninsula'. Hasdrubal signed because he did not want another Sardinian episode. The Carthaginian position in southern Spain was not yet so well established that he could have withstood a Roman invasion. The assurance demanded by the Romans cost him nothing to give, and although the treaty offered him no security for Rome's non-interference in Spain in the long run, it did represent a tacit admission on her part that she had no immediate intention of opposing his efforts to impose his rule upon the Peninsula south of the Ebro by military conquest. On the other hand, its wording did not constitute a formal recognition by Rome of the region south of the Ebro as a Carthaginian possession; recognition which would have precluded future Roman interference in the affairs of the peninsula should her interests demand it. Here again we should perhaps see the influence of the Massiliots and the Saguntines at work; although it is only reasonable to assume that there were many Roman senators who required no prompting to view a Punic conquest of Spain with grave misgivings.

However for the moment (which was all that the Senate was then concerned with) the situation had been satisfactorily clarified. The Senate could afford to dismiss Hasdrubal from its calculations and concentrate its attention on the Gauls, whom the consuls L. Aemilius Papus and C. Atilius Regulus routed with enormous loss at Telamon in Etruria. For his part Hasdrubal, confident that the Roman people would be unlikely to offend the gods by authorizing war against a 'friendly power' which had given an unequivocal indication of its desire for peace, could devote himself to the task of extending and consolidating his power in Iberia. If we take into account Hasdrubal's plenipotentiary position in Spain there is no need to suppose that the Carthaginian government was called on to ratify the Ebro Treaty. On the other hand the Romans are unlikely to have assumed that it was intended to have indefinite validity, or that it necessarily followed, because Hasdrubal had given an undertaking, that his successor would consider himself bound by it. It was a constitutional principle with them that a magisterial edict technically lost its force when the magistrate concerned went out of office. Nor, as events were soon to prove, were they prepared to reciprocate what Hasdrubal probably regarded as a gesture of positive friendship towards a late enemy.

Between 225 and 221 the Romans were occupied with a series of counter-strokes against the Cisalpine Gauls, which led to the temporary subjugation of the tribes of the Padus (Po) Valley. In the course of these operations several generals, who were later to pit themselves against Hannibal, earned distinction. Q. Fulvius Flaccus and his colleague subdued the Boii in 224 and crossed the Padus. C. Flaminius, as consul in 223, routed the Insubres on the Clusius River – a victory for which his enemies in the Senate and the senatorial historical tradition alike tried to deny him the credit. In the fighting around Clastidium in 222, M. Claudius Marcellus, the best soldier among them, gained the *spolia opima* (one of only three Romans to do so; another of the three was Romulus) and took part in the capture of Mediolanum (now Milan), the Insubrian capital. By 219 the Gauls were considered to be sufficiently subdued for Rome to risk authorizing two large Latin colonies to be planted at Placentia (Piacenza) and Cremona in order to police the Boii and Insubres, the most dangerous of the Gallic tribes.

In the same year the Romans found themselves once again embroiled with the Illyrians, who had given trouble ten years earlier and were now under the control of Demetrius of Pharos, who had married the mother of the heir to the throne. Why Demetrius, who had displayed a good politician's appreciation of the expedient in the previous war, should have chosen this moment to defy the might of Rome, attack the towns of her Adriatic protectorate and send his ships raiding into Greek waters, is far from clear. It is on the whole unlikely that he was influenced by the course of events in Spain; nor, since he had had the good sense to espouse the Romans' side at the right moment in 229 and had been established by them in a small principality at the end of the war, did he have anything to fear from the advance of Roman power into Gallia Cisalpina and, in 221, into Istria. The most likely explanation is that Demetrius was by nature a restless adventurer whose gambles had hitherto come off. He had supported and then betrayed Queen Teuta, and he had fought beside Antigonus of Macedon against Cleomenes of Sparta in the winning battle of Sellasia. Now he risked a more reckless throw, perhaps in the expectation of receiving Macedonian support, and in doing so miscalculated Rome's forbearance, being neither the first nor the last person to do so.

The faction currently wielding the most influence in the Senate was the Aemilian group of allied families, who favoured an energetic foreign policy, and the Senate reacted vigorously to what it interpreted as Demetrius' breach of the treaty signed with Queen Teuta. The consuls L. Aemilius Paullus and M. Livius Salinator moved against him, isolated him in his capital of Pharos and after routing his forces drove him to take refuge at the court of the young King Philip v of Macedon, whose adviser he became in an evil hour for Macedon, in whose service he later perished. Demetrius' own possessions, including Pharus, were added to the Roman protectorate and the Illyrian kingdom proper came under the rule of Scerdilaidas, a member of the royal house, who had shared in, and somehow extricated himself from, the ill-considered escapade of Demetrius.

Meanwhile in Spain Hasdrubal had been assassinated in 221 by a Celt who cherished a private grudge against him, and the army acclaimed as his successor Hannibal, the son of Hamilcar. It is reasonable to assume that at Carthage there was considerable opposition in the Council to the idea that the province of Spain and the army should pass, as if by inheritance, to a third generation of the house of Barca; but the Barcine faction was strong enough to insist that the decision should be left to the people, and the popular Assembly confirmed the choice of the army.

CHAPTER VIII

221-218 BC

Hannibal, Saguntum and the Second Punic War.

With the death of Hasdrubal and the succession of Hannibal to his command history took a new turn. The army of Spain passed from the control of a mature statesman, who valued the rewards and the renown accorded to a ruler who cultivates especially the arts of peace, into that of an impetuous young man in whom the principal motivating force was a burning desire for military glory. With Hannibal's accession the possibility of war between Carthage and Rome hardened into virtual certainty.

Not the least cruel element of the tragedy of Hannibal's career is the fact that he is known to history mainly through the tradition preserved by his enemies. No other foreigner, not even the Gaul, Brennus, who sacked the city, or Pyrrhus who trampled the legions under the feet of his elephants, made such an impact on Roman history or embedded himself so firmly in the national memory. It was not merely that he threatened the Roman confederacy with dissolution just when as a result of the Gallic threat it appeared strongest and most indissoluble; it was not merely that he remained for sixteen years at the head of an army in Italy without suffering a defeat in the field and sailed from Italy in Punic ships, unbeaten to the end. The bitterest aspect of the Hannibalic War was that for thirteen of those years the Romans did not *dare* to offer him decisive battle. He diminished not merely their majesty, but also – what was more galling to accept – their pride and self-esteem. And so, since the known facts forbade them to belittle his military achievements and since the ambition to conquer and the thirst for military glory – aspirations rather out of fashion nowadays – were not regarded as necessarily evil by the Romans themselves, they denigrated his personal character. They portrayed him as the minion of Hasdrubal, a man of inhuman cruelty and of a more than Carthaginian perfidiousness, devoid of all reverence for the gods, regardless of the sanctity of an oath and of the restraints imposed by religion. The aged Masinissa, too, recalled chiefly that he was fonder of money even than the ordinary run of his countrymen.

The reality, which constantly breaks through the Graeco-Punic and even the Roman tradition, was clearly something very different. To the Spanish veterans he appeared as the reincarnation of Hamilcar as he had been at the very height of his powers. All the forcefulness of the father's countenance, the fire of his eyes, his facial expressions, his very features were reproduced in the son. He was absolutely brave, yet quite collected in the face of danger; and Polybius, himself a soldier, notes his sense of responsibility as a leader in that he did not expose himself to danger unnecessarily: in this respect, if in no other, he was Alexander's superior. He was tireless as long as there was work to be done and when he slept he often did so upon the ground among his men, wrapped in his military cloak. Essentially a civilized, Hellenistic man, he was neither more cruel by nature than the best of his contemporaries nor more treacherous. Indeed his actions show him to have been both magnanimous and generous. Cruelty after all is inseparable from war and if towards the end he appears to have broken faith with friends and allies it was only when the exigencies of a deteriorating military situation made the further keeping of faith impossible. Nor is there any need to doubt his respect and reverence for the gods. A godless man does not make a journey of more than seven hundred miles, going and returning, on the eve of the greatest undertaking of his career in order to discharge and renew his vows to his guardian deity, as Hannibal did when he travelled from New Carthage to Gades to worship at the shrine of Melqart.

Pre-eminent, however, among all his virtues was the quality of leadership: he was what the Greeks called *hegemonikos*, a born leader. In different circumstances this quality might have been placed selflessly at the disposal of the government of his country and Hannibal, subordinating his individualism to the corporate will of the ruling class – which was his own – might have earned a paragraph or two in the histories of the time as the man who completed the pacification of Iberia. As it was he inherited the 'palatinate' position of the Barcas. Nominally the City's governor of Spain he became, at the age of only twenty-six, in effect the absolute ruler of the province and its army; and with the oligarchs of distant Carthage, engrossed in their business affairs and domestic politics, he can have had no very strong feelings of identity and class loyalty.

If we are to look for what was reprehensible in his character – the 'fatal flaw', to pursue the analogy of classical tragedy – it was his all-consuming ambition to excel in what his father had taught him, and what he had already experienced for himself, to be the greatest sport in the world: the terrible game of war, the only worthwhile occupation for a Barca. Unquestionably he would have agreed with Napoleon's view of war: 'C'est un grand jeu et une belle occupation!' If he were to confine his activity to the Iberian Peninsula he would have to spend his life winning obscure victories over faithless Iberian princelings, conducting boring sieges of small walled towns, eventually perhaps meeting an inglorious death in some petty skirmish, as his father had done. But the Romans were a worthy foe. They had beaten down the Etruscans, the Samnites, the Gauls, even Pyrrhus, reputedly the finest soldier of his age. Even Hamilcar had failed either to defeat them in the field or to force them to relax their grip upon the province of Sicily. To defeat the Romans would confer upon the son of Hamilcar both the supreme joy of achievement and the highest distinction in the Hellenistic world. Nor is it fanciful to assume that he was aware of the challenge presented to him by the career and fame of Alexander the Great, whom he considered the greatest general of all, and who, like himself, had when little more than a boy succeeded a famous father who had died leaving his greatest task unaccomplished – in his case the war against Persia, which was to be Greece's revenge for the invasion of Xerxes. Like Alexander Hannibal had inherited a war of retribution, and like Alexander he had inherited the means of waging and winning it: a secure base, abundant reserves, a full treasury, an unbeatable field army and a new technique of war.

Hannibal's early training had accustomed him to identify his ruling passion not only with his filial but also with his patriotic duty. Taught to look upon Rome as the implacable enemy of his country he rebelled against the policy of peaceful coexistence pursued by Hasdrubal. Hasdrubal had tried to show that peace with Rome was compatible with the policy of expansion in Iberia, and in this if in nothing else he and his sympathizers in the Council at Carthage will have had the support of the 'Libyan' party led by Hanno. Hannibal had to make Carthage share his conviction that Rome was only looking for the opportunity – for the justifiable *casus belli* – to strike again, this time in Spain, where the centuries-old enmity and rivalry with Massilia had received a new impetus from the Greek city's alliance with the Italian.

Hannibal had to play his cards in such a way that the Romans could be shown to be the aggressors and could be induced to confront Carthage with the choice between ultimately losing Spain, as they had already lost Sicily and Sardinia, and fighting Rome at a time when the circumstances with the choice between ultimately losing Spain, as she had already lost ready to his hand. The Carthaginians were not likely to forget how Rome had obtained her first and seemingly innocent foothold in Sicily by means of the treaty with Messana. If the Romans ran true to form it should not be difficult to make it appear that in the town of Saguntum the Romans had found their Iberian Messana.

After receiving the confirmation of his appointment Hannibal lost no time in completing the work of Hasdrubal and subduing those tribes that had not as yet been overcome by force. In 221 he crushed the Olcades, who are perhaps to be located in the La Mancha region, and took their chief city, Althaea, which Livy calls Cartala. In the following year he attacked the Vaccaei, capturing the city that is today called Salamanca as well as the mining town of Albocola (today, Toro). On his return journey he found a coalition of hostile tribes on his heels that included the powerful Carpetani from the region of the Sierra di Guadarrama. He gave a taste of his quality as a tactician by facing about, retracing his steps and putting the Tagus between his army and the enemy (probably not far from Toledo), thus forcing the latter to attack him across the river. He then used his forty elephants to destroy the barbarians who reached the bank and sent his cavalry in to overwhelm those still in the water. Finally he crossed the river in his turn and completed the rout of the Iberians on the further, or northern, bank. With the discomfiture of the Carpetani only the town of Saguntum was willing to resist the power of Carthage, south of the Ebro.

Saguntum (now Sagunto) was the chief town of a people who were perhaps called the Arsetani; and even in those days it may have claimed a kinship, as it did later, with the Greek town of Zacynthus – a connection which was perhaps suggested to it by the Massiliots purely on the strength of its name. It stood above the River Palancia about three-quarters of a mile from the sea, in a very strong position, being open to assault only on the west side, and had long enjoyed close trade relations with Massilia. When Hamilcar came to Spain the Saguntines must have shared the alarm of the Massiliots, and with even better cause; and it may have been the Massiliots who suggested that they should put themselves under the protection of Rome as many Greek cities of Magna Graecia had done.

Rome's pact with Saguntum presents a number of problems. The first concerns its date. Polybius states that it was concluded 'many years before Hannibal's time', and in another passage seems to imply that it was before the death of Hamilcar. Some modern historians however prefer to put it as late as 223/2. But if that were the case Carthage's apologists could hardly have failed to mention the fact, and the honest Polybius would not have written 'many years' without some qualification. Therefore it looks as if the relationship between the two states was established before (or at the latest, about the same time as) the signing of the Ebro agreement by Hasdrubal, and it may even go back as far as 231.

Then there is the question of the nature of the pact. Some writers believe that there was no formal alliance (*foedus*) but merely a *deditio in fidem* (a throwing oneself upon the protection) on the part of the Saguntines. However Polybius used the word *symmachia* (alliance), and Livy describes the Saguntines as *socii* (allies); and in a much later passage he talks of 'the obligations of an ally (*fides socialis*) observed by both parties'. It is not, therefore, safe to assume that a formal alliance did not exist.

Thirdly, did the pact between Rome and Saguntum (whatever its formal character), if it was concluded in or just after 226, constitute a breach of the Ebro agreement; and if it was concluded before 226 must we regard it as having been made void by that agreement? The answer to both questions must be no, the opinion of many eminent historians notwithstanding. The Ebro agreement – Polybius is quite emphatic on this point – was a unilateral undertaking on Hasdrubal's part; and it was probably never ratified by the home government. The wording – no doubt dictated by the Romans – was designed to avoid a specific recognition of Carthage's claim to Spain as a province, and it left Rome no less free than Carthage to form alliances with the cities and tribes of the Peninsula. If Hasdrubal had been in a position to assert, and if Rome had been prepared to concede, a Punic claim to the exclusive possession of Spain south of the Ebro, it seems inconceivable that the concession would not have been written into the treaty.

Lastly it must be asked, why did Rome accept Saguntum as an ally (or protectorate), when it must have been abundantly clear to the most insensitive senator that to do so – particularly after the rape of Sardinia – was to offend Punic susceptibilities and provide a bone of contention for the future? There does not seem to be any good reason to suppose that her action was dictated by imperialism and was intended to undermine Punic power in Spain with a view to driving the Carthaginians out of the Peninsula and seizing it for herself, any more than her treaty with the Mamertines had been concluded with the conquest of Sicily in mind. It is probable that the Senate was influenced by a variety of considerations. Rome was anxious to keep on good terms with Massilia, and Massilia was interested in safeguarding the independence of Saguntum. Then again, in view of the fact that Carthage was building up her power in Spain, Rome could hardly afford to turn down the offer of an alliance that would materially weaken her potential enemy's strength and ability to strike, and at the same time prove to the world that Rome was still the champion of the weak against the strong. However the Senate's chief reason for acting as it did was probably to demonstrate to Carthage that she no longer controlled the western Mediterranean and that she could not now exclude the Romans from any territory that they chose to take an interest in, as she had done before the late war. Saguntum in the Roman camp was intended to act not only as a check on Carthage's imperial aspirations but also as a reminder and a warning. The Romans were leaving Carthage in no doubt that they were not afraid of her and that they would judge her intentions towards themselves in the light of her behaviour towards their ally. But by showing that they distrusted her and accepted the possibility of war they measurably increased its likelihood.

It would certainly have been strange, with Saguntum lying within the Punic sphere of influence but being in alliance with Rome, if her domestic politics had not become polarized along the lines of the still-passive confrontation between Rome and Carthage. The party struggle came to a head in 221, probably as a result of the change of leadership in Punic Spain with all its implications for Saguntine independence. Rome, not Carthage, was asked to arbitrate and as a result several leading Saguntines – presumably members of the anti-Roman faction – were put to death. Although it is quite clear that both Saguntum and Rome were fully within their legal rights in this matter Hannibal chose to regard it as an act of unjustifiable interference on the part of Rome in Spanish and therefore in Carthaginian affairs.

But this was not all. With the pro-Roman party firmly established in power the Saguntines began to take a strong line against a neighbouring tribe, probably the Torboletae, which was a subject ally of Carthage and with whom they had come into conflict. The Roman tradition accuses Hannibal of stirring up this conflict in order to provide himself with a *casus belli* against Saguntum and it may be taken for granted that he took no steps to compose the dispute. Indeed the development of this incident as described by Polybius makes it clear that he must have sent an ultimatum to the Saguntines, probably in the autumn or early winter of 220/19; for the Saguntines, who for some time past had been wearying the ears of the Senate with complaints against Carthage, now intimated that they expected to be attacked in the following spring.

The Romans at once sent a mission to New Carthage, to discover at first hand what Hannibal's intentions were and to make it clear to him that an attack upon Saguntum would be regarded by Rome as an act of war. Hannibal rejected the Roman protest and in language familiar to both the ancient and modern worlds stated that he was acting in the best interests of the Saguntines themselves. The commissioners then left for Carthage to reiterate their warning, and Hannibal himself wrote to the Council, asking in effect for permission to coerce Saguntum on the grounds that, incited by the Romans, it was oppressing Carthage's allies. And his letter must have left the Council in no doubt that nothing less than the security of the whole province was at stake. We are not told what the Council's reply was, but presumably he was authorized to take whatever steps he thought to be necessary.

Accordingly, in the spring of 219 BC, he marched north and laid siege to Saguntum. Its territory was the most fertile in Iberia and he anticipated a handsome material reward from its capture, quite apart from considerations of imperial policy. It is clear that he did not expect to encounter the Romans in 219, for he took none of the precautions for safeguarding Spain and Africa that he was to take the following year. It is therefore possible that he did not commit his forces to the siege, and apparently not to operations against the Oretani and Carpetani either, until he was assured that Rome was fully committed to the war against Demetrius in the Adriatic. The Romans for their part must have realized as soon as their embassy returned that a serious incident which would probably result in war was going to be provoked by Hannibal in the following spring. Rome, however, could hardly move until Hannibal had shown his hand; Saguntum was at the other end of the Mediterranean and Hannibal in Spain posed no threat to the security of Italy. On the other hand Rome, with her new commitments in Gallia Cisalpina, could not afford to look on while the Adriatic was thrown into a state of turmoil and her stabilizing work of ten years before was undone. Understandably the Senate turned its attention to the nearer problem first.

Siege work was not one of Hannibal's strong points. The Saguntines, sustained by the hope of Roman assistance, rejected an offer of their lives and liberty if they would abandon their town, and held out bravely for eight months. In the end Saguntum was taken by storm. Hannibal acquired a vast quantity of booty in goods and property, as well as in money and slaves. He set aside a part of this for his war chest, distributed a further portion among his men, and shipped the rest to Carthage, so advertising the fact that he was acting as the City's viceroy and carrying out the instructions of the Council.

It is absurd to suppose that when the news of the fall of Saguntum reached Rome in January or even early in February, 218, the Senate did not discuss the matter in all its aspects – as Polybius would have us believe. The Aemilian faction, which was at the moment predominant in the Senate, was eager for war in vindication of Rome's fides, whereas the Fabians advocated a more cautious reaction to the crisis, and deprecated Rome's involvement in a war at such a distance from home, when the security of Italy was not directly threatened. There would be no question, at this time, of asking the people to authorize war – that would have to wait until after the accession to office on the Ides (15th) of March of the new consuls, whose task it would be to fight the opening campaign. However by the end of the debate it must have been quite clear that Aemilian consuls would be elected for 218, that Carthage would be presented with an ultimatum in March, and that war would almost certainly follow.

Indeed, it must by now have been realized by all the parties concerned, the Roman Senate, the Council of the Carthaginians and Hannibal, that whatever diplomatic activity ensued, war in 218 was a foregone conclusion. Each of these parties had its own notion of the shape that the war was going to take. Only Hannibal's came anywhere near the reality.

The Romans were going to fight because the capture of Saguntum and the enslavement of its inhabitants were matters affecting Rome's fides. Besides, the attack on Saguntum in the face of their explicit warning proved first that Carthage must herself be ready for war, and secondly that Hannibal could not be trusted to remain south of the Ebro. Marching into northern Spain he would threaten the colonies of Massilia and extend his dominion to the borders of Gaul. An alliance of Punic Spain, the Ligurians and the Gauls would keep alive the hostility to Rome of the Gauls of Gallia Cisalpina and would constitute a real threat to the security of Italy itself. We are not told what Rome's war aims were, but it seems likely enough, in view of the strength of the opposition to the war in the Senate, and taking into account the actual disposition of her forces in the spring of 218, that they were quite limited. They probably did not extend beyond the destruction of Hannibal's war machine (which might be achieved by a single decisive victory in the field, followed by the recall and crucifixion of the defeated general), the restoration of Saguntum, the establishment of a Roman protectorate in central Spain and the confinement of Carthaginian power to the south of the peninsula. The war itself was to be what the nineteenth century would have called a 'colonial war'. It would be fought at a comfortable distance from Italy and would cost relatively little in terms of Italian lives – the Romans had no great respect for Carthaginian armies – and nothing in terms of money (another swingeing indemnity would take care of that). It would furnish consuls of the Aemilian party with glory, triumphs and enhanced prestige, provide all who took part in it with abundant booty from the plunder of Spain and Libya, and the Republic and her allies, including Massilia, would reap the benefits accruing from the opening up of Iberia. It seems quite clear from the fact that the Senate committed only one strong consular army to the Spanish theatre that it had no conception of the magnitude of the undertaking upon which it was embarked. Indeed the Romans probably felt that with the respected Hamilcar and the respectable Hasdrubal out of the way, the youthful Hannibal would present few problems.

Carthage was going to war because the majority of her rulers had come to feel that no other course was open to them. There was a strong party – that of Hanno 'the Great' – which like the Fabians at Rome, was opposed to the idea of war. They believed that the dispute with Rome could and should be settled amicably, if only because war must vastly enhance the prestige and power of the hated Barcine faction and its political ally, the people. But apart from the Barcines in the Council there must have been many who felt that national honour as well as national interests were deeply involved in teaching Rome a sharp lesson. They would point out that militarily Carthage had not done badly in the earlier war. She had suffered two defeats on land in Sicily but she had destroyed the consular army of Regulus in Libya. The Romans had swept her navy from the seas during the decade following the battle of Mylae, but she, with the aid of the gods, had retaliated as effectively in 249; and many voices would be raised to assert that if the victories of Adherbal and Carthalo had been energetically followed up western Sicily at least would still be in Punic hands.

Carthage was now richer than in 264 and militarily stronger. Also she had fewer overseas commitments. Sicily had been lost because the Romans were able to sever its communications with Africa, but it would be virtually impossible for Rome to isolate Spain in this way, even though she did command the seas. Undoubtedly Libya would be exposed to raids from Rome's new bases in western Sicily, but the fates of Regulus and of the mercenaries had shown that Carthage could protect herself, and this time she would have part of Hannibal's huge professional army at her disposal. Spain – which was what she was going to war about – could be held indefinitely by Hannibal, who had short secure lines of communication with his base at New Carthage and with north Africa. He had virtually limitless resources in manpower backed by an adequate supply of silver to support a lengthy war if need be. The Roman citizen levies, with hundreds of miles of sea between them and home, fighting against vastly superior numbers of expertly led professionals, would wear themselves out in vain. At worst Carthage could anticipate a stalemate, with peace being concluded on the basis of a recognition of the status quo. At best, if the Romans suffered some spectacular disaster or series of disasters by land and sea a victorious Hannibal would be admirably placed to strike at Sardinia. Moreover the long life of King Hiero was drawing to a close and unrest could be expected to follow at Syracuse. Even Sicily might fall again into her hands.

In the splendid palace that Hasdrubal had built at New Carthage to be the administrative centre of his 'kingdom', Hannibal and his Council were making preparations for a totally different kind of war. He had not provoked the conflict with Rome simply in order to fight a defensive war for the protection of Spain and Africa. He thirsted for a fame the equal of Alexander's, and his father had trained and dedicated him to a hatred of the Romans. He must have felt that he had no alternative but to take his army into Italy and beat them on their own soil. Their allies, almost all of whom had been brought into the confederation by force, would then fall away and Rome would be left isolated and helpless. This was a calculation based on history and experience. History – the histories of Athens and Sparta, for example – showed that subject allies were always on the look-out for an opportunity to revolt. Carthage's African subjects had revolted when first Regulus and later the mercenaries had been masters of the field, and he was well aware that his own Spanish allies would fall away if the Romans once got a firm footing in the Iberian Peninsula. Hannibal was confident that he knew how to win over the Italian allies: if he had not learnt political wisdom from Hasdrubal he had certainly learnt the art of diplomacy. A Hellenistic – a Mediterranean – man, he had no contempt for Greeks or Italians, and as the son of Hamilcar and the brother-in-law of Hasdrubal he was accustomed to the idea of entering into partnership with the people – something that might prove to be very valuable for the detaching of Rome's socii from their allegiance.

At the outset, however, he would have to surrender the strategic initiative to the Romans. They had the command of the sea and so could strike – at least in theory – wherever they wished. Hannibal could not march on Italy leaving Spain and Africa at their mercy. In practice he knew that the Romans had only two courses open to them, since the formal cause of the war would be the rape of Saguntum. They could either put two consular armies supported by strong naval forces into northern Spain, where Emporiae offered a base, at the same time perhaps sending another fleet to raid the African seaboard; or they could send one consular army with a fleet to northern Spain and the other to effect a landing in Africa, perhaps with the object of establishing a strongpoint there and so bringing pressure to bear directly on Carthage, to make her sue for peace.

Hannibal therefore had to take both these possibilities into account. He decided to transfer to Africa sufficient forces either to deal with raiding parties or to constitute the nucleus and stiffening of any army that might have to be raised in order to contain a consular army for a single campaign. His younger brother Hasdrubal would remain south of the Ebro with enough men and elephants to keep the tribes there in order. He would also occupy himself with raising and training fresh levies. Hannibal himself would cross the Ebro with massive forces and subdue the tribes between the river and the Pyrenees in a lightning campaign conducted regardless of cost. He would then wait for the Romans on ground of his own choosing. With at least eighty thousand men at his disposal, to say nothing of his elephants, he would be in a position to crush even two consular armies with overwhelming numbers.

Having dealt with the invaders he would march straight upon Italy, aiming to arrive in Gallia Cisalpina before the campaigning season was over, with all the glamour and renown of a great victory upon him. The Gauls would rise and join him in their tens of thousands and the Romans would be chased out of the region, and in the following spring he would descend upon the Roman confederation, its morale already shaken, at the head of an irresistible army. Fighting for survival in Italy, the Romans would have no forces to send to Spain or Africa, which would thus be taken out of the war. Indeed Hasdrubal would be able to lead a second army from Spain across the Maritime Alps, to complete the dissolution of the Italian confederation and to bring Rome finally to her knees. The subjugation of Sicily would then be merely a triumphal progress, while Sardinia and Corsica could be reoccupied whenever Carthage wished.

Hannibal's war aim was thus neither more nor less than that of making the western Mediterranean permanently safe for the Carthaginians. It was an aim that justified the risks involved in achieving it – risks that probably did not seem so very great to Hannibal and do not seem excessive today. Hannibal had limitless faith in his own military genius and his plan involved meeting the Romans everywhere with an overwhelming superiority in numbers. With at least half and perhaps the whole of Rome's field army destroyed in Spain, he would be able to take the easy coast road into Liguria, whose tribesmen had for generations supplied Carthage with mercenaries, and thence march by easy passes into Gallia Cisalpina. In the following summer he might confidently expect to lead well over a hundred thousand fighting men to the overthrow of the Italian confederation; and he would still have Hasdrubal's reinforcements to come. And even if everything went wrong and he failed to conquer Italy, he could still claim that his plan would cost his country little beyond the price that she would ultimately have had to pay for not standing up to the Romans. The soldiers with whose lives he was gambling were professionals, Iberian and African hirelings whom he was leading to adventure, excitement and unlimited plunder. That they might be going to their deaths was something that he himself was risking together with them and something that they had taken into consideration when they enlisted.

As far as Hannibal was concerned the ensuing summer was to witness the beginning of the war with Rome, and he passed the winter and early spring in making preparations for it. For the defence of Africa he selected levies from the Spanish tribes, including the newly subjugated Olcades, replacing them with Africans, so that the representatives of the two nations supplied contingents to the armies of Spain and Libya and also hostages for the good behaviour of their respective peoples. He transferred fifteen thousand Spanish horse and foot to Africa, plus 870 Balearic slingers, stationing most of them in the coastal region that took its name from Cape Metagonium, on the western borders of the country of the Numidians. Here they served a threefold purpose: they could be employed to prevent the Romans from establishing a base from which to sever sea communications between Spain and Africa, they would keep an eye on the somewhat unpredictable Numidian chieftains, and they were well placed to reinforce the defences of either Spain or Libya in the event of Roman landings. The loyalty of the towns of the Metagonian region itself was assured by drafting four thousand of their young men to Carthage to serve on the garrison there.

The African and Numidian levies plus 800 Ligurians and Balearic islanders – 15,200 horse and foot – were assigned to Hasdrubal for training and for the defence of central and southern Spain. He was also left with 21 elephants and all the warships of the Spanish command, of which 32 quinqueremes and five triremes were fully serviceable. Hannibal himself recorded all these details for posterity on a tablet which he set up in the temple of Hera Lacinia, in southern Italy, some thirteen years later.

Polybius tells us that the Romans sent an ultimatum to Carthage 'immediately' after the arrival of the news of the fall of Saguntum. But we know from Livy that the embassy included the ex-consuls of 219 and that therefore it could not have set out until after 15 March. Moreover, Polybius himself states elsewhere that news of the Carthaginian rejection of the ultimatum reached Hannibal at New Carthage in the spring: that is, before mid-May at the latest. However he further confuses the problem of the chronology of the opening months of the war, and in this he is assisted by Livy, by asserting that the Roman Senate, although advised by its returning ambassadors that a state of war now existed – and the journey from Carthage to Rome need not have taken more than three days – waited until Hannibal reached the Ebro before deciding on the military dispositions for the war. He expects us to believe that the consuls of 218, who were to command the Roman armies and with whom the political initiative rested, were prepared to wait probably from the end of March until mid-June before asking the Senate to discuss the question where they were going to campaign.

The truth is that the crossing of the Ebro (undoubtedly a breach of the agreement signed by Hasdrubal) was quite irrelevant to the declaration of war. However the Roman historical tradition, which at this point influenced Polybius as well as Livy, being sensitive over the failure of Rome to come to the help of the Saguntines, was anxious to show that she did in fact react vigorously to a breach of treaty. The crossing of the Ebro was the first move in the war and marked the beginning of Hannibal's march on Italy. But the need to establish beyond doubt Hannibal's responsibility for the war led Roman apologists to bracket it with the capture of Saguntum as a cause of the war, and it is adduced as such in Polybius' account of the first Roman embassy of protest and in Livy's account of the second. Since the Senate had known from February at least that war with Carthage was virtually inevitable and since it would have to send an army into Spain whether Hannibal crossed the Ebro or not, it seems absurd to suppose that it waited until June (when he did so) before either sending an ultimatum, as some historians believe, or apportioning the consular provinces.

It is much more probable that one of the first actions of the consuls of 218, P. Cornelius Scipio and Ti. Sempronius Longus, was to obtain from the people a conditional declaration of war and to despatch an embassy, of which their political rival M. Fabius Buteo was the senior member, to present it at Carthage in the form of an ultimatum. Moreover since the rejection of the ultimatum was to be regarded as a foregone conclusion, the consuls will have lost no time in obtaining their provinces from the Senate and in starting to enrol the four legions that constituted the two consular armies, without waiting for an appreciable part of the campaigning season to pass while Hannibal marched to the Ebro. It was decided that Scipio should go to Spain, taking with him a strong army of 8,000 citizen infantry and 600 citizen cavalry and no fewer than 14,000 foot and 1,600 horse from the allies. His naval force of 60 quinqueremes was large enough to deter interference with his voyage by the Spanish fleet, of whose strength Rome had no doubt been informed by the Massiliots. Longus was to attack the Carthaginian homeland with the twofold object of preventing reinforcements from being sent to Spain and of bringing the war home to the Carthaginian people, and inducing them to throw over Hannibal. For this operation he was allotted, in addition to the same number of citizen soldiers as his colleague, 16,000 allied foot and 1,800 allied horse. With this force he would be able to establish himself on Punic territory, devastate the countryside and raise the natives in revolt. Since he might have to encounter the Carthaginian navy he was given 160 battleships and a dozen smaller craft.

The embassy duly presented Rome's ultimatum to the Council at Carthage. Either with or without the permission of his government Hannibal had attacked and destroyed an ally of the Roman people, contrary to the terms of the Treaty of Catulus. Therefore the Carthaginians must either repudiate him and surrender him and his advisers to the Romans for punishment or else accept responsibility for his action and with it war with Rome. The Carthaginians, who had in effect already made their decision and accepted the possibility of war when they authorized Hannibal to attack Saguntum in order to safeguard their hold on Spain, now offered merely a formal rejection of the Roman charge. Basing their argument also upon Catulus' treaty, they declared that, since Saguntum was not an ally of Rome in 241, they had committed no breach of the treaty by attacking it. As the Romans had made their position over Saguntum perfectly clear the year before Fabius contented himself with indicating the fold of his toga and telling the Council that it held both peace and war and that he would let fall from it whichever they chose. The presiding suffete (if he was Bomilcar, whose son Hanno was one of Hannibal's most trusted officers, he was probably a supporter of the Barcids) replied that they left the choice to him. Fabius, then, with a symbolic gesture said that he let fall war, at which many of the councillors shouted, 'We accept it!' In this apparently rather casual manner the two great powers of the western Mediterranean embarked upon a war of whose subsequent course, duration and significance neither can at that time have had the slightest conception.

CHAPTER IX

218 BC

Hannibal marches to Italy. Ticinus and Trebia.

At New Carthage, in the meantime, Hannibal was pushing ahead with his preparations for the war. He had arranged for all or most of the troop transfers between Spain and Africa. He travelled to Gades, where he paid to Melqart (the tutelary deity of his family) the vows he had already made and bound himself by new ones to ensure the success of his vaster undertaking. He now needed only the news from Carthage that the City had rejected the Roman ultimatum; and when that arrived he drew his forces out of their winter quarters (the Spaniards had been dismissed to their homes at the close of the Saguntine siege) and made ready to march. This was 'in the course of the spring season' – a rather vague phrase that probably represents a date in early May. He had sent emissaries to the chieftains of the Boii and Insubres in Gallia Cisalpina urging them with lavish promises to join him in his march on Rome, and also to those Alpine tribes through whose lands his road lay. He can scarcely have delayed his departure, as Polybius says he did, until the envoys should return, for he was committed to war in northern Spain anyway, and his messengers could rejoin him anywhere on the march. In fact they arrived with favourable reports before he left his base.

Probably before the middle of May then, he set out from New Carthage with ninety thousand infantry, twelve thousand horse and perhaps forty elephants. He took with him also, in emulation of Alexander the Great, two historians to chronicle his campaign for posterity, Silenus of Caleacte and Sosylus of Lacedaemon; and he arrived at the Ebro 'at the beginning of summer', between mid-May and mid-June. He crossed the river and began to subjugate the tribes and towns between the Ebro and the Pyrenees, speed being at this stage more important than economy of mercenary lives, since he might reasonably expect to see the Romans in Catalonia by the end of June. The Ilergetes, under their King Indibilis, who lived in what is today Huesca, were the most important tribe, and they, as well as the other peoples of the region, were compelled to submit to Carthaginian overlordship. The most obstinately hostile tribe, the Bargusii, was placed under direct Punic rule. He did not attempt to take Emporiae, the colony of Massilia, although it would clearly be used as a landing place by the Romans. He could not afford to commit a large part of his forces to a lengthy siege and indeed he had no wish to impede the Romans: once Catalonia was even superficially subjugated the sooner the Romans appeared in the field the better. But June passed away and then July and there was still no sign of the enemy.

What had happened was that one of the essential elements of Hannibal's master plan had recoiled upon him. In the previous year the Romans had decided to establish large Latin colonies at Cremona and Placentia in the upper Padus Valley, and the colonists, no less than twelve thousand in all, were instructed to present themselves at the two centres during the month of June in order to receive their allotments from the commissioners, whose leader was C. Lutatius Catulus, son of the victor of the Aegates. In order to prepare the sites and make them defensible, and also in order to cover the land apportionment and the settling in of the colonists, the Senate had sent into the area the peregrine praetor, L. Manlius Vulso. It looks as if they transferred to his command one of the two legions – the fourth – which Scipio had raised for his Spanish campaign and which he had probably instructed to assemble at Pisae, the port from which he intended to sail to Emporiae.

Scipio clearly did not expect to leave for Spain before early July: very likely he was waiting for definite news from Massilia of Hannibal's crossing of the Ebro before making the final plans for his own campaign. No serious opposition on the part of the natives had been anticipated; but in fact the Boii, encouraged by Hannibal's promise that he was coming to lead them to the overthrow of Rome, threw off their irksome allegiance to the Republic and raising the Insubres as well attacked the two infant colonies and chased the settlers – together with the three commissioners – into the allied Etruscan city of Mutina (now Modena) and besieged them there. When the commissioners came out to parley they were treacherously seized. Manlius hurried to raise the siege, was ambushed by the Boii as he passed through a wooded region and was driven into the village of Tannetum, a little over thirty miles short of his objective.

When the Senate learnt what had happened it despatched the city praetor, C. Atilius Serranus, to take Scipio's second legion and restore the situation in Gallia Cisalpina. Scipio was authorized to raise fresh forces, citizen and allied, to replace those tranferred to the Padus Valley. By now it was probably well into July, and the timing of Rome's war plan for 218 was completely thrown out. Scipio could not possibly be ready, now, to sail before early September and so Longus, whose attack on Libya was clearly intended to coincide with Scipio's invasion of Spain, was also delayed. It looks as if a part of the fleet destined for Libya was sent ahead to Lilybaeum (unless, indeed, it had been stationed there since the previous year), coming under the command of the praetorian governor of Sicily,

M. Aemilius Lepidus, and was therefore available for the defence of the province when Carthage made the first hostile move of the war by sea.

By the end of July news must have reached Hannibal in Catalonia that the tribes of Gallia Cisalpina were in revolt and that one of the consular armies had been diverted to suppress them. Coming from a Gaulish source, or perhaps from the spy who was, as we know from Livy, active at Rome during 218 and 217, the reports may well have exaggerated the Roman losses and the extent to which the Romans had lost control of the region. This news caused Hannibal to make a change in his plan that was to affect the subsequent course of history. Two essential elements of that plan had been the destruction of the Roman invasion force in Spain and the junction of his own forces with those of the Gauls for the invasion of Italy. Now it looked as if the Romans had committed the army intended for Spain to the pacification of Gallia Cisalpina. By the end of the summer the whole region would once more be under the heel of Rome, the fortresses of Placentia and Cremona would be firmly established and the opportunity of enlisting tens of thousands of Gauls for his attack on Rome would be lost, perhaps for ever. He therefore decided not to wait any longer for Scipio in Catalonia but to march as swiftly as possible to Gallia Cisalpina before the fires of revolt were wholly stamped out there.

He could not, however, leave Spain undefended. Hasdrubal had only fifteen thousand men south of the Ebro and the tribes of Catalonia were only superficially subjugated: the Romans could appear as liberators in northern Spain. He therefore appointed a Hanno as military governor of the region between the Ebro and the Pyrenees, and assigned to him ten thousand infantry and one thousand cavalry – the smallness of the force indicating that Hannibal did not expect to see a consular army in Catalonia that summer. In fact it is probable that he saw Hanno's main task, apart from policing the region, as being that of raising troops to reinforce the army of Italy. Hannibal also dismissed eleven thousand Spaniards to their homes, thus ensuring that he took only willing men with him on his march, and at the same time creating a reservoir of good will in Spain that would assist future recruiting there. These reductions also served to bring his invasion force down to a size that could cover the difficult ground between northern Spain and the Padus Valley with the greatest speed.

The view taken here, that Hannibal changed his original plan of campaign in the belief that the Romans were tied up in Gaul and therefore would not put an army into Spain in 218, is not the generally accepted one, according to which at the very outset 'he formed the bold scheme of sacrificing his communications with Spain and Carthage and swooping suddenly onto North Italy' (Scullard). However this view is only tenable if it is also accepted, first, that the Romans were waiting for Hannibal to cross the Ebro before making a move, and secondly, that Hannibal was so irresponsible as to be prepared to leave the province – which it was his first duty to protect – without its governor or its best officers and troops; and to disband thousands of his levies and entrust the area in which the enemy must arrive to the incompetent Hanno with barely the equivalent of a single legion to defend it.

It has already been argued, however, that the crossing of the Ebro was not a *casus belli*; that it was only later that Roman propaganda made it one. In 218 the Romans were not concerned either to saddle the Carthaginians with war guilt or to explain away their own failure to succour Saguntum when it was attacked. The destruction of an ally (or client) provided a good and sufficient reason for going to war; and they did so in March 218 with a perfectly clear national conscience, to punish an aggressor whom they had comprehensively defeated and humbled once already, and with the intention of restoring Saguntum. The Ebro Treaty was not even 'a scrap of paper'.

But if Rome declared war in March 218 a Roman army should have been in Catalonia by the end of June at the latest; and in fact Scipio's army was apparently enrolled and (probably) at Pisae by 1 June – as Hannibal very well knew. Therefore Hannibal had to expect to encounter it in northern Spain before he was ready to cross the Pyrenees. But if he really meant from the outset to give it the slip why did he spend so long in Catalonia? The answer would appear to be that he was not trying to give it the slip; he was waiting for it. And if, when he crossed the Pyrenees, he still believed that the Romans were coming to Spain, why did he not leave a proper force to deal with them? The answer must be that he no longer believed that they were coming.

So in early September he marched past Emporiae unencumbered with heavy baggage and with only 50,000 infantry, about 9,000 cavalry and 37 elephants, forced his way over the Pyrenees at their eastern end and pitched his first camp in Gaul at Iliberis (Elne). The Gauls had been alarmed (not surprisingly) by the subjugation of the peoples of Catalonia, and a coalition of tribes prepared to bar his path at Ruscino (Castel Roussillon). However he won over their chieftains and secured their friendly cooperation in his speedy march to the Rhône, which he reached at, or near, Beaucaire-Tarascon, below the confluence with the Durance, about the middle of September.

When he arrived at the Rhône, Hannibal found that the people of the region, the Volcae, who were no doubt well disposed towards their ancient neighbours, the Massiliots, had moved all their fighting men to the east bank and were preparing to contest his passage. He won over the people who stayed behind and got enough boats and timber from them to provide transport for his army. Although it is contrary to the rules of good generalship to divide your forces in the face of the enemy, Hannibal had the Rhône between him and the Volcae – and the latter were operating strictly on the defensive. Accordingly he detached a strong force, largely composed of Spaniards, under Hanno, son of the suffete Bomilcar; and these marched twenty-three miles upstream under cover of night, crossed the river on rafts and camped in a strong position from which they could descend at the tactical moment upon the right flank of the tribesmen holding the east bank. On the fifth night after leaving the main body Hanno moved down the east bank and indicated by smoke signal when he was in position to attack. At once Hannibal led his light forces across the river, with the cavalry swimming their horses behind the boats; and when the barbarians, who were thronging the bank in disorder, had their attention fully occupied by the enemy in the stream and on the further bank Hanno fell on their right flank and their deserted camp. The frontal attack completed their rout and Hannibal was left the master of the crossing. The cost in lives may, however, have been heavier than Polybius' narrative suggests.

This operation was the first of many that owed their success to the excellent quality of Hannibal's subordinate commanders – a class of officer in which the Roman army was sadly deficient. Before a general can plan an operation such as that which cleared the crossing of the Rhône he has to know that the officer to whom, for instance, an encircling movement is assigned will carry out his task competently and punctually. Hannibal brought with him out of Spain a splendid team of experienced soldiers whom he could employ with complete confidence as commanders of detachments. These men also formed his War Council. They included his brother Mago, Hanno, Maharbal, Hasdrubal, his quartermaster-general, Mago Saunites and Hannibal Monomachus, whom tradition holds responsible for those acts of cruelty that cannot simply be dismissed as Roman propaganda. The Roman system, on the other hand, under which (in the ordinary run of things) a general enjoyed his first taste of independent command only when he put himself at the head of his army as consul, did not provide subordinate officers who possessed any experience of tactical command, nor did it envisage the Roman manipular army manœuvring in the field in any other way than as a single body.

Once the east bank of the Rhône had been cleared Hannibal fetched across the remainder of his troops and arranged for the ferrying over by raft, on the next day but one, of the thirty-seven elephants. The following morning, however, the alarming news was brought to him that a Roman fleet had arrived at the mouth of the Rhône, little more than a day's forced march to the south. He at once sent off five hundred Numidian cavalry to reconnoitre the enemy, and he must have had some very bad moments when not very long afterwards only three hundred of these rode back into camp with a victorious body of Roman and Celtic horsemen at their heels.

Scipio had had to recruit two fresh legions from citizens and allies at a time when their fields were claiming the attention of the peasantry. It is also likely that he had been required by the Senate to remain in Italy until it was announced that Mutina had been relieved, Placentia and Cremona recovered and peace restored, at least outwardly, to Gallia Cisalpina. The result was that he had finally sailed from Pisae only a few days after Hannibal crossed the Pyrenees, and making good time along the coast had arrived at the eastern (the Massiliotic) mouth of the Rhône (at Fos or at Port St Louis) five days later. There he learnt that Hannibal had crossed the Pyrenees, but believing that the Carthaginians could not arrive at the Rhône – which was the obvious place to encounter them – for some time yet, he disembarked his men and allowed them to recover from the discomforts of the voyage. If he had taken the elementary precaution of at once sending even a handful of cavalry up the Rhône into the country of the friendly Volcae he would have been informed of Hannibal's arrival in time for him to have the legions in position to dispute the crossing unbeknownst to the enemy, and the outcome of the battle there might well have been very different. As it was, the news reached him only the day after Hannibal had got his army across the river, the same day that Hannibal heard of *his* arrival at the Rhône mouth. Belatedly he sent three hundred of his own cavalry, plus an unreported number of Celtic horsemen supplied by the Massiliots, to reconnoitre, and it was this force that encountered Hannibal's Numidians and after a bloody battle drove them back into their camp. They had a good look at the enemy and then rode back to Scipio to report that Hannibal was already on the east bank of the river, and the next day Scipio, who believed that Hannibal intended to fight him, advanced north with his army in a state of readiness to deploy for battle as soon as the enemy should be sighted.

Hannibal, however, had no intention of fighting. His army had been reduced by this time to something over forty-six thousand horse and foot and for all he knew to the contrary Longus might have been recalled and two consular armies might be marching on him from the south. As a defeat – or even a Pyrrhic victory – at this stage of his campaign could have been disastrous he felt that his business now was to put himself beyond the reach of the Romans as quickly as he could. On the day following the cavalry fight he got his elephants across the river on rafts (some that panicked and plunged into the water swam safely across, with the loss of their mahouts), and with these and his cavalry forming a rearguard he marched north up the line of the river. Scipio reached the scene of the crossing two days after his departure and rightly judged that it would be a fruitless and possibly dangerous undertaking to pursue Hannibal into the unknown country of south-eastern Gaul. He was now convinced that Hannibal was intending to invade Italy (interrogation of Numidian prisoners would have confirmed this fact), and accordingly he returned to the coast.

There he made a decision which was to affect the whole course of the war. The first duty of a consul was to ensure the safety of the Roman people. Therefore he decided to put the army and a part of the fleet under the command of his brother Gnaeus, who had been Marcellus' colleague in 222 and had campaigned with him in Gallia Cisalpina and who was now accompanying Publius as his lieutenant, with orders to take them to Spain and begin operations against Hannibal's base. In the meantime he would return by sea to Italy and assume command of the two legions with which the praetors had been operating in the Padus Valley. He would endeavour to keep Hannibal occupied there until his colleague Longus could be recalled with his army, so that eventually four legions could bar the road to Italy.

Hannibal marched upstream to a region known as the Island at the confluence of the Rhône and the Aygues, the tribal land of the Cavares. Before he left the crossing place he had been joined by emissaries of the Boii under a chieftain called Magalus, who no doubt had intended to guide him by one of the easier, more southerly passes over the Alps; they were not likely to be of much use to him now that military considerations had forced him to the northward. At the Island, however, he was able to make useful friends. Invited by Brancus, the elder of two contending brothers, to establish him on the throne, Hannibal threw his professionals into the tribal dispute and so secured the gratitude of the victor, who not only provisioned but also thoroughly refitted and re-equipped his army with new weapons and clothing suitable for their onward journey and provided a strong covering force to escort it through country exposed to the attacks of the hostile Allobroges.

Having rested his men Hannibal resumed his march up the left bank of the Rhône and when he reached its confluence with the Isere he turned north-east and followed the course of the latter river towards the mountains. His Gaulish allies left him when they reached the disputed frontier country and from that point he had to fight his way past the Allobroges, who gathered in great force and occupied ground commanding the ascent. Once again Hannibal showed the difference between the professional and the amateur in the game of war. No general has ever understood better than he the importance of reconnaissance. He fed the self-confidence of the tribesmen by making it appear that they had brought his march to a halt and then by night occupied with picked forces their positions, which he had thoroughly reconnoitred beforehand. Even so the army suffered heavy losses, especially in horses and baggage animals, from the frontal attack of the tribesmen when it resumed its advance, and Hannibal was obliged to charge down on the Allobroges from the heights and clear the upward path after a fierce struggle with heavy losses on both sides. He then attacked and easily took the almost deserted town belonging to the enemy (which has been identified as lying on or near the site of modern Grenoble), where he recovered many prisoners and animals that had been captured by the Gauls, as well as two or three days' supply of provisions.

His Boian guides could give him little assistance in these northern regions, and the mountaineers, impressed though they were by the defeat that the Allobroges had suffered, were treacherous and hostile. It has been plausibly suggested that Hannibal was intending to cross the Alps by the relatively easy Mount Cenis Pass, but missed the road and so was forced to cross a little further to the south by the much higher and more difficult Col du Clapier. His march continued to be harried right to the top of the pass by the tribesmen, who took advantage of every natural difficulty on the road to attack the column with missiles or in hand-to-hand engagements. These were continued by small predatory groups even after the attentions of the large, organized bodies had been left behind. It is worth noting that in this latter stage of his ascent the elephants – which Napoleon characterized as the source of all Hannibal's difficulties ('Les éléphants seuls ont pu lui donner de l'embarras') – were of the greatest value to him, as the mountaineers did not dare to approach such terrifying monsters.

After an ascent which took nine days and was conducted under such appalling conditions, the army reached the summit, from which Hannibal was able to hearten his men by showing them Italy, the goal of their march, and halted for a two days' rest during which many stragglers, men and beasts, rejoined the main body. It was now about the fourth week of October and snow had already fallen on the highest ground. The descent, we are told, was almost as costly as the climb had been, not because of hostile action but because of the difficulties of the ground aggravated by the fallen, and falling, snow. At one point he had to spend days laboriously clearing the path and then remaking it where it had been partly carried away by landslides. The losses in horses and baggage animals, and therefore in stores and provisions, were especially severe. The crossing of the Alps took at least fifteen days in all and when Hannibal at last descended into the territory of the Taurini in the upper Padus Valley, he had with him, by his own recorded admission, only 20,000 infantry – 12,000 Libyan and 8,000 Iberian – and 6,000 horsemen, out of the 46,000 horse and foot with which he had set off from the Rhône.

These losses are so enormous that some modern historians find them incredible. Yet the narrative of Polybius, based on eye-witness accounts of his struggle with men, mountains and the elements, enables us to understand how these figures may well be correct; and it must be remembered that a large proportion of the men that he led were Africans, men quite unaccustomed to the kind of conditions that they encountered in the Cottian Alps in the late autumn.

He camped, probably in the region of what is today Susa, and spent some time in restoring the morale as well as the desperately reduced physical condition of his army. However it was absolutely necessary for him to make contact with his allies the Boii, and with their allies the Insubres, as soon as possible, because his initial change of plan had led to his arriving in Italy with forces barely superior in numbers to a single strong consular army, instead of with enough men and horses to overwhelm two Roman armies if necessary. The Taurini among whom he had arrived were at odds with the Insubres and therefore hostile to Hannibal; they rejected his overtures of friendship and he accordingly besieged and took their tribal centre, Taurasia (Torino). He then quickly induced the peoples of the region to submit to him by a display of calculated ruthlessness.

It was probably whilst he was subjugating the inhabitants of the north bank of the Padus that the news reached him of the approach of the consul Scipio. This first report must have caused him considerable alarm, for he could not know that Scipio had not brought his legions with him. Indeed we are told that he found it quite incredible that a Roman army could have got back from the Rhône in the time. However subsequent reports will have told him that Scipio had with him only the forces that had been operating in Gallia Cisalpina under the praetors, and accordingly he pushed forward along the northern bank of the Padus, with the intention of raising the Insubres, as far as the east bank of the Sesites (Sesia). There he camped, having learnt from scouts that the Romans had already crossed the Ticinus and were close at hand. On the following day he went forward with the whole of his formidable cavalry force in order to carry out a personal reconnaissance of the enemy.

After leaving the mouth of the Rhône Scipio had lost no time in getting back to Pisae and joining the army of Gallia Cisalpina, which was probably camped in the region of Placentia. When he learnt that Hannibal had arrived among the Taurini he crossed the Padus at Placentia into Insubrian territory in order to forestall the Carthaginians and moving westwards threw a pontoon bridge across the Ticinus. After fortifying the western bridgehead he advanced to within five miles of Hannibal's camp, which Livy places at Victumulae; and the following morning he too set out with his cavalry, which included Gaulish contingents, and his javelin men in order to reconnoitre the enemy. The two scouting parties, Roman and Carthaginian, encountered each other, probably near Lomello, roughly midway between their respective camps.

If Hannibal had with him the whole of his cavalry, as Polybius states, the Romans were heavily outnumbered in the coming engagement, without taking into consideration the foot skirmishers, who in the event were more of an embarrassment than a help to their side. Hannibal made full use of his great superiority in numbers, employing his heavier cavalry to charge the enemy in front and sending the Numidians around their flanks to take them in the rear. The Roman javelin men, whom Scipio had stationed with the Gaulish cavalry in the van to break up the front of the enemy with their missiles, saw that they were going to be caught between two great masses of charging horsemen and fled to the rear without throwing a dart. A furious engagement ensued between the two cavalry forces, who had for the most part dismounted, since their stirrupless condition put men on horseback at a positive disadvantage in a hand-to-hand struggle with determined men on foot. The Romans were still holding their own when the Numidians appeared in their rear, riding down the javelin men and then falling on the knights. The knights broke and fled, but a small body held together and carried the consul Scipio out of the battle, severely wounded and only saved from death or capture by the bravery of his son Publius, an eighteen-year-old youth.

Scipio at once broke camp and retired by a night march towards Placentia where he intended to recross the Padus, making the new colony his base. Hannibal followed his retreat as far as the Ticinus, where he captured the bridge-guard but found the bridge broken. He then about-turned and marched back up the Padus until he came to a suitable place to construct a pontoon bridge. Leaving his quartermaster-general Hasdrubal to see the army across, he received deputations from the Celtic tribes who wished to come over to him and then advanced downstream until he reached the Roman camp, which was sited on the right bank of the river somewhere to the west of the River Trebia, covering Placentia. Scipio, who was now at a considerable disadvantage numerically as thousand of Celts had joined Hannibal, and who was himself incapacitated by his wound, naturally refused his enemy's offer of battle, and the Carthaginian retired and pitched his camp between five and six miles from the Romans.

The policy of their fellow countrymen had not been lost on Scipio's Gallic allies. They concerted their plans and at daybreak fell upon the guards, slaughtered many and decamped, two thousand foot and two hundred horse, to the enemy. Hannibal sent them off to raise their own tribes in his cause and was further heartened by the arrival of envoys from the Boii, whose lands lay to the south-east of Placentia, with whom he contracted a formal alliance. Scipio, now feeling that his forward position was too insecure, executed another retirement by night which brought him onto the high ground east of the Trebia, where he was in communication with Placentia, about eight miles to the north-east, and where the terrain was less favourable to cavalry. For already the inferiority of the Romans in this arm was beginning to exercise an influence on the course of the war. Only the freebooting instincts of the Numidians, who paused in their pursuit of Scipio to ravage the abandoned Roman camp, saved his baggage train from capture. Hannibal again followed up his enemy and camped about five miles from him, to the west of the Trebia. The whole plain westwards declared enthusiastically for him and his supply position was thus secured. A little later, when his troops approached the isolated Roman depot of Clastidium, its prefect, an ally from Brundisium, accepted four hundred gold pieces to surrender it, making the Carthaginians a present of a well-stocked granary.

Scipio was by temperament a fighter and when he first marched west from Placentia he no doubt intended to engage Hannibal in battle before he could strengthen his depleted army with Gallic contingents. Now, however, when the Carthaginian was already too strong to fight and was becoming stronger still every day, and when he himself was *hors de combat*, the only course open to him was to hold on at Placentia, where his army stood between Hannibal and the Boii and also covered the road south into Liguria, and wait for his colleague to join him.

In the southern theatre of the war, the postponement of Longus' departure from Italy as a result of the revolt of the Boii allowed the Carthaginians to make the first move at sea. Carthage's rulers had not gone out of their way to seek the present conflict, and their approach to it was characteristically hesitant. In 218 Carthage may have had about 130 serviceable ships, but fifty-seven of these were under Hannibal's control. If she had had the whole navy at her disposal or had built new ships in 219, when war with Rome became virtually inevitable, and if she had sent a fleet of even a hundred ships with an adequate landing-force to Sicily as soon as war was declared; in short, if she had behaved in a manner wholly out of character in such circumstances, the effect upon the course of the war might have been considerable. Lilybaeum might have fallen and other Sicilian cities might have revolted to her side. The Senate would have had to send Longus to Sicily, Boian revolt or no Boian revolt, and he might very well have become tied down there and been prevented from joining Scipio in Gallia Cisalpina.

As it was Carthage had too few ships ready for sea in the spring of 218 to hope to make any impression on Roman Sicily and so she thought only of defending Africa against Roman attack, not of pre-empting it by the seizure of Lilybaeum. It was not until the autumn, when the Roman expedition had been so seriously delayed, that she made the effort, and then, as so often in the past, the effort was too little and too late. Only fifty ships were despatched to take Lilybaeum, while at the same time a diversionary attack by twenty ships carrying a thousand soldiers was aimed at the Italian coast. Both fleets were driven off course by bad weather – a possibility which might have been avoided had the operation been mounted before mid-September – and three ships of the raiding force were captured by King Hiero's fleet off Messana and their crews interrogated. Hiero at once alerted the praetor, M. Aemilius Lepidus, to the danger threatening western Sicily and Lepidus took energetic steps to meet it. It has been suggested earlier that a portion of Longus' fleet may have been sent on ahead to Lilybaeum. At all events, when the Carthaginians sailed by night from the Aegates Islands (to which they had been driven by the storm) and attempted to surprise Lilybaeum, Lepidus had enough ships to hold them off and inflict a decisive defeat on them in the daylight battle that ensued. In it he captured seven ships and 1,700 prisoners.

Before the news of the battle reached Messana the consul Longus arrived in the straits with his huge expeditionary force. Hiero met him there with his fleet, appraised him of the military situation in the Sicilian theatre, reminded him that the Carthaginians would appear as liberators to many in the island, and assured him of his own continuing loyalty and active support. Consul and king then sailed to Lilybaeum, learning on the way of the praetor's victory. Hiero returned to Syracuse; but Longus, clearly disquieted by the Punic naval activity, sailed to Malta, which might be used as a base for operations against eastern Sicily and southern Italy by the enemy, and captured it along with its garrison and garrison commander, Hamilcar son of Gisco. From Malta he went north to the Lipareae Islands, hoping to intercept the Punic diversionary force, which was at that moment (although he did not know it) menacing the city of Vibo (Bivona) in Bruttium. Returning to Lilybaeum he was informed both of the attack on Vibo and, in despatches from the Senate, of Hannibal's march on Italy, and was instructed to bring his army immediately to Gallia Cisalpina. He left the praetor Lepidus a total of fifty ships with which to protect Sicily, detached twenty-five others which he placed under the orders of his legate, Sex. Pomponius, to deal with the Punic raiding force, and then, about the middle of October, proceeded to carry out the instructions of the Senate.

There are two mutually contradictory accounts of Longus' 'march' to Ariminum. One, that of Polybius, states that he sent his fleet 'home' (presumably to Ostia) and put his soldiers under oath individually to be at Ariminum 'on a certain day'. It appears from a later passage that consul and army made their way through Rome, greatly heartening the populace, and that the whole march, from Lilybaeum to Ariminum, took forty days. On the other hand Livy makes Longus send his army by sea to Ariminum, while he himself followed by sea when he had done all he had to do in Sicily. What Polybius does not say (although modern writers imply that he does) is that Longus put his men on oath to be at Ariminum within forty days. It is probable that the truth lies somewhere between the two accounts, albeit closer to Polybius', and we should perhaps assume that Longus shipped his army to Ostia and there put them on oath to muster at Ariminum 'on a certain day' and that the whole move from Lilybaeum to Placentia took forty days.

From Ariminum he proceeded by forced marches to Placentia where he joined his army with Scipio's in a double camp; this will have been towards the end of November. With the coming of Longus' army the balance of numbers tipped against Hannibal once more. Perhaps about 14,000 Celts had joined him, so that in all he commanded about 40,000 men, of whom over 10,000 were horsemen. The Romans probably totalled rather more, if we take into account the contingent supplied by the loyal Cenomani but also allow for quite substantial losses in the course of the year as the result of sickness, desertions, the detachment of men for garrison duty and battle casualties. One of the first results of the strengthening of the Roman position was that many of the Celts began to waver in their new allegiance to Hannibal, and Longus, who was in effective command of the combined armies, was able to inflict a defeat upon a strong raiding party that Hannibal sent to teach the waverers a lesson. The tradition followed by both Polybius and Livy is strongly pro-Scipio and in consequence anti-Longus; but it is in fact likely that Scipio, disabled and prevented from commanding his men in the field, was opposed to the idea of giving battle to Hannibal so late in the year, arguing that the present enthusiasm of the notoriously fickle Celts for the invader would not survive a winter's inactivity. Longus on the other hand, encouraged by his successes at Malta and against Hannibal's raiders, and naturally unwilling to forgo the unique opportunity of handling two consular armies and of earning a triumph as glorious as any in Rome's annals, was probably eager to fight a decisive battle before the deterioration of the weather and the state of the terrain made further campaigning impossible.

It is not improbable that Hannibal received intelligence, through his Celts, of Longus' frame of mind; if not, he was a sufficiently astute psychologist to work it out for himself. He, too, needed a spectacular victory before the end of the season, in order both to hearten his own men and to maintain and stimulate the enthusiasm of the Celts for his cause. But he proved his superiority as a soldier over Longus – the superiority of the professional over the amateur – by taking care, once he had decided to fight the Romans, that the battle took place on ground of his choosing, and that the enemy came to him.

He had marked out a suitable spot – a steep-banked, overgrown water-course – where a considerable body of troops might be hidden from sight. Under cover of darkness on the night following the skirmish mentioned earlier, he concealed there two thousand picked men, half of them cavalry, under the command of his young brother Mago, who like himself had been bred to soldiering from childhood. At daybreak he sent his Numidians across the river to harass the Roman camp, with the object of provoking Longus into accepting the challenge before his men could break their fast. His own army breakfasted and prepared for battle at leisure. The date was 'about the winter solstice'; that is, some time during the last week of December.

Longus fell into the trap. He first of all sent out his cavalry to engage the Numidians, then six thousand skirmishers (javelin men) to support them, and finally moved the legions out of camp. He marched about five miles down the east bank of the Trebia and crossed at a point that would bring his army out onto the plain in front of Hannibal's encampment.

Snow was falling and the water was breast-deep, fast-flowing and icy-cold. Already tired and dispirited, the Italians plodded towards the enemy who had been sitting comfortably around their watch fires until the time came to fall in and march the mile that separated their camp from the battleground that their general had selected. There, covered by a skirmishing force of about 8,000 spearmen and slingers, Hannibal drew up his army, placing his cavalry, who numbered over 10,000 in all, on the two wings and the 37 elephants in front of the wings of the phalanx, which numbered about 20,000 men, Spanish, African and Gaulish, with the latter nation forming the centre of his line. We cannot say for certain how many heavy infantrymen Longus had in the battle. Polybius tells us that he had 36,000, which would represent the strength of a strong double consular army, inclusive of about 10,400 light-armed. On the other hand we are told by Livy that the two consuls started the year with no fewer than 46,000 infantry. If we suppose that Longus left a fairly strong camp-guard behind with Scipio, a figure of 26,000 heavy infantry would perhaps be about right. Longus recalled his cavalry, who had been having rather the worse of the running fight with the Numidians, and drew up his infantry in the usual order of three lines of maniples in chequer-board formation with his cavalry, including the Cenomani on the wings. When all were in position Longus advanced in slow time towards the enemy with his skirmishers out in front, having done all that was comprised by the art of generalship as he understood it. What followed would depend on the will of the gods, the fighting qualities of the Italian infantryman and the example that he himself would set as a leader.

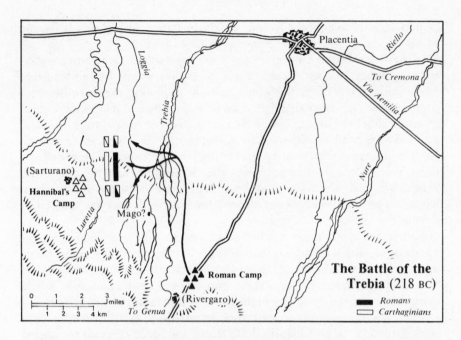

The Battle of the
Trebia (218 BC)

Romans
Carthaginians

(Sarturano)

Hannibal's
Camp

Mago?

Roman Camp

(Rivergaro)

To Genua

0   1   2   3   miles
1   2   3   4 km

Placentia

Riello

To Cremona

Via Aemilia

Loggia

Trebia

Luretta

Nure

Hannibal, on the other hand, in consultation with his war council, had planned every move of a battle that was intended to end in the annihilation of the Roman infantry. His very large force of light spearmen and slingers was first to clear the field of the skirmishers, who were severely handicapped by having already been in action under adverse conditions since daybreak, and then to deploy on the wings, join up with the Numidians and follow the charge of the bridled cavalry. The latter would drive off the enemy's horse, thus denuding the flanks of his infantry, which were then to be attacked by the light spearmen and the Numidians while the extremities of his front were trampled down by the elephants. The Punic centre, composed of expendable Gauls, would contain the attack of the best Roman troops and Mago's ambush party would emerge at the tactical moment and charge them from behind, so preventing the rear line, the triarii, from reinforcing the front lines. When the rout of the Roman wings was complete the virtually untouched Spanish and African heavy infantry – his best troops – would envelop the isolated Roman centre and assist in its complete destruction. The fugitives from the broken wings would be hunted down and killed by the elephants, the cavalry and the light infantry.

That this masterly plan, superbly executed, did not wholly succeed was due mainly to the inability of the Gauls – furious sword-fighters but unarmoured and untrained for the requirements of 'civilized' warfare – to contain the attack of the legions, who fought like lions under the eye of the consul. The Punic centre was broken and Longus and ten thousand of his men poured through the gap. But by then the battle was lost everywhere else. The Roman cavalry had made good their escape, but the infantry wings and the triarii of the centre had been overwhelmed, and the luckless Italians were being cut to pieces or trampled by the Punic cavalry and elephants on the bank of the Trebia to which they had fled, or else drowned in its icy waters. The survivors escaped across the river to the Roman camp. Longus' men were exhausted, whereas the Spanish and African infantry, superior in numbers to his own men, were almost as fresh as a reserve. Accordingly the consul retired in good order from the field, marched north to the bridge over the Trebia and so came safely within the fortifications of Placentia.

The other refugees from the battle, including the cavalry, either managed to rejoin Longus on his march or else made the best of their way across the river to the camp, which Scipio evacuated during the night, taking everyone in it to Placentia. He did not remain there long, however, but removed the remnants of his own army to Cremona in order to ease the burden of supply upon the colony.

The Roman losses have been estimated at about fifteen thousand killed and captured; no doubt they would have been even higher had not the appalling weather conditions – the battle had been fought in driving sleet and snow – prevented any pursuit of the main body. The invaders suffered very severely from the cold and wet; few of the badly wounded can have survived and many men and horses and almost all the elephants perished. In the fighting, however, the heaviest losses fell upon the Celts who formed the Punic centre.

In his despatches Longus at first attempted to hide the fact that he had been defeated, but the truth was probably known at Rome before he returned to the city to hold the elections for 217. Livy's description of the consternation when the news got out is probably exaggerated. The disaster was less serious than some that Rome had suffered during the century, the troops of the centre had routed the forces opposed to them, the cavalry had saved itself from destruction, and the consuls, secure behind the walls of Placentia and Cremona, were still between Hannibal and Italy. On the other hand, the greater part of Gallia Cisalpina (whose total population has been estimated at about 1,400,000 at this time) had declared for the invader and Rome, which had begun the war in such an aggressive spirit, had now been forced onto the defensive.

The Roman people had not, however, lost confidence in its leaders. It is true that Longus, who had achieved next to nothing in the Sicilian and African theatres and whose incompetence was rightly held to have been largely responsible for the defeat on the Trebia, was not employed again, unless perhaps as a legate in 215. But Scipio's imperium was prorogued and it was decided to send him to rejoin his brother and his army in northern Spain – a piece of boldness that was ultimately, if indirectly, to lead to Rome's winning the war. The consuls elected for 217, Cn. Servilius Geminus and C. Flaminius, both belonged to the Aemilian party, and Flaminius (tribune of the people, first praetorian governor of Sicily, consul in 223 BC, censor, and builder of the Circus Flaminius and the Via Flaminia) had campaigned against – and, by popular vote, triumphed over – the Insubres in his first consular year.

Flaminius, a man of enormous energy and political ability, represented the survival at Rome, two generations after the ending of the Struggle of the Orders, of a democratic movement which was strongly resisted by such conservatives as the Fabian party. Flaminius had come into head-on collision with the Fabians, as tribune in 232 and in his consulship; and again as recently as the previous year, when he alone supported in the Senate the bill of the tribune Claudius which in effect debarred senators from capitalist pursuits. Nonetheless his re-election contrary to the 'ten years rule' then in force probably reflected less a popular reaction against the nobility than a lack of new consular candidates on the part of the then-predominant Aemilian faction. There was also an understandable desire on their part, as well as on the people's, to utilize the services of an experienced and successful soldier, well known for his patriotism, his energy and his impatience with obstructionism.

That the Senate was now taking the war very seriously indeed is shown by the number of legions authorized. There were to be two for each of the consuls (those which had fought on the Trebia being brought up to full strength), two (from then on known as the 'urban' legions) for training and the defence of Rome, two for Sicily, where T. Otacilius Crassus was to be praetor, and one for Sardinia: eleven in all, counting the army of Spain. Garrisons were also sent to Taras and to other places. Sixty new capital ships were built, presumably to replace vessels damaged or found to be unsound in 218.

CHAPTER X

217 BC

Trasimene and Fabius Cunctator.

The disposition of Rome's forces in the early summer of 217 illustrates at once the strength and the weakness of her military organization. In 225, at the time of the Gallic 'scare', the Senate had taken an inventory of Italy's resources in manpower. Polybius (following Fabius Pictor) tells us that they totalled over 700,000 footmen and 70,000 horseman. Accepting Professor Brunt's emended figures of 580,000 foot and 54,000 horse, we can see that ideally Rome should have been able to put into the field more than twelve times as many fighting men as Hannibal was bringing into Italy – no fewer than 240,000 of them her own citizens. The Senate has been criticized by historians like De Sanctis for not throwing an army of 100,000 men against Hannibal at the outset, but the truth of the matter is that the politico-military character of Rome's army command effectively prevented it from doing so.

Imperium – power, and essentially the power to command the people under arms (the *exercitus*) – was the real basis of the Roman state. However it had come into conflict with the developing rights and liberties of the Roman people, and had accordingly been divided among two senior and (eventually) four junior magistrates; and certain restrictions had been placed upon their use of it, by custom and statute. Imperium, especially consular imperium, was also the object of the legitimate ambition of the ruling class, which was unwilling to dilute it by sharing it among a larger number of magistrates, and also unwilling to allow the same individual to hold it more than once (or at most twice) in a lifetime with the result that someone else, who as a member of the aristocracy had a prescriptive right to it, was excluded. Furthermore, in order to prevent the working of the constitution from being hamstrung, the consuls had to be prevented from neutralizing each other's effectiveness and also from poaching on the preserves of their juniors, the praetors.

As a result the regular Roman military establishment comprised not one but two or more distinct armies. A consular army consisted of two legions, a praetorian army normally of one (praetors were sent to the front only as an exceptional measure). Each army was commanded by a magistrate of the people, elected for one year and, except in the relatively rare case of a consul who had previously commanded an army as praetor, now having his first experience of independent command. As yet relatively little use was made – except, again, in exceptional circumstances – of the expedient of prolonging a successful general's tenure of command by prorogation, which was to become such an important feature of the Roman military system. The generals operated each in a separate province specifically allotted by the Senate, with only a very uncertain potentiality for cooperation between them. In order to place even four legions under a single command it was necessary to have recourse to the dictatorship; but by 217 the dictatorship was already going out of fashion on political grounds, being disliked for different reasons by both the nobility and the commons. Moreover custom decreed that the dictatorship should only be resorted to in an emergency – that is to say, only after a military disaster.

Because one consular army of two legions normally operated independently of the other, and because the two consuls enjoyed equal power, of which they were apt to be extremely jealous, even when two consuls joined forces so as to produce a four-legion army it tended to behave in the field as a pair of armies rather than a single body. The most that could normally be hoped of a four-legion army was that its two chief components would display a decent measure of cooperation under a rotating overall leadership – a basically unsatisfactory arrangement.

The absence of any tradition, much less any training and practice, of independent manœuvre by the separate sections of even a single consular army has been mentioned already. As far as tactics and tactical control on the battlefield went the Roman general was only little in advance of, say, the generals of fifth-century Athens or Sparta and his generalship was virtually limited to controlling the engagement and disengagement of the two front lines of maniples, the *hastati* and *principes*, and the use made of the tactical reserve provided by the third line, the triarii. In short the Roman system of army command, because of the political significance of the imperium upon which it was based, was suited only to the simplest manœuvres on the part of relatively small armies, and adapted awkwardly to the handling of a force of even forty thousand men.

In the present instance, therefore, although the Senate authorized the mobilization of about ninety thousand men, apart from the two legions in Spain, the consuls who were to confront Hannibal had each to be content with the traditional two-legion army. Moreover it was politically unthinkable to abandon at the outset to the ravages of the invader either the Roman territory of the Ager Gallicus and Picenum in north-east Italy or allied Etruria, vulnerable because of its large serf population, to the west of the Apennines. Therefore the Senate had to divide its forces forward so as to cover both Hannibal's possible axes of advance into Italy. The result was that, although Rome had six legions raised for the defence of Italy, when Hannibal entered Etruria with well over fifty thousand men he had less than half that number directly in front of him, and the discrepancy in cavalry was even greater.

It is not clear where in Gallia Cisalpina Hannibal wintered. He released the Italian socii captured in the battle, hoping in this way to influence their communities in his favour and weaken their allegiance to Rome, and with the arrival of spring he prepared to move south into Italy. His circumstances now were somewhat less satisfactory than he had anticipated when he left New Carthage a year before. He had entered Gaul more like a fugitive from the Romans than a conqueror; not at the head of perhaps ninety thousand men but with a weary army, halved by the rigours of a winter march through hostile tribes and mountains. It was true that he had won two battles since then, and that Gaul had risen against the Romans; but Polybius tells us that the natives were already eager to see the back of him. Perhaps this was partly the result of the Trebia battle, in which the Gauls had suffered a bloody defeat. Whatever the reason, it looks as if, from first to last and counting those who fell on the Trebia, less than half the seventy thousand warriors who had marched away south only eight years previously, to be cut to pieces by the Romans at Telamon, joined Hannibal – and these, we are told, did so mainly in the hope of booty.

His army, then, amounted in all to perhaps fifty-five thousand men, of whom something over ten thousand were horsemen. He had only one elephant left, which was destined to serve as his headquarters vehicle in the coming campaign, and so he would have to devise new tactics in order to win his next pitched battle. Instead of having behind him an open line of communication with Iberia, along which ample reinforcements of trained Spaniards and fresh elephants could reach him, he now had a well-led Roman army between himself and Hasdrubal. He still had high hopes of his City. Carthage might still make an effort to recover the command of the sea and so be in a position to send him reinforcements, including elephants, from Africa. But the attitude of the government at Carthage to his Italian expedition, which no one, unless perhaps his closest adherents, had envisaged when they opted for war with Rome, would be regulated by the extent to which it appeared to contribute to, or imperil, the security of Spain and Africa.

His original plan, had it come off successfully, would have made Spain and Africa safe. As things were he had left them exposed to invasion, and in the case of Spain, to the disruption of its commercial exploitation, and even to the danger of its conquest by the Romans. He had, indeed, relieved the pressure on Africa for the moment, but it remained to be seen whether or not his plan was well conceived in the long term. Its boldness – indeed, its effrontery – must have alarmed beyond measure the hard-headed businessmen, whose instinct and training would disincline them to invest too heavily in such an extravagant and hazardous speculation. They will have certainly hoped that Hannibal would do Rome the maximum amount of harm whilst he was in Italy; but they probably intended to use him as they had used his father in Sicily. If he could fight the Romans to a standstill, so that Carthage in her habitually rather leisurely way could restore her empire without Roman interference, securing Spain and recovering Sardinia and even Sicily, he would have done all that they required of him. From the moment that Hannibal crossed the Pyrenees he became expendable in the eyes of the rulers of Carthage. They cannot have viewed with very much satisfaction the prospect of his return to Carthage with the laurels of an Alexander adorning his brow. If with Spain, Sardinia and Sicily safe in Punic hands he and his mercenaries perished together in Italy, probably so much the better. So the Carthaginians, like the majority of the Gauls, waited to see what would be the outcome of his adventure. The only move they made at sea in 217 was in northern waters, striking at Rome's sea communications with northern Spain.

The account given by our sources of the opening of the year on the Roman side is somewhat confused. This is partly due to an attack by the Roman annalistic tradition upon the character and sense of responsibility of Flaminius, who is said to have sneaked away to Ariminum before the Ides of March so that he could enter on his consular duties unhampered by the demands and delays of religion and ceremonial. Flaminius' reputation has been blackened from several directions. The nobility disliked a man whom they stigmatized as a demagogue; the Fabians in particular hated him for his defiance of their leader Q. Fabius Maximus; and the Romans had already shown (in the case of P. Claudius at the battle of Drepana) that they preferred to ascribe their defeats to the impiety of the general. Yet more than a grain of truth may lie behind the charges levelled against him. His well-attested actions show him to have been an impatient and headstrong man, and he may very well have decided to get to the seat of the war as early as possible, leaving it to his colleague to tidy up such matters as the Latin Festival on the Alban Mount.

Let us therefore suppose that at some time before the Ides of March Flaminius had instructed Longus to bring what was left of his army from Placentia down to Ariminum. Then as soon as he had held his levy Flaminius hastened to Ariminum, collected Longus' men and marched them to Arretium (Arezzo), where he had ordered his own levies to muster; thus bringing his command up to the full strength of a consular army. His patrician colleague, Cn. Servilius Geminus, duly performed the various rites and ceremonies that devolved upon new consuls, and then hurried north to Ariminum with his levies, to take over Scipio's troops who had come from Cremona. Both ex-consuls must have left strong garrisons in the colonies of the Padus Valley, and so the bulk of the forces that were stationed to contest Hannibal's advance into Italy was 'new draft'.

Hannibal had a choice of three main routes south. He could march through Liguria and then down the west coast via Pisae, into Etruria; he could follow the line of the later Via Aemilia to Ariminum and from there take either the Via Flaminia into Umbria or the east-coast road through Picenum into the Samnite country; or he could cross the Apennines from the direction of Bononia (Bologna) by the Colline Pass and descend on central Etruria via Pistoria (Pistoia) and Faesulae (Fiesole). To the east of the Apennines there are many places on the road where the natural strength of a defensive position would more than compensate for any lack of numbers, and Hannibal was unlikely to try to force the Via Flaminia – although it had to be held, as a deterrent measure. The west-coast road could be cut at Pisae, where the Arnus enters the sea, and the Gauls may have had qualms about taking such an ill-omened path. Flaminius clearly expected Hannibal to follow a road into central Italy, but since the Colline was not the only pass through the Apennines he could not risk taking up a more advanced position at, say, Faesulae, for fear of being outflanked. At Arretium he could cover all the roads into Italy west of the Apennines and still be in a position to reinforce his colleague should Hannibal, contrary to strategic likelihood, elect to take the most easterly route. However, the non-professionalism of the Roman command, even of a man who had led an army previously, like Flaminius, is again illustrated by the fact that no cavalry patrols were established on the border of Gallia Cisalpina to shadow and report back the earliest movements of the enemy.

In May, by which time the passes were clear of snow and forage would be available for his immense number of animals, Hannibal moved off from the Padus Valley, crossed the Apennines by the Colline Pass and descended into the flooded marshes of the middle Arno. In the passage of these he lost an eye, most of his baggage animals, many horses, and a certain number of Gauls. As usual he treated these allies with disdain, leaving them the worst of the footing after it had been broken up by the Spaniards and Africans, and posting Mago and the cavalry as a rearguard to prevent them from deserting. Once clear of the marshes he pitched camp and rested his men, in the neighbourhood of Faesulae. Unlike his

(Grenoble)
(Susa)

INSUBRES

CENOMANI

Sesia

Ticinus

Taurasia

Cremona
Placentia

Padus

Trebia

Mutina

BOII

Savo

Genua

Ariminu

Faesulae

Fanum Fortunae

Massilia

Pisae

Arretium
Cortona

Metaur

UMBRIA

Populonia

ETRURIA

Perusia

Ilva

Cosa

Aleria

Tiber

Rome

Tibu

LATI

Cornus

Caralis

Italy

Tribes **INSUBRES**

0   20   100   200
                                  ⌐ miles
    50   100   300 km

Lilybaeum

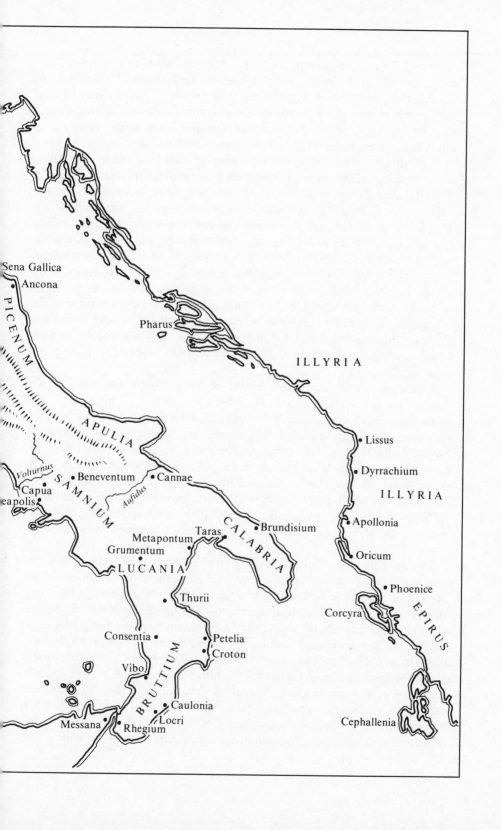

Sena Gallica
• Ancona

PICENUM

Pharus

ILLYRIA

APULIA

• Lissus

• Dyrrachium

ILLYRIA

Volturnus

• Beneventum   • Cannae

SAMNIUM   *Aufidus*

• Apollonia

Capua

eapolis •

Metapontum   Taras

CALABRIA

• Brundisium

• Oricum

Grumentum

LUCANIA

• Phoenice

• Thurii

Corcyra

EPIRUS

Consentia   • Petelia

• Croton

Vibo •

BRUTTIUM

• Caulonia

Messana   • Locri

Rhegium

Cephallenia

opponent he had his scouts out in front of his advance and knew that Flaminius was at Arretium. He also knew – for Hannibal appreciated to the full the importance of 'knowing your enemy' – that he had to deal with a man whom in all likelihood a variety of factors – self-confidence, over-impetuosity, pride and, not least, patriotism – would betray into allowing himself to be ensnared by a more astute and skilful adversary.

Accordingly when his army was ready to move he advanced south-west, keeping to the west of Arretium and trailing his coat before the Romans as if daring them to attack him, and then descended into the valley of the Clanis (Val di Chiana), destroying and burning as he went. The blow to Flaminius' pride was deeply felt – he had, after all, a triumph to his credit as well as being the trusted friend of the people. A skilful general, even with inferior forces, should be able to keep within fairly narrow bounds the ravaging of a hostile army which must, after all, move slowly and spread itself over a wide area if it is to do its work of destruction thoroughly, and an army dispersed is an army vulnerable. Moreover the invader was now between him and Rome and it was the first duty of a consul to defend the city. No consul's reputation, in 217, could have survived the spectacle of an unfought enemy devastating the plain of Rome.

Flaminius would have done better to have retired towards Perusia (Perugia) and awaited the arrival of Geminus, who had discovered the direction of Hannibal's march and was moving down the Via Flaminia to join his colleague. Instead he set off in pursuit of the enemy, who now swung eastwards, still devastating the land, to pass to the south of Cortona and along the northern shore of Lake Trasimene – away, that is, from the direct road to Rome but towards Perusia and the Via Flaminia. We shall never know what Flaminius thought Hannibal was up to, but it must have seemed to him that the gods were going to grant Rome another Telamon, with Hannibal caught between two consular armies.

The evening of 21 June, according to the Roman calendar, found the Carthaginians, with the Romans hard on their heels, in the neighbourhood of what is today the flourishing tourist resort of Passignano, which lies some three miles to the west of the north-east corner (for want of a better term) of Lake Trasimene, where the Cortonian hills come down in a high spur to the water's edge. Hannibal's genius perceived at once that before him lay a perfect ambush position. From Passignano a narrow plain skirts the lake, bordered on the left by hills; it curves round to the south and ends in a defile, up and through which the road runs to Magione and Perugia. Under cover of darkness – he had little to fear from Roman scouts anyway – Hannibal occupied the high ground surrounding the defile, posting his crack Spanish and African infantry on the hill at the top end and his slingers and spearmen on the slopes to the right of the defile, and on the right flank of an army entering it from the north. He extended their line so as to prevent any break-out from the trap along the shores of the lake towards Monte del Lago, and stationed the Gauls and the cavalry, who amounted all told to more than thirty thousand men, on the left, with their line curving round the hills to command the approaches to the defile through the lakeside plain.

Flaminius, pressing forward until sunset, had camped close to the lake, probably just outside the 'narrows' at Passignano, and as soon as it was day he broke camp and advanced along the shore of the lake, eager to make contact with the enemy – but apparently with no cavalry out in front. There was a heavy mist and the first indication that he had of his predicament was when his vanguard clashed with the troops at the head of the defile, whom he probably at first took to be the enemy's rearguard. Having been marching for only a couple of hours the Romans were probably still in fairly close column and a large portion of the army crowded into the defile, where they were fallen upon from all sides by an enemy suddenly appearing out of the mist. At the same time the part of the army that was outside the defile, still in column of route, was assailed by the Gauls and the cavalry on flank and rear. What ensued was less a battle than a massacre, with about 15,000 men being cut down in the defile or in the plain, or else being driven into the lake where they drowned or were despatched by the Punic cavalry. Flaminius fell fighting, run through by an Insubrian knight named Ducarius. About 6,000 of those caught in the defile broke out of the trap, but when the mists cleared and they saw no way of retrieving a day hopelessly lost, they pressed on to a village where, the next day, according to Livy, they surrendered to Maharbal on condition that their lives should be spared. The total number of prisoners amounted to 10,000, and of these Hannibal released the non-Romans (as he had done after the Trebia battle) and sent them home. His own losses are given by Punic sources as 1,500, and 2,500 by Roman; once again the majority of them were Celts.

The news of the battle must have reached Rome about two days later. The peregrine praetor, M. Pomponius Matho, told the vast and anxious crowd that had gathered in the place of assembly simply, 'We have been defeated in a great battle.' But this was not the end of the bad news. Geminus had sent on his cavalry, numbering about four thousand, in advance of his march down the Via Flaminia. Forewarned of the approach of this force, Hannibal sent Maharbal with a mixed body of horsemen and spearmen to waylay them. Neither the details nor the location of the ensuing engagement are known (De Sanctis placed it in the neighbourhood of Assisi), but the result was the death or capture of the entire Roman force.

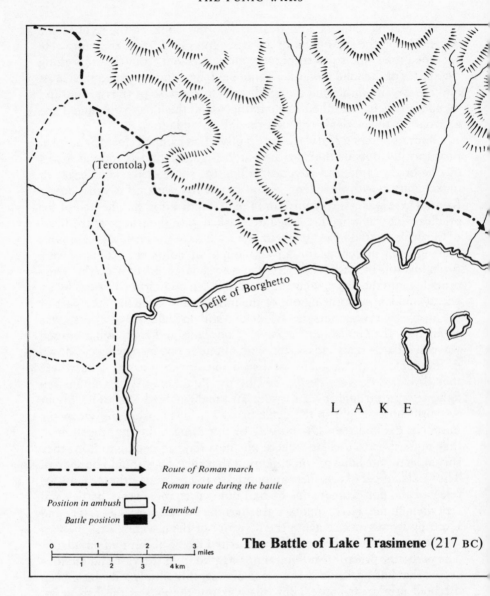

(Terontola)

Defile of Borghetto

L A K E

- · — · — · — ·→ Route of Roman march
- — — — — — → Roman route during the battle
Position in ambush ☐ ⎫
Battle position ■ ⎬ Hannibal

The Battle of Lake Trasimene (217 BC)

0   1   2   3
└─────┴─────┴─────┘ miles
  1   2   3   4 km

Trasimene and its sequel not only left Rome without an effective field
army but also largely discredited the Aemilian party. At all events it
enabled the Fabian faction in the Senate to demand the appointment of
a dictator; and to this solemn responsibility no one had a better claim
than their leader, Q. Fabius Maximus Verrucosus, censor in 230 BC, twice
consul, twice *interrex*, and once already dictator. The method of his
appointment is far from clear, for Geminus was out of touch with Rome,

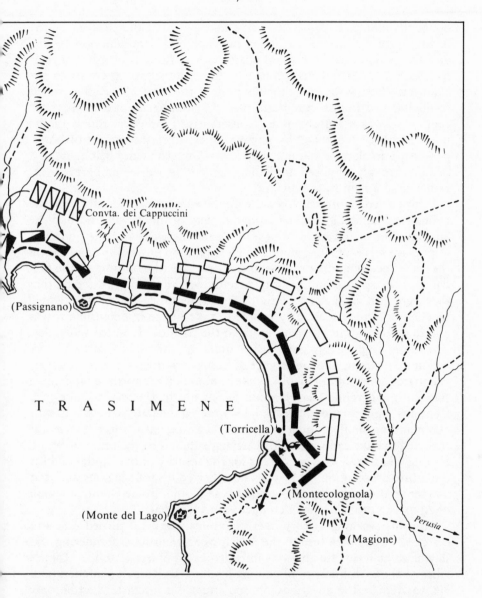

and a praetor could neither nominate nor hold an election to choose a magistrate with greater power than his own. Perhaps the Capitoline Fasti afford the correct explanation: that since both consuls were politically disabled, the senators had recourse to the interregnal procedure, and an interrex presided over the election of a dictator. If this is really what happened a kind of precedent will have been created for the election of Sulla to a very different sort of dictatorship, 135 years later. It was no doubt the influence of the Aemilians that procured the election by the Assembly of the master of horse, in place of his nomination by the dictator, which was the normal practice. As a result a member of their own faction, M. Minucius Rufus, who had campaigned as consul in 221 against the Istri, was chosen for the post. In this way, although a unified command had been secured and placed in the hands of a man whose caution was as notorious as his conservatism, the effectiveness of the move had been weakened by party politics, since the master of horse, possessing an elective and not a derivative imperium and belonging to a faction strongly opposed to Fabius', might prove an embarrassment rather than a help to the dictator.

Fabius acted vigorously to deal with the emergency. He attributed the blame for Flaminius' disaster to the impiety of the consul and had the Sibylline Books consulted in order to learn the wishes of the gods. An impressive series of rites, games, dedications and vows was enjoined on the state, including the promise of a *ver sacrum* (the offering of the first fruits of the spring) and the city praetor was charged with seeing that they were carried out. Then with the approval of the Senate Fabius issued an edict ordering all country people to take refuge in defensible towns and to destroy all houses and crops in the path of Hannibal's advance. This done he probably gave instructions for the raising of two more legions for training and the defence of Rome and ordered the two existing urban legions to Tibur (Tivoli), while he himself went north to Ocriculum (Otricoli), where the Via Flaminia passes out of Umbria, to take over Geminus' legions from the consul. He ordered the latter to Ostia to take command of the fleet there and pursue a Punic naval force which was reported to have captured ships carrying supplies to the army in Spain. Having taken these energetic steps for the security of the capital and for the future prosecution of the war, he collected his four legions at Tibur and set off down the Via Latina for Aecae (Troja) in the Daunian region of Apulia in order to make contact with Hannibal.

After his crushing victory over Flaminius Hannibal turned east and marched through Umbria to the Adriatic coast burning, plundering and slaying as he went; for this was intended as an object lesson to Rome's allies on the foolishness of remaining loyal to the Roman confederation. He was repulsed in an attack on Spoletium – a foretaste, had he only known it, of the loyalty to be displayed by the Latin colonies in the course of the war – and reached the Picene coast during the first week of July, laden with booty. As the army was suffering from scurvy as a result of the hardships and privations it had undergone since crossing the Alps, he spent some time there recruiting the health of his men and beasts, and he re-armed his Libyan infantry with the much superior captured Roman equipment. He also sent off news of his victories to Carthage, where there was great jubilation. When his army was restored to tip-top condition he set it in motion down the coast, ravaging as he went, until he came to the country of the Dauni in Apulia. He laid waste the territory of the Latin colony of Luceria (Lucera), and from a base in the hills near Vibinum (Bovino) he began a systematic devastation of the Tavoliere.

When Fabius arrived at Aecae, Hannibal at once offered battle, but Fabius had no intention of accommodating him. The army that he led probably contained a high proportion of raw recruits, it was short of cavalry and it was not yet accustomed to operating as an army; to have fought Hannibal then would have been to court disaster. But good and sufficient though these reasons were for avoiding battle, the temperament, qualities, and politics of the leader provided others as strong. Fabius, who as a child had been regarded as little better than a simpleton, was a slow-minded man who made up in tenacity of purpose and obstinacy for what he lacked in mental agility. He was well aware that in cleverness he was no match for Hannibal; but what, after all, did the invader's talent for trickery and ambush amount to other than Punic perfidiousness? To this he could oppose the true Roman qualities of which he was the very embodiment – courage, self-control, a dogged determination 'to see it through' – qualities which would preserve Rome from the dangers to which the recklessness, in gross and in detail, of the Aemilian faction had exposed her.

Hannibal, whose hopes of ultimate success in the war rested entirely on his ability to detach Rome's allies from her, badly needed another spectacular victory in the field. However, the nature of classical warfare and classical armies precluded the possibility of achieving one as long as his opponent declined battle and kept to parallel lines of advance, not following blindly on his heels (like the unhappy Flaminius). In the hope of either goading Fabius into fighting or of catching him off his guard Hannibal now struck across the mountains into the rich heart of Samnium. He laid waste the lands of the colony of Beneventum, took an unwalled but well-stocked town, probably called Venusia, and then, with Fabius dogging his advance at a safe distance, descended into Campania, marching by way of the Calor and Volturnus Valleys, Allifae and Cales, into the Campus Stellatis in the rich Ager Falernus, part of the territory of Rome ceded to her a century earlier by Capua. He camped on the north bank of the Volturnus, which forms the southern boundary of the Ager Falernus, and proceeded to devastate the plain systematically. Fabius was under great pressure from his master of horse – virtually his colleague – and from other magnates in the army to take advantage of the dispersal of Hannibal's forces to attack him. He adhered, however, to his chosen strategy, keeping to the high ground and merely policing the movements of Hannibal's forces in the plain below.

With the end of the summer approaching (it must by now have been late August) Hannibal had to think about winter quarters. It was out of the question to winter where he was as long as the strong cities of Campania, such as Capua (which was a Roman half-citizen community) and Nola, remained hostile. He had to get back to the wide, fertile but relatively thinly populated plains of Apulia. His army was heavily burdened with the spoils of the richest district in Italy, on which it proposed to subsist during the coming winter. By burdening itself in this way it gave a hostage to the enemy of which a better general than Fabius might have taken full advantage. Hannibal was in fact in a trap, for Fabius, in the hills, was in a position to close the exits from the Ager Falernus, with strongpoints at Casilinum (Capua) commanding the crossing of the Volturnus, on the Via Appia at Tarracina, and on the southern slope of Callicula (which has been identified as the Monte San Angelo–Monte Caievola–Monte San Nicola range) where his camp commanded the Via Latina north of Teanum. Fabius was weak in cavalry and in good subordinate commanders – a scouting group under a man called Mancinus allowed itself to be routed with the loss of its officer by Carthalo's Numidians – and this weakness made it impossible for him to set up an ambush like that of Trasimene. However he should at least have been able to compel Hannibal to fight his way out of the Campus Stellatis at the cost of heavy casualties and the loss of his plunder, which would have been a serious matter, both materially and because of its effect on the morale of his army (especially the Celts) and upon that of Rome's allies.

Fabius satisfied himself that Hannibal intended to break out by the same route as he had taken when he entered the plain, following the line of the Via Latina (and of today's *autostrada*) past Cales, leaving Teanum on his left and then taking one of two options open to him. He could either follow the Via Latina north-westwards or else strike north-east past Pietravairano to the middle Volturnus and so reach Samnium by way of Allifae (Alife). Fabius concentrated his forces, less garrisons, on the slopes south of Vairano and stationed four thousand men in the narrow pass leading to the Volturnus, so that he covered both Hannibal's escape routes. Hannibal advanced to within two miles of Fabius' camp and halted in the plain. He ordered his men to eat and then lie down and rest.

It is possible that Hannibal had already thought of the master-stroke by which he extricated his army from its predicament when he passed that way on his march into Campania. Under cover of darkness his quartermaster-general Hasdrubal collected two thousand strong draught oxen in front of the camp and at about three o'clock in the morning this great herd with blazing faggots of dry wood bound to the animals' horns was driven up onto a ridge that lay between the Punic camp and the Roman detachment guarding the pass. The light spearmen played the rôle of cowboys in keeping the stampede on course. The Romans in the pass abandoned their positions, thinking that the enemy was trying to break out over the hills, in the neighbourhood of Pietravairano, and rushed back to head them off. Some confused fighting followed between them and the spearmen and they withdrew onto higher ground to wait for daylight. Fabius, too, fearing a trick, remained quiet. In the meantime Hannibal marched the rest of his army through the pass unmolested and at first light sent some of his Spanish infantry from the rearguard to assist the spearmen to disengage from the enemy. In the course of this action the Romans lost a quarter of their number.

Fabius' reputation had suffered a serious setback, and the murmurings of his army, led by his master of horse, who expressed the sentiments of the Aemilian party and the radicals in the Assembly, were not unjustified. He had appeared to have the enemy almost at his mercy, but by an over-cautiousness that his opponents characterized as pusillanimity had allowed them to escape and cover the Romans with ridicule. However he again followed Hannibal's march, this time up the Volturnus Valley towards the country of the Paeligni, and from there into that of the Frentani, where Hannibal, after a short siege, had captured the border town of Gerunium, about twenty-two miles north-west of Luceria. The inhabitants had rejected an offer of alliance, and so he put them to death and made the town his magazine. He fortified a strong camp in front of it and brought into it the food and forage that his army set about collecting from the adjacent plain. Fabius brought his army into the territory of Larinum (Larino) and encamped on high ground at Calena (perhaps Monte Calvo). There he received despatches recalling him to Rome. The reason given by our sources – that certain religious ceremonies required his presence – is probably only half the truth. The anti-Fabian section of the Senate was no doubt pressing for a first-hand explanation of the escape of Hannibal from Campania, and there was also the matter of the election of a suffect consul to replace Flaminius.

Fabius handed over the army to his master of horse with a passionate injunction to abstain from fighting Hannibal; but M. Minucius Rufus, who embodied the aggressive spirit of the Aemilians, had several reasons for wanting to fight. Militarily it could be argued that the Roman army of four legions – probably over forty thousand men – was now seasoned by a summer's marching and counter-marching and fit to meet Hannibal's mercenaries and that it was bad for their morale and disastrous for Rome's position of *hegemon* of the confederation to allow Hannibal to ravage Italy unfought. At the level of party politics it was desirable to discredit Fabius and his policy by demonstrating that Hannibal could be fought.

When the Romans appeared at Calena Hannibal, assuming that he had nothing to fear from their then negative approach to war, moved some two-thirds of his army to a hill about two miles nearer the enemy in order to cover the activities of his foraging parties, and during the night threw forward two thousand light spearmen to occupy a hillock close to and commanding their camp. It must have come as something of a shock to him when Rufus attacked this advanced force next morning and drove it off, subsequently moving his whole army to occupy the hill. Clearly he expected the Romans to follow up this success by attacking his camp, and therefore kept his troops within its walls; but as the enemy remained inactive, after a few days he resumed his foraging. Rufus waited until midday and then led out his forces. He stationed his heavy infantry in front of Hannibal's camp and sent his cavalry and light infantry to cut up the scattered foragers. The spirit of the Roman soldiers was such that when the Carthaginians failed to come out of their camp they made an assault upon it, which was repulsed with difficulty. However Hasdrubal brought aid from the main camp before Gerunium, relieving the pressure on his general, who then sallied out from the camp and compelled the Romans who were attacking its walls to fall back.

Hannibal had suffered serious casualties both to his foragers and to the troops defending the camp – and at this stage of the war, with the Italian communities remaining obstinately loyal to Rome, he had no way of making good his losses. Realizing that he was now opposed by an aggressive enemy, he abandoned his forward position and fell back on the main camp before Gerunium, for if he had allowed the Romans to strike at his supply base his position could have become desperate.

Rufus was in high feather over the result of his operations. He moved forward and occupied the camp abandoned by the enemy and sent an exaggerated account of his success to the Senate. The prestige of the Fabian party was badly shaken, and on the motion of a tribune the plebeian Assembly passed a bill giving the master of horse authority equal to that of the dictator. Having thus destroyed the whole *raison d'être* of the dictatorship the Romans allowed Fabius to return to the front (presumably after he had hurried through the election of M. Atilius Regulus as suffect consul), so that the supreme command was once again divided, and this time between men who were personally as well as politically antipathetical to each other. Rufus saw in the action of the Assembly the endorsement of his opinion that Hannibal could and should be fought; Fabius was only the more hardened by the political tactics of his opponents in his determination to avoid battle. The dictator proposed that they should exercise command in daily rotation, but Rufus realized that this arrangement would enable his colleague to frustrate effectively his strategy of bringing Hannibal to battle. He therefore agreed to divide the army and Fabius took two legions off to the hill from which Rufus had driven the Punic light spearmen, a little over a mile distant.

It was not long before Hannibal's intelligence service had acquainted him with what had happened, and he decided to give Rufus the opportunity of walking into a trap that he appeared to be looking for. He sent about five hundred cavalry and five thousand foot soldiers by night to occupy ambush positions in the vicinity of a piece of rising ground between his camp and Rufus' and at daybreak he stationed the rest of his light infantry on the hill in full view of the Romans. Rufus swallowed the bait, sending in succession his light-armed and his cavalry, and lastly leading out his heavy infantry, to take the hill – a repeat, as he hoped, of his first successful performance. Hannibal kept throwing fresh forces into the battle, forcing Rufus to support his skirmishers with the legions. He then sent in the whole of his cavalry force with his heavy infantry following in close support. The Roman light infantry were flung back upon the legions and at the same moment the ambush was sprung and Rufus found his whole force threatened from all sides.

It is impossible to assess the true extent of the danger from which the approach of Fabius' army in battle order rescued him; the history of the period owes too much to the pen of the dictator's kinsman Q. Fabius Pictor and to the senatorial tradition. Yet we may take it that Rufus was very glad to fall back on his colleague's legions after sustaining considerable losses, although Hannibal, with his cavalry and light infantry in disarray, did not feel that it was the moment to try conclusions with the legions. However, he established a strongpoint on the hill with a ditch behind it, in order to deny it to the enemy and both armies – the Romans reunited in a single camp, presumably with the command now rotating daily – settled down to an interlude of skirmishes and 'affairs of outposts'. In his despatches Fabius had left the Senate and people in no doubt about the service that he had done the state and the superiority of his policy over Rufus'; while the latter had lost so much face that he was unable to assert himself any further against the dictator and was publicly reconciled to him. Probably in November both men abdicated their imperium and the consuls Cn. Servilius Geminus and M. Atilius Regulus arrived and took over the armies.

Geminus had not been inactive during the summer. When he had handed over his legions to Fabius he went to Ostia and there got a fleet of 120 ships to sea with which he set out in pursuit of the Carthaginian force of seventy ships that had been sent into northern waters in order to cut Rome's communications with Spain. This force had touched at Sardinia and then at Pisae (not so much because it expected to make contact with Hannibal, in all probability, as because Pisae was the port of embarkation for Spain), and from there it had sailed south to Cosa

(Ansedonia), where it had captured some of Scipio's transports. It had probably returned to Sardinia when it learnt of Geminus' approach and immediately made off for home. The consul took hostages from those Corsican and Sardinian communities that had received the enemy fleet and then, after putting in at Lilybaeum, sailed over to Africa, to the Lesser Syrtis (Gulf of Gabes). There he ravaged Meninx (Djerba) and extorted ten talents of silver from the people of Cercina. Encouraged by these easy successes he made a descent on African soil, but his men, carelessly dispersed for plundering, were attacked by the inhabitants and driven back to the ships with the loss of his quaestor and a thousand soldiers. He had a final success, however, in the capture of the island of Cossyra (Pantelleria) on his homeward voyage. Back in Sicily he handed over the fleet to the praetor, who subsequently sent it back to Italy for the winter, while he returned to Italy in time to receive back his legions and get them settled into winter quarters.

CHAPTER XI

216 BC

Cannae. The crisis of the war.

In the winter of 217/16 no cautious betting man would have offered any but the longest odds against Hannibal's ultimate victory. He had indeed won two battles and was at present wintering securely in Apulia, but he had not brought about the defection of a single Roman ally or taken a single important town. It is true that a measure of disaffection was growing both in southern Italy – the region most recently incorporated into the confederation – and in Campania, where there were social and political grievances; but Hannibal would have to do better than he had done so far if these sentiments were to lead to open revolt. The Romans had latterly held their own in Apulia, Carthage had made no serious effort to dispute their command of the sea, Hannibal had been losing men and horses without any means of replacing them, and the news from Spain was extremely encouraging. It is true that the strain of the war on Rome's economy had led to a further reduction in the weight of the bronze *as* (the monetary unit), which had already fallen in the course of the century from a pound (*libra*) to a half-pound. Nonetheless the Senate still felt confident enough in the economic strength of the Republic to refuse with thanks presents of gold from Neapolis and Paestum.

Neither of the consuls was prepared to return to Rome in the early spring of 216 to hold the elections and so a 'dictator to hold elections' was nominated, but was soon forced to abdicate on a technicality. Recourse was then had to the interregnal procedure, and the elections were conducted by P. Cornelius Scipio Asina. This represented a political victory for the Aemilian party, for we may be certain that Fabius had used his position of augur, as he was often to do, in order to bring about the abdication of the politically hostile dictator. The Aemilians were in fact back in favour, for Minucius' setback in Apulia had shown only that Hannibal could not be beaten by a single consular army, not that he was invincible. Senate and people were fully alive to the very real danger, to say nothing of the disgrace, of allowing Hannibal to ravage the lands of their allies with impunity, and in the run-up to the hotly contested consular elections the Aemilians and the radicals insisted that if

Minucius had been allowed a free hand in Apulia Hannibal would have been defeated.

The result of the consular elections suggests that there had been a pact between the Aemilian party and the 'popular' candidate C. Terentius Varro, whom the former were prepared to support against the Fabian candidates on the understanding that he would then use his influence to bring in their man. Consequently Varro was elected first and then took over the conduct of the elections from the interrex and secured the election as his colleague of the patrician L. Aemilius Paullus, who had triumphed as consul over the Illyrians in 219. (Was it perhaps his influence that caused an embassy to be sent to King Philip v of Macedon demanding the extradition of Demetrius of Pharos?) His re-election had been made legally possible by a tribunician law (perhaps inspired by Fabius as dictator) that removed the 'ten years rule' in order to enable the Republic to make use of the services of experienced soldiers. Varro was a 'new man', the son of a rich merchant or contractor, and his reputation has suffered from the hostility of the Fabian and senatorial tradition, which portrays him as a person of the lowest origins – the son of a butcher – who had risen in the state as a result of demagogy and by undertaking popular law-suits. His ability and even his courage have also been disparaged by the Aemilian–Scipionic tradition reflected by Polybius. In fact there is no good reason to suppose that he was an enemy of the Senate, that he was not as able and courageous as the ordinary run of senatorials, or that there was any fundamental discrepancy between his policy, strategy and tactics and those of his more experienced colleague, to protect whose reputation the Aemilians threw overboard that of their ally, after Cannae.

For the coming campaign season the Romans sent the two urban legions raised by Fabius after Trasimene into Gallia Cisalpina under the praetor L. Postumius Albinus, who as consul had warred against both the Ligurians and the Illyrians, and they raised two fresh urban legions and reinforced the consular armies in Apulia, bringing the strength of the individual legions up to five thousand foot and three hundred horse – although the latter figure poses certain problems. The allies were called upon to provide the same number of infantry but a considerably larger number of cavalry. Twenty-five additional ships were sent to Lilybaeum and put under the command of T. Otacilius Crassus, whose imperium was prorogued and who was given permission to attack Africa with his fleet, which now totalled seventy-five ships. The consuls of 217 had their imperium prorogued in order to provide the armies facing Hannibal with leaders until such time as the consuls should take them over. P. Cornelius Scipio in Spain and the governor of Sardinia were likewise continued in their commands. Old King Hiero of Syracuse demonstrated his loyalty and his faith in the Republic by sending as a gift to the Roman people a thousand light infantrymen, an immense shipment of wheat and barley and a golden statue of Victory. In the coming years the Romans were going to rely heavily upon imports of grain from Sicily and Sardinia.

The consuls of 217 BC had been 'advised' by the Senate to avoid a general action with Hannibal in the spring, prior to handling over their armies to their successors. However in the clashes that occurred between their forces and Hannibal's foragers the Romans more than held their own. Accordingly in early June, with his supplies running out, Hannibal left Gerunium, marched the sixty miles across the Tavoliere and seized the small abandoned town of Cannae, which stands upon an abrupt rocky eminence not far from the right bank of the Aufidus (Ofanto) roughly midway between the important city of Canusium (Canosa) and the sea and which the local inhabitants had been using as a granary in accordance with the general instructions issued by Fabius. With Cannae as his supply base Hannibal began to plunder the plain of the Aufidus, a country that was suitable for the employment of cavalry.

The narrative of Polybius – although not that of Livy – suggests, probably rightly, that the proconsuls had followed Hannibal part of the way to Cannae. They wrote repeatedly to the consuls and Senate asking for instructions, pointing out that they could not approach his camp without being obliged to attempt to check his depredations and that they could not do that without accepting battle. They were ordered to wait for the arrival of their successors and Varro and Paullus, having done what needed to be done at Rome, set off for the front with their levies, armed with the Senate's authorization to offer battle to the enemy. When they reached the camps they sent Regulus back to Rome on the grounds of his age and then marched directly across the plain to a point about six miles to the north-west of where Hannibal lay, and camped there. According to the Aemilian tradition, Paullus wanted to fight on ground of his own choosing – ground less favourable to cavalry – which would have involved pressing on to the south where the country rises slightly. However the consuls, when they began their march, can scarcely have been ignorant of Hannibal's position, which was probably between the hill of Cannae and the river. And since they marched directly towards him across the plain, although they could, if they had wished, have approached him over the hills, it is probably better to assume that this story is a part of the literary campaign, which also influenced the account of the Trebia battle, to shift the blame for defeat from the shoulders of the Aemilii–Scipiones, who are portrayed as circumspect and prudent, onto those of their colleagues, who are made to appear rash and impulsive.

On the day following their arrival – it was now the end of July – Varro, the commander of the day, moved the army towards the river, below Cannae. Hannibal attacked him on the march with his horsemen and light infantry, but Varro deployed some of his heavy infantry in support of his skirmishers and cavalry and the Carthaginians were driven off. The next day Paullus fortified a camp on the left bank of the river and threw a third of his forces across to occupy a smaller camp, a little over a mile higher up and about a mile and a half from the camp of Hannibal. From this position the Romans could cover the foraging parties from their main camp and harass those of the enemy. Hannibal countered this move by transferring his own forces to the left bank of the river, thus proclaiming his readiness to fight. Throughout his whole campaign he had attached so much importance to intelligence that we may be sure that he knew as much as he needed to know about the consuls and the current temper of Senate and people. He knew, in short, that the Romans had come to Cannae in order to fight. He had had plenty of time to make up his mind where he intended the battle to take place; the 'how' he left open until he saw what tactics the enemy proposed to adopt.

Two days after crossing the river Hannibal offered battle but Paullus, whose day it was, refused – why, it is impossible to say. Hannibal therefore sent the Numidians to harass the smaller Roman camp and prevent the men from watering; a move which produced precisely the reaction on the part of the enemy that he had hoped for. Next day, 2 August, Varro marched out his men at daybreak from both camps and drew them up on the right bank of the Aufidus. He was accepting the challenge that his colleague had refused.

Varro intended to apply the lessons of the Trebia. There the legions had crushed the Punic centre but had been prevented from exploiting their success by the rout of their wings by the elephants and cavalry. At Cannae there were no elephants to fear; but as Hannibal drew up his army his best troops formed the wings of his infantry and therefore the wings constituted the dangerous areas. The answer, as Varro saw it, was to have no wings – to mass all the heavy infantry in the centre, punch a hole a thousand yards wide in the middle of Hannibal's line, re-form and then – this is quite conjectural – hold off one of the isolated Punic wings with a part of his infantry and throw the rest with overwhelming weight of numbers against the other and annihilate it. The rôle of the cavalry was to protect the flanks and rear of the phalanx during its advance. For he was, in effect, going to sacrifice the flexibility of the manipular formation to the solidity and weight of the phalanx. To ensure that the Roman and allied horse, outnumbered and outclassed by the enemy, fought with the necessary spirit and determination the consuls themselves would lead them, leaving the command of the infantry to the proconsul Servilius.

Accordingly Varro drew up his infantry in mass formation, narrowing the gaps between the maniples, reducing their fronts, and deepening them correspondingly. The Roman cavalry under Paullus were stationed on the right flank of the infantry, with their own right flank protected by the river, which in those days was still flowing in early August, although today its bed is at that season quite dry. The left flank of the infantry was covered by Varro himself with the allied horse.

Polybius tells us that 6,000 cavalry took part in the battle on the Roman side; but then he, as well as Livy, also believed that the Romans had eight legions, and not four, in the line. However, since this figure of 6,000 horse does not fit the normal ratios of citizen cavalry to foot soldiers (300 to an over-strength legion) and of allied cavalry to citizen (three to one) – ratios which would give 4,800 for a four-legion army and 9,600 for an eight-legion army – it may represent the true number and

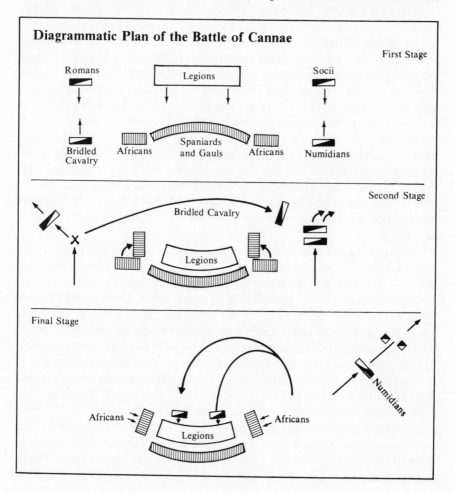

Diagrammatic Plan of the Battle of Cannae

First Stage

Romans   Legions   Socii

Bridled   Africans   Spaniards   Africans   Numidians
Cavalry   and Gauls

Second Stage

Bridled Cavalry

Legions

Final Stage

Africans   Legions   Africans

Numidians

not one deduced by the historian. On the other hand it may be the result of guesswork on the part of Polybius' Punic sources, and the Romans may have had no more than 1,200 citizen, and 3,600 – or even, if we follow Livy, only 2,400 – allied horse on the field. After all, the confederation had suffered serious losses in cavalry during the previous year. The skirmishers, who must have numbered about 10,000, were thrown forward to cover the whole front.

Hannibal led his men back across the river, and behind a screen of light infantry drew up his army in order of battle. The Spanish and Gallic cavalry under Hasdrubal faced the Roman knights; the Numidians under Hanno faced the allied horse. The two wings of his infantry were formed by the Africans, the cream of his foot soldiers, now armed in the Roman manner, while the Spanish and Gallic swordsmen, in alternate companies, comprised the centre; the naked torsos and the golden torques and armlets of the Celts contrasting strikingly with the purple-bordered linen tunics of the Iberians. The centre was the thinnest part of the line and was drawn up so as to form a fairly deep crescent-shaped bulge towards the enemy. Hannibal himself and his brother Mago commanded the infantry, and the course of the battle suggests that they took their stance on the wings among the Africans. We may safely disregard Polybius' statement that Paullus left 10,000 men behind on the left bank with orders to attack Hannibal's camp. The Punic tradition that he is following has confused the camp guards with the refugees from the battle who escaped to the Roman camps as related, correctly, by Livy. Hannibal must have had about 30,000 infantry in the line, apart from the light-armed, and the Romans must have had much the same number; but in cavalry Hannibal with some 10,000 horsemen enjoyed a decided advantage.

The battle commenced with the usual clash between the light forces on both sides that preceded the arrival on the scene of the heavy infantry and cavalry. On the Roman right the Roman knights, heavily outnumbered, were almost annihilated in a desperate dismounted engagement and the survivors were driven from the field, apart from a few who, like Paullus himself, attached themselves to the infantry in order to continue the fight. On their left the bridleless Numidians were content by attacking, retreating and attacking again to keep the allied horsemen occupied and to detach them from the flank of the infantry, which it was their business to protect.

However, it was in the centre that the battle was decided. The great mass of Roman heavy infantry crashed into the bulge in Hannibal's line and as the barbarians resisted with all the savage fury of their races the Roman front adjusted itself to the convex face of the enemy line. Slowly, stabbing and slashing, the Iberians and Celts fell back, the Punic front straightened, caved in, collapsed, and the whole body of Roman infantry, jammed into the space between one horn of the now reversed crescent and the other, pressed forward in pursuit. Another – but this time a successful – breakthrough, such as had been achieved on the Trebia, seemed imminent. Then the trap, the more deadly and unexpected from having been set and baited before the eyes of the whole army, was sprung. Hannibal's wings, the crack African heavy infantry, which had up till now been unengaged, entered the battle. Either the right and left wings turned left and right respectively, and then dressed ranks from the right and left, or else – less probably, in the light of the language of Polybius – they simply wheeled left and right. By this manœuvre, executed with parade-ground coolness and efficiency in the heat of the battle, the Africans, probably about ten thousand in number, changed front and positioned themselves so as to be able to attack the flanks of the Roman infantry. In the meantime Hasdrubal had re-formed his bridled cavalry – in itself no small achievement – and ridden across the rear of the Roman advance to fall upon the allied cavalry on the Roman left and drive them from the field without striking a blow. Leaving their pursuit to the Numidians, he now returned to the centre of the field and fell upon the rear of the Roman infantry at several places simultaneously.

It was here, among the triarii, that the consul Paullus fell fighting. And indeed the battle now became a massacre as Hannibal and Mago rolled up the flanks of what ceased to be an army and degenerated into a mere mass of men, huddled between the two inexorably advancing phalanxes of Africans, with the Celts and Spaniards, rallied and thirsting for revenge, assailing what had been its front while Hasdrubal's horsemen attacked it from the rear.

It is quite impossible to arrive at an accurate figure for the Roman losses. Wounded, other than those lightly wounded, who were left upon the enemy's field must always be included among the dead. According to Livy, some 19,000 fugitives escaped from the shambles to the two camps and to the rock of Cannae; but of these all except 4,200 were killed or (the greater number) taken. 6,400 surrendered in the small camp on the evening of the same day, and a similar number on the next day in the main camp. In all about 14,500 men are reckoned by the Romans to have got away. Of these 10,000 escaped to Canusium (this figure includes the 4,200 who made their way there from the main camp), and 4,500 to Venusia – to which the consul Varro, carried away in the rout of his cavalry, also escaped with only 50 knights. This figure of 14,500 represents, of course, only those fugitives who returned to the standards; there must have been many allies who went away home after the battle and remained there quietly. The precise number of prisoners taken is also irrecoverable, Livy estimating them at almost double Polybius' figure (itself suspect) of 10,000. However, if Varro started the day with about 46,000 men, it looks very much as if he left considerably more than half of them on the field – and half of these were Roman citizens. The consul Paullus, the commander of the centre Cn. Servilius Geminus, M. Minucius Rufus who had been Fabius' master of horse the year before, both the quaestors, the majority of the military tribunes and eighty men of senatorial rank were among the slain. The official Punic figure for their own dead was 5,700, of whom 4,000 were Celts. The wounded, however, must have amounted to two or three times this number, and of these, if we take into account the season of the year when the battle was fought and the state of medical knowledge at that time, we may reasonably conjecture that a great many subsequently died or suffered permanent disablement.

The year 216 constitutes the high-water mark of Hannibal's military career and Cannae his greatest battle. Even in the twentieth century it is cited as a classic. It has been suggested that the battles on the Trebia and in Spain near Ibera in the early summer of 216 were intended to anticipate Cannae, but failed to do so because the Romans broke through the Punic centre before the wings were able to encircle them. If that is so perhaps the basic battle plan was one that Hamilcar had taught to his sons. But it took the genius of Hannibal to perceive on the field of battle itself how Varro's massed infantry attack could be confined to the centre of the Punic line and held there long enough for the wings to move in un-impeded on its flanks. Cannae illustrated once again the ability of the various parts of Hannibal's army to manœuvre independently yet in con-junction with each other, when actually in contact with the enemy; an ability strikingly in contrast with the monolithic character of the Roman infantry and its powerlessness to respond to and counter the tactical moves of the enemy. It illustrated, too, the use that can be made, even in an infantry battle, of well-led cavalry – a lesson learnt from Alexander's campaigns – and the folly of surrendering the fringes of the battle to the enemy – although this was a mistake which the consuls did in fact try to avoid with the inferior cavalry forces at their disposal.

Cannae was in itself a major disaster for Rome. Few ancient states could have taken in their stride – or even recovered from – the loss of twenty thousand or more men in a single day; but on its own its effect would not have been so calamitous. It was, however, the culmination of a long series of disasters: the Ticinus, the Trebia (about 15,000 men lost), Trasimene (25,000 killed and captured), the rout of Servilius' cavalry (some 4,000 killed and taken) and now Cannae. In less than three full campaigns, including the fighting in Campania and Apulia, the con-federation had lost well over seventy-five thousand men, a high pro-portion of whom were of the knightly class; and not only had it lost almost twelve per cent of its available strength, it had apparently made no impression on that of Hannibal, who had gone from victory to victory. The most serious damage done by Cannae was to the myth of Roman invincibility. Cannae had been a formal trial by combat between the Roman confederation and Hannibal and the outcome seemed to indicate that Rome could not contain the invader or defend her allies. Punic propaganda asserted that Rome had committed eight legions to the battle and had left no fewer than seventy thousand dead upon the field, and this lie found its way into the Punic history of the war and was taken over by Polybius, the great weight of whose authority imposed it also upon Livy. But it is likely enough that the Fabian party was not unwilling to exaggerate Rome's losses in order to discourage the Senate and people from persisting in, or returning to, the policy of fighting Hannibal.

Now, for the first time, the solidarity of the confederation cracked. Several of the most important cities of Apulia – Salapia, Aecae, Herdonea and Arpi – declared for Hannibal. They had welcomed Rome's hegemony in the fourth century when the Samnites had posed the principal threat to the independence of the Italian communities; now, with the Samnites subjugated, they perhaps felt that they could afford to indulge their resentment of Roman domination, of which the Latin colonies of Luceria and Venusia were the visible symbol. But with the Carthaginians victorious in south-eastern Italy, fear must have played a significant part in persuading them to defect. Hannibal did not waste time or effort besieging the remnants of the Roman army in Canusium and Venusia; nor did he entertain the proposal eagerly advanced by Maharbal that he should strike directly at Rome. The cavalryman's protest that Hannibal 'knew how to win a victory but not how to exploit it', although expressing a deeper truth than he intended or was aware of, only served to illustrate by contrast the military acumen of his leader. An assault on Rome could be contemplated only when the total dissolution of her confederation was an accomplished fact.

Hannibal did not permit his triumph to deflect him from the policy that he had chosen as being the only one that could destroy the power of Rome. He rested his men and made arrangements for the disposal of the prisoners. The allies, as on former occasions, were set free while the Romans were allowed to send a deputation to Rome under Carthalo to plead for their ransoming. He then moved south-west into the territory of the Hirpini, a Samnite tribe, where a faction in the city of Compsa (Conza) betrayed the place to him. He made Compsa his baggage depôt and from there he extended the area of the revolt to include the Hirpini and their neighbours the Caudini, who were resentful, like all Samnites, of their subjugation by the Romans and of the presence, on what had been their land, of the Latin colony of Beneventum, which, like Venusia just across the border from the Hirpini, was a bastion of Roman imperialism. From Compsa Hannibal detached his brother Mago with part of his forces to march south through Lucania into Bruttium and to stir up revolt among the peoples of the extreme south, the most recently subjugated of Rome's allies.

Hannibal himself with the rest of his army marched through Samnium into Campania. His objective was the Greek city of Neapolis (Naples), a favoured ally of Rome for over a century, whose capture would give him what he most needed at the moment – a port on the Tyrrhenian Sea, looking towards Carthage. However he realized that the city was not going to go over to him, and as it was much too strong to besiege he directed his march towards Capua, after a cavalry skirmish that resulted in a defeat for the Neapolitans. His object now was to get control of a city whose extensive territory – some of the most fertile land in the peninsula – and flourishing industries made her probably the wealthiest and most highly cultured state in Italy, and second only to Rome in power and importance.

Capua was perhaps a pre-Etruscan foundation which was subsequently taken over in the sixth century by Etruscans and then, in the second half of the fifth century, by Sabelli from the hills. Threatened by Samnites in the fourth century it had placed itself under Roman protection, and between 339 and 338, after ceding the rich Ager Falernus to Rome, it became a half-citizen community (*municipium*), whose aristocracy (*equites*) received full Roman citizenship while the commons received citizen rights without the franchise. The Campani continued to govern themselves and their dependencies as before, electing their own magistrates (*meddices*), deliberating in their own Council and ratifying the rulers' decisions in their own Assembly. However their equites or knights could if they wished move to Rome, acquire property on Roman territory and contract marriage alliances with the Roman nobility, which opened up to them the possibility of enjoying a public career in Roman politics. Such were the political origins of the Atilii and the Otacilii, adherents of the Fabian party. The Campani served in the Roman army (we are told that they could provide thirty thousand infantry and four thousand cavalry) and were liable to pay the direct tax (*tributum*), but on the other hand they conducted their own census and probably farmed their own local revenues. Capua suffered badly from the kind of class warfare, exacerbated by racial differences between aristocracy and commons, that bedevilled the histories of so many Greek cities. In 318 this reached such a pitch that Rome was asked to intervene and the urban praetor sent his representative, his prefect, to the city to bring Capua's law code into a satisfactory relationship with that of Rome.

Anomalies are seldom satisfactory and Capua's position was

anomalous. She was neither a town of Roman citizens like Tusculum nor an autonomous and tribute-free ally like Neapolis. She was not even a true municipium, since her aristocracy enjoyed full Roman citizenship and their loyalties, like their fields of ambition, were divided. In the main they were good Romans as well as good Capuans, but the democratically minded commons – many of them industrial workers – bitterly resented the support that Rome gave to the knights, who were generously subsidized by the community. Their social grievances were, no doubt, much more bitterly felt than their own exclusion from political rights at Rome, which in the nature of things they could not have exercised, even if they had possessed them.

The chief magistrate of Capua (the *meddix tuticus*) of 217 was Pacuvius Calavius, who was allied by marriage to the Claudii and Livii at Rome but headed the popular faction in his own city. He took advantage of the fact that many of the knights were away serving in the Roman armies to carry out a species of *coup d'état* that depressed the authority of the aristocratic Council while it enhanced that of the popular Assembly and made him the virtual ruler of Capua. Immediately after Cannae a delegation was sent to Varro at Venusia and returned with such a gloomy account of Rome's military condition that it was decided to revolt, and the same delegation was sent to Hannibal to conclude a treaty of alliance. Hannibal granted Capua a treaty that secured her complete autonomy, and he undertook to hand over three hundred Roman captives to be exchanged for three hundred Capuan knights serving in Sicily. He made a triumphal entry into the city – all Roman officials and visitors had been arrested and imprisoned in the baths, where, perhaps accidentally, they appear to have met their deaths by asphyxiation – and next day at a plenary session of the Council he promised that Capua should take Rome's place as the *hegemon* of Italy.

Meanwhile what of the Romans? The refugees from the battle collected at Canusium, where a group of young military tribunes that included P. Cornelius Scipio took charge, and at Venusia, to which the consul Varro had escaped. When Hannibal moved out of the region Varro took his men to Canusium and there put together a force which numbered fifteen thousand men if we accept one set of Livy's figures and ten thousand if we accept another. We should probably take the larger estimate; in which case he had what amounted to a weak consular army – and indeed this force was subsequently known as the Cannae legions. At Rome, where the praetors presided over the Senate, energetic steps were taken to deal with the crisis, whose full extent had been revealed in a letter from Varro, while another despatch, from T. Octacilius in Sicily, had spoken of Punic fleets attacking the territory of Syracuse and threatening Lilybaeum from the Aegates Islands. Varro was summoned to

Rome and the praetor destined for Sicily, M. Claudius Marcellus (who had won the spolia opima and a triumph over the Gauls as consul in 222) was ordered from Ostia where his fleet lay to Apulia to relieve him. The gods were placated by a human sacrifice in the Forum Boarium, among other rites, and the future historian of Rome, Q. Fabius Pictor, was sent to Delphi to consult Apollo. Marcellus sent 1,500 men to Rome to strengthen the garrison of the two urban legions, and sent the rest of the marine legion (consisting of the marines of the fleet and drafts for the legions in Sicily) to Teanum Sidicinum on the northern borders of Campania to watch the Via Latina. Then, having handed over the fleet to the urban praetor P. Furius Philus, who had triumphed as consul in 223 over the Gauls and Ligurians, he hastened to Canusium. Varro returned to Rome, where he was honourably received by a Senate in which the influence of his political opponents, the Fabian party, now predominated, and nominated M. Junius Pera dictator. Pera, the last traditional military dictator in Rome's history, in turn appointed Ti. Sempronius Gracchus as his master of horse.

The dictator collected a force of twenty-five thousand men with which to oppose Hannibal in Campania. This consisted of the two urban legions and the corresponding allied contingents, who had by now all had some training, and eight thousand slave volunteers (volones), purchased from their owners and armed by the state. He also set in motion the raising of two more urban legions made up of youths, some below the military age, levies from Picenum and the Ager Gallicus, and gaol-birds, who provided no fewer than six thousand volunteers. These last were armed with weapons taken from the Gallic spoils carried in the triumph of Flaminius. Rome's determination to present an unyielding front to Hannibal had already been advertised by the Senate's refusal, on the motion of T. Manlius Torquatus, to ransom the Roman prisoners of war. There had been too much running away in battle and too much surrendering of late – Hannibal's victories must be made more costly. Moreover the ransom money would have been of immense value to the enemy, for the payment of his troops.

Pera led his twenty-five thousand men down the Via Latina to the borders of Campania to block the road to Rome. Perhaps it was now that the consul Varro took the marine legion across into Apulia, where we later find him, and where several important communities had remained loyal. In the meantime the praetor Marcellus had brought the Cannae legions up from Canusium into Campania, where he occupied Casilinum which commanded the crossing of the Volturnus. Hannibal, having secured Capua and its dependencies, Atella (the home of farce) and Calatia, now moved into the territory of the important city of Nola. There, as at Capua, the aristocracy remained loyal to Rome while the commons were eager to revolt to Hannibal, the friend of the people. The aristocracy got a message through to Marcellus, who promptly marched by way of a wide detour through the mountains to Nola, and on his arrival Hannibal, perceiving that the city was not going to be betrayed, moved towards Neapolis, to try his luck again there. But the Neapolitans had accepted a Roman garrison under a prefect, M. Junius Silanus, and once again the Carthaginian's hopes of an easy success were frustrated.

Hannibal now marched to Nuceria (Nocera), which was isolated and remote from assistance, and starved it into surrender, its inhabitants taking refuge in various Campanian towns. Since he still had hopes that Nola would be betrayed to him by the commons he returned there, but Marcellus held his own in what fighting there was and Hannibal retired disappointed to Acerrae, whose people abandoned the city to destruction by the enemy. Marcellus for his part identified as traitors and executed seventy citizens, withdrew from Nola and occupied as his winter quarters a strong position on the heights above Suessula which commanded the entrance to the Caudine Pass into Samnium and which was subsequently known as Castra Claudiana, 'Claudius' camp'. Pera and his legions wintered at Teanum.

Hannibal now received word that the dictator and his army were expected to arrive at Casilinum, and although the campaigning season was at an end he decided to secure this strategically important town before the Romans occupied it in strength. Casilinum was held by a garrison of about a thousand men composed of levies from Praeneste (Palestrina) and Perusia, who had missed the battle of Cannae and subsequently taken refuge in the town. They beat off the attacks of Hannibal's advance guard and defended the town so effectively that Hannibal had to abandon the attempt to take it by assault and retired for the winter to Capua, leaving a force behind in the camp to conduct a blockade of the town. Towards the end of the winter he returned and resumed the siege. Neither Gracchus – Pera had returned to Rome – nor Marcellus felt able to intervene and hunger forced the garrison to surrender, on condition that Hannibal allowed them to be ransomed. Casilinum was given back to Capua and received a garrison of seven hundred men from Hannibal's army.

While these momentous events were taking place in Apulia and Campania, the Carthaginian navy raided Syracusan territory and threatened Lilybaeum. It was perhaps ships of this force that conveyed Mago to Carthage, where he gave the Council a highly dramatic and exaggerated account of his brother's achievements, pouring out upon the floor from a sack the rings taken from the dead fingers of knights and senators. Enthusiasm for Hannibal swept the meeting and it was resolved to send him four thousand Numidians and forty elephants as immediate reinforcements and a much larger force as soon as it could be got ready. The Carthaginians however made no serious attempt to recover the command of the sea, which would have to be the preliminary to anything like an all-out effort on their part to ensure victory in Italy, and although the praetor Furius was severely wounded while making a descent on the coast of Africa there is no indication that the Carthaginians challenged his fleet at sea.

In 216 BC the Romans were forced to pay some attention to what was going on in the Adriatic. The previous year saw the ending, with the Peace of Naupactus, of the so-called 'Social War' between the Aetolians and their allies and the Hellenic League presided over by Philip of Macedon. Demetrius of Pharos, one of the young king's principal advisers, was anxious to embroil Macedon with Rome, in the hope of recovering his lost principality, and he encouraged Philip to take vigorous action against his former associate, the Illyrian prince Scerdilaidas, who had broken with Philip and seized certain districts in the western part of his kingdom. During the winter of 217/16 Philip built a fleet of a hundred light galleys, suitable for carrying out sea-borne raids and landings, and in 216 he brought them round into the Adriatic. Alarmed at the news, Scerdilaidas asked the Romans for help and just before the battle of Cannae T. Otacilius was ordered to send ten ships out of the seventy-five which he had at Lilybaeum into Greek waters. This put him at a disadvantage later when the Carthaginians attacked Sicily. However, these ten ships did all that could have been expected of them, for Philip fled precipitately at the mere report of them and withdrew to Cephallenia.

At Rome a dictator, M. Fabius Buteo, the consul of 245 and an ex-censor, was nominated by Varro who had been recalled for the purpose, in order to revise the list of senators. Predictably a proposal that would certainly have affected the course of Roman domestic history, that members of the Senates of the Latin communities should be enfranchised and admitted to the Roman Senate, was turned down. Buteo, protesting at the irregularity of the whole procedure, confirmed all living senators in their positions and selected 177 men who had held office or distinguished themselves in the war to fill the vacancies. As Varro had returned immediately to Apulia and as Buteo abdicated as soon as he had finished his task, the dictator Pera was summoned to Rome to conduct the elections, at which the praetor L. Postumius Albinus, who had been consul twice, and the master of horse, Ti. Sempronius Gracchus, were elected. Pera then returned to Teanum.

However, before the end of the consular year news arrived of the death of Albinus and the annihilation of his army of twenty-five thousand men by the Boii in an ambush in the Litana Forest near Mutina (Modena).

It is probable that he was on his way to throw supplies, and perhaps reinforcements, into the loyal cities of Gallia Cisalpina, such as Mutina, Cremona and Placentia. It is significant that although the Boii had inflicted on Rome a disaster equal to that of Lake Trasimene they made no move to invade Italy or to reinforce Hannibal. From then on the gold-mounted skull of Albinus served as a libation vessel and sacred drinking-cup in the principal shrine of the Boii.

Gracchus as consul conducted the election to choose a replacement for Albinus and M. Claudius Marcellus was elected. However possibly as the result of an understanding between him and Q. Fabius – the Claudii seem to have been in political alliance with the Fabii at this time – his election was declared invalid by the augurs, of whom Fabius was one, and at a second election Fabius himself was chosen. The Fabian party was now in a position of almost unchallenged predominance in the state. The Aemilii, with Flaminius, Minucius and Paullus dead and the Scipios in Spain, had no established soldiers to put forward for the consulship and although they were still popular (as the career of the younger P. Scipio was to demonstrate) their aggressive line in both foreign policy and military strategy was held accountable for Rome's present critical situation, and was therefore discredited.

The influence of the Aemilii was not the only political casualty of Cannae. The popular movement – the opposition by the commons to the preponderance of authority enjoyed by the Senate in the state and by the nobility within the senate – was another. The strongly entrenched position of the Senatorial Order could only be sapped effectively by opposing its policies and its consular candidates, and after Cannae the people wished neither to fight Hannibal again nor to entrust the command of its armies to new men unless they had the confidence of the nobility. Since policies and strategy could only be discussed and decided in the Senate, where the authority of the consuls, the ex-consuls and the great families outweighed that of the tribunes of the plebs, by ceasing to elect 'popular' leaders to the consulship the people in effect abdicated its participation in the government. The supremacy of the Senate, which was to become the essence of the Ciceronian Republic, dates in its completeness from Cannae.

CHAPTER XII

215-213 BC

The strategy of cunctatio: *Rome hangs on.*

Q. Fabius Maximus and the policy of *cunctatio* ('putting off' the trial of strength with Hannibal) which Cannae appeared to have endorsed so dramatically now dominated the thinking of the Senate. To the foreign, un-Roman endowments of Hannibal, to his astuteness, his versatility, his quickness, his cunning – his genius, in short – Fabius opposed the true Roman qualities of which he himself was the very embodiment: discipline, courage, tenacity and patriotism. As long as Hannibal had been the only enemy, cunctatio was tantamount to total avoidance of battle, with disastrous results both for Rome's prestige and for the morale of the army. Now, however, Rome was offered a multiplicity of military objectives, and the strategy that General Moreau was to suggest to the enemies of Napoleon could be employed against Hannibal: 'Always fight him where he is not.' Even the seemingly invincible Punic army was divided, and the part of it not commanded by Hannibal was a permissible target. The reconquest of Apulia, Samnium, Campania, Lucania and Bruttium provided ample scope for offensive operations, while even Hannibal could be defied from behind strong walls and earthworks or from unassailable positions in order to deny the enemy further gains.

Thus Hannibal had himself provided the Romans with the kind of war that dogged determination and a total dedication to winning could win in the long run. Every month that passed saw some diminution, as the result of battle, sickness and desertions, of Hannibal's professional army. The revolted Italians were, like the Romans, militiamen, part-time soldiers, but they lacked the Roman spirit and were more concerned with defending their own territories than with winning the war for Carthage. If Rome could mount a counter-offensive in southern Italy, Hannibal's allies would quickly become military liabilities rather than assets and his prestige would suffer – as Rome's had already suffered – from any failure on his part to protect them. Nor was the revolt of the south as complete as it might have been. Below a line drawn from Arpi in Apulia to Capua in Campania the Latin colonies and many Italian and Greek communities remained loyal. Hannibal had not gained control of a single worthwhile port, while the strong walls and steadfast courage of the Latins provided

PROSPECTVS FRETI SICVLI,
vulgo il Faro de Meſſina.

*Mare anguſtum, atque anceps, alterno curſu modo in
Tuſcum, modo in Ionium pelagus influens, verticoſum.*
SCYLLAE et CHARYBDIS
ſæuitia inclytum.

A calabria .
B. Rhegium Iulium .
C. Sicilia .
D. Meſſana, vulgo Meſſina .
E. Ætna, vulgo Monte Gibello .

A sixteenth-century impression of the Straits
of Messana, from *Civitates Orbis Terrarum*
by Braun and Hogenburg, *c.* 1572–1618.

Hiero II of Syracuse, *c.* 306–215 BC.

Coin of the Mamertines of Messana. On the
obverse, the head of Zeus; on the reverse, a
naked warrior, with the legend
'Mamertinon'.

Ivory plaques from Praeneste, showing Latin soldiers (3rd century BC).

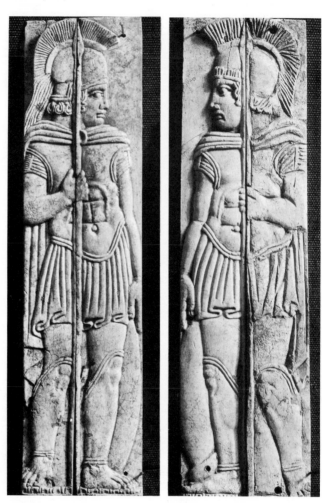

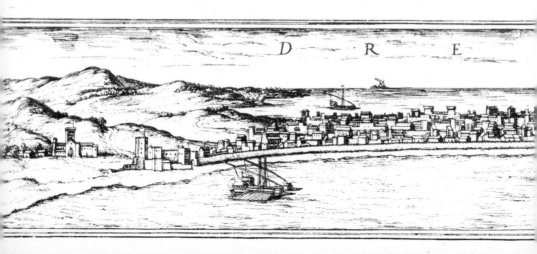

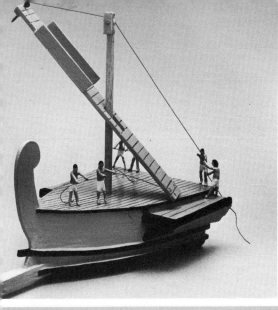

Model to illustrate the working of the *corvus*, as described by Polybius. It is possible that the bow ornament (*acrostolion*) was removed in order to allow the boarding bridge to fall directly over the bows.

The siege of Lilybaeum, 250–241 BC. The spit of land running north from the foreground divided the ancient harbour area from the open area to the left.

Below A sixteenth-century impression of Drepana, from *Civitates Orbis Terrarum* by Braun and Hogenburg, *c.* 1572–1618.

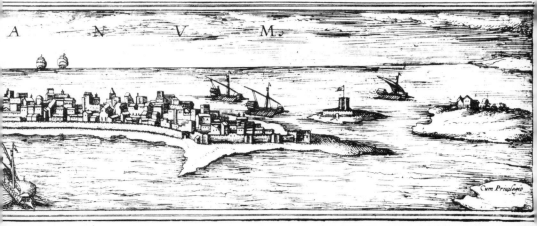

The battle of Drepana, 249 BC. The Bay of Drepana, looking west from the summit of Mount Eryx. The harbour lay to the south (*left*) of the sickle-shaped promontory from which the city took its name (*drepane* = sickle). The fighting took place off the salt flats to the south of the harbour.

The summit of Mount Eryx, looking towards the site of the temple of Aphrodite.

Hannibal.

Left Coin struck by the mint at New Carthage believed to show Hamilcar Barca, and on the reverse, a war elephant.

Saguntum from the east. The theatre is Roman of the imperial period. The medieval castle and walls probably correspond to the ancient citadel and walls.

The battle of Lake Trasimene, 217 BC. The view from the high ground south of Torricella across the lake to Passignano shows the head of the ambush position.

The battle of Cannae, 216 BC. The hill and town of Cannae from the west.

The plain of Aufidus, looking north-east from the hill of Cannae.

A sixteenth-century impression of Puteoli (Pozzuoli), from *Civitates Orbis Terrarum* by Braun and Hogenburg, *c.* 1572–1618.

Philip v of Macedon, 238–179 BC.

Hieronymus of Syracuse, 215–214 BC.

Bronze *as*, *c.* 235 BC, showing the prow of a war galley.

Right The new silver *denarius*, *c.* 211 BC, worth ten *asses*, showing on the obverse, the head of Roma, and on the reverse, the Dioscuri (Castor and Pollux), with the legend 'Roma'.

The ruins of the fortress of Euryalus above the Epipolae of Syracuse.

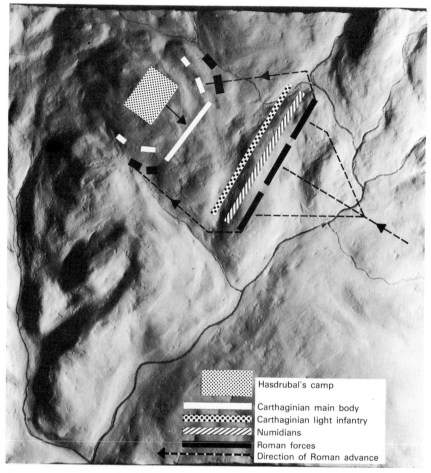

▦	Hasdrubal's camp
▬	Carthaginian main body
∞∞∞	Carthaginian light infantry
⁄⁄⁄	Numidians
▬	Roman forces
◀---	Direction of Roman advance

Contour model of the site of the battle of Baecula, with a superimposed battle plan, from H.H. Scullard, *Scipio Africanus*, published by Thames & Hudson Ltd.

Conjectural portrait of Scipio Africanus on a coin minted at New Carthage.

Hasdrubal Barca.

The battle of the Metaurus, 207 BC. The probable site of Hasdrubal's last stand, looking west from Sant' Angelo.

Above A coin of the Bruttians. On the obverse, the head of Nike (Victory); on the reverse, Poseidon (Neptune), with the legend 'Bruttion'.

King Masinissa, on a Numidian coin.

A Numidian coin showing on the
obverse, King Syphax; on the reverse,
a Numidian horseman.

Below The site of Carthage, looking south towards the harbours and the Gulf of
Tunis. The Byrsa is in the middle distance, on the extreme right of the photograph.

Carthage from the Byrsa, showing the remains of the harbours.

The last coins of Carthage, struck during the Third Punic War. On the obverse, the head of Tanit; on the reverse, a horse, the symbol of the City.

Rome with strongpoints of inestimable value for the immediate intimidation and ultimate recovery of rebellious areas.

With the benefit of hindsight we can see that the year 215 was one of those years in which the history of western civilization has hung in the balance. Hannibal had done all that even he could do to win this war; it is doubtful if Alexander himself could have done more. But he had lost the strategic initiative, and in bringing about the revolt of southern Italy he had given hostages to the god of war that might prove his undoing. Beaten by him on three bloody fields, the Romans still confronted him along the line of the Volturnus and in southern Italy with about forty-five thousand men. He knew that Fabius would not offer him the chance of another Cannae and he did not have the resources to take by siege any of the major Roman strongholds in the south. Nor could he venture up into the loyal centre and north of Italy, for such a move would give the enemy a free hand in the south and alienate his Italian allies. But unless he could enlarge the area of revolt and detach Umbria, Etruria and Picenum from Rome, he could not hope to win the war.

Now, more than anything else, he needed help from abroad. The resources of the Punic empire in men and material were probably equal to – indeed, after the revolt of southern Italy, probably superior to – those at Rome's disposal. It was essential that Carthage should make an effort to recover the command of the sea and send him substantial reinforcements, including elephants, and money : that was what he had sent Mago home to tell the Grand Council. Hasdrubal, too, had to dispose of the Scipios and bring his army from Spain. And there were other possibilities. The Roman defeat at Cannae had decided King Philip of Macedon to take a hand in the game and he had already opened negotiations with Hannibal. Unfortunately Philip, with so many enemies and potential enemies in Greece, was not likely to commit very large forces to the war against Rome; his intervention might, however, affect the attitude of the Greek cities and even of the Sicilians.

The situation in Sicily was distinctly promising. The cities were already weary of Roman suzerainty, so much more pervasive and permanent-seeming than that of Carthage, and in Syracuse events had taken a turn since the summer of 216 decidedly in Carthage's favour. Hiero, Rome's most loyal ally and friend, died some time after Cannae, having been predeceased by his son Gelon. The Council of Regency for his grandson Hieronymus (then aged fifteen), who on his mother's side was also a grandson of Pyrrhus, was dominated by his son-in-law Adranodorus, the commander of the mercenaries, whose sympathies were pro-Carthaginian. If Syracuse were to throw off her allegiance to Rome the Republic would be forced to divert ships and men to Sicily. Yet over all these possibilities hung the unpalatable truth, which can scarcely have escaped

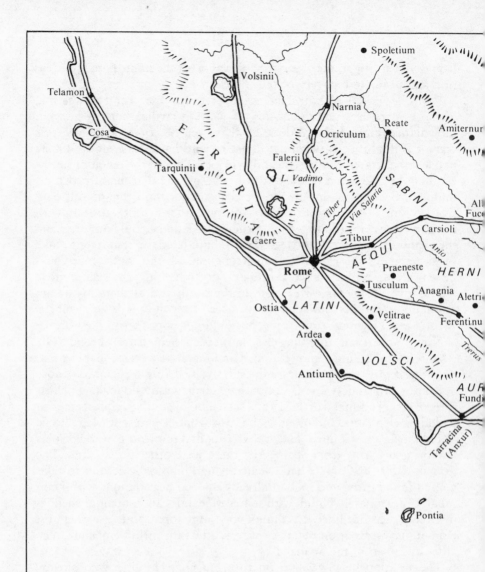

Spoletium

Telamon

Volsinii

Narnia

Cosa

Ocriculum

Reate

Amiternur

E T R U R I A

Falerii

S A B I N I

Tarquinii

L. Vadimo

All
Fuc

Via Salaria

Carsioli

Caere

Tibur

A E Q U I

Anio

HERNI

Rome

Praeneste

Tusculum

Anagnia

Aletri

Ostia

LATINI

Velitrae

Ferentinu

Ardea

Trerus

VOLSCI

Antium

AUR

Fund

Tarracina
(Anxur)

Pontia

Central Italy

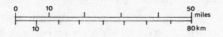

Tribes M A R S I

0   10   50
|--------|----|----|----|----|----| miles
   10   80 km

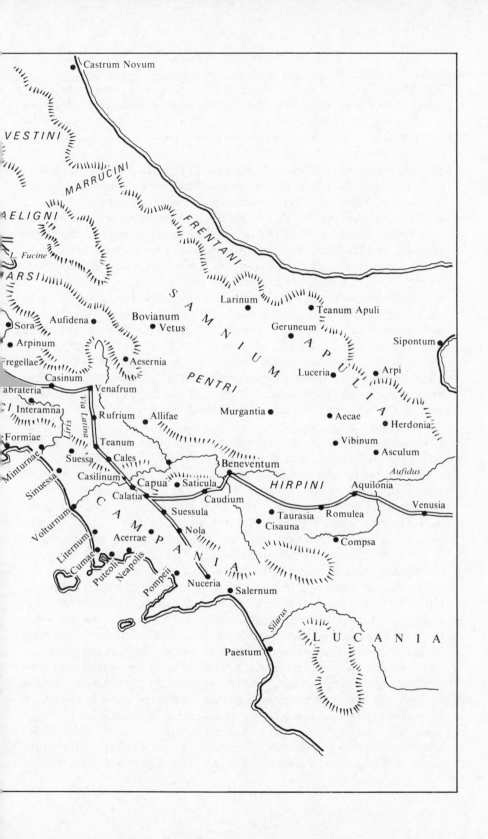

Castrum Novum

VESTINI

MARRUCINI

ÆLIGNI

FRENTANI

L. Fucine

ARSI

SAMNIUM

Larinum

Teanum Apuli

Sora

Aufidena

Bovianum
Vetus

Geruneum

APULIA

Sipontum

Arpinum

Fregellae

Aesernia

PENTRI

Luceria

Arpi

Casinum

Venafrum

abrateria

Via Latina

CI Interamna

Liris

Rufrium

Allifae

Murgantia

Aecae

Herdonia

Formiae

Teanum

Vibinum

Asculum

Minturnae

Suessa

Cales

Casilinum

Beneventum

Aufidus

Sinuessa

Capua

Saticula

HIRPINI

Aquilonia

Calatia

Caudium

Romulea

Venusia

Volturnum

CAMPANIA

Suessula

Taurasia

Liternum

Nola

Cisauna

Compsa

Cumae

Acerrae

Puteoli

Neapolis

Pompeii

Nuceria

Salernum

Silarus

LUCANIA

Paestum

Hannibal in his comfortable winter quarters in Capua, that while it was going to be harder for him in the coming year to impress his will and direction on the course of the war than it had been up till then, if he was not at least in sight of final victory by the end of it he was not very likely to win the war at all.

There was nothing dilatory about Rome's preparations for the coming campaign season. The tributum was ordered to be doubled, and the twelve available legions were assigned to the most important theatres of war. Fabius took over Pera's two legions at Teanum, and Gracchus the eight thousand volones. The two scratch legions raised after Cannae were assigned to Marcellus, who was invested with proconsular imperium; he was to take them to Castra Claudiana, while the Cannae legions which he had led as praetor were to return to Rome and then go to Sicily to relieve the legions there, remaining for the duration of the war. This was regarded as punishment for their failure to die like Romans on the field of Cannae. The Sicilian legions were earmarked for Apulia, where the peregrine praetor M. Valerius Laevinus was sent to take over Varro's legion until they should arrive. He was also given twenty-five quinqueremes and the duty of guarding the coast of Calabria, which meant keeping an eye on the movements of Philip's warships and also guarding against any attempt by Carthage to send ships into the lower Adriatic. Ap. Claudius Pulcher, son of the Claudius who had lost the battle of Drepana, was sent to Sicily as governor, while T. Otacilius was entrusted with the bulk of the fleet and permission to raid Africa. There was still a legion in Sardinia, and once again P. Scipio had his imperium renewed and remained in Spain with the two legions that he had commanded when he first left Italy. Although it had been reluctantly decided to make no attempt to retrieve the situation in Gallia Cisalpina, Varro was sent to Picenum to raise a legion and to be prepared to counter any threat to north-eastern Italy on the part of the Boii. The urban praetor was given twenty-five ships for the defence of the coast near the city.

The first successes of the war in Italy went to the Carthaginians. Himilco and his Bruttian allies took the Bruttian cities of Petelia (Strongoli), and after a protracted siege, Consentia (Cosenza), while the Greek town of Locri Epizephyrii capitulated to Hanno, the Roman garrison being allowed to escape. Later in the year Caulonia and Croton (Cotrone) were also lost to the Romans. Ap. Claudius, however, was able to save Rhegium by sending troops across from Messana, and vigorous action by Laevinus across the border of Apulia recaptured three towns of the Hirpini. In the Campanian region the Romans held their own. Fabius moved to Cales on the edge of the Ager Stellas, closer to Casilinum; Gracchus took his volones down to Liternum (Tor di Patria) on the coast, covering Cumae and Neapolis; and Marcellus was dug in at Castra

Claudiana. Hannibal, when he moved out of Capua, also occupied a strong defensive position on Mount Tifata (Monte di Maddaloni) above Capua. The first offensive move was made by the Capuans under their meddix tuticus Marius Alfius, who attempted first to win over Cumae and then to seize the senate, and subsequently the city, by treachery. The loyal Cumaeans, however, got word of the plot to Gracchus who turned the tables on the Capuans, capturing their camp in a night attack and killing Alfius himself. He then withdrew into Cumae, and Hannibal, who had hurried down from Tifata hoping to catch the Romans in the open, was obliged to retire without achieving anything.

However he yielded to Campanian pressure and returned to Cumae with siege equipment, and made a regular assault upon the town which was beaten off with some loss by Gracchus. Hannibal made a formal offer of battle which the consul, unsupported – for Fabius was employing every device of religion to deter himself from stirring out of Cales – was in no position to accept even if he had wished to do so. Hannibal therefore abandoned the siege and returned to Tifata.

The reason why Hannibal had allowed his allies to make the first move in the campaign of 215 was that he was entertaining an embassy from King Philip, led by an Athenian, Xenophanes, which had travelled over-land from the neighbourhood of Croton. They had come to negotiate an alliance; ostensibly an offensive and defensive alliance with no time limit (which was an un-Greek feature of the agreement) but one which in fact committed neither party to giving any specific assistance to the other, mentioning neither the despatch of troops to Italy by Philip nor of ships to Greek waters by Carthage. Indeed it is not certain that the government of Carthage was a party to the agreement at all. It stipulated that any peace treaty signed by Hannibal with Rome should require the latter to renounce her claim to the Greek cities of the Illyrian coast, and this would encourage Philip to attack and 'liberate' the Roman protec-torate. It would also enable Hannibal – already known as the friend of the people – to pose as the champion of Hellenic liberty in southern Italy. Philip for his part hoped to be allowed to get on with the liquidation of the Roman protectorate unimpeded by Rome. It is significant that the wording of the treaty (which we know from Polybius) implies the survival of Rome – and even her survival as a power against whom a permanent defensive alliance was thought necessary.

Unfortunately the Macedonian embassy together with three Punic envoys was captured at sea on its return voyage to Philip by Laevinus' admiral P. Valerius Flaccus, and who sent it in swift galleys to Rome. Gracchus intercepted the flotilla off Cumae and forwarded the documents to the Senate himself, while the captives continued their journey by water. Flaccus' squadron was now strengthened by thirty ships and he was instructed to reconnoitre Greek waters to get first-hand information of Philip's intentions. If it appeared that Philip was contemplating war Laevinus, who was based at Luceria, was to hand over his army to his legate at Taras, and take charge of a naval offensive against Philip. This episode was of the utmost importance to Rome, as the capture of Philip's envoys prevented him from knowing that the treaty had been successfully concluded, and by the time a second embassy had visited Hannibal and a new document had been prepared, the summer was over and the Romans were spared the attentions of Macedon in this critical year.

With Hannibal safely back in Tifata, Fabius found the auspices favourable for crossing the Volturnus. He sent Marcellus to garrison Nola, where the commons were again intriguing with Hannibal, while he occupied Castra Claudiana. Hannibal's position had been strengthened by the arrival at Locri of what purported to be the first instalment of considerable reinforcements from Carthage but what was in fact the only assistance that he was to receive in the whole course of the war. Bomilcar probably brought him the four thousand Numidians and some, at any rate, of the forty elephants voted by the Council the previous year. He just missed being caught at Locri by Ap. Claudius, who made a dash on the town from Sicily. However, as we have seen, Claudius' presence at Messana enabled him to frustrate a Punic attempt on Rhegium. Hannibal now moved the bulk of his army into the territory of Nola in order to take the pressure off the Caudini and Hirpini who had been suffering from the attentions of Marcellus. He was joined before the city by Hanno, who had with him the newly arrived reinforcements and the elephants. An attempt to talk the leading citizens into betraying their city failed, and so did an assault on the place, although it is generally considered that the impressive victory attributed to Marcellus before the walls is an annalistic exaggeration. Hannibal was in no position to undertake a lengthy siege of one of the strongest cities in Italy and so he dismissed Hanno to Bruttium while he took his own army over to Apulia and into winter quarters near Arpi. There he could draw upon the produce of the fertile plains of Apulia without burdening the Campanians; also he was nearer to his new ally Philip. On his departure Fabius undertook a systematic devastation of Capuan territory until it was time to retire for the winter to Castra Claudiana, now much strengthened and well stocked with provisions. Marcellus was ordered to send back to Rome any men who were not needed for garrison duty at Nola, while Gracchus took his volones across to Luceria to watch Hannibal. Laevinus, who had received the two legions from Sicily during the summer, moved down to Brundisium.

Although there had been plenty of minor activity in Italy, the most dramatic events of the year 215 took place overseas. A decisive victory gained by the Scipios in Spain caused the Carthaginian government to countermand the force of 12,000 foot, 1,500 horse, 20 elephants and 60 warships which, together with 1,000 talents of silver, was intended for Hannibal. They were sent instead to Spain, under Mago Barca. At the same time it received a message from the principal chieftain in Sardinia, Hampsicora, indicating that the Sardinians, wearied of the oppressive rule of the Romans and their exactions of grain and tribute, were ready to revolt. Accordingly it sent Hasdrubal Calvus with a force almost equal to Mago's to raise a rebellion in the island.

Circumstances were most propitious, as the newly arrived governor, Q. Mucius Scaevola, had fallen sick and was quite incapacitated. However the Senate took vigorous steps to counter what was reported by the retiring governor as a critical situation. The urban praetor, Q. Fulvius Flaccus, was instructed to raise a force of five thousand foot and four hundred horse for Sardinia and to appoint a deputy for Scaevola with imperium. He selected the man who had originally subjugated the island, T. Manlius Torquatus, who had been consul twice and censor. Then the gods took a hand and Hasdrubal was driven by a storm to the Balearic Islands and compelled to waste precious time repairing his ships, so that Manlius arrived in Sardinia before him. With the men he had brought, the legion already there and the rowers of his fleet he put together a force of twenty-two thousand foot and 1,200 horse and set out from Caralis (Cagliari) for Hampsicora's country on the west side of the island. The chief, who was trying to recruit fighting men in the interior, had left his son Hostus to hold the camp and he was unwise enough to accept battle and was heavily defeated.

However the arrival of Hasdrubal's fleet at Cornus caused Manlius to retire to his base, and the Carthaginian, after dismissing his ships and joining forces with Hampsicora, proceeded to march on Caralis, devastating the lands of loyal Sardinian communities as he went. Manlius was obliged to take the field to stop him, and in the ensuing engagement Hasdrubal's Sardinian allies were routed, and the Romans encircled and annihilated the Punic force. Hasdrubal and several prominent Carthaginians (including Mago, a kinsman of Hannibal) were captured, Hostus fell in the battle and Hampsicora not long afterwards. Cornus and the other rebellious towns were taken or capitulated and were punished, and Manlius was able to take his army, his captives and his booty back to Rome and announce the subjugation of the island. In the meantime T. Otacilius had raided Carthaginian territory from Lilybaeum and on his return voyage caught Hasdrubal's fleet returning from Cornus and captured seven ships.

Once again with the benefit of hindsight, we may say that Carthage in effect lost the war in 215. The minor gains made by Hannibal's lieutenants in Bruttium did not extend the area of revolt, and Hannibal himself, apart from the capture of Casilinum, was almost wholly ineffectual in Campania – in striking contrast to his series of brilliant successes in the three preceding years – and had already shown himself unable to protect his Samnite and Campanian allies from devastation by the Romans. The Carthaginians had again made no attempt to drive the Romans from the sea and had not only failed to send Hannibal the reinforcements he so urgently needed but had actually committed more than twenty-five thousand men to Spain and Sardinia – a clear enough indication of where their priorities lay. And in both these preferred theatres they had suffered staggering reverses. Nor had the alliance with Philip borne any practical fruit. On the other hand the Romans had had a year without disaster at home and had won two most heartening successes abroad.

Almost the only matter calculated to cheer the Carthaginians was the elimination of the pro-Roman influence at the court of Syracuse and the decision taken by the unbalanced Hieronymus to throw in his lot with Carthage. Agents went to and fro between him and Hannibal; a proposal on the part of the praetor Ap. Claudius to renew the treaty that had existed between Hiero and Rome was rejected derisively and an alliance was negotiated with Carthage. This recognized his suzerainty over the whole of Sicily, which the Carthaginians were to assist him to secure in return for the promise of his aid to Hannibal in Italy. We need not suppose that the Carthaginian government, who had got the measure of their new ally, had any intention of abiding by the terms of this agreement once the greater part of Sicily was in their hands. On the strength of this treaty Hieronymus, apparently contrary to the feeling of the majority of his Council but with the support of Adranodorus and two Syracusan exiles, Hippocrates and Epicydes, whom Hannibal had sent to win him over, replied to a second Roman embassy in terms that were tantamount to an ultimatum and both Syracuse and Carthage prepared for war in Sicily. However even this important diplomatic success was marred by the assassination of Hieronymus by a group of conspirators at Leontini early in 214. Syracuse fell into disorder as the regicides, who were republicans, clashed with Adranodorus and the monarchists. This gave Ap. Claudius a breathing space in which to organize his frontier defences and alert the Senate to developments in eastern Sicily.

Q. Fabius Maximus was determined that nothing should be allowed to jeopardize the pursuance of the strategy of cunctatio. By going straight to the Campus Martius without entering the city he was able to conduct the elections for the consular year 214/13 with all the state and with the unrestricted imperium of a consular army commander. When the first voting century (*centuria praerogativa*), whose suffrage almost invariably decided the choice of the whole Assembly, chose T. Otacilius and M.

Aemilius Regillus as consuls, Fabius intervened. He told the Assembly to think again, and caused himself to be re-elected with Marcellus as his colleague. Otacilius received a second praetorship and the continuing command of the fleet as a consolation. Another of the praetors was Fabius' son Quintus. All outgoing force commanders had their imperium prorogued, so that Gracchus remained in Apulia at the head of his volones, Ap. Claudius continued to command the Cannae legions in Sicily (although a fresh governor had been appointed) and Laevinus remained in Calabria to keep watch on Philip and the southern Adriatic. His two legions, however, were transferred to the younger Fabius. In all, Rome prepared to fight with 20 legions and 150 ships in 214, building 100 new vessels to replace those lost or taken out of service. Owing to the shortage of seamen, due largely to the revolt of southern Italy, the Senate adopted the extraordinary expedient of ordering all citizens assessed at over fifty thousand asses to purchase, equip, train and pay from one to eight slaves (according to their wealth) for service as rowers.

The determination of the Senate to prosecute the war to ultimate victory found further expression in the severity with which the censors of the year dealt with those who had lost heart after Cannae or had improperly avoided military service, over two thousand of whom were degraded and sent to serve 'for the duration' with the Cannae legions in Sicily. They recorded numerous instances of patriotic generosity on the part of contractors, slave-owners and trustees, while it became the practice for knights and centurions to agree to serve without pay. They named M. Fabius Buteo leader of the Senate (*princeps senatus*), thus further strengthening the Fabians' grip on the state.

As soon as the campaigning season opened Hannibal returned to his western base on Mount Tifata and from there moved part of his force into the Baiae peninsula. Having sacrificed on the shores of Lake Avernus he devastated the promontory and made a sudden attack on Puteoli (Pozzuoli), which had become Rome's principal supply base in the south. However Fabius had strengthened its defences only a few months previously, and Hannibal's assault was beaten off. Meanwhile Fabius hurried back from Rome to his army and summoned Gracchus up from Luceria to Beneventum, so that while two armies confronted Hannibal in Campania a third should be in position to bar the road against a Punic army coming up from Bruttium and moving so as to threaten the Romans from the east. Once again the class conflict flared up at Nola, and while the commons invited Hannibal to 'liberate' the city, the aristocracy sent for Marcellus, who had mustered his legions at Cales. Although delayed by the swollen waters of the Volturnus, he succeeded in throwing 6,300 horse and foot into the town. Fabius meanwhile advanced to threaten Casilinum.

Hannibal delayed committing himself to an assault on Nola, because he was waiting for the arrival of his lifelong friend and trusted lieutenant Hanno, who was bringing 1,200 African horsemen and 17,000 Bruttian and Lucanian infantry up the Via Appia from Bruttium, through the friendly Hirpini country. Hanno pitched camp on the Calor River about three miles south-east of Beneventum, and Gracchus, whose army had evidently been brought up to something like the full two-legion strength, marched out, and on the next day gave him battle. The slogging-match that ensued ended in a victory for the Romans and the capture of Hanno's camp. Hanno himself escaped with only about a tenth of his force, mainly horsemen, according to the Romans. The slaves, including even those who had fought half-heartedly in the battle, were given their liberty by a decree of the Senate, as Gracchus had promised before the battle.

Hannibal made a demonstration before Nola and his forces and those of Marcellus clashed; but Hannibal was even less in a position to undertake siege operations now than he had been a year earlier, and the territory of the Campanians could not easily support his army. Therefore, since the Romans would not accept battle in circumstances that would ensure him victory and as the security and even the loyalty of his southern allies might have been shaken by Hanno's costly defeat, he withdrew from Campania into the coastal region around the Gulf of Tarentum. He had a positive reason also for moving there, for certain Tarantines, whom he had freed without ransom after Trasimene and Cannae, had approached him with a proposal to betray the city to him. The acquisition of Taras would have been of great potential value as it possessed a magnificent harbour which, if occupied by a Carthaginian fleet, would neutralize Brundisium and provide a bridgehead for a possible invasion of Italy by Philip. He devastated the lands belonging to Rome's allies but not those of the Tarantines, and advanced to within a mile of the city. However he found the defences, commanded by Laevinus' prefect M. Livius, alert and ready and therefore moved away into Apulia where he intended to winter, and sent his African horsemen to forage in Calabria. Their booty included four thousand unbroken horses.

When Hannibal left Campania Fabius summoned Marcellus to Casilinum, and with the greater part of two consular armies assaulting it the place was stormed – apparently while the Campanians were under the impression that a truce was a in force. The capture of this town, which commanded the crossing of the lower Volturnus, was an important success strategically and also morally, since it illustrated Hannibal's powerlessness to protect his gains and Rome's ability to recover lost ground. Fabius next carried fire and sword into Samnium and retook several towns, including Compsa and Aecae, just over the border in Apulia, where the younger Fabius also made some gains. Gracchus, on the other hand, suffered a setback at the hands of his old enemy Hanno in Lucania.

Although Marcellus had been operating in Campania, his province – that is, the theatre of operations assigned to him by the Senate – was the kingdom of the late King Hiero in Sicily; and after a period of forced inactivity at Nola owing to illness he went there late in 214 or early in 213 with one of his legions. The situation at Syracuse had become chaotic following the murder of Hieronymus. Adranodorus, receiving prompt information of what had happened at Leontini, at first occupied Ortygia, the island citadel of Syracuse; but when leading regicides arrived and roused the citizens to arms to vindicate their liberty he surrendered the citadel and treasury to the Council and people and was elected as one of the generals in the restored Republic. His ultimate aim was now to acquire the kingship by popular acceptance.

Hannibal's two agents, the exiled brothers Hippocrates and Epicydes, who had been sent by Hieronymus with four thousand troops to liberate the Sicilian cities from their Roman garrisons and had been deserted by their men, now also returned to Syracuse, where they began to stir up hostility against the Council. A conspiracy formed by Adranodorus and Themistus, a brother-in-law of Hieronymus, was betrayed to the Council and both men were cut down as they entered the council chamber and their murder was followed by the precipitate slaughter, on the orders of the Council, of the women of the royal family. Although Hannibal's men were elected generals at an unruly Assembly of the people, envoys had already been sent to Ap. Claudius (who was still waiting to see if war could be avoided, while Otacilius' ships kept watch on Syracuse itself) to negotiate the renewal of the treaty with Rome; and when Marcellus arrived on the scene he sent a mission to Syracuse to conclude an agreement.

The year 214 saw the first move made by King Philip in the game. Perhaps assuming that the attention of the Roman navy was wholly concentrated on Sicily and the Tyrrhenian Sea, he brought his 120 biremes into Illyrican waters and attacked the Roman protectorate, taking Oricum and laying siege to Apollonia, which stood about seven miles from the sea and at a little distance from the right bank of the river Aoüs. Laevinus at Brundisium responded promptly. He now had fifty quinqueremes under his flag and for soldiers the so-called marine legion, in addition to a certain number of garrison troops. He crossed the Adriatic with the bulk of his forces and retook Oricum without difficulty. He then put two thousand picked men under a prefect into Apollonia by night, and the following night these, together with the men of Apollonia, stormed and sacked the Macedonian camp, King Philip only just escaping, half-naked, to his ships. Laevinus brought his fleet round to the mouth of the Aoüs intending to bottle Philip's ships up in the river. But the king, knowing that his light galleys were no match for the Roman quinqueremes and with his army seriously short of weapons and equipment as a result of the sack of their camp, burnt his fleet and retired overland into Macedonia, leaving Laevinus to winter undisturbed at Oricum. It was to be nearly two years before Philip gave the Romans any further cause for concern.

It had been another good year for Rome, with Hannibal suffering a serious blow to his prestige in Campania and the Romans making gains in Samnium and Apulia and so weakening his hold on both these regions. Abroad, Syracuse might still return to her allegiance, Philip had been driven out of the Adriatic and the Scipios, profiting by the withdrawal of Punic forces to put down a revolt in Africa, were consolidating their position in Spain. Once again an important contributory factor to Rome's escape from her post-Cannae perils was the inactivity of Carthage herself in the Hannibalic theatre. She had begun to make preparations for a war in Sicily before the assassination of Hieronymus, but the damage and losses sustained by her fleet in the disastrous Sardinian expedition, the closing of her important recruiting grounds in Liguria, Gaul and Spain (where the native levies were needed for home defence), and finally the revolt of the powerful King Syphax in Numidia, all contributed to prevent her from reaching a state of readiness to intervene in those areas – such as Syracuse and the Adriatic – where her navy might have played a decisive rôle.

Fabius, therefore, had good grounds for continuing to represent his policy to the people as their best hope of ultimate victory, and at the consular elections he secured the success of his son Fabius and of his former colleague Gracchus. The consuls took over the armies of their predecessors, while Castra Claudiana, Marcellus' old stronghold, was entrusted to the praetor Gn. Fulvius Centumalus with the urban legions. The latter, as had become the custom, were replaced by two newly levied legions. In all, twenty-two legions were enrolled in 213 BC; with these forces, which can hardly have amounted to less than 190,000 men, Rome should have been able, while avoiding a clash with Hannibal himself, to undertake a vigorous offensive campaign.

The consul Fabius (to whose headquarters the Cunctator had attached himself as legate in order to ensure that he attempted no action incompatible with Fabian policy) marched from Suessula into Apulia and attacked the important city of Arpi, the third-largest city in southern Italy, one of whose leading men had already deserted back to the Romans. The city wall was assaulted by night at its strongest point, after heavy rain had driven the guards to take shelter, and after some street fighting the Arpini changed sides and joined in the attack upon the Punic garrison, five thousand strong. Of these a thousand Spaniards deserted to the consul and the rest were permitted to withdraw to Salapia, where Hannibal lay. After the fall of Arpi the Carthaginian moved south into Calabria, for he was still angling for the betrayal of Taras and Calabria had been left unguarded as a result of the departure of Laevinus. A number of Sallentine communities went over to him while in Lucania a force of allies under a prefect, T. Pomponius Veientanus, was routed by Hanno. Gracchus, meanwhile, made some unimportant gains in this region, while in Campania the Romans did no more than harry the countryside and interfere with the farming activities of the Capuans.

CHAPTER XIII

213-212 BC

Syracuse, Taras and the fighting in Campania.

In the spring of 213 the Syracusans, with Roman ships anchored off the town and a Carthaginian fleet lurking about Cape Pachynus, opted for a return to the Roman alliance. It was decided to get rid of Hippocrates as well as the more turbulent mercenaries and the Roman deserters – a particularly intransigent bunch – by sending them as a garrison to Leontini. But a series of raids carried out by Hippocrates against Rome's allies across the border culminated in an attack upon a Roman outpost, and Marcellus, whose proconsular imperium had been renewed, sent an ultimatum to Syracuse. Epicydes left for Leontini to join his brother, and the two men persuaded the Leontinians to renounce their connection with Syracuse. Marcellus, who still had only one of his legions with him, and Ap. Claudius, who was propraetor under Marcellus' command, moved their armies against the town and took it by assault. The two brothers escaped to Erbessus. A force of eight thousand men had set out from Syracuse to assist Marcellus and to ensure, by doing so, that Leontini was returned to Syracusan control, but this force was won over by Hippocrates and Epicydes by means of reports – only partly false of a massacre of the garrison at Leontini, and the same means were employed to inflame anti-Roman passions at Syracuse. The authorities tried to exclude the returning column from the city, but the Hexapylon – the principal gate in the wall of Dionysius – was opened by sympathizers inside and the troops burst in and were joined by the military in the city. A slaughter of the magistrates ensued, slaves and gaol-birds were liberated, and the mob elected Hippocrates and Epicydes generals. A Roman embassy sent by sea was attacked and one of two vessels seized.

Marcellus now marched on Syracuse and camped near the temple of Olympian Zeus, a little over a mile to the west of the Great Harbour, where the Athenians had camped almost two hundred years earlier. His ultimatum was rejected and he prepared to try to take the city by assault, although the strength of its situation and of its fortifications, which had been repaired and improved by Hiero, gave it the reputation of invincibility. Syracuse had been founded by Corinthians in the eighth century. It had outgrown its original site on the island of Ortygia (Quail Island),

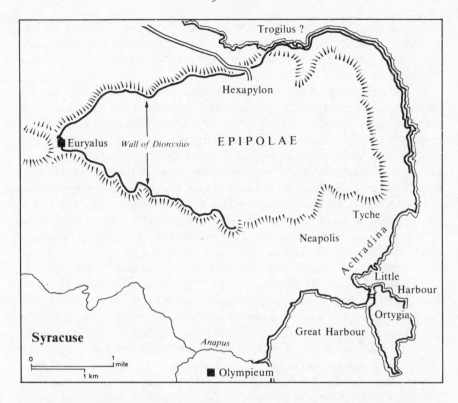

Syracuse

climbed the rugged slopes of Achradina on the mainland, and in the early fifth century spread over the suburbs of Tyche and Neapolis. Finally, under Dionysus I, it took within the circuit of its walls the triangular plateau of Epipolae, at whose apex the fortress of Euryalus crowned the whole mighty system of fortifications.

Marcellus directed his efforts against the sea wall of Achradina, on the north side of the Little Harbour. He employed sixty quinqueremes, from some of which, keeping their distance, bowmen and slingers swept the wall of defenders, while the attack was driven home by pairs of galleys lashed together, each pair carrying a movable assault ladder called a *sambuca* or harp, the invention of Heracleides of Taras. But the ingenuity of Heracleides was outmatched by that of a yet greater mathematician, Archimedes. He sited missile throwers of differing power to deal with each stage of the attack, opened scientifically designed loopholes in the walls for the safe discharge of arrows and light artillery and devised ingenious engines to repulse the sambuca-carriers which under cover of darkness were brought up as far as the wall. The attack by sea was beaten off, and an assault by land delivered by Ap. Claudius with his two legions upon the wall of Epipolae near the Hexapylon – a position of immense natural strength – had no better success, for there, too, Archimedes had planned the defences. Frustrated in their attempts to storm the city the Romans settled for a blockade, cutting Syracuse off from her supplies by land and sea.

In the meantime Himilco, who had commanded the Punic fleet at Pachynus, had returned to Carthage and had urged the government to take immediate action; his arguments being energetically seconded by envoys from Hippocrates and a letter from Hannibal. As a result he was sent back to Sicily with an army of 25,000 foot, 3,000 horse and 12 elephants, which he landed at Heraclea Minoa, and from there quickly won over Acragas, thus giving fresh heart to Carthage's friends on the island. The Syracusans were so encouraged that Hippocrates slipped out of the city by night at the head of ten thousand infantry and five hundred horse to join forces with Himilco. As luck would have it, Marcellus with his one legion had made a foray into the interior, receiving the surrender of Helorus and Erbessus and taking Megara by assault. Then learning of Himilco's arrival at Heraclea he had hastened to Acragas to try to forestall him there but had been too late. Now making his way cautiously back to Syracuse he stumbled upon Hippocrates' force as it was engaged in pitching camp at Acrillae, and from the ensuing slaughter only the Syracusan cavalry escaped with its general to join Himilco.

The Carthaginians advanced to within eight miles of the Roman position at the Olympieum and camped by the River Anapus, while fifty-five ships under Bomilcar entered the Great Harbour. No part of the information that we possess about the siege of Syracuse is more unsatisfactory than that which relates to the rôle played in it by the Roman fleet. T. Otacilius Crassus was appointed each year by the Senate to its command and in spite of the fact that he is nowhere mentioned in the account of the siege it is best to assume that in fact he led the fleet, under Marcellus' commandership-in-chief. It also seems likely (although it is nowhere so stated) that the fleet was not permanently based at Syracuse but rather at Messana, perhaps withdrawing to Lilybaeum for the winter, Livy's account notwithstanding. It is clear that manning problems had forced the Romans to lay up many of their ships, some had been damaged by Archimedes' engines and thirty had been sent, or possibly taken by Otacilius himself, to escort Marcellus' second legion to Sicily. The Carthaginian fleet therefore enjoyed a temporary numerical superiority over their enemy at Syracuse. When news was received that the legion had arrived at Panormus Himilco hurried across country to cut it off; but the Romans marched by the northern coast road with their left flank protected by the ships as far as Cape Pelorias, where Ap. Claudius met them with his army and escorted them to Syracuse. With the return of these thirty vessels Otacilius' fleet would again outnumber Bomilcar's, and as the feeding of his crews would impose a strain on the resources of the town the Punic admiral – who had little stomach for a fight under any conditions – took his ships home.

As something of a stalemate had now developed at Syracuse Himilco withdrew into the interior and brought about the revolt of the town of Morgantina which the Romans had been using as a magazine, and this was the signal for widespread defection. The strong and important town of Enna (famous, too, for its connection with Demeter and Persephone) was saved for Rome only by the action of its garrison commander, who had the men of the town massacred in the theatre, to which he had invited them to discuss their grievances with him. Then the town was sacked. However this brutal desecration of a holy place had the effect not of deterring other towns from defecting, as Marcellus had hoped, but rather of spreading the fires of revolt still wider. At the end of the campaigning season Himilco retired to Acragas and Hippocrates to Morgantina. Marcellus garrisoned Leontini and fortified a strong winter camp at Leon to the north-west of Syracuse, about four and a half miles from the Hexapylon. The camp by the Olympieum was entrusted to the legate T. Quictius Crispinus, so as to allow Ap. Claudius to return to Rome to canvass for the consulship of 212.

Except in the Sicilian theatre the year had produced few incidents of importance in terms of the numbers of troops mobilized by the combatant powers. Early in 212, however, Hannibal scored his most important success since the defection of Capua; and for this the Romans themselves were largely responsible. They had been keeping under rather careless guard in the Hall of Liberty a number of noblemen from Thurii and Taras as hostages for the good behaviour of their communities. A certain Phileas, who belonged to the anti-Roman faction in Taras and who had been sent to Rome on some mission, talked the hostages into making their escape. They got down the Appian Way as far as Tarracina, where they were overtaken and arrested. They were brought back to Rome, scourged and cast from the Tarpeian Rock. That the Romans committed this incredibly short-sighted act of retaliation is a sign of the extent to which their nerve had been shaken by the events of the last three and a half years. They ignored the fact that the Tarantines were a proud, indeed an arrogant, people, conscious of their ancient descent from Lacedaemon and of their Hellenism: that is to say, of their superiority to all non-Greeks. Within the memory of very old men still living Taras had been a sovereign power – in her own estimation a great power. The Greek passion for liberty was fed by the traditions and literature of the race and in spite of the fact that Taras had nothing to gain and much to lose by breaking away from Rome there was a faction within the city which dreamed of regaining for her her former independence. But their hands were tied as long as Rome had the hostages in her keeping. Now the Romans had at one and the same time thrown away this advantage and further in-flamed anti-Roman feeling in the two cities, and the result was the forma-tion of a serious conspiracy to betray Taras to Hannibal by a group of young noblemen. Hannibal for his part promised to respect the autonomy of the city and to sequestrate Roman property and citizens to the Taran-tines. His winter camp was situated at what was reckoned to be a safe three days' march from the city; but when the time for action arrived he was able to put himself, with a picked force of eight thousand foot and two thousand horse, within striking distance of the walls in a single day, employing a screening force of Numidians to prevent a rumour of his approach from reaching the garrison. The conspirators inside had fixed a day on which the prefect, M. Livius Macatus, was due to attend a party in the Museum near the marketplace, and by nightfall he was in no condition to evaluate properly accounts of Numidians overrunning the countryside.

About midnight fire signals were exchanged between Hannibal from the tomb of Apollo Hyacinthus, some three-quarters of a mile from the walls, and the conspirators inside the city; whereupon the latter rushed to the Temenid Gate, killed the guards and admitted the Carthaginians. At the same time (for Hannibal left little to chance in such essentially chancy operations) a second force entered, also as the result of treachery, by another gate. The cavalry remained outside, to deal with any relief force that might try to interfere. Getting his infantry together near the marketplace Hannibal gave the necessary instructions for taking the city. Livius was just sober enough to realize, when the mounting uproar and confusion announced that the enemy were within the walls, that the most he could hope to do was to preserve himself and the citadel, and so he escaped to it by boat. The braying of a Roman trumpet, blown by the conspirators, sounding 'to arms' from the theatre brought the men of the garrison running in disorder from their billets into the streets that led, through a bottleneck, to the citadel, and a great many were killed.

It was not until daybreak showed the roads littered with Roman bodies that the Tarantines fully appreciated what had happened. The pro-Roman elements fled to the citadel while the rest gathered in the market-place and there learnt that their city was now the ally of Carthage. A systematic pillage of Roman property followed. A palisade was con-structed to cut the town off from its citadel and a sortie by the garrison was severely punished. The earthworks were then strengthened and a strong wall built behind them, so as to prevent the Romans from breaking into the town. Hannibal then withdrew the greater part of his force to a camp about four and a half miles east of the city, as he was anxious to be seen to be abiding by his undertaking to respect the independence of the Tarantines, and made preparations for the siege of the citadel. Livius, however, who appears to have been an able soldier when sober, having received reinforcements from the garrison at Metapontum, made another sally and destroyed the siege engines. Hannibal then suggested to the Tarantines that they could effectively blockade the Romans if they were to transport their ships by land from the Inner Harbour (the Mare Piccolo), whose entrance was commanded by the citadel, to the Outer Harbour (the Mare Grande), by moving them on carriages from sea to sea by a street that crossed the western end of the town. When he had thus put the citadel in a state of siege Hannibal returned to his winter camp and remained there until the end of the spring. As a result of the transference of troops to Taras Metapontum threw off its allegiance and joined Hannibal.

At Rome the elections were conducted by a dictator (to save the consuls from having to leave their armies) and the master of horse, Q. Fulvius Flaccus, who had twice campaigned as consul against the Ligurians and the Gauls, was chosen consul, with Ap. Claudius Pulcher as his colleague. Although the consular and praetorian elections marked a triumph for the Claudii and the Fulvii, who were political allies of the Fabians, the younger Fabius did not have his imperium prorogued. It was no doubt widely felt that the policy of cunctatio had been carried too far and that Rome's failure to assert herself in Campania, in Apulia (where there had been a praetorian as well as a consular army – four legions in all) and elsewhere, had helped to substantiate the myth of Hannibal's invincibility and so indirectly contributed to the loss of Taras. Gracchus, however, did have his command extended, possibly because it was felt that no one else could get the best out of the volones. The latent resentment of the commons over the monopolization of political authority by the sena-torials found expression, early in the consular year, in an attack by certain tribunes upon a flagrantly dishonest contractor who had the support of his order, the Equestrian Order, and the tacit protection of the Senate, which did not wish to offend the capitalist class at this juncture. However by causing an Assembly to be broken up the equites played into the hands of their accusers, the Senate was able to rebuke and dissociate itself from disturbers of the peace and the tribunes took strong measures against the offenders. The shortage of recruits this year was so serious that two commissions were appointed to scour Rome's territory and enlist all men capable of bearing arms, even if they were under the statutory age. With twenty-five legions under arms, Rome must have mobilized about 225,000 men in 212, excluding those serving as marines and seamen.

After the celebration of the Latin Festival on 27 April the consuls ordered their legions, which had been disbanded for the winter, to muster near Bovianum (Bojano) in northern Samnium, no doubt in order to leave the enemy in a state of uncertainty about their intentions. However the Capuans rightly conjectured that they were not going to be left in relative peace for another year and appealed to Hannibal to provision the town before the blockade commenced. Hannibal, whose attention was still directed towards the Tarantine region, ordered Hanno to throw supplies into Capua and Hanno marched up from Bruttium and fortified a strong camp on high ground about three miles west of Beneventum. He directed the neighbouring people to bring grain into his camp and appointed a day – and subsequently a second day – for the Capuans to come and collect it. Beneventum reported these events to the consuls and Flaccus marched from Bovianum and entered the colony by night. Next day he ascertained that Hanno was absent from his camp with part of his army, foraging, that the camp itself was crowded with wagons and peasantry and that order and camp discipline had broken down. Moving out under cover of darkness he attacked just before first light and after a desperate struggle, during which the consul himself is said to have despaired of success, the camp was stormed, the defenders slaughtered and an immense booty captured. Hanno retired at once into Bruttium.

Both consular armies now concentrated at Beneventum and the consuls sent orders to Gracchus to bring his cavalry and light infantry up from Lucania. Unfortunately Gracchus had been betrayed by the treachery of a Lucanian guest-friend into an ambush set by Mago near the River Calor and killed, his body being accorded a hero's funeral honours by Hannibal. Obscurity envelops the subsequent history of his army. According to Livy it simply disintegrated on the death of the only man who could hold it together. However we are also told, first that Cn. Cornelius Lentulus brought this army into Campania, and secondly that the Senate entrusted to a veteran centurion, M. Centenius Paenula, a force of eight thousand men with which to carry on the war in Lucania and that Paenula almost doubled this body by local recruitment. The likelihood is, therefore, that Paenula was in fact assigned what remained of Gracchus' army and that a large number of deserters returned to the colours when he took the field.

The Capuans, who had managed to get in one consignment of grain from Hanno's dump, sent another urgent appeal for aid to Hannibal, who sent on ahead two thousand horsemen under Mago, who was already near the Campanian border, to protect their farmers, while he followed with his army. So effective was this advance force that the consular armies suffered a costly reverse when they began to devastate Capuan territory, and Hannibal was able to make his way past Beneventum to Capua without interference on the part of the Romans. He offered battle and had the better of a cavalry engagement; whereupon the consuls, thoroughly infected with the Fabian doctrine of Hannibal's invincibility in the field, evacuated their camp by night; and while Flaccus fell back to cover the supply base of Puteoli Claudius marched south into Lucania. Hannibal could not allow a consular army to range at will among his allies nor did he have sufficient supplies to maintain his own army in Campania, and so he hurried in pursuit of Claudius, who managed to give him the slip and return to Campania. Paenula came upon Hannibal's army as it was resting, and made the mistake of believing that he could reverse the verdict of Cannae. In the ensuing battle and rout the leader and virtually the whole of his army were wiped out.

Although it was clearly in Hannibal's interest to get back to Campania before the Romans could invest Capua he could not afford to neglect appeals from his other allies. Reports came in from Apulia of the activities of the praetor Cn. Fulvius Flaccus, the brother of the consul, who was in the neighbourhood of Herdonea (Ordona) about thirty-five miles from the borders of Lucania, and Hannibal marched to encounter him. We are told that the discipline in Flaccus' two legions was very bad, for apart from Flaccus' inadequacies as a disciplinarian and a commander this was their third summer in Apulia, having served under the younger Fabius and the peregrine praetor M. Aemilius, and having achieved nothing of note during the whole period. They were spoiling for a fight and Hannibal, who probably though by no means certainly had more men with him than the enemy, was ready to accommodate them. He chose his battlefield and planted about five thousand light infantry and cavalry in ambush positions. Flaccus drew up his army in two lines with a very extended front which collapsed before the Punic onslaught, and the greater part of his army was cut to pieces. Flaccus fled from the field, and there were only about 2,200 survivors. At the beginning of the following year Flaccus was arraigned on a charge of treason (*perduellio*) by a tribune and went into exile. The survivors of his army were shipped to Sicily on the same terms as the Cannae legions.

When Appius Claudius returned to Campania the two consuls occupied themselves with the investment of Capua. They established depots at Casilinum, at Puteoli and at the mouth of the Volturnus (on the site of the later town of Volturnum) and in them they stored grain sent from Sardinia and from Etruria, where the praetor M. Iunius Silanus was making a show of strength and collecting supplies, in preparation for a winter's siege. They also summoned the praetor C. Claudius Nero from Castra Claudiana, where he commanded the legions that Varro had raised in Picenum; and the three armies – six legions – set about constructing a circumvallation that should cut Capua off from the rest of Italy and also provide an impregnable ring of defences from behind which the besiegers could fight off any army coming to the relief of the place. It was apparently in the course of the siege of Capua that the Romans began to give some thought to the training and scientific employment, after the Punic fashion, of the light armed components of the legion, the *rorarii*. They were taught to operate in conjunction with the cavalry and were thenceforth known as *velites*, in allusion to their quickness of movement.

The Capuans, who at first did their utmost to impede the siege work, got messages through to Hannibal, who had returned to Calabria because he had been led to believe that he might be able to get the citadel of Taras or Brundisium into his hands – either of which successes would have represented a military gain far outweighing the moral effect of the loss of Capua. He promised to raise the siege, although it was by now too late in the season to think of invading Campania before the spring, and the Capuans were sufficiently heartened to reject with contempt a senatorial offer of an amnesty for all those who left the city before the end of the consular year. In fact 112 knights had already gone over to the Romans in 213.

The year just ended marked a swing of the balance of success in Italy in Hannibal's favour. He had captured the town of Taras and could hope to capture the citadel eventually, although the Romans managed to get a shipment of grain through the blockade. Thurii, too, was moved by the same grievance as Taras to intrigue with the enemy, and Hanno and Mago between them were able to rout the Graeco-Roman force that the prefect M. Atinius led out against them when they approached the city. The townsfolk closed the gates against the retreating Romans, but for personal reasons allowed Atinius and a handful of his men to enter and escape by water. With the defection of Metapontum, Thurii and (about this time) Heraclea, the Carthaginians had gained possession of all the Greek cities of the south except Rhegium. The Carthaginians had also cleared Lucania and Apulia of Roman forces and had killed a good soldier in Ti. Sempronius Gracchus. There were ominous indications, too, that the strain imposed by the Fabian strategy upon Rome's resources, particularly in manpower, was beginning to tell. On the debit side, Hanno had suffered a defeat in Samnium and Capua was closely invested by six legions sitting behind the kind of fieldworks that only the Romans could build.

In Sicily the Carthaginian army displayed the same dilatoriness and lack of enterprise in 212 that had lost Carthage the island in the earlier war. When spring arrived Himilco still lingered in western Sicily when he should have been harassing the Romans besieging Syracuse. Meanwhile the Romans were themselves reduced to ineffectualness by the strength of the city's defences and the impossibility of preventing the flow of supplies brought in by sea from Carthage, whose admiral, Bomilcar, dominated Syracusan waters with his ninety ships. A formidable conspiracy was indeed painstakingly engineered by Marcellus, whose imperium had again been prorogued, involving the exiles in his camp and sympathizers within the city; but this was betrayed to Epicydes, who was in charge of the defence of Syracuse, and the traitors were cruelly executed. However it happened that lengthy negotiations were entered upon at the harbour of Trogilus between representatives of both commanders with a view to the ransoming of a Lacedaemonian envoy sent by Epicydes to Philip and captured by the Romans. Lacedaemon was the ally of the Aetolians, themselves the traditional foes of Macedonia, and Rome was anxious not to offend her. One of the Roman party convinced himself – and subsequently Marcellus – that the wall was scalable at the spot where the discussions were held. Taking advantage of a major feast of Artemis which was being celebrated within the city and for which wine in abundance had been supplied to the populace by Epicydes and the well-to-do (there was a scarcity of bread), Marcellus sent a picked force to scale the wall which the guards had deserted and to make their way along to the Hexapylon Gate and secure it. At daybreak he brought his army into Epipolae and occupied the plateau that dominates the city.

Epicydes hastened up from Ortygia expecting to have to deal with a scaling party merely; but when he perceived the extent of the disaster he retired as hurriedly as he had come, in case treachery should lock him out of Achradina and the island. Marcellus, who is said to have wept as he gazed upon the doomed city and reflected how much history the flames must consume if it had to be taken by storm, appealed to the populace through the exiles in his camp to surrender the place. But Achradina was held by desperate men, including Roman deserters who had only a shameful death in store for them, and his appeals were disregarded. Marcellus therefore marched to Euryalus, to summon the supposedly impregnable fortress that overlooks Epipolae on the west and commands the gate and road leading to the interior of the island, by which Himilco would have to come, if he marched to the relief of the city. The captain of the citadel, Philodemus of Argos, procrastinated, expecting Himilco's arrival from one day to the next, and so Marcellus brought his army down to the quarters called Tyche and Neapolis and after fortifying his camp and giving orders that no free blood was to be shed loosed his soldiers to sack the upper town. Bomilcar slipped out of the harbour on a night of storm with 35 ships and returned to Carthage to ask for aid for their allies. Before long he was back with 100 galleys. Otacilius could not man more than 60; and so Carthage, because of the difficulty that Rome was experiencing in raising seamen, was able to establish temporarily her command of the sea.

But Philodemus had already despaired of Himilco's arrival and had surrendered Euryalus, and Marcellus, now confident that he could not be taken from the rear, devoted his energies to besieging Achradina.

Belatedly – for the summer was by now far advanced – Himilco and Hippocrates arrived before the city. They fortified a camp on the marshes at the mouth of the Anapus and arranged a concerted attack by land and sea on the Romans. It was arranged that Epicydes should make a sortie against Marcellus, while Hippocrates assaulted the winter camp where the legate Crispinus commanded the Cannae legions and Bomilcar landed a force from the sea to cut Crispinus off from the city. Both attacks failed completely. And now pestilence came to the assistance of the Romans just as, 185 years earlier and in the same place, it had come to the aid of the Syracusans against a namesake of Himilco. It proved a capricious ally and many Romans sickened and died; but the Romans had been camped before Syracuse for two summers now and had acquired a certain degree of immunity. Moreover Marcellus withdrew Crispinus' men within the walls where conditions were healthier. The Carthaginians, deserted by their Sicilian allies – though not by Hippocrates – at the first serious onset of the plague, perished to a man. Bomilcar now took his fleet back to Carthage for the winter and persuaded the authorities to make an even greater effort to relieve Syracuse the following year.

With the destruction in southern Italy of two armies (one, indeed, largely composed of expendable volones) and with substantial casualties being sustained by the armies besieging Capua and Syracuse and by the garrisons of Taras and Thurii, the year 212/11 had been for Rome one of the most costly of the war in terms of human life. Yet once again the overall final balance of loss and gain was narrowly in her favour; the partial capture of Syracuse, the destruction of Himilco's army and the continued success of the Scipios in Spain outweighing the slight advantage that Hannibal had achieved in Italy. Yet if Himilco had been a more enterprising – or even an ordinarily efficient – general, or if Philodemus had held out a little longer in Euryalus, the picture might well have been a very different one.

CHAPTER XIV

211-210 BC

The Roman Successes in Italy, Sicily and Greece. Disaster in Spain.

Towards the end of the consular year Ap. Claudius returned to Rome to hold the elections and Cn. Fulvius Centumalus was chosen consul with, as his colleague, a man who had previously held no curule office, P. Sulpicius Galba – an indication of a shortage of 'consular material' such as the Roman political system was liable to produce. In fact in this most eventful year all the main armies and the fleets of the Republic were commanded by proconsuls and propraetors.

In the late spring of 211 Hannibal moved out of Bruttium with a light column to redeem his promise to raise the siege of Capua. He brought with him thirty-three elephants. There was no Roman army in Apulia or in Lucania to challenge him and he marched swiftly to the neighbourhood of his former base on Mount Tifata and from there seized the town of Calatia. He succeeded in getting a message through to the Campani, so that his lieutenants in the town Bostar and Hanno could co-ordinate a sortie with his assault upon the Roman lines. Both attacks failed, although Ap. Claudius received a wound from which he later died whilst repulsing the Capuans. Hannibal's attack was not pressed home, being intended to goad the Romans into coming out of their lines and offering battle, which would not only have given his cavalry an opportunity of causing them loss but would have provided a diversion that the Capuans might have been able to turn to good account. As he dared not remain indefinitely in the vicinity of Capua and so risk being surrounded by five armies should the consuls decide to bring the urban legions from the capital, and as there was insufficient forage in Campania for his army with its large contingent of animals, he decided to make a dash on Rome. He did not expect to take it but hoped merely to create sufficient panic there to induce the Senate to recall one or both of the proconsuls, or to cause them to return on their own initiative to defend the city.

Accordingly on the fifth day after his arrival in Campania Hannibal got a heartening message through to the besieged and slipped out of his camp by night and marched north across Samnium. Then making a wide detour so as to avoid the Via Latina he struck through the country of the Paeligni to Alba Fucens, from there to Reate (Rieti) on the Via Salaria, and from Reate south, to cross the Anio before the Romans were aware of him and pitch his camp less than four and a half miles from the walls. His appearance caused considerable alarm in the city, not least because it might imply the defeat of the Roman armies in Campania. However Rome was not short of defenders, for the consuls had at their disposal the urban legions of 212 BC, newly returned from their winter's leave, and the recruits recently levied to make up the urban legions of the current year. They paraded this force before the walls to discourage the enemy from attacking the city. Hannibal contented himself with laying waste the country around Rome and then, having no wish to be caught between the city walls and the returning proconsular armies, he withdrew north-wards. At the fording of the Anio – for the consuls had succeeded in destroying the bridges – he lost some men and was forced to abandon a large part of his immense booty. His route back to Campania can only be conjectured, but perhaps he went, very quickly, by way of Tibur, Treba, Sora and Aesernia. Galba, encouraged by his success on the Anio, followed his retreat, keeping to higher ground, but paid for his temerity when Hannibal, learning that the proconsuls had not budged from their lines and that there was therefore no further need of haste, turned on him and in a night attack drove his legions with loss out of their camp. The Carthaginians then continued their march into Bruttium and almost captured the town of Rhegium by a surprise attack.

Hannibal's march had advertised two facts: first that he could march and countermarch at will in southern Italy and the Romans dared not oppose him, and secondly that he was powerless before the defences of a city and could make no impression on the siege-works of a Roman army – that he could neither beat a loyal ally of Rome into submission nor protect an ally of his own whom the Romans exerted themselves to re-capture. Hannibal's retirements from Campania, followed by the detec-tion of a fifth column formed by Numidian 'deserters' in the Roman camp, broke the spirit of the Campani. Under pressure from the com-mons a plenary session of the Senate debated the question of surrender and the majority voted in favour. Twenty-seven senators followed Vibius Virrius home (he had taken the lead in proposing the defection of the city from Rome) and there, after feasting together, poisoned themselves. The following day the Romans were admitted to the city.

With their surrender the Capuans became *dediticii* – people without any political status – to do with as the Romans pleased. They had not been ordinary allies but citizens, although without right of franchise; they had revolted on the morrow of Rome's greatest military disaster since the Allia, when the Republic desperately needed all the loyalty and every soldier that she could call upon. They had set an example which, if it had been universally followed, would have left Rome at the mercy of her implacable foes They had killed scores, perhaps hundreds, of fellow citizens in battle and, that very spring, had slain a proconsul. Each and every one of them was guilty of treason, for which the accepted penalty was death. It is scarcely to be wondered at that the Romans were not in a forgiving mood and that the punishment of the Campani was exemplary. The fact that for two summers the Senate had thought it advisable to keep an army stationed in Etruria is a sign that mutterings of disaffection had been heard even in northern Italy; the present was no time for mildness and clemency.

The guiltiest, seventy in number, among the senators of Capua and of her dependencies Atella and Calatia (which soon capitulated), were summarily executed by Flaccus, disregarding a 'recommendation' from the Senate reserving them as citizens for the judgement of the Roman people. The fate of the remainder of the population was decided in the following year by the Senate. Most of the aristocracy – apart, of course, from those who had remained loyal or who had previously returned to their allegiance – were placed in captivity and died from various causes without recovering their freedom. Of the proprietary class, those who had actually fought alongside the Carthaginians were sold as slaves; the rest retained their liberty but remained dediticii, and it was decreed that they should be expelled from Campania and resettled in Etruria. The mass of freedmen, manual workers and petty tradesmen was left undisturbed and the town was left intact. The land – some of the most fertile land in Italy – became Roman public land, leased out by the censors and bringing in a valuable revenue to the treasury. Capua was permitted no civic institutions, becoming a prefecture administered by a prefect for Capua elected by the Roman Assembly. The manner of Capua's recapture and the punishment of its citizens were a grim object lesson on the folly of putting trust in the Carthaginians that was not likely to be lost on any waverers.

The capitulation of Capua had been preceded by the fall of Syracuse. In the spring of 211 Bomilcar sailed from Carthage with the biggest Punic armada of the war: 130 galleys and seven hundred supply ships. With a south-easterly wind blowing his huge convoy of sailing ships was able to make Heraclea Minoa in western Sicily but could get no further. Bomilcar himself proceeded along the coast with his galleys, but with weather conditions worsening he stopped short of Cape Pachynus. When the news of his approach reached Syracuse Epicydes, who knew his Bomilcar and feared that he would not wait indefinitely for a shift of wind, sailed with his own force to meet him and persuade him to come north with his warships and fight it out with the Roman battle fleet.

Marcellus' position was not too happy. The survivors of Hippocrates' army, who had established themselves in two strongholds close to the city, were gathering strength for a land campaign in conjunction with Bomilcar's projected landing, and if the Carthaginians had been allowed to gain the command of the sea Marcellus might have found himself beleaguered on all sides. The Romans could man only one hundred ships, but Marcellus ordered these south as far as Cape Pachynus, presumably under the propraetor Otacilius, who was still the fleet commander. Otacilius waited on the eastern side of the promontory for the wind to drop sufficiently to allow a battle to be fought, should Bomilcar put out to sea. Bomilcar, however, instead of rowing to meet the Romans when the wind abated, headed south from his anchorage, and when he was well clear of Cape Pachynus he hoisted his sails, sent orders back to the convoy at Heraclea to return to Carthage, and stood away to the northeast for Taras.

It is to be presumed that Bomilcar had been ordered to relieve Syracuse first, and then to proceed to Taras, but that – not being a great 'fighting' admiral – he was only too glad of the excuse afforded by contrary winds and by Epicydes' report of conditions at Syracuse to avoid battle, even with the odds heavily in his favour, and sail directly to Italy. When he arrived there he was content merely to prevent supplies from reaching the Romans and made no attempt to crush Laevinus' small force and so gain the command of the Adriatic. The Aetolians were quite as much alarmed as the Romans by the possibility that Philip might receive the support of a huge Punic fleet, and consequently Bomilcar's presence at Taras served to throw them into the arms of Rome. Moreover his horde of seamen consumed more food than the townspeople could import, with the result that they suffered more than Livius' men from his blockade and were heartily glad to see him go home. Epicydes, despairing of the safety of Syracuse, parted company with the Carthaginians and sailed to Acragas.

The withdrawal of Epicydes, who, with his brother, had been the mainspring of the Sicilian revolt, and the precipitate flight of the Carthaginians decided the Syracusans to try to come to terms with Rome. Those under arms outside the city treated first with Marcellus and finding him inclined to moderation proceeded into the city and won over their kinsmen and friends there. They killed Epicydes' lieutenants and easily persuaded an Assembly of the citizens to elect an interim government to represent the community in dealings with Marcellus. The most the Syracusans could hope was that their city would not be destroyed and that they would not be sold as slaves, and this Marcellus promised. But while the envoys were away the Roman deserters in the city talked the mercenaries into seizing Achradina and the island, after massacring the newly elected magistrates. However one of the leaders of the mercenaries, a Spaniard, was persuaded by the peace party to admit a body of Roman troops, under cover of darkness, to the region of the city that he was responsible for guarding, and following an attack by land and sea Ortygia and a part of Achradina were occupied by the Romans. The Syracusans then opened the remaining gates and capitulated and the city was sacked, Marcellus having first made sure of the royal treasures. One of those who fell victim to the destructive frenzy of the victorious soldiers was the man who had played so large a part in keeping them for so long outside the walls, Archimedes son of Phidias, the greatest mathematician of antiquity, who is said to have been killed while engrossed in a problem. His planetarium became part of the enormous booty of one of the richest cities of the classical world.

A threat of famine which hung over victors and vanquished alike was dispelled by the action of T. Otacilius, who took his fleet back to Lilybaeum when Bomilcar removed his warships from Sicilian waters, and from there sailed across to Utica and captured, among other booty, 130 cargo vessels loaded with grain, perhaps part of Bomilcar's aborted relief fleet. The grain was sent at once to Syracuse. There Marcellus received the envoys of the various Sicilian communities and dealt with them as he felt they deserved. The faithful, and those who had returned voluntarily to their allegiance, were restored to their former status while those who now capitulated out of fear had to pay for their disloyalty. Not that Sicily was wholly pacified. Acragas was still in full revolt and the Punic commander Hanno and Epicydes had been joined by another of Hannibal's lieutenants, a man of mixed race from Hippou Acra named Myttones. This man, who was an accomplished soldier, operated so effectively at the head of a force of Numidian cavalry that the Carthaginian cause in Sicily began to show signs of reviving, and Hanno and his colleague felt encouraged to move out of Acragas to the Himera River. Marcellus advanced to within a few miles of the enemy, where he pitched camp, only to be seriously harassed by Myttones' horsemen. Fortunately for the Romans, Hanno's antipathy to the half-caste Myttones led to a mutiny among the Numidians; and the Carthaginian, crossing the river and giving battle in the absence of his cavalry commander, saw his horsemen, on whom he chiefly relied, stand aloof from the fighting and was easily routed. Marcellus then marched back to Syracuse (summer was by now almost at an end) and handed over the command to his successor, the praetor M. Cornelius Cethegus, and returned to Rome. Since he had left his army in Sicily the Senate, no doubt persuaded by the jealous Fabius, decreed that he might not celebrate a triumph. And so, after all his victories and in spite of the vast quantity of booty and works of art with which he enriched the city (to her moral detriment, said the reactionaries), he had to be content with an ovation, and perhaps an unofficial Alban triumph.

Cethegus did not succeed to any easy command. The morale of the army was understandably low, Marcellus' legions being indignant that they had not been permitted to return home to triumph with their leader and the Cannae legions chafing at the continuation of their punishment service. Otacilius may already have been incapacitated by the illness which was to kill him before the end of the consular year. Moreover Punic reinforcements of eight thousand foot and three thousand Numidian horse were landed in western Sicily (no doubt after the return of Bomilcar from Italy) and several cities went over to the enemy. Meanwhile Myttones and his Numidians were ranging through the land ravaging and burning. Cethegus however pacified his troops and recovered the revolted towns, assigning possession of Morgantina to those Spaniards who had betrayed Achradina to Marcellus in the final assault, in conformity with a decree of the Senate.

Some time before the fall of Capua Rome had been deeply grieved by the receipt of a despatch sent from Spain by a knight named L. Marcius Septimius who, styling himself 'senatorial propraetor', announced that he was holding the northern bank of the lower Ebro with the remnants – less than half – of the Roman army in Spain. The remainder (he wrote) had perished with their commanders, and the survivors had chosen him to lead them. He asked for food and clothing for his army. The news of this disaster was the more distressing because Rome had become accustomed to receive heartening tidings from Spain, for this was a theatre of war in which her army had been uniformly successful since the outbreak of hostilities. She had sent to Spain two soldiers of above the Roman average of competence, the brothers Publius and Gnaeus Scipio, the latter acting as legate to his younger, consular brother. Gnaeus had arrived at Emporiae with his brother's army in early October 218. Hanno, whom Hannibal had left in command in Catalonia, took no offensive action against the Romans when they landed; and when Gnaeus Scipio, who fully appreciated that Rome had not declared war in order to stand on the defensive, pushed south along the coast road towards the mouth of the Ebro, Hanno allowed himself to be defeated and taken prisoner near Cissa, which may be identical with Tarraco (Tarragona). Tarraco provided the Romans with what they most needed at that time: a good base less than fifty miles from the Ebro, from which next year they could strike down the coast road towards Saguntum. Hasdrubal, who had hurried north to reinforce Hanno, succeeded in surprising the Roman naval camp but then withdrew across the Ebro and wintered in New Carthage.

In the following spring Hasdrubal came north again with his army and a fleet of forty ships under Himilco. They camped near the mouth of the Ebro and there Himilco was surprised by a mixed force of Roman and Massiliot galleys (for Publius Scipio had taken at least half his fleet back to Italy). The thirty-five vessels under the Roman flag gained a complete victory – the Massiliots were experts in naval warfare and had an old score to settle with Carthage – and twenty-five of Himilco's ships were driven ashore and captured and four sunk. The Roman fleet followed up its success by raiding the enemy-held coast and the Balearic and Pityussae Islands. The victory at sea was an important one, for it gave Scipio the command of the Spanish waters. The Carthaginian home government sent a fleet into northern waters to cut the sea communications between Italy and northern Spain, but it retired before the consular fleet from Ostia after a trifling success and allowed Publius Scipio, with twenty warships, eight thousand men and a large supply convoy, to sail from Italy and rejoin his brother in Spain. It says something for the good long-term strategic sense of the Roman Senate that it was prepared to send so many men out of Italy to reinforce the Spanish theatre immeditely after the disaster of Lake Trasimene. However its decision may have been partly influenced by a wish on the part of the dictator Fabius to have his ablest political rival and the chief proponent of the aggressive strategy out of the country.

On his arrival Publius assumed the command of the army. Hasdrubal was occupied in suppressing a native revolt, and so the Romans were able to advance across the Ebro as far as Saguntum. There they released a number of important Iberians who were being held as hostages by the Carthaginians and restored them to their own people, thus establishing a valuable fund of good will. However, having no base south of the Ebro they fell back on Catalonia for the winter, during which further supplies reached them from Italy. The following year produced no outstanding military event. The Scipios were engaged in extending their influence north of the Ebro while Hasdrubal was obliged to suppress a revolt of the Turdetani, a powerful tribe living in the Baetis Valley, the heartland of the Punic province. Since the Scipios' primary duty was now to ensure that no reinforcements reached Hannibal from Spain they were forced to adopt a defensive strategy towards Hasdrubal, allowing him to come to them so that they could always put their army across his path and bring him to battle, with their base close behind them and his three weeks' march away.

In the spring of the next year (215) Hasdrubal received reinforcements from Africa and also, according to Livy, specific instructions to reinforce Hannibal in Italy; for the prestige of the Barcine faction stood high after Cannae. He therefore marched north and found the Scipios besieging the important strategic town of Ibera which stood on the south bank of the Ebro which with Dertosa on the north bank commanded the river crossing. The two armies were evenly matched, with about twenty-five thousand men on each side, for what was to be a critically important battle, for if Hasdrubal won he would be able to re-establish Carthage's shaken suzerainty over the tribes of Catalonia and the road to Italy would be open. It has been suggested that he intended to repeat his brother's success at Cannae, using the same tactics; but his centre, which consisted of Spaniards (regarded as expendable, like Hannibal's Gauls), broke under the impact of the Roman charge, his cavalry fled from the field and the greater part of his African and mercenary infantry which composed the wings – the flower of his army – was cut to pieces. The Scipios had won Rome's first important victory of the war in the field, a victory as crushing as Lake Trasimene and one whose long-term effect upon the course and outcome of the war was most significant. Hasdrubal had lost his army and had to appeal for help to Carthage. Carthage, more concerned about the security of Spain than about the welfare of Hannibal, sent him 12,000 infantry, 1,500 cavalry and 25 elephants, which had been intended for Italy and which his younger brother Mago now brought to Spain, together with 1,000 talents of silver for the hire of Iberian mercenaries. The 60 ships that escorted this convoy might have been of decisive value to the Spanish command had they remained in Spain, but Carthage was short of ships – or perhaps, like Rome, short of rowers – and they returned home. Not only, therefore, had Hannibal no immediate prospect of seeing his brother enter Italy: he could expect no reinforcements from Carthage either.

Even after the victory of Ibera, however, the Scipios did not feel strong enough to undertake an offensive against southern Spain, where the native tribes would be less likely to favour the invader. A lack of repair-and-maintenance facilities and a shortage of rowers had apparently caused the Romans to lay up their warships and without additional troops and adequate naval support it would have been very dangerous to strike down the coast road at southern Spain. Therefore the Scipios, after receiving further stores from home supplied by three companies of Roman contractors, occupied themselves between 215 and 212 with steadily enlarging the area of Roman sovereignty south of the Ebro, winning over many tribes and finally recovering Saguntum, the key to the largest fertile plain on the east coast, which would provide a valuable forward base for a subsequent offensive against New Carthage and the Baetis Valley. After 214 Hasdrubal had been able to offer no serious resistance to their advance because he had been obliged to withdraw troops and even go himself to deal with a defection from his alliance on the part of Syphax, King of the Masaesyles. Syphax was at this time engaged in uniting the nomadic tribes under his rule and building them

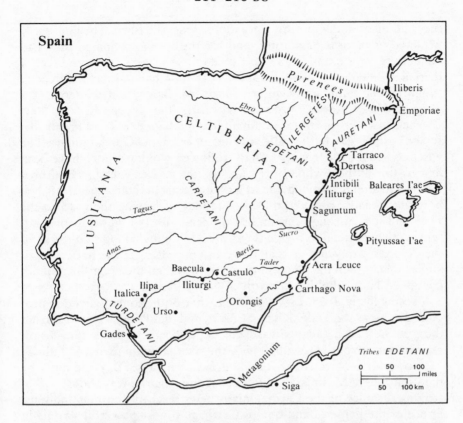

Spain

Pyrenees
Iliberis
Emporiae
Ebro
CELTIBERIA
ILERGETES
EDETANI
AURETANI
Tarraco
Dertosa
Intibili
Iliturgi
Baleares I'ae
Saguntum
LUSITANIA
CARPETANI
Tagus
Sucro
Pityussae I'ae
Anas
Baetis
Tader
Acra Leuce
Baecula
Castulo
Ilipa
Iliturgi
Italica
Orongis
Carthago Nova
Urso
TURDETANI
Gades
Tribes EDETANI
Metagonium
0   50   100
—————— miles
50   100 km
Siga

up into a formidable Numidian kingdom that should enable him to treat
with the Carthaginians as one Mediterranean power with another. It
seems likely that he had now taken advantage of Hasdrubal's defeat in
Spain to encroach on Carthage's dominions, and he negotiated with the
Scipios, who sent him a Roman centurion to train his people in infantry
fighting, in return for which he brought about the desertion of many
Numidians from the Carthaginian army in Spain. Following a Carthaginian defeat Hasdrubal encouraged Syphax's eastern neighbour and
rival kingdom-builder, King Gaia of the Massyles on Carthage's south-
western borders, to make war on him – a war in which Gaia's seven-
teen-year-old son Masinissa distinguished himself. However by the end of
212 Syphax appears to have returned to his allegiance, for we find
Hasdrubal back in Spain and the young Masinissa there, too, commanding a body of Numidian horse.

The Scipios knew that the enemy had regrouped for a vigorous resump-
tion of the struggle in 211; but this time, having a strong base at
Saguntum and the aid of Iberian tribes, they decided to risk taking the
offensive against the Carthaginians rather than abandon the gains that

they had made and withdraw once more across the Ebro. They probably wintered at or near Saguntum, and for the spring campaign they had about twenty thousand Roman and allied troops and the same number of Iberian auxiliaries. It would appear that they had no naval forces in support. One Punic army, under Hasdrubal Barca, had wintered at a place called Amtorgis, probably covering the approaches to New Carthage, two other armies, commanded by Mago Barca and Hasdrubal son of Gisgo, were in the valley of the upper Baetis (Guadalquivir). The wiser course for the Scipios to have followed would seem to have been first to throw their whole force against the nearer enemy, Hasdrubal Barca, and after destroying him to march against his colleagues. Possibly, however, because they did not like the idea of leaving the road to the Ebro and Italy through central Spain open, with two Punic armies unfought, they decided to divide their forces; Publius taking two-thirds of the legionary army and marching to crush the enemy in the Baetis Valley while Gnaeus with the remaining one-third and all the Spanish auxiliary contained Hasdrubal Barca north of New Carthage.

It seems likely, from Livy's account, that both Roman generals proceeded as far as the Tader River (Segura), and that Publius marched from there up the Tader Valley towards the upper Baetis, and that Gnaeus remained to confront Hasdrubal, with the river between them. As Publius got closer to his objective he found his march harassed day and night by the attentions of Masinissa's Numidians; and when he was almost within striking distance of the Carthaginians news reached him that Indibilis, Prince of the Ilergetes and one of Carthage's most powerful vassals in Spain, was approaching with 7,500 men to reinforce the enemy. Deciding that he must at all costs prevent this junction of hostile forces he made a night march with the bulk of his army, leaving his legate Ti. Fonteius in charge of the camp, and fell upon Indibilis on the march. Unfortunately Masinissa discovered what was happening and rode up in time to take the Romans in flank, and the three bodies of troops were still locked in untidy combat when the main Punic army came upon the scene and charged the Romans in the rear. Scipio fell fighting, his army broke and fled, and only a small portion of it was saved by the fall of night from the pursuit of the horsemen and light infantry, and escaped to join Fonteius in the camp. The next day the Carthaginians proceeded by forced marches to unite their armies with that of Hasdrubal Barca on the Tader.

Gnaeus Scipio had been having his troubles, too. Hasdrubal, well acquainted with the ways of Spaniards, had made contact with Gnaeus' allies and persuaded them by means of lavish bribes not indeed to change sides but to withdraw into neutrality, so that Scipio found himself deprived in a single day of nearly three-quarters of his fighting strength. Livy says that he at once retreated, closely followed by Hasdrubal, but it is perhaps better to suppose that he remained in his camp with his front protected by the river until the arrival on the scene of Hasdrubal's colleagues. He now had in front of him a concentration of enemy forces many times as strong as his own and he realized that if his brother's army had been destroyed (as he more than suspected) his position was hopeless. Accordingly he withdrew by night up the Tader Valley, but once again, with the return of daylight, the remorseless attacks of the Numidians brought the Roman column to a halt and Scipio decided to make what he must have known would be his last stand on a low hill near Ilorci (Lorqui). The hill-top was too bare and its covering of soil too thin to permit the construction of defensive fieldworks; but the Romans threw up an improvised breastwork of pack-saddles and baggage and fought well enough against overwhelming odds for a large number to escape from the trap into the forest and so make their way to Fonteius' camp. The very inconsequentiality of the tradition that Gnaeus Scipio was killed on the twenty-ninth day after his brother lends it a certain credibility.

Fonteius made good his retreat across the Ebro and there a camp was fortified. As their commander the soldiers elected Septimius, who had served under Gnaeus Scipio and had displayed great energy and efficiency in collecting the refugees from the battles and from the garrisons of the various towns. Septimius still had the bases at Tarraco and Emporiae behind him and his sea communications with Italy were open. It is possible that Saguntum, too, continued to hold out.

The Carthaginians, however, failed to exploit their victory. Our authorities tell us that the three generals quarrelled and therefore failed to cooperate against the Romans, but this may be a somewhat simplistic explanation of the situation. If, as seems likely, Hasdrubal II was the son of the Gisgo who had met his death at the hands of the mutineers, owing, as Hamilcar's enemies would say, to the egoism of Hamilcar, he would have had family reasons for hating the Barcids. If that is so it is possible that he was sent to Spain by the home government, who continued to trust him almost to the very end, for the express purpose of preventing the re-establishment of a Barcid 'palatinate' in Spain and of ensuring that the interests of Carthage were given priority over the sending of reinforcements to Hannibal. Carthage's hold on Spain, never very secure, had been severely shaken by the successes of the Scipios, and it was of prime importance to her to re-establish her sovereignty and to get the flow of silver going again. Silver was the essential sinew of war for a state that depended on mercenaries, and the fact that Mago had brought silver to Spain seems to show how seriously the production of the Spanish mines had been disrupted.

It is not so difficult, therefore, to envisage how a bitter hostility could have developed between the three generals. Hasdrubal Barca probably pressed for action in support of Hannibal, but was unable to take it without the cooperation of the others; Mago may very well have resented the seniority claimed by an older brother who had consistently failed to perform the tasks assigned to him by Hannibal (whereas he, Mago, had played no small part in the conquest of southern Italy); while Hasdrubal Gisgonis insisted on the total subjugation of Spain before any move towards Italy could be made. Thus although they established a footing north of the Ebro and Hasdrubal II took hostages from Indibilis and his brother, who had been restored to the status of independent allies as a reward for their services, they devoted most of their efforts to the strengthening of Carthage's hold on the regions south of the river. This failure to drive the Romans out of Catalonia was to prove one of the costliest of all Carthage's mistakes in the war.

The humiliation of Hannibal, the reconquest of Campania and the success of Marcellus in Sicily gave the Senate the confidence to send reinforcements to Spain. The propraetor C. Claudius Nero was instructed to select twelve thousand Roman and Allied infantry and 1,100 cavalry from the two legions he had commanded before Capua and ship them from Puteoli to Spain. When he arrived at Tarraco he laid up his ships and armed the crews for land service and then marched to the front to take over the command. Either late in the same year or in the spring or early summer of 210, he apparently outmanœuvred Hasdrubal in the territory of the Ausetani and had him at such a disadvantage that the Carthaginian agreed to evacuate Catalonia and withdraw his forces south of the Ebro.

In the Adriatic theatre, M. Valerius Laevinus, who had his imperium prorogued each year, with Greece and Macedonia as his province, continued to watch events from his bases in the Roman protectorate. During 213 and 212 Philip was occupied in subjugating the tribes of the Illyrian hinterland; and in one of these years, probably in 212, he captured Lissus, and so not only drove a wedge between Scerdilaïdas' principality and the Roman protectorate further south but also, by giving himself an outlet to the sea and a naval base, opened up the possibility of future cooperation between his land forces and a Carthaginian fleet. This possibility became much stronger when Hannibal captured Taras (even though its citadel remained in Roman hands), and stronger still when Bomilcar brought his 130 ships into the port in the spring of 211.

Laevinus accordingly put himself in touch with the Aetolians, Macedon's inveterate enemies among the Greek powers. They had been alarmed by Philip's recent activity in Illyria and by the presence of Bomilcar's fleet at Taras, and they were also anxious to recover Acarnania, which they had lost some nineteen years earlier. Laevinus sounded their

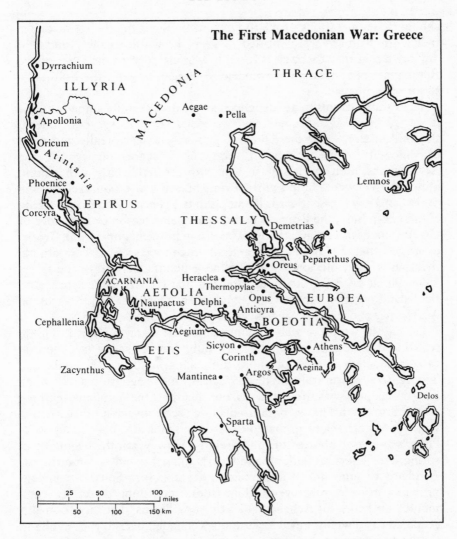

The First Macedonian War: Greece

leading men, and in the summer of 211 attended in person an extra-ordinary meeting of the synod of the confederation, where he concluded an offensive and defensive alliance against Philip. He showed himself to be a singularly skilful diplomatist, and for the trifling price of Rome's participation in the war against Philip with not less than twenty-five quinqueremes (which was probably as many as he could find crews for), and the promise to assist in the conquest of Acarnania and to hand it over, when conquered, to the Aetolians, he ensured that Philip would be kept fully occupied in Greece for the next few years and thus be prevented from either assisting Hannibal or attacking Rome's allies. Nor should these operations prove too expensive, since, by the terms of the treaty, the Romans were entitled to keep the whole of the plunder of any town that they themselves took. It was left open to the allies of the Aetolians – Elis, Messene, Lacedaemon, Pergamum and the Epirotes – to join the alliance.

The validity of this treaty depended solely on Laevinus' imperium, for it was not ratified at Rome until two years later. It was not, indeed, the kind of treaty that the Romans' public conscience really approved of, since it involved them in unprovoked aggression against the Acarnanians, and, inevitably, in war with the Achaeans, with whom, although they were Philip's allies, Rome herself had no quarrel. On the other hand it was essential for Rome's safety to keep Philip from helping Hannibal in Italy, the Romans had no particular reason to be tender of Greek feelings in 211, and there was nothing in the history of the Greeks to suggest that they needed any external encouragement to fight among themselves. Laevinus lost no time in implementing his part of the agreement. He at once attacked and captured first the city of Zacynthus on the island of the same name, and then Oeniadae and Nasus in Acarnania, and handed them over to the Aetolians.

During the winter, which Laevinus passed at Corcyra (Corfu), Philip, realizing that he was going to have trouble on his hands in Greece in 210, conducted a series of short campaigns in Illyria, Thessaly and Thrace, so as to forestall and discourage any move against his rear when he was occupied with the Aetolians. For their part the Aetolians, learning that Philip was in Thrace, organized a large-scale invasion of Acarnania, which the Acarnanians prepared to resist to the death; but the report of Philip's approach aborted the undertaking. However at the beginning of spring 210, Laevinus sailed round to Naupactus and summoned the Aetolians to join him in attacking Anticyra (Aspra Spitia) in Phocis, probably in order to prevent Philip from establishing direct sea communications with his Achaean allies through Phocis. The city soon surrendered to Laevinus' naval force and was handed over to the Aetolians, the Romans taking the booty. Shortly afterwards the news came that Laevinus had, in his absence, been elected consul for 210 and that the proconsul P. Sulpicius Galba was on his way to replace him.

By the end of the consular year 211/10 it must have been clear to almost everyone concerned that the tide of war had not only turned in Rome's favour but was now flowing strongly. The spectacular failure of Hannibal to relieve Capua, coupled with his failure to take Rhegium and the citadel of Taras, and the reduction and punishment of the Campani, had damaged beyond immediate repair his hopes of extending the area of revolt. It is true that there had been rumblings in Etruria and Umbria, where the propraetor Silanus still maintained an armed presence, but there was little likelihood of serious revolt there unless Hannibal came north to foment it. However Hannibal could not come north, because the Bruttii and Lucani who now supplied the bulk of his army would not march so far from their own country. In Sicily, Carthage had suffered a military defeat, and the fall of Syracuse – a city which had in its time defied the greatest naval powers of the classical as well as of the Hellenistic world – helped to rub home the awful lesson of Rome's invincibility. At sea, although the fact that Carthage's fleet could spend the summer with impunity in an Italian port must have heartened the southern rebels, yet the Roman navy had not been destroyed, and it had even struck a heavy blow at Africa. In the Adriatic, Laevinus' diplomacy and ruthless activity had virtually taken Philip out of the Hannibalic War. On the debit side (from Rome's point of view) there was the disaster in Spain. Rome's economy, too, was still showing signs of strain and steps had been taken, probably this year, to stabilize the currency. The weight of the bronze as, the standard monetary unit, was fixed at two ounces (it had been six in 216) and a new silver issue, that of the *denarius*, was introduced, with a value of ten asses.

If the Scipios had continued their successful progress in Spain Hannibal might perhaps have been ordered to put the poor remnants of his splendid Spanish army onto Bomilcar's ships and bring them home. There must have been moments during that summer when Hannibal was sorely tempted to do so, without waiting to be ordered. It might have been better for him and for his City if he had done so; for provided that he escaped crucifixion, the customary penalty for failure – and his following among the people might perhaps have ensured his safety – he would have been able to unify and revitalize the command in Spain and drive the Romans out of Catalonia. With his departure from Italy the Fabians would probably have been prepared to make a negotiated peace with Carthage, and the final settlement of accounts between the two greatest powers of the western Mediterranean would have taken place under very different conditions from those of 149 BC. Yet it was by refusing to admit defeat that the Romans had remained undefeated, and the Romans had shown that they were still afraid to meet Hannibal in the field. As long as there was hope of Hasdrubal's bringing into Italy a fresh army with elephants, and that hope had in 211 become a much better one, there was still a possibility, however slim, that the genius of Hannibal could win a war that now was beginning to look as good as lost.

At the elections for 210, Marcellus and Laevinus were elected consuls, following the withdrawal of T. Manlius Torquatus, and received the Sicilian and Italian theatres respectively as their provinces, which they subsequently exchanged following complaints against Marcellus' harshness by the Syracusans. Of the outgoing consuls, Galba replaced Laevinus and Centumalus returned after conducting the elections to Apulia, where he commanded two legions. Although both the new consuls had imposing reputations as men of action the year started quietly, for Laevinus fell seriously ill in Greece and Marcellus refused to conduct any public business until his arrival. Twenty-one legions were enrolled – the first reduction in their number since the outbreak of war – but a proposal once again to pay for the manning of the navy by a levy on all property owners rated at over fifty thousand asses provoked an outcry. However, on the motion of Laevinus, the senators set an example of patriotism by voluntarily handing over the greater part of their valuables to the banking commission that had been established in 216, and their example was followed first by the equites and then by the people, so that sufficient funds were made available.

In Italy Hannibal began to reap the consequences of his failure to save the Campani. The people of Salapia made overtures to Marcellus and surrendered the city to him and only fifty of the five hundred Numidians who formed the garrison and who resisted furiously survived, to fall alive into the hands of the enemy. Militarily disastrous as the loss of this large body of irreplaceable horsemen was, the blow to Hannibal's prestige was more serious, and with four legions operating in northern Apulia, he retired into Bruttium. Marcellus now moved into Samnium, where he captured two of the enemy's garrisoned supply depots, leaving the pro-consul Cn. Fulvius Centumalus encamped before the important road centre of Herdonea, whose government, after Hannibal's withdrawal, was preparing to follow the example of its neighbours.

Hannibal could not afford to let another ally go so easily. Knowing that the consul was occupied in Samnium he executed one of those forced marches that helped to make his name a terror, and was advancing upon Centumalus' camp with his army in order of battle before the proconsul could get a message to Marcellus. Centumalus would have done better to refuse battle – his army was the weaker and he had no battle experience – but he decided to fight and drawing up his legions one behind the other attacked the enemy gallantly. Hannibal allowed the Roman infantry to become fully committed to the clash of the centres and then loosed his cavalry in an encircling movement onto the rear of the enemy and against his camp. The result was the rout of the proconsular army, the death of its general and the capture of its camp. Roman losses may have been as high as thirteen thousand; the survivors made their way to Marcellus' camp in Samnium. Even so Hannibal was compelled to acknowledge the grim military truth – that with Aecae and Salapia in enemy hands, he had lost his hold on northern Apulia. Accordingly he burnt Herdonea and evacuated its population to Metapontum and Thurii, and he put to death the leading men, on the grounds that they had been negotiating with Centumalus. These actions should be regarded as deterrent rather than retributive: they were intended as a warning to his remaining Apulian and Samnite allies. The whole of the great fertile plain of the Tavoliere was now back under Roman control.

The various points of similarity between this Roman disaster and that of 212 have led many modern historians to dismiss the earlier one as a 'doublet' or retrojection of the later, following the lead of De Sanctis, a great believer in 'doublets'. There is, however, no really good reason to do so. The coincidence of name and place is not all that remarkable, given the facts that Herdonea was a key town of Apulia and that both Fulvian generals undoubtedly operated in that region. On the other hand it would be remarkable, ancient historiography being what it was, if in the tradition some of the details of the one event did not become confused with those of the other.

After the battle Hannibal retired over the border to the neighbourhood of Numistro in Lucania, and Marcellus marched south to confront him. An inconclusive engagement between the two armies, in which Hannibal's elephants played a part, was followed by the withdrawal by night of the Carthaginians into Apulia, where the two armies played a kind of game of tag for the remainder of the summer, with Hannibal trying to lure Marcellus into a trap and Marcellus, sticking tenaciously to his enemy, refusing to be lured. At Taras the situation of the garrison had become little short of desperate following Bomilcar's sojourn in the outer harbour the previous summer, and the prefect at Rhegium, Decimus Quinctius, assembled a scratch squadron of twenty ships in order to escort a supply convoy from Sicily. Nico, the Tarantine admiral, who also had twenty ships, met the Romans at the entrance to the Gulf of Taranto and after a fierce engagement Quinctius was killed and his fleet sunk or driven ashore and subsequently captured. Later in the year, however, a convoy carrying grain and a thousand soldiers got through from Ostia.

In 210 Laevinus completed the pacification of Sicily. Arriving late in the year he first established some kind of order at Syracuse and then marched to Acragas, where the former hostility between Hanno and the half-caste Myttones had developed into an open breach between them. Myttones, dismissed from his command, negotiated with Laevinus and then opened the harbour gate to the Romans. Hanno and Epicydes made their escape to Africa with a handful of companions, the garrison (apart from the treacherous Numidians) was butchered and the city was taken. The leading Acragantines were executed and the remainder sold – many, no doubt, being purchased and restored to liberty by neighbouring communities, as had been done fifty-two years earlier. Following the capture of Acragas the remaining Sicilian towns, apart from six that were stormed, were betrayed or returned voluntarily to their allegiance. Laevinus punished and rewarded as circumstances dictated, and exerted himself to get the island's agriculture back to full production and the flow of grain to Italy restored. A band of four thousand deserters, broken men and criminals of every kind, who had occupied Agathyrna was shipped over to Rhegium and told to indulge their criminal proclivities at the expense of the Bruttii. Myttones was subsequently given Roman citizenship by a tribunician law and as M. Valerius Myttones did good service as a commander of Numidian auxiliaries under L. Scipio in Asia. M. Valerius Messalla was sent with fifty ships on a reconnaissance raid to Utica and brought back reports of Carthaginian preparations to reinforce Spain and recover Sicily. In fact the Punic fleet which was said to be intended for Sicily later raided Sardinia and carried off considerable plunder.

The reaction of the Sicilian cities in favour of Carthage during the war was no doubt primarily due to the realization, born of nearly thirty years' experience of Roman suzerainty, that under Rome political liberty, as the Greeks understood the term, was a thing of the past. This feeling, so easily aroused in Greeks and encouraged by Carthaginian promises of complete autonomy, was stimulated to the point of revolt by the barbarity (according to the advanced standards of Hellenistic civilization) of Rome's treatment of captured cities and revolted and even wavering allies. Yet in most cases we may be sure that faction (*stasis*) – party politics taken to excess, the ancient curse of the Greek *polis* – was responsible for the fatal change of allegiance. From first to last Carthage sent some thirty-nine thousand men to Sicily, almost the equivalent of two consular armies. It was Rome's good fortune that she chose careless and dilatory men to lead them and a coward to command her fleet. The Romans were allowed to keep the initiative throughout the war in Sicily and in Marcellus they had a soldier who knew how to take advantage of the gift. All Sicily became a Roman province, in which two cities enjoyed the status of allies and five that of free cities. The rest were subjects, paying tithes according to the system previously employed in the kingdom of Hiero (*Lex Hieronica*), or (where their land had become Roman public land) both tithes and rent.

In Greece, the war moved out of the western theatre into the eastern, where Philip was active in securing his communications with Euboea and central Greece. The proconsul P. Sulpicius Galba took his ships into the Aegean, and although he failed to prevent the capture of Echinus and Phalara on the Maliac Gulf, he took Aegina. This island was sold to King Attalus of Pergamum for thirty talents and became Rome's base in the Aegean. The Romano-Aetolian alliance was further strengthened this year by the adherence of Sparta, now ruled by the tyrant Machanidas, Elis and Messene. King Attalus was chosen generalissimo for the ensuing year.

The most significant event of the year, however, occurred at Rome itself, in connection with the choice of a long-term commander for Spain. In the eyes of the Senate and of the leading military men Spain was essentially a side-show, like Greece. The primary rôle of the Spanish army was defensive – to prevent reinforcements from reaching Hannibal over-land. And Spain was also uncomfortable and dangerous. Only five new families had been admitted to the nobility since 225, and by 210 men experienced in military leadership, mostly ex-consuls, were running very short indeed and could not be spared – and had no wish to be spared – for peripheral commands. C. Claudius Nero was needed at Rome to win a consulship for the Claudii. Casualties among ex-consuls had been heavy, particularly among the Aemilian party, who, with the deaths of the Scipios, had become almost wholly dependent upon the younger generation, which was not a numerous one. They were, however, making the beginnings of a recovery with the assistance of popular favour, for war-weariness, now that the immediate danger had receded, was finding expression in popular dissatisfaction with the inconclusiveness of the Fabian policy and with its exponents. So young P. Cornelius Scipio, the son of the consul of 218 and son-in-law of the L. Aemilius Paullus who fell at Cannae, who had shown a soldier's courage at the Ticinus and outstanding qualities of leadership after Cannae, gained the curule aedile-ship in 213, in spite of tribunician opposition on the grounds of his youth and administrative inexperience. He repaid the people and established a counter-claim on their gratitude by giving them a largesse (*congiarium*) of oil on the occasion of his games, in the manner of a Hellenistic king. In 212 the young P. Licinius Crassus Dives not only achieved the aedile-ship but also the office of chief priest (*pontifex maximus*), against such formidable Fabian opponents as Torquatus and the consul Q. Fulvius Flaccus. In 210 he was elected to the censorship, never having held a curule office, with L. Veturius Philo (the consul of 220), and they rein-stated M. Livius Salinator, Paullus' colleague of 219, in the Senate. When, therefore, in 210 the Senate decided that the Centuriate Assembly should be left to choose someone to go as proconsul to carry on the war in Spain and P. Scipio put himself forward he was unanimously elected.

The granting of proconsular imperium to a man who had never held magisterial imperium was an unprecedented step, for Marcellus, consul and triumphator in 222, had at least been elected consul in 215, even though he was obliged to abdicate almost at once. It was therefore prob-ably a feeling of legal disquietude that caused the Senate to associate with Scipio the propraetor M. Iunius Silanus, who had commanded as prefect the garrison at Naples and subsequently, as praetor and propraetor, an army in Etruria. The true state of affairs is obscured by the intrusion of the 'Scipionic legend'; but it may be that Silanus was formally given Spain north of the Ebro as his province, while Scipio was entrusted with the war against the Carthaginians – a similar state of affairs to that which obtained in Sicily under the commands-in-chief of Marcellus, Cethegus and Laevinus. Scipio was given ten thousand infantry and one thousand cavalry, probably drawn from the legion disbanded in Campania, and an escort force of thirty quinqueremes, and towards the end of the year sailed from Ostia to Emporiae, where he landed his army. From Emporiae he marched to Tarraco, where Nero handed over the province to Silanus and returned to Rome. Scipio now had over thirty thousand men in winter quarters, not counting the crews of the ships, and could plan with confidence an offensive to be undertaken in the following spring against the enemy, whose three winter quarters were widely dispersed over central and south-west Spain.

CHAPTER XV

210-208 BC

Scipio in Spain.

When the time for holding the elections for 209 came around, neither consul wished to leave his province; Marcellus because he did not consider it advisable to lose touch with Hannibal, Laevinus in view of the report of Carthaginian preparations for an invasion of Sicily brought back by Messalla. Laevinus did in fact visit Rome and agreed to appoint a dictator to hold the elections, but a deadlock ensued over the question, whom should he appoint? And so Laevinus, refusing to be dictated to by the Assembly, returned to Sicily and left it to his colleague to nominate the people's choice, Q. Fulvius Flaccus, who was currently engaged as proconsul in settling the affairs of Capua. Flaccus appointed Crassus as his master of horse and in the elections which he conducted, Flaccus himself, after a sharp legal tussle with the tribunes, was chosen consul for the fourth time, together with Q. Fabius Maximus, for the fifth. With the aggressive Marcellus back in Italy and the people – and, indeed, the whole of Italy – clamouring for an end to the war, it was clearly desirable from Fabius' point of view to reinforce by personal authority the sacrosanctity of the Fabian strategy.

War-weariness was beginning to find expression in the Councils and Assemblies of the Latins and allies; for although Rome laid a relatively much heavier burden upon herself than upon the confederacy, the direction of the war, and with it the responsibility for its many defeats and appalling casualties, rested entirely in her hands. The bulk of the Cannae legions was made up of Latins and allies, and the survivors of both the Herdonea disasters, similarly constituted, had been sent to Sicily on the same penal terms for the duration of the war. It was one thing, the allies felt, for Rome to adopt a draconian policy towards her own citizens and quite another to do so towards theirs. Now twelve out of the thirty Latin colonies formally declared that, having been bled white of men of military age, they could not contribute their required quotas of soldiers. All, with the exception of Cales in Campania, were situated in areas remote from the theatres of war; and it is clear that they had been called upon to make good the deficiencies of the south, where the loyal cities had been less seriously hit by the levy, both because of the difficulties of conducting it and because they had the tasks of defending their own territories, policing the adjacent areas of revolt and providing food for themselves and for the armies operating in their neighbourhood. The Senate was naturally alarmed by what to many looked like the beginning of the break-up of the confederacy; but the spontaneous expressions of loyalty on the part of the remaining Latin colonies restored its confidence and it decided that the most dignified rejoinder was to ignore the existence of the twelve 'rebels' and so hope to shame them into voluntary compliance with their obligations – at least until the proper time arrived for dealing with them more sternly. They were not in fact punished until 204. Yet a further sign of the long-term effect of Fabianism upon the economy was the withdrawal of four thousand pounds of gold from the fund reserved for extreme emergency, the *aerarium sanctius*.

However Fabianism did not discountenance limited offensive operations that did not involve giving battle to Hannibal, and it was decided this year to retake Taras. Fabius had that task assigned to him, using the army that had been training and at the same time policing Etruria. Flaccus, with Laevinus' legions sent from Sicily, was to command in Lucania, and Marcellus, whose imperium had been prorogued, in Apulia, in order to keep Hannibal from interfering. Thus six legions, over fifty-five thousand horse and foot, were concentrated in southern Italy. Laevinus, retained as commander-in-chief in Sicily, sent thirty quinqueremes to assist in the siege, while his four thousand Sicilian brigands, supplemented by as many Bruttian deserters, were let loose upon Bruttium, first to ravage the countryside and then to attack Caulonia.

In the early summer Hannibal marched to Canusium, hoping that it could be induced to revolt, but on the approach of Marcellus, who had C. Claudius Nero as one of his legates, he retired, repeating the tactics of the previous summer. Finally, however, the two armies camped in such close proximity that serious fighting became unavoidable, and the Romans appear to have had the worse of a slogging match of the kind that they could afford better than Hannibal. At all events Hannibal, who now withdrew into Bruttium, was able to keep the field for the rest of the summer, while Marcellus' force had been so severely handled that it retired to Venusia and stayed there. The Roman tradition admits the loss of 5,700 men killed – and if that is so there must have been at least as many wounded.

Meanwhile Flaccus was reconquering the Hirpini, making some progress in Lucania and conducting negotiations with certain of the Bruttii. In southern Bruttium Hannibal was summoned to the rescue of Caulonia and captured the attacking force. Nonetheless the latter, like Marcellus and Flaccus, had done what was required of them and kept Hannibal away from Calabria, where Fabius first took the town of Manduria and then marched to Taras and camped at the entrance to the harbour. A Carthaginian naval force had earlier put in at Taras but had then moved off to Corcyra to assist King Philip, so that Laevinus' thirty battleships commanded the Gulf; and it was from the sea that the consul prepared to attack the city, using warships and merchantmen as artillery platforms and assault vessels. However things were made easy for Fabius, as the infatuation of the commander of the Bruttian detachment in the city for the sister of one of Fabius' soldiers gave the consul an ally within the walls. Under cover of darkness he took his land forces around to the east side of the town, and when mock attacks from the directions of the citadel and the sea had stripped the wall on his side of its defenders he broke into the sector held by the Bruttians and by first light had his men in battle order in the marketplace. A massacre followed in which Carthalo, the garrison commander, was killed, and the city was sacked. An immense quantity of gold and silver was seized – a godsend for Rome's empty treasury – while the works of art taken away almost rivalled those seized at Syracuse.

The subsequent treatment of Taras was lenient, the city being restored to the pro-Roman elements and preserving its treaty with Rome. It was, however, obliged to surrender a large part of its fertile territory to the Roman people, and it never recovered either its former prosperity or its importance. Hannibal had hurried up from Caulonia to raise the siege, and pitched camp less than five miles from the city. He then retired to Metapontum and endeavoured to lure Fabius into an ambush, but the consul's suspicions had been roused and the plan was discovered. For his success – a remarkably cheap one in terms of Roman lives – Fabius was awarded a triumph.

In Spain Scipio ordered his land and sea forces and the contingents of his Iberian allies to muster at the mouth of the Ebro at the beginning of spring. His plan of campaign – as logical as it was audacious – was to seize New Carthage, the capital of the Spanish province and its principal arsenal and treasury. By doing so he would secure what his father had always lacked, a maritime base in the south of the Peninsula, whose capture would at once deprive the enemy of their best and most convenient port for the maintenance of sea communications with Numidia and Carthage, give Scipio control over the silver-mining area in the hinterland and provide a springboard for the invasion of the Baetis Valley. Moreover the moral effect of such a success upon the Spanish tribes could not fail to be tremendous. But to achieve success he would have to move with the celerity and plan his actual attack with the ingenuity of Hannibal himself. Of his capacity, with the help of the gods, to do both these things he did not entertain a doubt.

P. Cornelius Scipio was, like Hannibal, a military genius. To a splendid intelligence and breadth of vision he added the same personal magnetism which causes men to continue to follow one leader and die for him long after they would have given in under another. He also had that mysterious gift which is sometimes called 'timing': the instinctive awareness of what stroke to play and of the precise moment to play it. All genius is rare and military genius cannot, in the nature of things, be rarer than any other kind. It only seems to be so because it demands certain conditions in order to enable it to manifest itself, which are only very exceptionally encountered in advanced societies; for military genius is a flower of civilization, not of primitive barbarism. Given that a man has the natural endowments, five things more are needed if he is not to remain 'mute, inglorious'. He needs a war of some magnitude, swift elevation to high command, a tenure of command extending over several years, complete freedom of action and an adequate supply of human raw material out of which to forge the tools of his trade.

Stable societies, democracies and oligarchies alike, are inimical to military as to political genius. They are jealous of the individuality, the egoism, the unconventionality of genius. Military genius is only permitted to flourish in 'frontier' conditions, either when it is implanted in an autocrat – or in the trusted servant of an autocrat – or when the stability of a society has broken down, as in time of revolution, or when it is transplanted to a physical frontier – to a distant theatre of war in which it is given the time and the untrammelled freedom to develop. So it had been with Hannibal in Spain and so it was now with Scipio. If it had not been for the destruction of his father and his uncle, and if the Roman political system had not left the nobility so short of experienced leaders, Scipio would never have been given the opportunity of realizing his full potentiality as a general. Released however from his father's control by the latter's death, and set free, in Spain, from the watchfulness of envious colleagues, jealous tribunes and a suspicious Senate, he was allowed to become what Rome had such need of at that juncture: a general at least the equal of Hannibal. Like Hannibal he enjoyed the game of war, but as a means only, not as an end. His family, for all its popular sympathies, had not broken free from the bonds of class and society, nor had he been brought up on 'the frontier'. Scipio could not have rejected the nobility or subordinated Rome's interests to his own. He looked to his country to reward him for his services with honour and distinction, but unless these were freely bestowed he would not demean himself by contending or intriguing for them, much less would he lend himself to an attack upon the established order.

It is sometimes asked whether Scipio really believed in the gods whom he regularly invoked, or even, if he was a mystic. Polybius, who talked to men who had known Scipio, attributed to him characteristics of which he himself approved – and indeed helped to inculcate – in Scipio's adoptive grandson Aemilianus, and in particular Hellenistic rationalism, coupled with the calculating pragmatism that was prepared to exploit superstition in others. But the elder Scipio, born in 236, belonged to a generation that was mentally closer to Aeschylus than to Polybius. The gods were an established fact, part of the furniture of the universe and of the city; beings with very similar attitudes of mind and sympathies to his own, the magnates of an aristocratic society. It would be natural for them to assist one of their own kind who displayed the sense of duty (*pietas*), the prudence and the audacity that would win their approval. Brought up in a world of aristocratic alliances Scipio will have regarded his relationship with the gods, and especially with Jupiter, to whom he showed a special devotion, as that between one uniquely gifted aristocrat and another; as, no doubt, Hannibal viewed his relationship with Melqart.

Scipio had fought against Hannibal at the Ticinus, perhaps at the Trebia, and at Cannae, and he had devoted, we may be sure, a great deal of thought to the identification of what it was, apart from the genius of the commander, that made the Punic army superior to the Roman. When he found himself with truly independent command, he set about transforming an army that had hitherto been regarded tactically as a single monolithic body of infantry with weak cavalry support into a composite body, made up of separate heavy infantry, light infantry and cavalry units, each of which might be required to manoeuvre independently on the field of battle. In order to achieve this aim, he had to train a team of unit commanders, and for material on which to work he had Silanus, his own brother Lucius, C. Laelius and L. Marcius Septimius, whose good will he had been at pains to cultivate. These men were to be to him what men like Mago, Hanno and Maharbal had been to Hannibal.

As previously in Spain, and as in other theatres, the Carthaginians were proving a very convenient enemy. Scipio had learnt from Hannibal the importance of intelligence and reconnaissance, and his intelligence service told him that the three Punic armies were still widely dispersed, with Mago in the region of Gibraltar, Hasdrubal Gisgonis near the mouth of the Tagus and Hasdrubal Barca engaged in suppressing a local revolt among the Carpetani on the upper Tagus. Clearly the Punic generals, quite apart from their mutual antipathy, were finding that they had enough to do in keeping down the native tribes, and had decided to allow the Romans to come to them, in the belief that they would have ample warning of their approach down the coast road and therefore ample time to concentrate their forces to destroy them. Not one of them was within ten days' march of New Carthage.

Silanus remained north of the Ebro with 3,000 foot and 500 horse, while Scipio took the rest of his army, 25,000 foot and 2,500 horse, by forced marches south to New Carthage. C. Laelius brought the fleet of 35 ships, all seriously undermanned, into the harbour at the same time. Possession of the command of the sea meant that even if Scipio failed to take the town before the Carthaginian armies arrived on the scene he could still maintain himself in his camp, pitched on the neck of land that connects the city with the mainland on the east. During the winter Scipio had made himself thoroughly acquainted, by interrogation of fishermen and others possessed of local knowledge, with the topography and peculiarities of New Carthage. He had learnt that it was built on a hilly isthmus, like so many Phoenician cities and that the circuit of its walls was about twenty *stades* (2,300 yards). The northern section was washed by the waters of a shallow lagoon (today the marshy plain of Almajar) and the southern by those of the Gulf of Cartagena, at the head of which the city stands, while a man-made canal connected lagoon and sea on the west side. Scipio's camp occupied the whole width of the isthmus (about four hundred yards) and was fortified on the eastern side but not on the side facing the city, where the difficulties of the terrain were considered to offer sufficient protection to the besiegers against a sortie by the garrison, which numbered only a thousand soldiers. However Mago, the garrison commander, had also hurriedly armed two thousand of the townsfolk, who were for the most part tradesmen, merchants and fishermen, and posted them by the gate, and as soon as the Romans left their camp to assault the gate Mago threw his two thousand men against them. The fight was a hot one, but as more and more Romans poured out of the camp the townsmen, hopelessly outnumbered, were driven back and trampled underfoot, and the counter-attack almost carried the gate. Under Scipio's personal command the Romans now assaulted the walls, but it seems that they had misjudged their height. The scaling ladders proved too short and too few in number, while for their part the defenders, once their first panic had subsided, became bolder as they perceived the difficulties besetting the enemy. Consequently, although the fleet had also made a diversionary demonstration against the southern wall, the attack failed and the recall was sounded.

However the defenders were allowed only a very brief respite. Among the useful items of information that Scipio had acquired was the fact that when a strong north to north-east wind blew the water level in the lagoon dropped appreciably, and it became possible to wade across to the city. As these conditions now prevailed, he gave orders to renew the onslaught upon the isthmus wall with many more ladders, while the fleet pressed home its attack on the south side. At the height of the assault five hundred picked men were sent with local guides to cross the shallowest part of the lagoon and mount the unguarded northern wall towards its western end – and the valour both of this party and of the navy was stimulated by their general's assurance that Neptune was on the side of the Romans. It was subsequently adjudged that a legionary and a marine mounted the wall at the same moment. The wading party rushed towards the isthmus, sweeping the wall of defenders, the gate was opened and the wall stormed. The Romans poured in and the customary massacre of all living things followed, ending when Mago surrendered the citadel. The city was then plundered.

Of the captives those with citizen rights were given their freedom. Of the non-citizens those who were tradesmen were declared public slaves but with a conditional promise that they would be restored to liberty at the end of the war. Out of what remained of the captive population Scipio selected the best physical specimens to make up the full complements of his galleys and to man eighteen Punic ships laid up in the docks. These men, too, were promised their liberty as the reward of loyal service. A vast quantity of war material, six hundred talents' worth of gold and silver (public property), considerable stores of grain and no fewer than sixty-three merchant ships were among the booty of the town and harbour. The money and precious metals were taken in charge by the quaestor C. Flaminius, the son of the consul who had perished at Lake Trasimene.

Of all that fell into Scipio's hands at the capture of New Carthage nothing was more valuable to him than the hostages, more than three hundred in number, who had been taken by the Carthaginians from noble Iberian families and detained in the city. They included the wife of Mandonius and the daughters of Indibilis, the Princes of the Ilergetes; and the generosity and self-control of Scipio (who had the reputation of a womanizer) towards the women now in his power won him high regard in the army and among the Spaniards, and provided the material for a charming romance to be included in the already-forming Scipionic legend. He sent C. Laelius back to Rome by sea, taking with him Mago and the more important prisoners, who included two members of the Gerousia of Carthage and fifteen senators; their presence in the city showing the extent to which the home government was interesting itself in what had once been virtually a Barcid fief.

For the remainder of his stay in New Carthage, Scipio was busy training and exercising both his fleet and his army, paying particular attention to the physical fitness of his troops and to weapon training; and while it is likely that the Spanish-pattern sword came in during the First Punic War, the possibility that it was now introduced into the Roman army by Scipio cannot be ruled out. He may also have modified the throwing spear (*pilum*) incorporating features of the heavy Spanish *phalerica*. Moreover the workshops of what we may from now on call Carthago Nova were set to work under Roman management and under his own personal supervision, producing munitions of war, so that the town became a Roman arsenal established in the heart of the Punic empire. The mint was reopened to strike silver coins, now bearing the head of Scipio himself in place of that of Hannibal.

It may be said that by the end of his first campaign Scipio had shown that he possessed all the qualities that were to make him the equal of Hannibal: first-rate organizational ability, appreciation of the importance of intelligence and reconnaissance, celerity (to use the word that was applied to that 'portent', Caesar), an eye for country, personal magnetism, psychological insight, tenacity of purpose and self-control. Above all, in addition to his natural endowments he embodied the professionalism that had made Hannibal superior to the noble amateurs of Rome.

Probably late in the summer, having repaired the fortifications of the city, Scipio marched back to Tarraco taking with him the hostages and leaving Carthago Nova strongly garrisoned. On his arrival at his base headquarters he held a levee attended by all his Iberian allies, not only from north of the Ebro but from the south as well. That the three Punic armies in Spain had made no attempt to oppose his march to the south, or to make any move against New Carthage when it was in his hands, or to intercept his heavily burdened army on its return march to the Ebro, suggests that there was widespread unrest in the province inflamed by the harsh and repressive treatment with which the Carthaginians, contrary to their former practice, were attempting to re-establish their sovereignty. This hostility on the part of the natives was to prove of the utmost value to Scipio in the following summer.

In Italy Marcellus was forced to come up to Rome towards the end of the consular year in order to defend himself against an attack upon his conduct as a general by a tribune – an attack which developed into an indictment of the whole nobility. He exculpated himself so successfully that at the elections conducted by Flaccus he secured the consulship for 208 (his fifth), with his former legate in Sicily T. Quinctius Crispinus as colleague. At the same time extremely disturbing news arrived from Etruria, where the propraetor C. Calpurnius Piso was looking after internal security. Arretium was the danger point, and Marcellus was at once sent there to examine the situation, but being no doubt anxious to get back to the active front he reported that all was quiet. That it was not really so became apparent in the spring, and the new propraetor C. Hostilius Tubulus, was ordered to take hostages for the city's good behaviour. The attitude of the Arretines was so unsubmissive that even after 120 hostages had been sent to Rome C. Terentius Varro, the survivor of Cannae, was given propraetorian imperium and sent with one of the urban legions to occupy the town. The rumours which continued to come in from Africa of an intended Punic naval offensive caused orders to be sent to Scipio to send fifty ships to reinforce the defences of Sardinia; to Laevinus in Sicily to collect his whole fleet of a hundred ships and operate against Africa if he thought fit; and to the urban praetor, to commission fifty galleys for home defence. Altogether Rome had over 250 ships in, or ready for, service in 208. Twenty-one legions were mobilized.

The consul Crispinus took over Flaccus' army in Lucania. From there he proceeded south to besiege Locri, now the most important city still in Carthaginian hands, and sent to Laevinus' prefect in eastern Sicily, the future historian L. Cincius Alimentus, for artillery and ships. When Hannibal moved down to Lacinium, however, Crispinus raised the siege and retired into Apulia. There he joined forces with Marcellus, who had been detained at Rome by religious impediments and had only now – it must have been late summer – rejoined his old army and led it out of Venusia. Hannibal followed Crispinus, and he and the two consuls faced each other between Venusia and Bantia. The Romans offered battle, which Hannibal declined, but the wily Carthaginian continued to look for an opportunity to take the enemy at some disadvantage that would neutralize their superiority in numbers. However to try and achieve something before summer was over the consuls wrote to Cincius to bring his ships back to Locri and to cooperate with troops from Taras in besieging the city. Unfortunately Hannibal was warned of this move and sent a detachment to ambush the men coming from Taras, near Petelia. The Romans, moving as they so often did without reconnaissance, fell into the ambush and lost about 3,500 men, killed and captured. The survivors of the rout returned to Taras.

Then disaster overtook the consuls. Betrayed by that fatal weakness of the Roman army, the lack of subordinate officers trained to take responsible decisions in the field, Marcellus and Crispinus, with only two squadrons of allied cavalry, thirty light infantrymen and their lictors, rode out to reconnoitre a wooded hill that lay between their camps and that of Hannibal. The hill was in fact already occupied by Numidians, apparently posted there in the hope of picking off foragers or scouts, and these surrounded the reconnaissance party. Marcellus was killed and the surviving horsemen and footmen fled back to their camps, bearing with them Marcellus' colleague, mortally wounded, and his son, also hurt.

Marcellus was a grave loss to his country. Over sixty years of age, five times elected consul, the veteran of thirty-nine fights, he enjoyed the confidence of the army and of the people. As a result he had the stature in public life to defy what was coming to be regarded as the dead hand of Fabianism: the mere prolongation of the war against an enemy who, brilliant soldier though he still was, no longer possessed the superiority in cavalry that had so greatly contributed to his victories, and who was now largely dependent upon Bruttian militiamen for his phalanx. Yet the death of Marcellus exemplified once again the non-professionalism of the old Roman aristocrat. A general should not risk his life needlessly; Hannibal did not do so, nor did Scipio. That reconnaissance should have been carried out by a subordinate, or if the general felt that he needed to make it in person he should have taken all his horseman with him as Hannibal did on the Ticinus. Hannibal the professional had worn down his opponent's concentration; Marcellus, in the language of the cricket pavilion, had taken his eye off the ball.

Hannibal did not fail to use the advantage he had gained. He moved forward onto the fatal hill, where he found and buried the body of his most dangerous enemy. Crispinus, disabled, did the only possible thing and withdrew into the hills; but he was astute enough to warn the cities of the region against the possibility that Hannibal might attempt to trick them by the use of Marcellus' signet-ring. In fact this was precisely what Hannibal did, writing to the people of Salapia over Marcellus' seal and announcing that the consul would be paying them a visit. The Salapians, forewarned, admitted Hannibal's vanguard of six hundred Roman deserters and then dropped the portcullis behind them and cut them to pieces. Hannibal then evacuated Apulia and hurried south to raise the siege of Locri, whose resistance Cincius had almost beaten down. Hannibal sent his Numidians on in advance, and on their approach Mago, the garrison commander, made a sortie which, with the arrival of the dreaded horsemen, drove the Romans in panic to their ships. Cincius himself was taken prisoner.

On Hannibal's departure from Apulia Crispinus sent Marcellus' legions, under the command of his son, back to Venusia, where they were later taken over by the younger Fabius. He retired to Capua and from there wrote to the Senate an account of what had happened and asked for instructions. It was by now late in the year, so the Senate advised Crispinus to appoint a dictator to hold elections and to hand over his army to the praetor commanding among the Sallentini, Q. Claudius. Towards the end of the year the propraetor C. Hostilius Tubulus was sent from Etruria to take temporary command of these legions. The Fabian party did not omit to point the moral to be drawn from the deaths of the consuls (for Crispinus died before the year was out): that rashness – that is to say, deviation from Fabianism – led inevitably to disaster, and that Rome should be grateful that the gods had visited their displeasure only on the heads of the erring consuls.

Although in Italy the year 208 had proved to be one of the gloomier years of the war, with the deaths of both consuls, two minor defeats in the field, a revolt in Etruria, a pestilence afflicting Rome and the surrounding countryside and no compensatory gains, the arms of the Republic continued to prosper overseas. Laevinus, who brought to everything he did a thoroughness that suggests that if he had been allotted a more central rôle in the conflict he might have made a greater name for himself in history, had carried out a complete reorganization of the province of Sicily. The two Cannae legions, supplemented by the survivors of the Flaccan legions, had been brought up to almost two-army strength by the addition of large auxiliary forces recruited from the beaten Carthaginian Sicilian armies. It was with one of these 'armies' that Cincius had been operating in Hiero's former kingdom and against Locri. Laevinus himself had toured the island, escorted by Muttines' Numidian cavalry, to inspect the farms and encourage grain production, to such good effect that Sicily began once more to export grain to Rome and to the army operating in the Calabrian theatre. In the summer of 208 Laevinus made a descent with his whole fleet of a hundred ships on the African coast at Clupea on the east side of the Cape Bon peninsula and plundered the estates of the Carthaginian governing class. The Carthaginians had only eighty-three ships available for home defence (they still had a fleet in Greek waters) and offered battle with these, but were totally defeated, losing eighteen ships, and Laevinus returned to Lilybaeum laden with booty.

In the Macedonian theatre the proconsul P. Sulpicius Galba, with twenty-five ships and perhaps one legion (and a contribution from the sacred treasury), was doing as much as could be expected of him: at least he was helping to keep Philip fully occupied. The Romans played only a minor rôle in the serious fighting around Lamia in 209, which resulted in two defeats for the Aetolians but also in the failure of Philip to break through the Pass of Thermopylae. Galba with the fleet had probably been engaged in transporting Aetolian raiding parties across to Achaea and in watching the movements, or rather the non-movement, of the Punic fleet that had come by way of Taras to Corcyra. Attempts were made by neutrals, anxious for the preservation of the balance of power, to bring the war to an end; and Philip came under truce to Argos, where he was chosen to preside over the Nemean games, prior to attending a peace conference at Aegium, the Achaean federal centre. The Aetolians, however, emboldened by the presence of Galba's forces at Naupactus and by the arrival of King Attalus of Pergamum with thirty-five ships at Aegina, made unacceptable demands and the war was allowed to continue. Philip hoped for naval reinforcements from Attalus' enemy King Prusias of Bithynia; and with these (when they arrived) and five Achaean battleships added to the Punic fleet at Corcyra he confidently expected to drive the Romans from Greek waters.

Philip returned to Argos, but the festival atmosphere of the Games was disturbed by the descent of the Romans upon the fertile area that lay between Sicyon and Corinth. However Philip fell on them with his cavalry and chased them back to their ships. From Argos he moved into Elis in conjunction with the Achaeans and only narrowly escaped with his life in a clash with a Roman detachment which Galba had brought across from Naupactus. He was then recalled from southern Greece by reports of war and invasion on the borders of Macedonia, and hastened back to Thessaly, leaving 2,500 men to assist the Achaeans. Galba took his ships to Aegina and wintered there in company with King Attalus.

In the early summer of 208 Philip's forces mustered at Demetrias where he received reports of threats developing on all sides against his kingdom and allies and of the blocking of Thermopylae by the Aetolians. Philip reacted energetically. He threw forces into Boetia and Euboea and raced south to Heraclea Trachinea, hoping – but failing – to surprise a session of the Aetolian confederacy attended by Attalus. Attalus and Galba, who had been plundering the territories of Lemnos and Peparethus with their sixty ships, then attacked Oreus in Euboea, which commands the southern entrance to the Maliac Gulf and the sea approaches to Thermopylae, and took it by treachery, going on from there to take Opus, the chief city of the Opuntian Locrians. However, after Galba's departure to Oreus, Attalus was driven from Opus and almost captured by Philip, who had broken through at Thermopylae and outpaced any rumour of his approach. Attalus now retired from the war in order to defend his Asiatic possessions against the Bithynians and Galba withdrew to Aegina.

Fresh peace talks were interrupted by a report that Machanidas, the tyrant of Sparta, was preparing to attack Elis during the Olympic Games – to which Rome had sent an observer, with instructions to try to persuade Tarantine and Sicilian exiles to return home. Philip hastened to the Peloponnese and learning that Machanidas had returned to Laconia went on to Aegium, hoping to find the Punic fleet there to meet him. But the Carthaginians had received reports that Attalus and Galba had sailed south from Oreus and, believing that they were bound for the Corinthian Gulf, had moved off to Acarnania so as not to be trapped inside. For the moment, however, with six Achaean galleys and seven heavy and more than twenty light galleys of his own, Philip commanded the Corinthian Gulf. He raided the territory of the Locrians and then, sailing to Corinth (from where he sent his army overland through Boeotia) and transporting his own ships into the Saronic Gulf, he proceeded, under the nose of Galba at Aegina, by way of the Euripus Channel to Oreus, which he recovered. Back in his own kingdom, he put in hand the construction of a hundred warships at Cassandria which were however destined to play no part in the war.

In Spain in 208 the war took a decisive turn. Scipio had spent the winter winning over Iberian tribes to his side, employing bribery, personal charm and the politic restitution to their families of the hostages that he had acquired at Carthago Nova. The first to approach him had been Edeco, probably Prince of the Edetani who lived between the Ebro and the Sucro. His example was followed by all the peoples north of the Ebro and even Indibilis and Mandonius finally withdrew their force by night from the camp of Hasdrubal Barca in the territory of the Carpetani. These defections – of which this last was the most serious – made Hasdrubal anxious to fight while he still had an army to fight with. Scipio on the other hand was able to add to his army the most able-bodied of the seamen that he had left after sending fifty of his ships to Sardinia, and he was joined by contingents from his Iberian allies. After the return of C. Laelius from Rome in the spring of 208, no doubt bringing the news that his and Silanus' imperium had been extended, he marched south and was everywhere welcomed by the natives. Indibilis and Mandonius came to him, hailed him king – probably the title by which they had addressed their Carthaginian overlords (the Punic word *shofet* (judge) is rendered as 'king' in Greek) – received back their families, and concluded a regular treaty alliance with him. They then joined him with their forces, and were admitted into the Roman camp.

Hasdrubal, who had fallen back so as to cover the eastern approach to the Baetis Valley, was now camped near the town of Baecula (Bailén), south of the silver-mining area of La Carolina, with cavalry pickets in front of his position. These were driven in by Scipio's vanguard and during the night Hasdrubal moved to a stronger position on a steep-sided plateau about a mile to the east of the town, between which and the Roman camp flowed a small river (Rio Guadiel); two tributaries of which (mere streams) marked the boundaries of what was to become the scene of the action. Scipio did not at all like the look of Hasdrubal's chosen battlefield; but whereas Hasdrubal could afford to wait until his colleagues came up, Scipio could not. Accordingly after a two-day delay he prepared to mount an assault, first posting detachments to close the nearest escape routes from the plateau. In the coming battle Scipio must have had between 35,000 and 45,000 men. Hasdrubal's numbers can only be guessed at: 25,000 is widely accepted by modern historians but is possibly too low an estimate.

Scipio first threw forward a strong force of velites stiffened by picked legionaries against the front of Hasdrubal's position. These fought their way through a hail of missiles hurled by the men holding the top of the slope – light infantry, Balearic slingers and dismounted Numidians – and gained a footing on the plateau. Scipio at once sent in the rest of his light forces to reinforce this initial success, while he and C. Laelius each took a half of the heavy infantry in a double flanking movement that brought them onto the plateau and in a position to fall upon the left and right flanks respectively of the Carthaginian infantry of the line, which Hasdrubal, taken completely by surprise by the success of the frontal assault upon what he had believed to be an impregnable position, was belatedly arraying in order of battle. Through all the vicissitudes of the war in Spain Hasdrubal had never lost sight of the fact that one day he must bring an army to his brother in Italy; and it is probable that he had made up his mind to do so this summer, whatever the outcome of his encounter with Scipio. Now, with total disaster staring him in the face, he decided to salvage from it what he could. Accordingly he collected as many as he could of the heavy infantry of the centre – who were already in retreat – and abandoned the position. He had probably not brought his elephants onto the plateau, from which it might have been difficult to extricate them in case of defeat, but had left them, together with his war chest, somewhere well clear of the battlefield.

He retreated north by the Pass of Valdepeñas into the Tagus Valley. It is probable that his two colleagues, however little love may have been lost between the three of them, had moved to support him when they learnt of Scipio's offensive; and it would be logical for Mago to rendezvous with Hasdrubal Gisgonis on the upper Tagus, which lay in the line of Hasdrubal's retreat. At the ensuing conference between the three generals it was decided (according to Livy) that Hasdrubal should take out of Spain all the Spanish soldiery already serving with the Carthaginian armies, on the grounds of its unreliability, and march to Italy. Mago would go to the Balearic Islands to hire mercenaries and Hasdrubal Gisgonis would withdraw with his own and Mago's armies into Lusitania – a region unaffected by the defeats and defections of northern and eastern Spain. Masinissa with three thousand picked horsemen was to assist Carthage's allies generally and harry her enemies. Hasdrubal's losses in the battle are said to have been 8,000 killed and 12,000 captured. These figures have been doubted, but given the circumstances and the nature of the encounter they are not in themselves implausible. If in fact Hasdrubal had rather more than 25,000 men in his camp and if he added some thousands of Spaniards to his force before leaving Spain it is not difficult to reconcile his reported heavy losses at Baecula with his having a sizeable army in Gaul in 207. One thing does seem clear: that in the battle of Baecula Hasdrubal lost all or nearly all his cavalry. From the Tagus Valley he marched north so as to avoid the pro-Roman areas of Spain, and passing through Navarra crossed the Pyrenees at their western end and so reached Gaul. Scipio, having lost touch with him, did not waste time or endanger his army by pursuing him through the length of the Peninsula; he did, however, send a force – probably from Tarraco, after his return there – to the Pyrenees in order to obtain accurate information about Hasdrubal's movements.

Scipio moved his camp onto the site of Hasdrubal's, as being more defensible than his own, and probably spent some time in the area consolidating his position as the new master of eastern Spain. He released the Spaniards taken in the battle without ransom, but ordered the Africans to be sold. Among the latter was Massiva, the young nephew of Masinissa, and Scipio set him free with handsome presents. He was hailed once more as king by his Spanish allies – whom, beginning with Indibilis, he rewarded with gifts of horses – and by those who had so recently been his captives, although he mildly rebuked them for using a word so unacceptable to a Roman, kingly though he might be. He told them to call him imperator as his soldiers did. This is the first instance that has been recorded of a victorious Roman general's being so greeted by his troops and it may be the first.

Baecula has been described as a tactical victory for Scipio but a strategic defeat. This however would only be true if it could be shown that Hasdrubal managed to extricate a considerable part of his army. But if, as seems likely, he lost four-fifths – or even only two-thirds – of it the victory must be regarded as being at any rate as complete as that of Cannae, the ten thousand survivors of which subsequently played an important part in the capture of Syracuse and the expulsion of the Carthaginians from Sicily. Tactically the battle marks the coming of age of Roman military science. Scipio had learnt from Hannibal but was not content to copy him slavishly. Baecula was an exercise in the manner of Cannae, but the Barcine manœuvre was modified for employment in an attack upon an enemy standing on higher ground, using a citizen army no portion of which was expendable. So the velites, normally used merely as skirmishers to be removed from the field before the serious fighting began, were employed in a primary tactical rôle, pressing home their attack on the enemy centre and forcing the opposing general to take them seriously, while the heavy infantry, half of it under the leadership of a subordinate commander without imperium, moved around the enemy's wings and rolled up his line from the flanks. If Hasdrubal had stood his ground and fought it is probable that hardly a man of his army would have escaped. Scipio showed at Baecula that he had trained not only an army capable of carrying out an unorthodox manœuvre but also a junior commander competent to direct it. Now having completed his business in southern Spain, he marched back to Tarraco for the winter.

CHAPTER XVI

207 BC

The Metaurus and the beginning of the end.

The news that Hasdrubal had succeeded at last in breaking out of Spain and was on his way to Italy reached Rome before the consular elections. It caused considerable alarm and afforded the Fabians, conscious that their hold on the government was growing yearly weaker, an opportunity of criticizing the generalship of their political opponents. It also focused attention on the fact that the death of Marcellus and the inherent short-comings of the Roman politico-military system had left the state peril-ously short of experienced army commanders with which to encounter this new and as yet incalculable threat. The cunctator was by now too old to take the field and Varro still bore the stigma of Cannae. Laevinus might have been recalled from Sicily – although that would have been dangerous as long as there remained a possibility that Carthage might launch a diversionary attack in that theatre – and he could have been given as his colleague Q. Fulvius Flaccus, who had been consul for the fourth time the year before. However a new political alignment of the Aemilii and the Claudii produced a different solution. C. Claudius Nero, who had commanded armies before Capua and in northern Spain, was to be one of the consuls and in order to provide him with a plebeian colleague (Laevinus was a patrician) they turned to a man who had triumphed over the Illyrians twelve years earlier as the colleague of L. Aemilius Paullus, but had been condemned on a charge of embezzlement arising out of the division of the spoils and driven out of public life. This was M. Livius Salinator. Crassus and his colleague as censor had brought him back into the Senate and he had spoken in defence of his kinsman M. Livius Macatus, the ex-prefect of Taras. With considerable difficulty, for he was a deeply embittered man, he was persuaded to stand for the consulship, and was elected. With equal difficulty he was persuaded to lay aside (temporarily, as things turned out) a personal enmity and resentment towards Nero and agree to a formal reconciliation.

With the cooperation of the Massiliots the Senate had been able to follow Hasdrubal's movements from his arrival in Gaul to his winter quarters (wherever they may have been) and was aware that he was only waiting for the passes of the Alps to become practicable to bring his army, whose size had become grossly exaggerated by rumour, into Italy. It was decided that he should be opposed in northern Italy by the consul Livius, by the praetor of Gaul, L. Porcius Licinus whose base was at Ariminum and by M. Terentius Varro (who had replaced Tubulus in command of the two legions in Etruria), with the imperium of a propraetor. Hannibal likewise faced six Roman legions, more battle-tried than those in the north. Two of these were to be commanded by Nero, two by Flaccus (proconsul) in Bruttium and two by Q. Claudius (propraetor) near Taras. C. Hostilius Tubulus (propraetor) would lie in reserve with one legion at Capua. Two urban legions were also enrolled. Not surprisingly, there was an unusually fine crop of portents to be expiated (no year of the war had been without some). The levy was conducted most rigorously, for the census rolls of the previous year had shown a fall of almost fifty per cent in the number of citizens since 220, and although this figure is partly to be accounted for by the non-registration of soldiers serving out-side Italy it still represented a serious drop in available manpower. The consuls also enrolled slave volunteers, who were drafted into the army operating in Etruria, and they cooperated without acrimony in exchang-ing men from one command to another so as to provide a better balance between north and south. Livius is said to have also received reinforce-ments of 9,800 auxiliaries (including 1,800 cavalry, part of them Numi-dians) and 2,000 legionaries from Scipio in Spain, while 3,000 archers and slingers were sent over from Sicily, presumably to Nero.

Hasdrubal probably followed his brother's route and in April crossed the Alps by the Mont Cenis Pass. He had to cope with none of the diffi-culties that had made his brother's crossing a nightmare on an epic scale, and arrived in the Padus Valley, where he was to be met by eight thousand Ligurians, earlier than had been anticipated. He then advanced to Pla-centia and laid siege to it. Licinus wrote to the Senate to say that he (Licinus) was penetrating into Gaul with an army that was not up to full strength.

It will be helpful to attempt to reconstruct the Barcine war plan for 207 BC in the light of what was militarily practicable. It is a reasonable assumption that Hasdrubal had communicated to his brother his basic plan of campaign, either by a letter sent before he left Spain or by one sent from Gaul. What cannot be assumed is that Hannibal got any message through to Hasdrubal after the battle of Baecula, although of course he may have managed to do so. However we may assume that the brothers had been in communication down to that time and that Has-drubal was fully aware of the situation in Italy. He knew that Hannibal was now in effect penned into the foot of Italy and that the south no longer provided the power base from which the Roman confederacy might be overthrown. But he must also have known before leaving Spain that there was serious unrest in Etruria and that there, if anywhere, lay Carthage's hope of re-stoking the fires of revolt. The Etruscans had once been the active allies of Carthage, there were probably Etruscan exiles in both the brothers' camps, and if party strife could lead one of the great cities to open its gates to the invader the Carthaginians might recover the military initiative in Italy that they had lost, and render Rome's position very hazardous.

Three important factors limited the brothers' freedom in their choice of strategy. One was the strength of the Roman armies that stood between them, and the determination of the consuls to fight – even to fight Hannibal – rather than allow them to join forces. Another was the unwillingness of the Bruttii, who now composed the bulk of Hannibal's army, to engage in a protracted campaign far from the borders of their own country, menaced as it was by Roman armies in Messapia, in Lucania and in Sicily. The third was the uncertainty about how many Gauls of the Padus Valley would attach themselves to Hasdrubal. There had never been any question of the two brothers operating independently. Either Hannibal must march north and join Hasdrubal in Etruria or Umbria, or else Hasdrubal must come south in order to make the junction of forces; and since Hannibal could not guarantee the destruction of the armies opposing him, and as his Bruttians would refuse to go so far from home, it would be Hasdrubal's task to fight his way down to Apulia. But Hasdrubal could only hope to do that if the Ligurians and Gauls joined him in their tens of thousands. When the brothers first made and later reviewed their plans it would have been assumed that Hasdrubal would be bringing a victorious army of infantry, numerous cavalry and elephants into an Italy in which the Romans were already at least half beaten. The reality in 207 was very different. Rome would put fifteen legions into the field – something like 150,000 men – between Gaul and Apulia. Hasdrubal is unlikely to have brought much more than 10,000 men out of Spain, and these, in common with their general, carried with them the stigma of defeat. He needed at least 50,000 men if he was to have a hope of destroying whatever army the Romans threw across his path and still being able to bring his brother sufficient reinforcements to turn the tide of war.

But if the Gauls did not flock to his standard there still remained a third alternative, and this was probably the one that offered the best chance of success in 207. Hasdrubal would bring his army into northern Italy. He would avoid battle and would endeavour to shake off the Romans for long enough to enable him to effect a junction with Hannibal. The latter would leave the Bruttians behind in Apulia, give the slip to the armies policing his movements and dash north with as many men as would follow him – the remnants of his Spanish army, the exiles, the adventurers, the deserters. It would then remain to be seen if the terror and glamour of Hannibal's name would raise the north of Italy in revolt. Hasdrubal's success or non-success in recruiting Ligurians and Gauls – and he had brought his treasure with him for this purpose – would determine which of the two plans should be adopted, and Hasdrubal undertook to let his brother know in good time for him to make his moves. The outcome in either case would be a gamble, but so was the whole Italian adventure, and the Barcas were nothing if not gamblers.

When Hasdrubal came into Gaul he laid siege to Placentia. The only logical reason for his doing this is that he wanted to win the favour of the Gauls, whose former enthusiasm for the Carthaginian cause had been dissipated by the failure of so many of their countrymen who had accompanied Hannibal to return, and by the reports that had reached them of Rome's recovery. Hasdrubal's failure to take the place, which can have been only weakly defended, played its part in deciding the tribes not to aggravate the Romans further by joining in such an unpromising invasion of Italy. A good many Gauls did indeed enlist in the hope of plunder, but they were poor material; and when Hasdrubal had marched the length of Gallia Cisalpina he probably found himself with not very much more than thirty thousand men, Spaniards, Ligurians and Gauls, and of these only the Spaniards and the Ligurians were to prove of any fighting value. Accordingly he sent off six despatch riders to his brother to inform him that he must come north and appointed a rendezvous in Umbria. He had chosen to enter Italy by the eastern coast road, first in order to recruit among Rome's old enemies, the Boii, and secondly in order to avoid being faced by a possible concentration of seven legions in Etruria. The praetor Licinus with his weak army – perhaps between ten and fifteen thousand men – fell back before his advance, keeping to the high ground and harassing his column whenever he had the opportunity.

Livius is one of the most unfortunate of Romans in that his fame has been sacrificed twice to that of others. The part that he played in the Illyrian war of 219 has been passed over in silence by Polybius in the interest of Paullus, the grandfather of Scipio Aemilianus, and we are told virtually nothing about his movements in the northern campaign of 207, so engrossed is Livy in recounting the more dramatic march of an ancestor of his friend, the future Emperor Claudius. We can only surmise that Livius waited, with the urban legions of the preceding year, perhaps at Ocriculum or perhaps further forward, until despatches from Licinus told him for certain which road Hasdrubal was taking. He then marched swiftly to Ancona (he will not have gone by the Via Flaminia to Fanum (Fano), since he could not risk having Hasdrubal slip south past him), and moved up the coast to the vicinity of Sena Gallica (Sinigaglia), a Roman citizen colony.

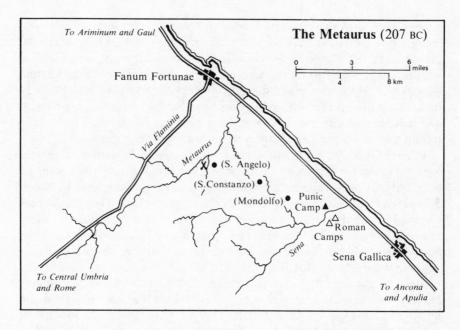

To Ariminum and Gaul

The Metaurus (207 BC)

0   3   6 miles
    4   8 km

Fanum Fortunae

Via Flaminia

Metaurus

X ● (S. Angelo)

(S.Constanzo) ●

(Mondolfo) ● Punic Camp ▲

△ Roman
△ Camps

Sena

Sena Gallica

To Central Umbria
and Rome

To Ancona
and Apulia

In the meantime Hasdrubal had been marching south past Ariminum, with Licinus moving along the line of the hills of his right flank. This meant that when Hasdrubal reached Fanum, Licinus was in a position to retire down the Via Flaminia before him if he chose to take the high-road through the Apennines into Umbria, and close it against him as soon as the terrain permitted. Hasdrubal wanted to keep the Via Flaminia open, so he pushed on south across the Metaurus, forcing Licinus to follow, until he found Livius in front of him. About three miles north of Sena the little river of the same name (today the Cesano) flows into the sea through a small plain lying between the low hills that come down to within a short distance of the sea, and Livius was probably strongly encamped on the southern edge of this plain. Licinus pitched his camp alongside the consul's and Hasdrubal pitched his on the northern edge of the plain, intending to wait there until a message should reach him from Hannibal telling him that his brother was in Umbria. He would then fall back, probably by night, and either cross the Metaurus or more likely make his way up its right bank until he hit the Via Flaminia, down which he would then march to his rendezvous with Hannibal.

Nero had already gone down to Venusia and taken over the army that Marcellus had commanded in 208. The propraetor Tubulus brought Crispinus' army up to Venusia from Taras, perhaps after a brush with the enemy on the way, and Nero selected the best elements from the four legions so as to give himself a full, if not actually over-strength, army with which to confront Hannibal. Tubulus then continued his march to Capua and turned over his two legions to Flaccus. Hannibal collected his forces and moved north into Lucania, to Grumentum (Saponara), and Nero marched down and camped less than a mile from him. There was some fighting between the two armies, the details of which as recounted by Livy are quite unreliable, and then Hannibal slipped away by night towards Apulia but was overtaken by the consul near Venusia.

The plan that he must put into effect if Hasdrubal failed to raise the Gauls – which was to leave the greater part of his army behind to contain Nero while he himself flitted north with a picked force – demanded every soldier that he could lay his hands on. Accordingly he now fell back in the direction of Metapontum and incorporated in his own army the men with whom Hanno had been holding the region, telling Hanno to replace them with Bruttian levies. Nero continued to police his movements, and by now Flaccus, whose rôle in the events of 207 has also been played down by Livy, had brought his legions into Lucania as well. Therefore when Hannibal moved north again by way of Venusia to Canusium in Apulia he found the roads into central Italy closed by four legions – about forty thousand men – while far behind him, among the Sallentini, were two further legions under the propraetor Q. Claudius.

At this juncture the worst happened from Hasdrubal's point of view. His despatch riders, having travelled the whole length of Italy, missed Hannibal and were captured by Q. Claudius' men and were sent by him to the consul. This was a great stroke of luck for Nero. It confirmed what he must have partly known and partly guessed for himself already – where Hasdrubal was and what the Barcids intended to do. But it also told him – and this was much more important – that while he, Nero, knew where Hasdrubal was, Hannibal did not. He could, therefore, be confident that Hannibal would not move far from his present position but would continue to wait for word from his brother. Nero decided that he would take a leaf out of Hannibal's book. He would leave the greater part of his army and the whole of Flaccus' to contain Hannibal, while he himself with a picked force of infantry and cavalry raced north to join Livius and destroy Hasdrubal before Hannibal realized that he had left his camp.

He sent Hasdrubal's despatch to Rome, with instructions to send the urban legions up to Narnia, in case Hasdrubal should elude Livius and came down the Via Flaminia, and to bring Tubulus up from Capua to cover Rome. He also sent messages to the peoples who lived along the line of his proposed march, instructing them to have provisions and transport ready at the roadside so that his force of men and animals, six thousand foot and one thousand horse, could march light, eat well, and not have men falling out on the march. He announced publicly that he was going to attack one of the enemy-held towns of Lucania and then, leaving his camp in the charge of his legate, he set out by night and marched with the greatest possible speed to Sena, picking up numerous volunteers from the communities through which he passed and adding them to his strength. At Sena, again under cover of night, he brought his force into Livius' camp without Hasdrubal's being aware of his coming. The consuls and the praetor held a council of war and lost no time in offering battle, but Hasdrubal became suspicious at the appearance in the Roman line of equipment and horses that he had not seen there before. He therefore refused battle and ordered a close reconnaissance of the Roman camps, which confirmed his worst fears: two trumpets sounded in Livius' camp, indicating that there were two consuls there. This discovery left Hasdrubal in a state of terrible uncertainty about what might have happened in Apulia. We cannot say for sure what he had in mind when he gave the orders for a night retirement, but the most probable explanation is that he intended to cross the Metaurus and retreat into Gallia Cisalpina, to await there more certain news from the south.

He did not like to risk moving up the coast road to the bridge, since Roman patrols might be out on it, so he struck north-west across the low hills (by way of San Costanzo), intending to ford the river. But the luck of the Barcids was running out. His guides, who were no doubt locals impressed for the purpose, gave him the slip and daylight found his army straggling up the right bank of the Metaurus, having already lost a considerable number of men, mostly Gauls, who had strayed or deserted. The Romans came in hot pursuit, Nero leading with all the cavalry – an arm in which Hasdrubal was particularly weak – followed first by Licinus with the velites and then by Livius with the heavy infantry, and they forced Hasdrubal to turn to bay. According to Ovid it was 23 June, the day after the anniversary of Lake Trasimene.

Hasdrubal had started to fortify a camp, probably on the high ridge above the river that terminates in the farmstead of Sant' Angelo, but the Romans were upon him in order of battle before it was defensible, and so he drew up his own men to make a fight of it. His left wing, composed of the Gauls, rested on Sant' Angelo, and the nature of the ground in front made it almost unassailable. The Ligurians, numbering perhaps eight thousand, were in the centre, either further south along the ridge where the more level ground in front would allow the enemy to approach, or more probably on the gently sloping fields a little further to the west and separated from Sant' Angelo by a short, steep-sided coombe. He himself commanded the right wing, made up of the Spaniards. He stationed his ten elephants in front of the Ligurians, or possibly in front of both the centre and the right wings; and the nature of the terrain rather than any other consideration caused him to draw up his army in depth, on a very narrow front. On the Roman side Livius took the left wing of the combined armies, giving the right to Nero and the centre to Licinus. For some time the fighting was confined to the centre and right of the Punic line, for the steep and in places precipitous little valley of the Sant' Angelo brook prevented Nero on the Roman right from getting to grips with the Gauls. Accordingly, as Livius and Licinus were making no progress and suffering heavy casualties, Nero withdrew his men behind the Roman centre and led them around the left wing of his own army, reformed and fell upon Hasdrubal's right flank and rear, rolling up the Carthaginian line. The Gauls, many of whom had already deserted while others were lying in a drunken stupor, put up only a feeble resistance. The elephants, after an initial success against the advancing Romans, had subsequently become an equal menace to their own side; six of them were killed, the majority by their own mahouts when they became wholly uncontrollable, and four were captured.

Hasdrubal had done all that a gallant soldier could do to save the day, but when he saw that it was irretrievably lost he spurred his horse into the Roman ranks and died in a manner worthy of his house. A man of very ordinary ability as a strategist and tactician, he would seem to have had some administrative capacity but hardly a spark of the genius or a scrap of the personal magnetism that made Hannibal almost unique. Yet his tenacity, his loyalty to his brother and his personal courage win our admiration. He must, however, bear some of the responsibility for the loss of the war in Italy; for without his army it was probably never winnable. If he could have broken through in northern Spain in 215 he would certainly have met with more support from the Gauls (who had just destroyed a Roman army), the Romans were still groggy from the effects of Cannae, and he would probably have succeeded in bringing into southern Italy forces that might have turned the scale. What would have been the outcome of a successful junction between his forces and Hannibal's in 207 can only be matter for conjecture; what is certain is that his defeat put an end to any hopes his brother might still have entertained of winning the war.

Some ten thousand of Hasdrubal's men fell in what was the only crushing victory in the field that the Romans won in Italy in the whole course of the war. Probably as many were captured and later sold, realizing three hundred talents for the treasury. The rest, Celts and Ligurians, who had either deserted during the night or fled from the field, were allowed to make good their escape to Gaul. The dead on the Roman side amounted to eight thousand. The sack of the Punic camp yielded not only considerable booty but also four thousand Roman citizen captives – colonists, no doubt, prisoners taken in skirmishes with Licinus and Livius and fieldworkers. The news of the victory relieved the Senate and people of Rome of a weight of anxiety that had been mounting ever since the receipt of

Nero's despatches, and the whole city became a scene of joy and thanks-giving to the gods. From that hour life at Rome began to return to normal, with the conviction that the war was at last won.

Nero returned to his camp in Apulia in less time even than he had taken to reach Sena (although he must have taken more than the six days of the 'Claudius legend'), and announced to Hannibal the news of his brother's death by having Hasdrubal's severed head thrown into his pickets. He also released two African prisoners to give him detailed con-firmation of the disaster. Shattered by this terrible, final blow to all his hopes, Hannibal retreated into Bruttium, evacuating the inhabitants of the Lucanian towns which remained faithful to him and which he could no longer defend, including Metapontum. He now prepared to fight a wholly defensive war while he waited on the outcome of events elsewhere. That he could expect no help from Carthage was emphasized by Lae-vinus, who once again took the home fleet across from Lilybaeum to Africa and ravaged the countryside around Utica and the capital. As before, the Carthaginian navy came out and fought and, as before, was defeated, losing twenty-one ships, taken and sunk. Laevinus returned home, again laden with booty, having made the seas safe for Roman commerce.

In the Macedonian theatre a new soldier statesman, Philopoemen of Megalopolis, 'the last of the Greeks', had emerged as the successor of Aratus to direct the affairs of the Achaean confederation. In 207, having reorganized the army during the previous winter, he was ready to try conclusions with Machanidas of Sparta. In the last major battle between Greek forces, at Mantinea in Arcadia, Machanidas was totally defeated and slain by Philopoemen himself, and the predominance in the Pelopon-nese of the Achaean confederation was firmly established. These were not matters that greatly interested Rome any longer, and as Attalus did not return to Greece with his fleet Galba withdrew his ships from the Aegean and was content to watch the approaches to the Adriatic. There was virtually no likelihood now that Carthage would send another fleet to cooperate with Philip, nor that Philip, occupied in beating down the Aetolians in central Greece, would show any further interest in the fate of Hannibal. On the other hand he could not be permitted to overrun the Roman protectorate and establish a hostile presence on the further side of the Adriatic.

Following Hasdrubal Barca's withdrawal from Spain the home govern-ment sent out another general, Hanno, with reinforcements for the army of occupation, and he, joining forces with Mago, went into the Celti-berian country and started to raise recruits there. Hasdrubal Gisgonis, who had wintered in the region of Gades, moved up into the Baetis Valley, the loyalty of whose inhabitants had been shaken by the events of the previous year. Scipio, whose imperium, like that of Silanus, had been prorogued again, sent his colleague at the head of ten thousand foot and five hundred horse to deal with Hanno. Silanus marched as fast as he could through difficult country, using Celtiberian guides, and arrived in the Punic training area without the enemy's being aware of his approach. The Celtiberian recruits, about nine thousand in number, were in one slackly guarded camp, the mercenaries, observing proper camp discipline, in another a little further off. Silanus was able to approach to within three miles of the former, dump his baggage, feed his men and then put them in order of battle without being seen by the enemy. Then he advanced to the attack. Mago barely had time to ride over from his own camp and get the Spaniards into some sort of order before the Romans were upon them. The broken ground covered with thickets compelled the two armies to fight in open order, and the battle became a murderous affair of single and group combats, in which the weapon training which Scipio had imposed on his men paid a handsome dividend. Hanno appears to have sent his soldiers across piecemeal from the Punic camp, with the result that they were swept away in the rout of the Celtiberians; and Hanno himself and those who joined the battle when it was all but over were captured. Mago, with most of the cavalry and those of the infantry who had seen a battle before and could gauge the inadvisability of lingering upon the field, escaped to join Hasdrubal in the Baetis Valley.

Scipio had perhaps already begun to march south. Hasdrubal, however, finding himself deprived at the beginning of the campaign season of most of his reinforcements, retired precipitately to Gades, having dispersed his army among the towns of the province. Since problems of commissariat – always a determining factor in ancient warfare and nowhere more so than in Spain – prevented Scipio from committing his large army to a series of sieges deep in enemy territory, he retired with the bulk of his forces, perhaps to New Carthage. However he left his brother Lucius with eleven thousand foot and horse to besiege Orongis, the chief city, and the wealthiest, of a silver-mining area on the edge of the upper Baetis Valley, which had been serving Hasdrubal as a base. The townspeople and the garrison at first put up a strenuous resistance, but the former lost heart and rushed out by one of the gates intending to capitulate. The Romans mistook their purpose, cut them down and burst into the city. However there was no sack, and only the garrison and the actively pro-Carthaginian elements were taken away captive. Following this success Scipio withdrew to his winter quarters in Catalonia and sent Lucius to Rome with Hanno and the other important prisoners.

At Rome Livius and Nero celebrated a joint triumph, Livius' army taking part in the procession and subsequently being disbanded, but Nero's remaining in southern Italy to watch Hannibal. Nero was anxious to return to his army, and left Livius to conduct the elections; and in order to reinforce the authority of his plebeian colleague, he nominated him dictator. L. Veturius Philo and L. Caecilius Metellus, the master of horse, who had both distinguished themselves on the Metaurus and had brought the consuls' despatches to Rome, were elected – a political victory for the Aemilii. Livius, reverting to his consular status, departed for Etruria and Umbria in order to conduct an enquiry to discover what communities there had been in treasonable communication, or worse, with Hasdrubal.

Only in Spain in 206 was the atmosphere not one of almost complete anticlimax after the dramatic intensification and then dissipation of the national peril in the previous year. Hannibal, who had until recently loomed so large and so menacing, had dwindled to the stature of a chieftain of Bruttian brigands, himself too dangerous to be attacked by the young and inexperienced men to whom the nobility could now afford to entrust the consulship, but too isolated and too remote to constitute more than a public nuisance. Indeed the most alarming event of the year at Rome was the extinction of the sacred fire through the negligence of a vestal. The peregrine praetor Q. Mamilius Turrinus took Licinus' old army into Gallia Cisalpina in order to teach the Gauls a lesson and to protect the colonies of Cremona and Placentia, to which – and to their farms everywhere on Roman territory – the peasants who had taken refuge in the cities were ordered to return by the consuls. Laevinus was recalled from Sicily, leaving only thirty ships for the use of the praetor C. Servilius Geminus. Rome could ill afford, after twelve years of such a war, to find and pay crews for a large fleet; but this ill-timed piece of parsimony gave the Carthaginians the freedom of the seas without a battle. The consuls, both assigned to Bruttium, ravaged the territory of Consentia and after a brush with the enemy's light forces retired with their booty into Lucania; the whole of which returned during the course of the summer to its allegiance to Rome, now that the Carthaginian garrisons had all been withdrawn.

In Greece the Aetolians, abandoned by Rome and Pergamum and with Philip in possession of Thermum, sued for peace. Galba did not have the strength to intervene, but in the following year (205) P. Sempronius Tuditanus succeeded to the Macedonian province, bringing thirty-five ships and eleven thousand foot and horse. He arrived in the Roman protectorate and from Dyrrachium moved to Apollonia, sending part of his force into Aetolia to try to rekindle the war. Philip, too, marched to Apollonia and offered battle, which Sempronius declined. Philip desired nothing better at this juncture than a general peace and accordingly returned into his own kingdom, from which, following a diplomatic approach on the part of the Epirotes, who were weary, like everyone else, of the war, he came down to Phoenice in northern Epirus and concluded with

Sempronius the Peace of Phoenice, in which the allies of both parties (apart from the Aetolians) were included and which was subsequently ratified by the Roman people. Apart from gains made at the expense of the Aetolians and their allies, Philip acquired Atintania from the Roman protectorate; but insofar as Rome had gone to war chiefly in order to prevent Philip from implementing his agreement with Hannibal, she could regard the outcome of the First Macedonian War as entirely satisfactory.

CHAPTER XVII

206~205 BC

Roman victory in Spain.

The year 206 saw the conclusive military defeat of Carthage in Spain. Hasdrubal Gisgonis had taken no part in the war against Rome since the defeat of the Scipios, concerning himself with the re-establishment and extension of Carthage's sovereignty, at first over the whole Peninsula (apart from the Roman enclave) and latterly over the south and west. Nothing stamps him more clearly as a true son of Carthage than his apparent belief that after their shattering defeat the Romans would go away; it was a repetition of the attitude and behaviour that had lost his countrymen Sicily. But he had not been idle during these last four years and apart from imposing his authority – often, it would seem, harshly – upon the natives, he had built up a formidable army, the more modest estimate of whose size puts it at 50,000 foot, 4,500 horse and 32 elephants. Hitherto he had refused battle, but he could no longer go on refusing: he had reached the point beyond which an empire in retreat must soon cease to be an empire at all. Accordingly Hasdrubal, with Mago as his second-in-command, chose a battlefield deep inside the old province – and concentrated his forces on the southern edge of a fairly level plain near Ilipa, on the right bank of the Baetis, about ten miles north of Seville.

There was nothing Scipio desired more than the opportunity of finishing the war at a single stroke. He sent Silanus to collect a force of horse and foot that an Iberian prince, Cukhas, had agreed to provide, and drew together all his forces, Roman and Iberian, to the number of forty-five thousand foot and only three thousand horse, at Castulo (Cazlona) at the head of the Baetis Valley. From there he marched downstream until he caught sight of the enemy, whereupon he halted and proceeded to fortify a camp on the hill called Pelagatos, about three miles north-east of the high ground across the plain on which Hasdrubal was encamped. Mago and Masinissa, with most of their cavalry, attacked the Romans as they worked; but Scipio had foreseen some such move and had his own horsemen drawn up in readiness behind a low spur of the hill. These charged the Carthaginians and after a sharp fight, in which they were supported by the infantry, drove them off in disorder.

Both generals had come to Ilipa to fight; but whereas Hasdrubal was content to bring the two armies into collision in the orthodox manner and to trust to his superior numbers, his elephants, and the greater reliability of his Spaniards compared with Scipio's to give him victory, Scipio had set himself a nice tactical problem to which he had to find an answer before accepting battle. He had seen, and proved for himself, that it is the flank attack that wins battles most effectively and cheaply. He had now to find some way of outflanking an army more numerous than his own, without placing too much reliance on his Spanish auxiliaries who must have made up at least a third of his total force. Spaniards, in his own experience of them, other than well-trained mercenaries, were not particularly impressive in battle, and he was not likely to forget how they had betrayed his father and his uncle to their deaths.

Accordingly over the next few days he allowed Hasdrubal to offer battle daily. He noted his invariable formation, with the best troops, the Africans, in the centre and the Spaniards on the wings with the elephants in front of them; and he invariably drew up his own army to correspond, with the legions in the centre and his Spaniards also on the wings. But he did not advance into the plain, and when the cavalry and spearmen on both sides had had their fill of skirmishing between the two armies he would allow Hasdrubal to retire into his camp first, as he had been first to take the field. At last, when he was quite ready, he passed the word around his army at first light, and after his men had breakfasted he led the heavy infantry out onto the plain, while the cavalry and velites advanced right up to the enemy's camp and attacked it with missiles. Flustered by this reversal of the usual order of events Hasdrubal emptied his camp without pausing for breakfast and, while his light forces engaged those of the Romans, drew his army up in its customary order of battle on the level ground. Presumably he saw nothing sinister in the fact that this time the Romans, drawn up and waiting in the centre of the plain, had changed their order of battle, bringing the Spanish allies into the centre and the legions onto the wings. The right wing was commanded by Scipio himself, while Silanus, with Septimius as his second-in-command, led the left.

Scipio was in no hurry to open the ball. His men were fed, coolly and deliberately marshalled, and confident. Hasdrubal's were hungry, hustled into their lines and nervous. When he judged that the right moment had come Scipio recalled his light forces, who had, as usual, been playing tag with the enemy skirmishers in the middle, and re-formed them behind the wings, with the velites in front of the cavalry. He then gave the order for the whole army to advance. When it was a little under half a mile from the enemy he gave the signal and the maniples of the legions changed direction, the right wing moving to the right, the left wing to the left, by either wheeling or turning the individual maniples, while the centre, the Spanish phalanx, continued at a slow pace towards the enemy. The cavalry, with their attendant velites, repeated the movements of the infantry.

When the two wings had moved right and left in column sufficiently far to bring their right and left maniples opposite the extreme ends of the enemy line they were given the signal to change direction left and right respectively; the three leading maniples – those of the hastati, principes and triarii – wheeling as one: in effect, as a cohort – with the rest of the maniples wheeling round successively by cohorts in their wake. The cavalry and velites again performed the same evolution as the infantry, except that the three leading troops of horse with their velites were probably stationed at the head of each infantry column. Having completed their turn, the two columns marched rapidly towards the enemy while the Spaniards of the centre continued to advance in line in slow time. When the columns were only a short distance from the enemy they deployed into line, the maniples of the right wing either turning half-left or wheeling left, while those of the left wing reversed this manœuvre. The cavalry column of each wing reversed the movement of its own infantry, so that the completed evolution brought the Roman legions into order of battle facing the ends of the Punic line, with the cavalry extending beyond the ends and in position to carry out an enveloping movement. The centre was deliberately held back and out of contact with the enemy.

We must assume that Hasdrubal, who as a general fell far below the level of the least able Barcid, was totally confused by Scipio's unorthodox approach, as Scipio had intended. The elephants, which we should naturally expect to have been thrown against the Roman infantry in the middle of its deployment for battle, were driven back into their own ranks by the cavalry and velites covering the advance of the columns, and perhaps scattered the Punic cavalry, of whose activity in the battle we hear nothing. Hasdrubal's Spaniards fought gallantly, but they were up against the best trained and best led infantry that Rome had put into the field during the course of the war, and the Roman cavalry and velites – too few in number to strike a decisive blow – were harassing their flanks. The centre, the flower of the Punic army, was unable to play any part in the fighting. If it had gone forward to engage Scipio's centre it would have run the risk of being cut off from its camp by the collapse of the wings; if it had changed front so as to support the wings it would have exposed its own flanks to a devastating charge by Scipio's Spaniards. The heat of the day, their unfed condition and their impaired confidence – for they were aware that the enemy had seized the initiative – all contributed to the defeat of Hasdrubal's men, whose fighting retirement degenerated first into full retreat and finally into total rout, as they broke and fled to their camp. Only the intervention of a violent cloudburst prevented the Romans from storming the works, and drove them back to their own lines.

If anyone in Spain had still entertained a doubt that the gods had at last provided Rome with a general who could defeat Hannibal it would have been dispelled by Ilipa. Ilipa embodied a subtlety beyond that of Cannae. When Hannibal drew the legions into the concave centre of his line to be crushed by the enveloping wings he knew that his Gauls and Spaniards would fight hard enough to contain the legions until the wings had completed their evolutions. Scipio, with his father's fate always before his eyes, could not trust his Spanish allies. He could not risk throwing them against their fellow Iberians on the wings of Hasdrubal's army and was therefore obliged to renounce what had been the common practice of generals at least since Leuctra: to attack the enemy's best troops with his own best. The result of such a move might very well have been a second Trebia but with no walled city to retire to. Nor, using the dispositions that he decided on, could Scipio afford to allow the crack African troops to engage and chase his Spaniards from the field. Lighter-armed and more mobile than the legionaries, they could have returned to give decisive support to their struggling wings. Therefore he had to find a way of containing the Punic centre without fighting it, while he destroyed the wings. His advance in columns and line disguised the nature of his plan until it was too late for a general of Hasdrubal's mediocrity to do anything to counter it. We need not doubt that Scipio, like Hannibal, appreciated to the full the importance of the dictum: 'know your enemy'.

The Punic army spent a miserable night strengthening the defences of their camp in the pouring rain; but many of the Spaniards realized that the rule of Carthage in Spain was coming to an end and went over to the conquerors. Prince Attenes defected with the contingent sent by the Turdetani, two fortresses surrendered to Scipio, and Hasdrubal withdrew his army by night towards the Baetis, intending to make for Gades. Scipio, however, having been advised of a shortcut, reached the river-crossing ahead of him, and so the Carthaginians turned south-west and a running fight ensued with the Roman cavalry and skirmishers, until finally what was left of Hasdrubal's army was brought to bay by the legions and all but annihilated. Hasdrubal got away with about six thousand men and fortified a camp on a hill not far from the sea, from which the Romans were unable to dislodge him. However hunger and exposure began to do their work for them, and as desertions became more frequent the general fled by sea to Gades, leaving Mago to hold the camp. Scipio left Silanus with eleven thousand men to besiege him and withdrew to Carthago Nova. Mago also now got away by sea to Gades and the army dissolved and vanished. Prince Masinissa seized the opportunity of having a secret conference with Silanus, at which he suggested that he might go over to the Romans and bring his people with him. It looked as if the serious fighting in Spain was at an end.

We have noticed already that the traditional policy of the Aemilian faction leaned towards overseas adventurousness, whereas the Fabians were 'little Italy' men. It was inevitable that the conflict between these two policies would be reopened with the utmost bitterness when Scipio returned to Rome as a candidate for the consulship of 205. Old Fabius, now almost at the end of his days, might be prepared to admit that now, at last, after the Fabian strategy had worn Hannibal down to a shadow of his former menace, it might be feasible to destroy or expel him by direct assault. But he would insist that the war should end with the defeat of Hannibal, and that the work of post-war restoration, including the re-establishment of Roman sovereignty over Gallia Cisalpina, should begin. A peace signed with Carthage recognizing the Roman conquest of Spain would be in the old Roman tradition and would enable the Republic, with its resources augmented by the wealth of Spain, to make good the devastation of Italy while preserving intact from foreign, and especially Greek, contamination the religion, laws, customs and habits of its people. It would also preserve the nobility in particular from adulteration by 'new' families who might rise to the top as a result of real or pretended military ability.

Scipio took the broader view that we should expect him to take. Hannibal might to all intents and purposes be beaten, but Carthage was by no means beaten. The loss of Spain was, no doubt, a very serious blow to her prosperity, but she was still the mistress of an extensive empire in Africa, and it had always been her practice when thwarted in one direction to branch out and expand in another. Deprived of all her overseas possessions she might develop her African empire to such an extent that the next generation of Romans would find themselves involved in another conflict, no less serious than the two preceding. For no Roman could doubt that the present war at least was of Carthage's making. If Rome was to have peace with her southern neighbour that neighbour's teeth must be drawn. Scipio's private interest was in harmony with these public considerations. The victor of Carthago Nova, Baecula and Ilipa would not wish his consulship to be an anticlimax. If he accepted the Fabian point of view he would be obliged as consul to take Bruttium as his province – he, whose province was currently the whole of Spain south of the Ebro. He would have to confront Hannibal, not with the Spanish army that he had trained to manœuvre on the battlefield, but with last year's consular army, taken over from a general who would have taught it only how to march and countermarch and pitch camp. He would require at least one season in order to make such an army into an instrument of victory; but with the return of normal conditions to Roman political life and the consequent hardening of the opposition to iteration of command, he might well find his command in Italy limited to a single year. Thus if he failed to defeat Hannibal as consul – and Hannibal would probably refuse to come out and fight – he might find that his military career had ended with Ilipa and that he had merely perfected an army with which his successor as consul gained the supreme glory. He needed another overseas command of two or three years' duration, freed from the interference of colleagues, tribunes and Senate, in which to train a second Scipionic army. In short, he needed to be given Africa as his province. If he prospered in Africa Carthage would have to recall Hannibal to defend her, and in defeating Hannibal in front of Carthage he could crown his career with the defeat of both.

From Carthago Nova Scipio sent his most trusted subordinate, C. Laelius, to sound King Syphax of the Masaesyles, with whom his father had had dealings, about his readiness to defect from the Carthaginians. Syphax sent him back with a message to the effect that he would be pleased to accept the friendship of Rome, but would negotiate only with Scipio himself, to whom he extended safe conduct. It would have been the height of irresponsibility for Scipio to have undertaken such an adventure before Ilipa; now, however, it was, like almost everything in war, no more than a calculated risk. He left Septimius in charge of the base camp at Tarraco and Silanus at Carthago Nova and sailed with Laelius across to Siga (Takembrit), Syphax's western capital, taking two quinqueremes. He came within an ace of disaster, for Hasdrubal, who had abandoned Spain, had just entered the harbour with a much larger force, and Scipio was barely able to bring his ships into port before the Carthaginians cleared for action. Syphax, swelling with self-importance, saw himself as the mediator between the two greatest powers of the *oecumene* and entertained the two generals and their aides to dinner. Even Hasdrubal was captivated by Scipio's charm and force of character, declaring him to be even more formidable in conversation than he was in arms. Syphax was won over and concluded a treaty with Scipio, who then returned to Carthago Nova.

It was felt that certain Spanish towns outside the small Carthaginian enclave had, by their treachery to the elder Scipios, merited exemplary punishment. Conspicuous among these was Ilorci, whose inhabitants had massacred the fugitives from Cn. Scipio's army five years earlier. Scipio undertook the assault on Ilorci in person; and although the inhabitants, men, women and children, resisted with the courage that is born of desperation, the place was stormed, his African auxiliaries (deserters) taking the citadel, and burnt to the ground, with the massacre of all inside. Scipio then marched towards Castax, a town which had defected from its alliance in 211, which Septimius was besieging. The report of the sack of Ilorci, however, and of the approach of Scipio himself broke the resistance of the townspeople and they voluntarily surrendered the town and its Punic garrison to the Romans. Having capitulated and having no Roman blood on their hands they were treated with leniency and placed under a native ruler sworn to allegiance. Septimius was then sent to bring under Roman rule any towns and tribes that had not submitted as yet. Only the people of Astapa, whose habits of brigandage gave them small hope of mercy, showed fight and after a desperate resistance destroyed themselves, their families and their town with all its contents. Meanwhile Scipio returned to Carthago Nova and there held magnificent funeral games for his father and uncle. The gladiators who fought in them were volunteers, or represented their rulers, one pair even consisting of contending claimants for a chieftaincy.

Shortly after Septimius returned to Carthago Nova offers came to Scipio to betray the town and garrison of Gades to the Romans, and accordingly Septimius with a land force and Laelius with one first- and seven second-class battleships, which was all that crews could be found for in a hurry, were sent to seize the city. Septimius encountered Hanno, the prefect of Gades, recruiting along the Baetis, captured his camp and scattered his forces. However the conspiracy to betray Gades was brought to light, and the conspirators were shipped to Carthage for trial and punishment. Laelius intercepted the Punic squadron, which was slightly stronger than his own, in the Straits of Gibraltar. His flagship dominated the battle, sinking two Carthaginian triremes, and the survivors of the Punic squadron fled under sail to Africa. From Carteia, Laelius informed Septimius of the miscarriage of the conspiracy and the two commanders returned to Carthago Nova.

On arrival they found a very serious state of affairs. Scipio, who had clearly overtaxed his strength in the heat of the Spanish summer, had fallen seriously ill and was widely reported to have died. The repercussions of this rumour were widespread and alarming. Indibilis and Mandonius – who had helped the Hasdrubals to destroy the elder Scipios and had then helped Scipio to crush the Hasdrubals, in the hope that they would be rewarded with the restoration of the sovereignty of which Hannibal had deprived them now raised their tribesmen, and together with the Celtiberi began to devastate the lands of Rome's allies north of the Ebro; but when they discovered that Scipio was not after all dead they withdrew into their own kingdom. Their rising, however, in conjunction with the report of Scipio's death, encouraged Mago in Gades to hope that he might be able to recover Spain for Carthage, and he wrote to the home government asking for reinforcements. At Sucro on the river of the same name (the Júcar) inactivity, boredom and arrears of pay bred first disaffection among eight thousand legionaries in camp there and then, with the rumour of Scipio's death, open mutiny. On his recovery Scipio first collected tribute from his allies and then summoned the mutineers to Carthago Nova to be paid. He caused a report to be spread that the army was marching out of the city to chastise the rebellious Spaniards and so the mutineers entered it without misgiving. The ring-leaders, thirty-five in number, were segregated and arrested and the city gates closed and guarded. Next day the mutineers were summoned before the general's tribunal in the forum. They were at once surrounded by loyal troops and after receiving a tongue-lashing from Scipio were obliged to watch the summary execution of their leaders. They were then granted a formal amnesty and each man, on renewing his military oath, was paid in full.

When it was made clear to the princes of the Ilergetes that death was the penalty for fomenting revolt against Rome they again called out their fighting men and their allies, and invaded the lands of the Edetani with twenty thousand foot and 1,500 horse. Scipio wasted no time. He led an all-Italian army by forced marches to the Ebro and crossed it, the Iler-getes falling back on his approach, and after a four days' march upstream he confronted the Spaniards across a narrow valley. He enticed the enemy's light-armed troops down into the valley by driving into it the cattle that his army had lifted from their farms, engaged them with his own velites and then charged them in front and rear with Laelius' cavalry, which had been posted in readiness behind a spur of the hills, and routed them.

As he had hoped, this rather costly reverse stung the enemy's pride and provoked him into sending down into the plain the next day not only his heavy infantry but also his cavalry, his best troops, and offering battle. Scipio reduced his front to the width of only four cohorts in close order – the battlefield was too narrow to accommodate more – and sent out his velites to contain the enemy's light infantry, who had remained at the foot of the hill on which they had their camp. Meanwhile Laelius took the cavalry across the high ground that bordered the valley and fell upon the rear of the Spanish horse, who thus found themselves trapped between their own infantry, the legions in front and Laelius' horsemen behind. Almost all the Spanish heavy-armed troops and cavalry died, but not without putting up a good fight, in which the Romans lost 1,200 killed and three thousand wounded. The camp of the Spaniards was captured, the princes making good their escape with the light-armed troops. In-dibilis then sent his brother to beg for peace, and Scipio, who was des-perately short of time for all the things that he had to get done before the consular elections, made a virtue of necessity and said that he would not disarm the Ilergetes or take hostages from them, but would receive them back into allegiance on condition that they provided money with which to pay his troops. He sent Silanus to Tarraco and Septimius (probably with the greater part of the infantry and the baggage) back into southern Spain; and when he had collected the money from the Ilergetes he set off after him and overtook him before he reached the vicinity of Gades.

His reason for going so far at the end of such a full year was to effect a meeting with Masinissa, for which the ground had long been prepared. Masinissa persuaded Mago to allow him to take his horsemen on a plundering raid on the mainland, ostensibly so that they should not deteriorate as a result of being cooped up on an island, and there he met Scipio – a momentous meeting for both of them and for Rome and Carthage. Masinissa, whose succession to his father's kingdom was at this time in great danger, promised Scipio his full assistance if he should come to Africa and then, with Scipio's permission, carried out his raid while Scipio returned to Tarraco. It may have been at this time (unless it was earlier in the year, after Ilipa) that Scipio broke his march northward in order to found a settlement for his veterans at Italica (Santiponce), only a few miles south-west of the battlefield of Ilipa. In this, as in so many other directions, he was establishing an imperial precedent. The settlement provided a refuge for the sick and wounded, a home and farms for those who did not feel like resuming their old lives in Italy and a bastion of Roman sovereignty in Baetica against the as yet untamed tribes of Lusitania. From this – Rome's first overseas colony – were to come three of her greatest emperors; Trajan, Hadrian and Theodosius the Great.

The government at Carthage was at last beginning to realize that this war, which it had entered upon so lightly, might end by costing Carthage more even than the loss of Spain. Hasdrubal will have brought back alarming accounts of Syphax's understanding with Scipio; and the reinforcement of Hannibal, a matter of secondary importance until then, suddenly acquired priority when it became a question of keeping the war out of Africa. Mago was ordered to take his ships and men from Gades to Liguria, to hire mercenaries (for which purpose he was sent money) and to stoke up the dying fires of war in Italy. He accordingly laid his hands on all the gold and silver that he could in Gades, public and private, sacred and profane, and sailed up the coast to Carthago Nova, hoping to surprise the place and add its treasure to his own. However the Roman garrison was alert and ready for him and his landing force was driven in rout back to its ships with considerable loss. Mago now sailed back to Gades, but he found that the oldest Phoenician city in the west had had enough of Carthaginian rule and had closed its gates to him. He seized the city suffetes and the treasurer when they came to confer with him and crucified them, before withdrawing to the Pityussae Islands, where he took on board supplies and recruits. From there he made his way to the Baleares (which, like the Pityussae, were still, at all events nominally, a Carthaginian possession). The tough slingers who inhabited Majorca, however, were also by this time less enthusiastic for a lost cause and drove him away to the smaller island, where he landed and camped for the winter above the harbour to which he has given his name (Port Mahon). From there he sent two thousand recruits to Carthage. As soon as Mago turned his back for the last time on Gades the town surrendered to the Romans.

CHAPTER XVIII

205-203 BC

Scipio takes the war into Africa. The Tower of Agathocles, the burning of the camps, the Great Plains and the fall of King Syphax.

Scipio returned to Rome early in 205 BC, leaving Silanus in charge of the province with Septimius commanding the army. The Senate greeted him, as was customary in the case of generals returning victorious from the wars, in the precinct of Bellona, outside the city, and received his formal report of his victories and of the conquest of Spain (Lucius Scipio had earlier brought the news of Ilipa, when only Gades and perhaps a few isolated strongpoints still remained unsubdued). As a non-magistrate invested with imperium Scipio was not by law or custom entitled to a triumph, and so he entered the city on foot, and paid into the financially embarrassed treasury no less than 14,342 pounds of silver, in addition to a large amount of coin.

At the consular elections which followed, conducted by L. Veturius, the Aemilian party – not surprisingly in the circumstances – were triumphant, and Scipio was elected, with P. Licinius Crassus as his colleague. When the question of the assignment of the provinces came up at the first session of the Senate a bitter confrontation ensued between Scipio and the leaders of the Fabian party over the proposal that Scipio should be given Africa as his province. Fabius, because he really had little choice in the matter, was prepared to acquiesce in the cruel possibility that his political enemies who (to his way of thinking) had brought the Hannibalic War upon Italy, should now, at the end of his days reap the glory of winning it – a dénouement made possible only by years of tenacious adherence on Rome's part to his policy of cunctatio. Scipio, however, by asking for Africa as his province was demanding not merely to be allowed to win the war but to tie Rome again to the lamentable policy of his father's generation. With so much to do in Italy and Gallia Cisalpina, he was proposing to involve her in adventures abroad, ill-omened, as the fate of Regulus attested, and which if successful would be conducive only to his own glory.

There was also another reason for the bitterness of Fabius' attack. It was rumoured that if he were refused permission to invade Africa Scipio

230

would appeal directly to the people who had elected him aedile while he was still under age and had given him his imperium as a private person, in order to go to Spain. Fabius, the intransigent conservative aristocrat, had all the shrewdness of the dedicated politician. The Fabian policy had done more than merely prevent Hannibal from winning the war. It had also killed the democratic movement at Rome and had secured – for more than three-quarters of a century, had he only known it – the complete predominance of the Senate and within it of the nobility in Roman politics. And it was this ascendancy that Scipio, with his 'popular' family tradition, was threatening to challenge. Flaccus loyally supported his leader and shrewdly got the tribunes on his side by making the issue one of senatorial privilege. Next day a compromise was arrived at, by which Crassus, who as Pontifex Maximus was not permitted by custom to leave Italy, received Bruttium, and Scipio received Sicily together with the thirty warships stationed there, with permission to cross over to Africa 'if he judged it to be in the public interest'. Metellus had his imperium prorogued in order to command the other consular army in Bruttium.

Scipio was anxious that his projected expedition to Africa should not impose a serious financial burden on the state, and therefore he appealed to the allies for contributions towards the fitting out and provisioning of his invasion force. Etruria and Umbria were well to the fore in giving aid – partly no doubt in order to display their loyalty, now that the final defeat of Hannibal was only a matter of time, and partly in order to hasten the return to normal conditions, in which trade and industry could flourish again and the danger of a revolt of their serfs would recede still further. In this way, without putting the state to any expense (an important matter, in the light of Rome's current financial difficulties), Scipio was able to equip and man thirty of the warships lying idle at Ostia, and to transport his army to Sicily. On his arrival he put the thirty ships of the Sicilian fleet into commission, and when these were ready for sea he sent Laelius to raid Africa with them.

Laelius landed his men at Hippo Regius and plundered the surrounding region. Masinissa, who was by this time an exile from his own country, had a meeting with him there and pressed for an invasion of Africa as soon as possible. Laelius' descent on Hippo Regius did in fact give rise to an invasion scare at Carthage; and when the true state of affairs was ascertained and the first alarm had subsided, the government began to take active steps to counter what had now to be regarded as a serious contingency. Embassies were sent to Syphax and to other princes to confirm their allegiance, and an attempt was also made to bribe Philip of Macedon to attack Italy, where Hannibal and Mago were instructed to do all they could to prevent Scipio from being allowed to cross to Africa. Mago had arrived unopposed in Liguria with 30 ships and about 14,000 foot and horse, as there were no Roman ships in commission in Italian waters to intercept him. It is in the circumstances likely that these forces included the 25 galleys, 6,800 men and 7 elephants which, we are told, Carthage sent to him, together with money, after Laelius' raid. He captured Genua (Genoa) and Savo (Savona) which he made his base. He sent 20 of his 30 warships back to Carthage, having heard reports of Scipio's proposed invasion, and he allied himself with the Ingauni and assisted them in a war that they were engaged in against their neighbours, intending in this way to build up and train an army for an attack on Italy. The Carthaginian government sent 100 merchantmen carrying grain and other supplies to Hannibal, but this convoy was blown off-course into Sardinian waters and most of it was captured by the praetor of Sardinia, Cn. Octavius, a collateral ancestor of the Emperor Augustus.

While Scipio was at Syracuse, indulging his taste for Hellenistic culture, reading the Greek authors, dressing after the Greek fashion, visiting the gymnasium and exercising in the Greek manner (all reprehensible activities according to the stern old Roman code of Fabius and Cato), he was approached by some Locrian exiles from Rhegium with a plan to recapture Locri by utilizing the services of certain sympathizers inside the town who enjoyed the confidence of the Carthaginians. Scipio, we are told, instructed two military tribunes to take three thousand men from Rhegium to Locri and to recover the city and he wrote to his legate, Q. Pleminius, to cooperate in the attempt. We must suppose either that Rhegium, which had been totally isolated in southern Bruttium since 215 and was largely dependent for survival on the support of the army and fleet in Sicily, was considered to come within the province of Sicily for operational puposes, so that, by explicit or tacit agreement between the consuls, Scipio could give orders to its garrison; or else – which is perhaps more likely – that Livy has simply omitted to say that the troops were shipped across from Messana for this operation, Pleminius being Scipio's commander there. Be that as it may, the attempt was at least partially successful and one of the two citadels of Locri was occupied. However Hamilcar, the Punic captain of the city, held out in the other and collected reinforcements from outside, which caused the townspeople – ancient foes of the Bruttii – to side with the Romans. When Scipio heard that Hannibal himself was hastening from Lacinium to the relief of his garrison he went to Messana and sailed directly to Locri, arriving some hours after Hannibal, but found the Carthaginians camped outside the walls. The next day Scipio launched a sortie against Hannibal's men as they approached the walls and Hannibal, accepting defeat, broke camp and withdrew the following night. He was joined on his march by the garrison, who had evacuated the citadel after firing it to cover the retreat.

Scipio now dealt with the Locrians, punishing the pro-Carthaginian party and turning their property over to the loyalists. He reserved any decision about the city's future for the Roman Senate and returned to Messana leaving Pleminius in charge. The wretched townspeople soon had good reason to regret their change of masters. Pleminius set his men an example in robbing them of their belongings, animate and inanimate, sacred no less than profane. Even the treasury of Persephone, untouched by the Carthaginians, was plundered. Finally the troops took to fighting among themselves, the tribunes' men against Pleminius', which resulted in Pleminius ordering the tribunes to be scourged and the mutilation of the legate by their infuriated soldiers. When Scipio heard of these disorders he sailed to Locri, to investigate the affair. Characteristically he supported his legate and arrested the tribunes for transference to Rome for trial. No sooner was Scipio's back turned than Pleminius had the unhappy men barbarously tortured and put to death, and then proceeded to treat the Locrians even more brutally than before.

In Bruttium itself, where Crassus commanded what had been Veturius' army while the proconsul Metellus continued to lead the army which he had led the year before, no progress was made, as a serious epidemic had afflicted not only the Roman armies but also the enemy. Indeed Metellus' army was disbanded before the end of the year in order to save it from annihilation. In Gallia Cisalpina and northern Italy precautions were taken against the possibility of Mago's attempting an invasion. The praetor in Gaul, Sp. Lucretius, was reinforced by the proconsul Livius with the two slave legions from Etruria, and Laevinus was instructed by the urban praetor to bring the urban legions up to Arretium. Thus six legions in all stood between Mago in Liguria and southern Italy.

The most serious fighting of the year occurred in Spain – which Scipio, somewhat prematurely, had described to the Senate as subjugated. In fact the final defeat of the Carthaginians and the departure not only of Scipio himself but also of his veteran army, encouraged Indibilis to make another bid for independence. Accordingly he raised his own people, the Ilergetes, and their neighbours the Ausetani, and mustered thirty thousand foot and four thousand horse in the territory of Rome's allies, the Edetani. Scipio and Silanus had been succeeded by L. Cornelius Lentulus and L. Manlius Acidinus, both with pro-consular imperium. They combined their forces – two legions, plus Spanish auxiliaries – and marched to confront the enemy. Diplomacy failed to prevent a clash between the horsemen of the opposing armies and the Spaniards offered battle which the Romans accepted, with both sides drawing up their lines so as to allow ample scope for their cavalry. A fierce infantry slogging match was turned into a Roman victory largely by the action of their cavalry, who rode through the gaps which the enemy had left in their line for their own horsemen, forced the latter to dismount in order to fight, and threw the Spanish line into confusion. Indibilis died gallantly while trying to rally his retreating followers and the Spaniards were driven in rout from the field and from their camp. The tribes then asked for peace and were told that they must surrender Mandonius and the other surviving leaders of the revolt. This was done, and they were then granted peace on the further condition of paying a double tribute and six months' supply of grain and clothing for the army. About thirty tribes were required to give hostages for their good behaviour.

Metellus conducted the elections as dictator so that neither consul should be obliged to leave his province. M. Cornelius Cethegus and P. Sempronius Tuditanus, who was still in Greece, were elected consuls; a result at best only half-favourable from Scipio's point of view since Tuditanus belonged to the Claudian alliance. However he was continued in his command; the man chosen to be the praetorian governor of Sicily was a relation, M. Pomponius Matho; and his first cousin, Publius Scipio Nasica, was judged to be the 'best man in the community', and as such worthy to receive on behalf of the Roman people the sacred stone that represented the Idaean Mother (Cybele). The Sibylline Books, confirmed by Delphic Apollo, had instructed the Romans to establish this stone at Rome in order to obtain final victory, King Attalus had obtained it for them from Pessinus and an embassy headed by Laevinus, with a squadron of quinqueremes, had brought it to Italy.

Scipio needed all the political support he could get, to survive the savage attack made by the Fabians in the Senate upon his conduct as consul in Sicily and his 'Hellenism'. This followed the accusations of the Locrian envoys, who maliciously declared that Scipio was too busy with his invasion preparations and too prejudiced in Pleminius' favour to listen to any complaints of theirs. The element of sacrilege in the charges levelled against Pleminius was particularly damaging at this juncture, and if Fabius' proposal had been carried Scipio would have been recalled to Rome and his imperium abrogated. Metellus, however, came to his rescue with a compromise proposal, that Scipio's cousin Pomponius should conduct an enquiry into the whole business on the spot, with the assistance of ten senatorial commissioners, two tribunes and an aedile; and if Scipio was found to be blameworthy he should be brought home, even if he had already crossed over into Africa. Metellus himself was selected as a member of the commission.

The commission went to Locri and did everything it could to ensure that all stolen property was returned to its proper owners. The Locrians were restored to their former status of autonomous allies and invited to lodge material complaints against Scipio; but they were too prudent to do this, being content to insinuate that his preoccupation with military affairs and his partiality for the accused had made him blind and deaf to their representations. Pleminius on the other hand and thirty-two others were accused of crimes 'against gods and men' and sent to Rome for trial. If the facts of the matter are as Livy presents them we have to admit that Scipio was seriously at fault in not conducting a rigorous enquiry into the state of affairs at Locri. But it is absurd to suppose that he had any idea of what was really going on there. Communications between Locri and Syracuse were not easy, and Pleminius, whom he trusted, undoutedly pooh-poohed any complaints that may have reached his leader's ears, dismissing them as the whinings of men who were being very properly punished for their rebelliousness.

That he was prejudiced in Pleminius' favour is undeniable, but also understandable. Like any member of his order he would automatically support a subordinate who was his personal representative – and possibly, in addition, a client of his clan – against attack by outsiders, particularly if they happened to be foreigners who had broken their oaths of allegiance. To win his battles Scipio needed loyal and devoted subordinates, and he repaid loyalty in its own coin. That he should have made such a grave error of judgement as to trust Pleminius so completely might appear less remarkable if we knew the man. It is, however, a failing to which the patrician is especially susceptible, as witness the case of the Emperor Tiberius (also a 'professional' soldier) and Sejanus. It was, at all events, wholly in keeping with Scipio's character that having given Pleminius his confidence he should support him against the accusations of those outside his circle.

From Locri the commission went on to Syracuse to see what truth there was in the Fabian allegations that army and general alike were in a state of military unpreparedness and indiscipline. However Scipio was on safe ground here, and the commission was lost in admiration of the state of high efficiency and readiness for war of both army and fleet, as well as at the quantity of supplies and war material collected in readiness for the invasion of Africa. On its return to Rome it reported to this effect to the Senate, which accordingly authorized Scipio to employ whatever troops stationed in Sicily he needed for the invasion of Africa, thus freeing the Cannae legions from the eleven-year-old ban on their removal from the island.

The Carthaginians had not been idle during the winter. They built watch-towers along the coast, and through the efforts of Hasdrubal concluded an offensive and defensive alliance with Syphax, cemented by the marriage of the king to Hasdrubal's beautiful daughter Sophonisba (Saphanba'al). Syphax then sent an embassy to Scipio to try to dissuade him from bringing the war into Africa. This was a blow to Scipio, for Syphax, on whose cooperation he had been relying, was a king in possession of a kingdom, whereas Masinissa, his other Numidian ally, was a homeless exile. However to prevent the news of the Numidian's *volte-face* from leaking out and discouraging his soldiers, he announced that Syphax had in fact been urging him to sail, and he ordered all his ships and men and all the merchantmen in Sicilian ports to muster at Lily-baeum, and requested Pomponius to meet him there, to discuss with him the division of the forces stationed in the island.

The question, what troops did Scipio take to Africa, is not very easily answered. Livy tells us that he was not permitted to hold a levy in Italy and that accordingly he took only seven thousand volunteers to Sicily, where there was already a large army composed of the Cannae legions and the miscellaneous elements recruited by Laevinus. The simplest solution of the problem is to accept Livy's positive statements and to ignore certain discrepant passages which appear to suggest that at least one of his sources believed that Scipio had brought a regular consular army to Sicily. According to Livy, then, Scipio decided to take to Africa the veteran Cannae legions (which were actually under the imperium of Pomponius, as governor of Sicily), replacing the old and unfit with men whom he had brought as volunteers from Italy, and bringing each of them up to a strength of 6,200 foot and 300 horse. These, together with the allies brigaded with them, gave him a total strength of at least 26,000 men. If this represents the truth of the matter we have to assume that Pomponius was left to hold Sicily with Laevinus' irregulars, plus the unfit from the Cannae legions – an assumption not inherently improbable, since Carthage no longer posed any threat to the province – and that at some subsequent date two regular legions were sent to Sicily. It would, however, be unwise to disregard Professor Brunt's suggestion that the story of the 'volunteers' is 'a retrojection of Aemilianus' recruitment of volunteers in 134', and that Scipio in fact took a consular army to Sicily but made the veteran Cannae legions the basis of his invasion army as suggested above, leaving behind with Pomponius the two legions (less the drafts) that he had brought with him.

His invasion fleet amounted to about four hundred transports and the escort to two squadrons each of twenty galleys, of which he and his brother Lucius were to lead the right-hand division, and C. Laelius as prefect of the fleet, and the quaestor M. Porcius Cato, the left. As Scipio made no secret of his intentions and as the embarkation and the departure of the armada were in the nature of public spectacles, we must assume that he had reliable intelligence of the Carthaginian navy's unpreparedness to intercept him. It must in fact have been badly hit by the drying up of the flow of silver from Spain and the diversion of the available funds to other undertakings, such as Mago's invasion of Italy. After a slow, foggy but uneventful crossing the expedition, having sighted land off Cape Hermaeum (Bon), came to shore at Cape Pulchrum (Farina) and camped on high ground, some sixteen miles north-east of Utica (which is about thirty miles from Carthage). The landing caused widespread panic and an exodus of the rural population and their beasts from the countryside into the cities, and considerable alarm in the capital itself.

The next day Scipio's cavalry pickets routed a Punic reconnaissance force and killed its commander, and the army began to devastate and plunder the region, taking a town and thousands of captives, who, together with the booty, were shipped back to Sicily. The Romans were now joined by Masinissa with about two hundred horsemen. The prince had fallen on evil times since he went to Spain as commander of Hasdrubal's cavalry in 212. On the death of his father Gaia the kingdom of the Massyles had passed to a pretender, and although Masinissa had returned and driven him out he had himself been expelled by Syphax, who, with Carthaginian encouragement, had added the Massyles to his own kingdom. Masinissa had waged guerilla warfare against the conqueror, but had been twice defeated by superior numbers and had fled to the Lesser Syrtis region, from which he now came north to join Scipio.

Scipio decided to acquire the important city of Utica as a winter base

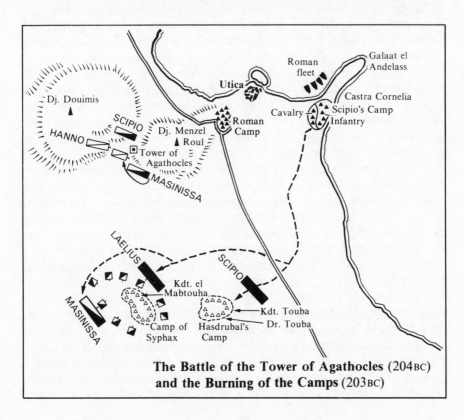

The Battle of the Tower of Agathocles (204BC)
and the Burning of the Camps (203BC)

and advanced to about a mile's distance from the walls, pitching his camp on the line of hills at whose northern end the town stood. The Carthaginians had no considerable forces available for the defence of the region but they had raised a body of cavalry, largely Numidians but including over two hundred Carthaginians, some of noble family, under a Hanno, son of Hamilcar. This force was billeted in the town of Salaeca (probably Henchir el Bey) about fifteen miles west of the Roman camp. Scipio sent Masinissa with a body of horse to ride up to the town, draw the enemy out and entice them, by a tactical withdrawal, to pursue him past the southern foot of a range of hills, behind a saddle of which he would be waiting with the rest of the cavalry. The ambush was entirely successful. Masinissa's men, after putting up a stiff fight, retired in good order towards Utica with the enemy in close pursuit, and when the latter reached the place where Scipio's cavalry waited, hidden from view behind the high ground, they were taken in flank, while Masinissa wheeled his horses about and attacked them in front. Hanno and a thousand of his men were killed in the battle and two thousand more killed or captured in the pursuit of the routed force. Following this battle – which is known to history as the battle of the Tower of Agathocles, from an old fort that commanded the ambush position – Scipio occupied and garrisoned Salaeca and spent a week devastating and plundering the whole region before returning to the more serious matter of besieging Utica.

In those days Utica was a port, although today it lies some five miles inland, because the River Bagradas (Medjerda) has shifted its course since classical times, and its deposits have caused the coastline to recede. Utica was the oldest Phoenician city in north Africa, and had for centuries been a privileged ally of Carthage. However, as it had taken the side of the mercenaries in the Truceless War, and had offered itself as an ally to Rome almost within Scipio's own lifetime, he probably expected it to fall into his hands fairly easily. He brought up artillery and siege engines, some imported from Sicily, some manufactured on the spot, and attacked it from the sea and from the land, but without effect. The Uticans were relying upon relief from Carthage, and although the Carthaginian fleet (no doubt even shorter of rowers than the Roman) made no attempt to intervene Hasdrubal, now the established war leader, marched to its relief. He had been busy raising an army in the interior, and had encamped before Carthage to wait for Syphax. When the king joined him with his Numidians he advanced to a camp to the south of the Roman position, and so forced Scipio to raise the siege after forty days in order to avoid being sandwiched between the Punic armies and the defences of the town. He withdrew to a ridge a couple of miles to the east of Utica and separated from it by a marsh. There he fortified a winter camp (which in Caesar's day was still called Castra Cornelia) at the base of what was in ancient times a promontory formed by a continuation north-eastwards of the ridge. He hauled his ships ashore on the northern side and stationed his cavalry on the southern, and enclosed all his forces within the one circuit of fortifications. He suffered from no shortage of provisions, as Cn. Octavius, who was on coast defence duty with forty ships, brought him stores and clothing from Sardinia, in addition to the grain which he had collected from the surrounding countryside.

In Italy in 204 there was some fighting in the territory of Croton in Bruttium between Hannibal and the consul Tuditanus, the latter subsequently supported by the proconsul Crassus, in which Hannibal, after an initial success, appears to have had the worst of it. Tuditanus vowed, and later dedicated, a temple to Fortuna Primigenia for his victory, and Hannibal retired to Croton. The Romans were then able to recover Clampetia as well as several other places. The other consul, Cethegus, was occupied in Etruria, where widespread disaffection was brought to light, and numerous leading men were condemned or driven to save themselves by flight, on charges of intriguing with Mago – a circumstance which helps to explain why, right up to the moment when his brother's head was thrown into his lines, Hannibal had still entertained hopes of dismembering the Roman confederation. Mago himself made no move this year to challenge the Romans in Cisalpine Gaul and northern Italy.

The elections for 203 were conducted by the consul Cethegus, and the successful candidates for the consulship were Cn. Servilius Caepio and C. Servilius Geminus; both adherents of the Aemilian party, but also eager for their own advancement. They were to prove themselves unreliable allies of Scipio. Scipio himself had his command extended 'until his task should be completed' and Pomponius and Octavius, who had both loyally supported him, likewise had their imperium extended, so that he could be sure of naval and commissarial assistance from Sardinia and Sicily in the year to come. It is likely that one result of the 'treason trials' of the previous year had been to alert the Senate to the probability that Mago would invade Italy in 203. Accordingly one consul, Geminus, was assigned to Etruria and Liguria, while the other faced Hannibal in Bruttium supported by Tuditanus as proconsul. Cethegus remained in Gaul as proconsul with two legions, and the praetor P. Quinctilius Varus was sent to Ariminum, also taking over two legions, so that once again six legions were stationed in the north of the peninsula. The Republic, besides putting no fewer than twenty legions into the field this year, made a special effort at sea, for it was known that Carthage had got a fleet ready for service. Three Roman fleets of forty ships were commissioned to guard the waters of Sicily, Sardinia and Italy.

During the winter Scipio did not limit his preparations for the coming season merely to the military. He also reopened negotiations with

Syphax, in an endeavour to detach him from his allegiance to Carthage – perhaps, in view of the dynastic nature of his relationship, one should rather say, to Hasdrubal – but the uxorious Numidian, apart from being still under the spell of Sophonisba, was well aware of the advantage to himself if his kingdom held the balance between Rome and Carthage, rather than if one of the super-powers emerged as the undisputed mistress of the western Mediterranean. Accordingly he applied his diplomacy to the achievement of a peace under whose terms Carthage would evacuate Italy and Rome would evacuate Africa. So Scipio, whose ambition could not possibly have been satisfied with such a tame ending to the war, quite apart from any consideration of his country's interests, changed the direction of his own plan, from the detachment of Syphax to his destruction.

He pretended to be veering towards the king's way of thinking and multiplied his embassies to the latter's camp, mingling with the negotiators officers disguised as slaves, who carefully reconnoitred all the ways of the sprawling town of palm frond and matting shelters that housed the Numidian contingent, which, we are told, amounted to 50,000 foot and 10,000 horse. These figures are certainly much too high: it is probable that Syphax himself did not know how many men he had camped within and without his lines. Moreover the numbers that we are given for Hasdrubal's army, camped in wooden huts a mile and three-quarters away to the east, namely 30,000 foot and 3,000 horse are also exaggerated. But if Hasdrubal, after his experience at Ilipa, was prepared to face Scipio's army in pitched battle in conjunction with Syphax we may reasonably assume that the combined armies did enjoy a significant numerical advantage, particularly in cavalry.

At the first sign of spring Scipio began to make overt preparations for a renewal of the siege of Utica, mounting siege engines on his ships and sending a force of two thousand men to reoccupy the hill commanding the town and to construct fieldworks so as to discourage a sortie on the part of the besieged. He forestalled any move by the enemy to interfere with the execution of his plan by giving Syphax the impression that he was on the point of making peace and wanted to know what Hasdrubal's reaction to the proposal would be. Both the king and Hasdrubal were completely taken in. The Carthaginian must have believed that, with the navy at last ready to play its part in the defence of Africa, he had Scipio cornered at Utica and that the Romans would be very glad to be allowed to make their escape. On the other hand a cornered wolf is no laughing matter, and if he could secure peace – and a peace that was not of Hannibal's making – he would be content to see Scipio go without trying to even the score between them. Even if he were to destroy Scipio Rome would not be likely to allow the war to end on a note of Carthaginian triumph, and it had always been his city's policy to look for a negotiated peace when it once became apparent that a quick and profitable victory was not to be gained by continued fighting. While Scipio intensified his preparations for carrying on the war, Syphax and Hasdrubal allowed their vigilance and their military preparedness to relax.

On receiving the news that Hasdrubal would agree to make peace on the basis of Syphax's proposals, Scipio replied that while he personally was still in favour of the peace his War Council was opposed to it – a quite brilliant piece of disingenuousness which had the twofold effect of keeping his enemies' eyes averted from their own peril – for it was not to be expected that the Roman army would make a hostile move while its leader was still searching for a way to end hostilities – and at the same time morally freeing Scipio's hands by implying that the peace negotiations had broken down. Bitterly disappointed but in no way alarmed, the two Punic leaders began to discuss the strategy that they should adopt in order to force a military decision.

When Scipio's preparations were complete – probably about the beginning of March – he moved his army out of its lines after the sounding of the last post and marched to the vicinity of the enemy's encampment, about ten and a half miles distant. From there Laelius, with Masinissa as his second-in-command, took half the legionaries and all the Numidians to Syphax's camp, while Scipio with the rest of the army proceeded more slowly, having a shorter distance to go, to positions commanding the camp of Hasdrubal. When they reached their objective Laelius and Masinissa divided their forces. Laelius moved to the windward side and threw fire onto the highly inflammable frond and matting huts. Masinissa, who knew the layout of the encampment and understood the ways of his people, posted his men at all the exits not already covered by his colleague, and butchered the panic-stricken Africans as they bolted from the holocaust, dazed with sleep or fuddled with alcohol, naked and weaponless. When Hasdrubal's men saw from their own hutment the fire sweeping through the Numidians' camp, they streamed out of their lines; and while some started to run to help their allies, supposing the disaster to be the result of an accident, the rest collected to gape at the blaze. Upon this unarmed, unsuspecting mob Scipio loosed his swordsmen, and chasing those that they did not kill back into their lines they fired the Carthaginian camp as well.

It is impossible to assess the losses suffered by the allies in this catastrophe. No doubt several thousand were killed or burnt to death and five thousand may have been taken prisoner. Both the leaders escaped and took little more than a handful of men with them. The rest of the host fled into the night, and while many subsequently rejoined their king and their general we may be certain that a very large number made the best of their way back to their villages and took no further part in the war. However it was not the number of killed and taken that makes the burning of the camps one of Scipio's most brilliant exploits but the fact that, as a result of one night's work and at almost no cost to himself, two enemy armies temporarily ceased to exist and the attempt to raise the siege of Utica had been defeated.

Hasdrubal halted at the nearest town (possibly named Anda) and some fugitives from the disaster joined him there, bringing his 'army' up to 2,500 foot and horse; but he could not trust the townspeople, and on Scipio's approach he retired to Carthage. The town surrendered to the Romans and was treated leniently. However two other towns which resisted were sacked. Scipio then returned to the coast, and when he had completed his preparations for the siege moved his army back into its positions in front of Utica.

As might be expected the Carthaginians' resolution was at first badly shaken by what had occurred; but as the fugitives from the disaster continued to come in, so that before long Hasdrubal, who had not lost heart, had the nucleus of another army, they determined to fight on. Accordingly they sent Hasdrubal into the interior to recruit and train, and got in touch with Syphax, who had halted at Abba, a town in the lower Bagradas Valley, and begged him to remain true to his allegiance. Syphax, whose heart had never really been in the war, had decided to cut his losses and go home, turning a deaf ear to Sophonisba's entreaties. However, the arrival at Abba of a body of four thousand Celtiberians who had been hired by Carthage and were on their way to the capital presumably from somewhere like Hippo Regius where they had been disembarked, caused him to change his mind. He added the newcomers to the force that he had managed to salvage from the great burning and marched to rejoin Hasdrubal in an area called the Great Plains (Souk el Kremis) on the upper Bagradas, between seventy and eighty miles west-south-west of Utica. The army mustered there totalled about thirty thousand men.

When, probably towards the end of April, the news reached Scipio that the enemy were concentrated on the Great Plains he left a sufficient force to maintain the siege of Utica (for this purpose he could also employ the crews of his forty ships) and marched his legions, unimpeded by heavy baggage, to a hill about five miles from Hasdrubal's camp. The next day he paraded his army, covered by a cavalry screen, on the plain, and after two further days of skirmishing both sides moved down onto the level ground for a pitched battle. Scipio drew up his legions in the traditional order, with the lines of hastati, principes and triarii one behind the other. He stationed his Italian cavalry on the right wing and the Numidians under Masinissa on the left. It is clear that by now Masinissa's original contingent of only two hundred horsemen had been very largely augmented – no doubt by his own tribesmen and deserters from Syphax, and perhaps (although we are not told so) by Muttines' followers brought over from Sicily by Scipio.

Hasdrubal put his best troops, the Celtiberian heavy infantry, in the centre, with Syphax's infantry on their left and his own on their right, and with the Punic and Numidian cavalry covering the flanks of their respective contingents. When the two armies clashed Scipio's horse at once drove Hasdrubal's from the field, thus exposing the flanks of his phalanx; and while the hastati contained the front of the enemy's infantry, the principes and triarii moved sideways out onto the wings, a manœuvre that at once doubled the strength of the Roman wings and extended them. They routed the Punic and Numidian foot soldiers opposed to them and then enveloped the Celtiberians of the centre and assisted in their annihilation. The Spaniards died where they stood, having nothing to hope for from flight in a strange land, or from surrender to the man who had 'pacified' Spain.

The Great Plains battle, in which the three lines of maniples manœuvred independently while in contact with the enemy, has rightly been described as the most sophisticated of Scipio's battles. No doubt, if we take into consideration the fact that in fighting quality and equipment the legions were vastly superior to Hasdrubal's infantry apart from the Celtiberians, Scipio could have achieved victory in the traditional Roman manner by engaging in a straightforward slogging match. But Scipio was a 'soldier's general' in this as in other respects, that he was sparing of the lives of his men; and although Syphax got away to his own kingdom with most of his horsemen, and Hasdrubal was able to reach Carthage with what was left of his contingent, Scipio had once again wiped a Carthaginian army off the map at what was probably a relatively small cost to himself.

The subsequent history of Hasdrubal cannot be established with certainty, but it seems likely that he was dismissed from his command and replaced by Hanno the son of Bomilcar, who had been sent home from Italy to prepare the way for Hannibal's return, and that he was condemned to death. He is said to have fled from Carthage and to have collected and trained a 'private' army. On the strength of this he tried but failed to be taken back into favour by his compatriots. When Hannibal returned to Africa he took over Hasdrubal's army and had his death sentence revoked. However, he was still afraid to appear in public at Carthage, and during the winter or spring of 203/2 he committed suicide to escape lynching by an ultra-nationalist mob. A courageous and determined man, loyal to his city and to his class, a good diplomat and administrator, Hasdrubal must surely rank as one of the worst generals that the

war produced. He was, of course, unfortunate in being opposed throughout almost his whole career by the genius of Scipio.

After the battle Scipio consulted with his advisers and decided that
while he with one part of the army should move deliberately back towards
Carthage, subjugating the towns and villages on his march, Laelius and
Masinissa with the other part, including the Numidians, should follow
Syphax and allow him no time to consolidate the defence of his kingdom.
When he approached Castra Cornelia, Scipio sent on there the great mass
of booty that he had collected after the battle and from the sacking of
the towns that had not voluntarily surrendered to him. He then marched
to Tunis, and encamped in front of the city, in full view from the walls
of Carthage, ten miles away across the lagoon. The garrison decamped
and Scipio occupied the town, thus cutting Carthage off from the interior
of Libya.

He was hardly established in this strong position when he was
thoroughly alarmed to see the Punic fleet putting out to sea from Carthage. He had not expected that the Carthaginians would venture to attack
his camp from the sea without the cooperation of an army; and having
left in a hurry in order to catch Hasdrubal on the Great Plains before
his army got any larger, he had made no arrangements and given no
orders for the defence of his naval station. The sailing of the fleet was
in fact only one outcome of a crisis debate in the Carthaginian Council,
at which it had been decided to strike at the Roman camp in the absence
of the general and the bulk of his army, to prepare the City to withstand
a siege and to recall Hannibal and Mago from Italy and Gaul to defend
their fatherland.

Scipio acted with his customary decision and speed. He at once
marched his army back to Castra Cornelia, which he reached in ample
time to make the necessary preparations for its defence before the enemy
(who had taken all day over the voyage) arrived and beached their ships
for the night at Rusucmon (Porto Farina), just inside the bay of Utica.
Scipio's fleet had been prepared for siege work and was in no state to
undertake a naval battle, so he moored the warships close inshore and
constructed a boom composed of supply ships lashed together to protect
them, with a gangway running from ship to ship throughout its length
and gaps left between many of the vessels to serve as sally-ports for light
craft. The next day the Carthaginians put to sea at sunrise and offered
battle, and only much later, when they realized the condition of the enemy
fleet, did they sail in to attack the boom, and, after a hard fight, succeed
in towing off sixty of the merchantmen by means of grappling irons.
There can be very little doubt that if they had made this attack while
Scipio was away in the interior, or if the admiral (whose name may have
been Hamilcar) had displayed even ordinary promptness and resolution

in carrying out his task, they could have inflicted the most serious damage on Scipio's fleet, even if they did not succeed in destroying or capturing the whole of it.

Meanwhile Laelius and Masinissa had arrived, about fifteen days after the battle of the Great Plains, in the former kingdom of Masinissa's father, and without much difficulty drove out Syphax's prefects and garrisons. Back in his own kingdom Syphax hurriedly raised fresh levies and prepared to contest the approaches to his eastern capital, Cirta (Constantine). When the Romans came up a skirmish between cavalry pickets developed into a full-scale cavalry battle, in which the Masaesyles more than held their own until the velites joined in and then the legionaries came onto the field, whereupon Syphax's men fled and Syphax himself, unhorsed, was taken prisoner. The rout and the capture of the king were followed by the capture of the enemy's camp. Masinissa then pressed ahead with the cavalry to Cirta, which surrendered to him when the king was paraded in chains before its leading men. Syphax's queen, encountering the victor in the forecourt of the palace, rose superbly to the occasion; and when Laelius arrived with the infantry he discovered that Sophonisba, in order to protect her virtue from the Romans, had become the wife of Masinissa. Laelius was most indignant, but he agreed to refer the matter to the commander-in-chief; and after sending Syphax and their most important prisoners to Scipio the two leaders attacked and captured a number of places in eastern Numidia. However the rest of the kingdom to the north and west remained in the hands of Syphax's son Vermina.

When Laelius and Masinissa returned to Castra Cornelia they found that Scipio, having talked to the vindictive Syphax, was in no mood to permit Sophonisba to bring her dangerous charms to bear on Masinissa as well. Bending all the force of his personality upon the prince he reminded him that Sophonisba, like Syphax himself, his kingdom and everything in it, was the lawful booty of the Roman people and hinted that the fate of Syphax was a heavy price to pay for the pleasures of a marriage-bed. With rather less impulsiveness but no less emotion than he had displayed when he married her, Masinissa sent her the poison that he kept for his own direst extremity, and she drank it with the same resoluteness with which she had always worked for her father's and her city's interests. The next day Masinissa received the reward of his perspicacity. At a public ceremony, at which Laelius and other officers were decorated for their services, Scipio addressed him as 'king' and presented him with triumphal ornaments, and the prince was given to understand that he was approved as the successor of Syphax to the kingdom of all Numidia.

Laelius was then sent to Rome with the distinguished captives and with envoys of Masinissa while Scipio moved back to Tunis. The Roman Senate approved all that Scipio had done, confirmed Masinissa in his title of king and sent Syphax for internment to the town of Alba Fucens (he was subsequently moved to Tibur, where he probably died before Scipio's return from Africa). At Carthage the overthrow of Syphax caused the views of the 'peace party' – in general identifiable with the big landowners – to prevail; while the 'war party' – which included the Barcine faction but was not identical with it – took a leaf out of Scipio's book and agreed to negotiate pending the arrival in Africa of Hannibal. The thirty members of the Inner Council (the *Gerousia*) were sent to Tunis to prostrate themselves before Scipio and, in language with which the world of diplomacy has always been familiar, to lay the blame for the war on someone else – in this case on Hannibal and his advisers – and to sue for a lenient peace. Scipio's terms, apart from the customary clause dealing with captives, deserters and fugitives, were that Carthage should withdraw all her forces from Europe and the islands, surrender the bulk of her navy, pay an indemnity (probably of five thousand talents) and supply food and perhaps double pay for the Roman army, until its final withdrawal. It is probable that there were also clauses delimiting Carthage's possessions in Africa and recognizing Masinissa's claim to the kingdom of Numidia. The Carthaginians agreed to these conditions, arranged an armistice with Scipio and sent an embassy to Rome to treat with the Senate.

Scipio was a realist and he knew very well that the Roman people, exhausted by the war in Italy, would not allow it to drag on simply in order to afford him the satisfaction and glory of capturing Carthage. Old Fabius died this year, but political opposition to Scipio from other quarters was growing. Former allies no less than old enemies had become envious of his success, and there were those in the Senate who wondered whether he might not even come to constitute a danger to the established order. And above all personal considerations, Rome and Italy desperately needed peace. The terms that Scipio had proposed would ensure that Carthage could never aspire to threaten Rome's supremacy in the western Mediterranean, as she would from then on be policed by a powerful, independent but pro-Roman Numidia.

The year 203 saw Italy finally freed from the presence of the African enemy. In the course of the summer Mago had at last launched his offensive against the Romans in Cisalpine Gaul and advanced with about thirty thousand men into the territory of the Insubres. He was brought to battle by the armies of P. Quinctilius Varus, the praetor, and the proconsul Cethegus. The fight was a stubborn one, and Mago's elephants proved most effectual against the Roman cavalry. However the Romans gradually gained the upper hand in the infantry battle, and when the general fell wounded the orderly retirement of his men degenerated into a rout. The Roman losses appear to have been about three thousand dead, including three military tribunes. Mago made good his retreat to Savo, where he found envoys sent to recall him to Africa. Accordingly he embarked his army (it was now autumn) and sailed; but he did not live to see his fatherland, for he died at sea. Some of his ships were captured by the Sardinian squadron – the attentions both of the governor of Sardinia and of the admiral Octavius were directed to the provisioning of Scipio's army – but his army was brought safely to Africa, to Leptis Minor, where it was incorporated with that of Hannibal. The consul Geminus had also advanced from Etruria into Gaul and had the personal satisfaction of releasing from captivity two of the colonial commissioners seized by the Boii in 218, one of whom was his own father. The Roman armies pursuing Mago's retreat took Genua, which Mago had destroyed, and Sp. Lucretius (propraetor) was instructed to rebuild it.

In Bruttium the consul Caepio received the surrender of the principal town, Consentia, as well as of many other places. Hannibal was now confined to a small region around Croton, his camp being near the temple of Lacinian Juno. He had nothing left to hope for in Italy, but he dared not return to Carthage without an assurance of his welcome there and his safety. He received this in the late summer of 203, in the form of a message delivered by envoys from the Council recalling him to defend his country. He had acquired and built ships, and no doubt others had come with the envoys; indeed, Appian tells us that the govenment sent their admiral with ships. The apparently total absence of the Roman navy from the waters between Croton and Africa suggests that the Senate intended to put no obstacle or discouragement in the way of Hannibal's removal from Italian soil; and for this, and for Mago's departure from Liguria, a five days' thanks offering was made at Rome. Hannibal distributed as garrisons those of his men, mainly Bruttians, no doubt, who were unwilling or too unfit to go with him, among the few towns that were still holding out, and in the autumn embarked the remainder for Africa, arriving without incident at Leptis Minor on the east coast of Punic Africa. He moved from there with Mago's army as well as his own to Hadrumetum (Sousse), where he established his winter quarters.

When the Carthaginian peace envoys arrived in Rome they were granted an audience with the Senate in the temple of Bellona and in spite of opposition on the part of Laevinus and Livius, formerly supporters of the Aemilian party, the Senate and subsequently the people ratified the treaty formulated by Scipio. In the meantime, however, a crisis had arisen in Africa. Cn. Octavius had brought a huge supply convoy across from Sicily, which had been scattered by a sudden storm when almost in sight of land, and the merchantmen had been driven ashore on

Carthaginian territory, within sight of the hungry populace. The latter persuaded the Council to order their admiral, a Hasdrubal, to put to sea and collect the vessels and bring them to Carthage, where the demands of Scipio's army under the terms of the armistice and the increase in the number of mouths to be fed due to the influx of refugees from the country had combined to cause a serious shortage of food. Scipio, who had just received unofficial news of the ratification of his treaty, sent an embassy of protest. But the Carthaginians, their optimism restored by the recent arrival of Hannibal, not only rejected Scipio's protest but arranged that the quinquereme in which the envoys were returning to Castra Cornelia should be attacked not far from the camp, with the result that the ship was driven ashore with heavy loss of life, although the envoys escaped unharmed. As a result the armistice was considered to have been broken and a state of war to exist once more. When, somewhat later, the Carthaginian peace envoys arrived at Scipio's camp in the company of the Roman priestly officials (*fetiales*) who were sent to conclude the peace, they feared for their safety; but Scipio had the good sense to treat them in the prescribed manner and to send them to their city unharmed.

At Rome the elections for 202 were conducted by P. Sulpicius Galba as dictator, since one of the consuls, Caepio, had apparently taken the view that as his province comprised Bruttium and the war against Hannibal, he was entitled to pursue his adversary to Africa, and had accordingly crossed over into Sicily. Meanwhile the other consul, Geminus, was fully occupied in Etruria with his treason trials. The master of horse, M. Servilius Pulex Geminus, and Ti. Claudius Nero were elected consuls. It is possible that before abdicating his office Galba, at the request of the Senate, wrote to Caepio ordering him, by virtue of his superior authority, to return to Italy. When the consular year began the consuls made an effort to have Africa designated a consular province and Claudius was indeed instructed, since hostilities had now recommenced there, to prepare a fleet of fifty ships, take it across to Africa and cooperate with Scipio. Scipio, however, was to have the responsibility and the glory of formulating the final treaty of peace. In the event Claudius was so dilatory in his preparations that it was late in the year when he sailed, and he was then forced by stress of weather to lay up his ships for the winter in Sardinia. The other consul was required to remain in the vicinity of Rome in case he should be needed, although Etruria had been allotted to him as his province.

CHAPTER XIX

202-201 BC

Zama and the end of the Carthaginian empire.

Scipio had passed the winter between Castra Cornelia and Tunis, and with the opening of the campaigning season he left the naval camp in the keeping of his legate L. Baebius and marched into the interior taking town after town and selling the inhabitants – a policy of calculated harshness intended to force the Carthaginians to summon Hannibal to their defence before he could build up and fully train a new army. Hannibal, however, was not to be hurried. He was waiting for the arrival of a Numidian prince, Tychaeus, a kinsman of Syphax and perhaps the leader of the Areacidae, and of Syphax's son Vermina, and he did not intend to move until his preparations were complete. Scipio, too, was short of cavalry and wrote repeatedly to Masinissa asking for his support. After the signing of the armistice, Masinissa had gone with Scipio's legates, his own men and a body of Roman horse and foot to recover control of his father's kingdom and to seize as much of Syphax's as he could. In order to expedite the junction of their armies, and also to avoid being brought to battle before Masinissa joined him, Scipio had moved south-west into the upper Bagradas basin, to the vicinity of Naraggara (Sidi Youssef).

Hannibal, after being joined by Tychaeus and two thousand horsemen, marched westward from Hadrumetum to the neighbourhood of Zama Regia (Seba Biar) and from there sent three spies to reconnoitre Scipio's army. These were detected, given a conducted tour of the camp and then sent back to their master. By this seemingly artless piece of magnanimity Scipio encouraged Hannibal to believe that Masinissa had let him down, although we may be quite certain that he had been informed that the king, with six thousand foot and four thousand horse, was then only a few days' march away. Hannibal then sent a herald to suggest a parley, to which Scipio, after Masinissa's arrival, agreed, and appointed as the meeting-place a battlefield of his own choosing, for he must have known quite well that nothing would come of the proposed colloquy. This was in the plain of Draa el Metnan, to which he advanced and camped on a hill at the western end, while Hannibal moved from Zama and pitched his camp on rising ground a little less than three and a half miles distant.

The two generals met on the plain and talked alone together, through an interpreter. Hannibal spoke of the notorious fickleness of Fortune, tactfully citing his own career as an object lesson and suggesting that peace should be made on the simple basis of Carthage's agreeing to confine her empire to Africa. Such a proposal, more favourable to Carthage than the terms of the broken treaty, was quite unacceptable; yet it was worth Hannibal's while to make it. There was a remote possibility that Scipio might allow himself to be overawed by the noble presence and the fame of his adversary – especially if (as Hannibal believed) he had been deserted by Masinissa over a hundred miles from his base. At least Hannibal could tell his own people that he had done his best to make peace and that the favour of the gods would be with them.

At daybreak the next day – it is generally reckoned to have been a day in October – both armies deployed for battle in the plain, 'the Carthaginians fighting for their own safety and for the control of Africa, the Romans for the empire of the world' (Polybius); which was certainly a true enough statement from the standpoint of history, although the Romans at that time were hardly conscious of its truth with reference to themselves. Hannibal throughout his career had made it his business to 'know his enemy' and he will certainly have discussed Scipio and his tactics with survivors of the Great Plains battle and possibly of Ilipa, too. He knew that he was up against a man who was both a 'professional' and a master tactician. It is therefore interesting that he drew up his heterogeneous army in three lines in the Roman manner, although not, of course, in maniples. He stationed the twelve thousand mercenaries, who must have included the survivors of Mago's expedition – Ligurian and Gaulish swordsmen, Balearic slingers and Moroccan archers – in the first line, the Libyan and Carthaginian levies (including Hasdrubal's men) in the second, and in the third the troops that he had brought over with him from Italy, mainly Bruttians. These last, his 'Old Guard', the flower of his army, were drawn up at an interval of about a furlong behind the rest of the army. The left flank was covered by his Numidian horse, the right by the Carthaginian; and in front of his whole array he stationed his war elephants, more than eighty in number. Modern historians are inclined to dismiss as exaggeration estimates of the size of Hannibal's army which would give him between 40,000 and 50,000 men; but Scipio's tactics are difficult to understand unless the rearmost of Hannibal's three divisions was almost as strong as Scipio's whole heavy infantry force after it had suffered appreciable casualties – that is to say, it numbered between 10,000 and 12,000 men. In that case we may assume that Hannibal had in all between 32,000 and 35,000 'heavy' infantry, many of whom, however, although put into the line, should really be regarded as light infantry, while the whole of the second division were very poor fighting material.

Scipio clearly took Hannibal's elephants much more seriously than he had taken Hasdrubal's at Ilipa. When he drew up his three lines of legionaries he placed the maniples of the principes and triarii directly behind the maniples of the line in front instead of behind the gaps in it (thus abandoning the customary chequer-board formation). This provided passage-ways through his army from front to back, and the gaps between the maniples of the hastati were filled, at the start of the battle, by velites. Gaius Laelius commanded the Italian cavalry on the left while Masinissa led his Numidians, horse and foot intermingled in the native manner, on the right. The Roman army may have amounted to some thirty-five thousand men, but in cavalry they were undoubtedly superior to the Carthaginians. That Scipio was prepared to fight a more numerous enemy is evidence of the confidence that he felt in the superior quality of his own soldiers and in his own genius as a leader.

After the customary harangues by both generals to their troops, skirmishing began on the Carthaginian left and then Hannibal launched his elephant attack, his Numidians coming forward in support. The elephants were in all probability inadequately trained. Some were at once scared off by the braying of the Roman trumpets and bugles, and bolted to the left where they helped Masinissa to complete the rout of Tychaeus' Numidians. The rest, after a bloody combat with the velites, who had poured out into the space between the two main bodies, were driven either through the corridors which had been left in the Roman ranks and so harmlessly to the rear or else away to the right. There Laelius took advantage of the confusion that they caused among the Carthaginian cavalry, and charging with his own men drove the enemy's horse from the field. The situation now resembled that at the end of the opening stage of Cannae – only this time the boot was on the other foot and Hannibal, who had won so many battles with his horsemen was left completely without cavalry.

Meanwhile the two great masses of heavy infantry – all, that is, except Hannibal's third line, the veterans, who remained where they had first been stationed – rolled slowly together, shouting their war-cries and the Romans beating upon their shields. The front ranks clashed and remorselessly the hastati drove the Punic mercenaries back, the principes and triarii trudging behind and yelling them on, while Hannibal's second division, the Libyan and Carthaginian levies, hung back and made no attempt to reinforce the collapsing front. Finally the mercenaries broke and in trying to force their way to the rear came to blows with their own second division. These were now forced to fight for their lives against their own men as well as against the hastati, who still carried the whole weight of the Roman attack, while the second and third lines stood firm and maintained their formation unshaken. In the end Roman discipline and courage told, and the survivors of the slaughter of Hannibal's two leading divisions, confronted when they turned to run by the levelled spears of the third line behind them, were driven out towards the wings and out of the battle, thus leaving a clear space between Scipio's men and the army of Italy.

There now followed a pause in the fighting. Scipio's bugles sounded the rally and the hastati, thoroughly disorganized by the confused nature of the fighting and by the completeness of their victory – for some of them were still pursuing the broken remnants of Hannibal's front lines while others were scattered among the piles of the slain – fell back and re-formed. They closed the gaps between the maniples and sent their wounded to the rear. The hastati now constituted the centre of Scipio's reorganized line, and the principes and triarii, also in close order, were brought up on their flanks and into line with them. When everybody was ready Scipio gave the order to advance over ground encumbered with bodies and weapons and slippery with blood, and the second phase of the battle began. The veterans of Italy, fighting under their general's eye, and having before them death in battle or a lifetime of slavery as the only alternatives to victory, were now pitted against the veterans of Cannae, who had fourteen years of disgrace to expunge. The struggle between the two bodies of men, almost equal in number, similarly armed and well matched in courage and determination, was a bitter one, but it was brought to an end when Scipio's cavalry returned opportunely from its pursuit of the enemy and fell upon the rear of the Punic phalanx. The army of Italy was cut to pieces, the fugitives from the shambles being for the most part run down and killed by the horsemen in that open, level country. Hannibal himself escaped with a handful of cavalry. Estimates of the Punic losses vary between 20,000 killed and almost as many captured and 25,000 killed and 8,500 captured. The Romans lost 1,500, or 2,500, and Masinissa may have lost over 2,500 of his men.

Zama (as the battle is called) certainly paid for Cannae. This time it was a superbly drilled Roman body of veteran infantry, supported by a powerful cavalry arm commanded by experienced cavalry officers, that defeated – indeed, annihilated – a larger force, weak in cavalry, much of it composed of raw recruits and with a recent history of defeat almost everywhere. Yet Hannibal had done everything that a great soldier could have done with the material at his disposal. Clearly he had expected better things of his elephants, who should have been able to disrupt the Roman front ranks as they had done on the Trebia, and so made things easier for his own infantry. The mercenaries, expendable in any case, were intended to dispose of the hastati (whom they heavily outnumbered) and with the support of their second line to rout the principes as well. That would have left Hannibal the master of the battlefield, with his reserve – his best troops, at least ten thousand strong – fresh and in a position to launch a devastating final charge against the 2,400 or so triarii and whatever remained on the field of the first two lines, the latter weary, beaten and with blunted swords.

But at Zama, Hannibal had not encountered a Longus or a Varro or a Fulvius; his elephants were not the noble beasts that had crossed the Pyrenees, the Rhône and the Alps; his cavalry, inferior in number, had apparently no Hasdrubal, Hanno or Maharbal to lead them; his Balearic slingers and Moroccan bowmen were of little use in hand-to-hand fighting and in retreat; and his second line, which might have done useful work if the mercenaries had succeeded in driving back the enemy in disorder, were not the stuff to stem an advance that was carrying all before it. However a lesser general than Scipio might still have lost the battle, for Hannibal's dispositions left him with a reserve with which to launch a counter-attack which, if the Romans had come on in disorder, might still have given him the victory. But Scipio had his whole army well in hand, and so the final clash was between two well-ordered bodies of infantry; and the army of Italy, instead of having mainly tired and dispirited troops to deal with, met an enemy with three-fifths of their men as fresh as they were themselves, and all of them flushed with victory. Had it been possible for Hannibal to throw his veterans against Scipio's army while it was still in the process of re-forming and re-deploying, he might have won the day; but the probability is that the wreckage of his forward divisions obstructed his advance even more than Scipio's and that both generals were equally aware of the fact.

At Zama Hannibal experienced the truth that was to be put into words two thousand years later by Napoleon: that in war the balance of moral over material advantage is in the proportion of three to one. Of all Hannibal's army only the veterans of Italy had the quality to stand up to the legions, and they could not win the battle by themselves. It was fitting, however, that the legions of Cannae should be the instrument of Hannibal's overthrow, and that, as at Cannae, it was the attack from the rear by cavalry that had chased their adversaries off the field that made the victory complete. The accounts of the battle that have come down to us try to heighten the tension by implying that Scipio's cavalry arrived only in the nick of time. It is however more likely that Scipio had made allowance for the notorious difficulty of controlling cavalry on the field of battle and that Laelius and Masinissa were no more dilatory in delivering their final attack than Hasdrubal had been on the banks of the Aufidus.

Hannibal rode straight to his base at Hadrumetum and from there was summoned to Carthage, which he had not seen since he left it thirty-five years before to join his father in Spain. He advised the Council that they had now no alternative but to ask for peace. Scipio plundered the enemy's camp and then returned to Castra Cornelia, where he found a convoy of fifty galleys and a hundred supply ships brought by the propraetor P. Cornelius Lentulus. He sent Laelius off to Rome with the news of the victory, and then, collecting all the warships at his disposal, a total of 120, sailed for Carthage to make a show of strength, while the propraetor Cn. Octavius, whose ships had been incorporated in Scipio's fleet, marched there at the head of the army. While he was at sea Scipio fell in with a ship carrying envoys sent to sue for peace, and he ordered them to appear before him at Tunis. When he had carried out his naval and military demonstration before the city he returned to Castra Cornelia, and from there marched to Tunis. Reports reached him on the march that Prince Vermina was coming belatedly to the help of Carthage with a force of cavalry and foot soldiers, and so he detached the cavalry and some of the infantry – including, no doubt, the velites – to deal with him. They intercepted the Numidians, according to tradition on the first day of the Saturnalia, in mid-December, and cut them to pieces, Vermina himself escaping with a few of his men.

At Tunis the thirty elders again prostrated themselves with lamentations before Scipio, whom they found unsympathetic towards their troubles but inclined to make peace. Scipio must have been fully aware of the strength of the opposition, bred of envy and nervousness, that was building up against him in the Senate. If the war were allowed to continue he would find Carthage a tougher nut to crack than Syracuse, and it had taken Marcellus three years to take the latter. Even if Scipio were not recalled he would certainly find himself saddled with a colleague – and probably a hostile colleague – in the shape of a consul, who at best would share with him the glory of bringing the war to an end. Moreover there were strong arguments, based on Roman tradition, on the conduct expected of a civilized Hellenistic man, and on political expediency, for not destroying Carthage. Carthage might prove a useful ally in the struggles which must inevitably follow in the eastern Mediterranean, for the Greeks were already complaining at Rome of violations of the Peace of Phoenice by Philip and the Senate had sent him a strong protest.

Scipio therefore dictated his revised peace terms. Carthage was to retain her autonomy and all her possessions intact 'within the Phoenician Trenches' – the dyke which delimited the territory of Carthage. She was to make reparation for the seizure of the Roman ships and the attack on the embassy; to hand over all prisoners of war, deserters and runaway slaves; to surrender all her galleys apart from ten triremes, and all her trained elephants, and she was not to train any more; she was not to make war on any nation outside Africa, or on any nation in Africa without Rome's permission; she was to hand over to Masinissa all towns, property and goods that had belonged to him or to his ancestors within certain limits to be subsequently decided; to furnish Scipio's army with corn for three months and with pay until the Senate and people approved (or rejected) the proposed treaty; to pay a war indemnity of ten thousand talents over a period of fifty years; and she was to give a hundred hostages, to be chosen by Scipio from the nobility, between the ages of fourteen and thirty.

These conditions were intended to render Carthage harmless to Rome for the foreseeable future. They gave Masinissa a free hand in north Africa to create a kingdom stretching from the borders of Mauretania to the Phoenician Trenches, and Carthage's only defence against his further depredations was the good faith of Rome and her willingness, in the name of justice, to defend someone who had been her most hated enemy against an ally. It is probable that all the implications of the sinister words 'everything that had belonged to Masinissa and to his ancestors' did not occur to Scipio, who would be thinking only of the kingdoms of the Massyles and the Masaesyles. In intention, the terms of the treaty were reasonable and even lenient if considered from the Roman point of view, that Carthage had provoked the war in the first place and that she had inflicted appalling loss of life and material damage on Rome and her allies during the sixteen years of hostilities.

The thirty took these terms back to Carthage and laid them before the Council. Hannibal dragged from the rostrum with his own hands a councillor who was advocating rejection of the terms (Livy tells us that his name was Gisgo, and it is tempting to believe him and to suppose that this was the son of the late Hasdrubal, the leader of the non-Barcine war party), and declared that the terms were better than they had any right to hope for and must be accepted. Accordingly the Council voted to accept them, an armistice was granted by Scipio and a deputation that comprised the most reverend and most distinguished members of the nobility, led by one of the chiefs of the anti-Barcine faction, Hasdrubal Haedus, was sent to Rome with an escort that included Lucius Scipio. The Senate gave audience to the party in the temple of Bellona, where L. Veturius Philo, who had brought the news of the Metaurus battle to Rome in 207, now had the privilege of describing Zama and the events which, it was hoped, would lead to the ending of the war.

The Carthaginians made most moving pleas for peace, which the Senate was disposed to accept. However one of the consuls for 201, Cn. Cornelius Lentulus (who should have been a supporter of the Cornelian Scipio), who had had a fleet assigned to him and the right to cross over to Africa if peace negotiations broke down, interposed his veto on the senatorial proceedings. Two tribunes friendly to Scipio then brought before the plebs, as the Senate had decreed, the questions, whether Scipio should grant the peace and whether he should bring back the army from Africa (and therefore be allowed to triumph for the war). The plebs voted unanimously in favour of Scipio, and accordingly the Senate empowered him to make the peace, assisted by ten senatorial legates. Furthermore the Senate, in a burst of generosity, freed two hundred noble Carthaginian prisoners without ransom. The fetiales were sent to Africa and the peace was concluded on Scipio's terms. Four thousand captives were released and all Carthage's war fleet, apart from the ten triremes, was burnt at sea before the eyes of the citizens. Scipio, at a public meeting, presented Masinissa with Syphax's capital of Cirta, as well as with all the late king's other cities and lands and with a number of war elephants – a further reminder to Masinissa that he was king only by the favour of Rome – a 'client' king. Then after having all his actions formally confirmed by the Senate and people of Rome, he took his army across to Lilybaem and from there to Italy, probably coming ashore himself at Puteoli and making a triumphal progress through Italy to Rome, where he celebrated the most distinguished triumph witnessed down to that time. Polybius states that King Syphax walked in it, but other writers say that he died at Tibur shortly before. Setting an example that was to be followed in the next century by others Scipio assumed the cognomen Africanus, from the country that he had conquered.

No war is inevitable until after the fighting has started. However from the day that Rome concluded a treaty with Saguntum a positive effort was going to be required if a renewal of hostilities between Rome and Carthage was to be prevented, and by 219 none of the three leading actors in the drama was prepared to make that effort. Rome did not fear war with Carthage; she had beaten her once and she could beat her again. Apart from other considerations, the treaty with Saguntum was intended to remind Carthage of that fact – to remind her that she no longer controlled the western Mediterranean and was no longer in a position to exclude Rome from Spain. Carthage herself had done well enough in the first war to feel that she might be able to do better in a second; she was deeply resentful of Rome's 'perfidious' behaviour over Sardinia; and she had an active 'war party', not exclusively Barcine. Yet neither Rome nor Carthage would have sought an excuse for war – yet.

The will to war, however, existed in Hannibal. As a patriot he wished to make the world safe for Carthage; as the son of Hamilcar, he was determined to reverse the decision of the First Punic War, in which his father's army had lost the war only because it had been stabbed in the back by a supine home government (as the German army believed, after the 1914–18 war); as Hannibal, he burned to equal the exploits and the fame of Alexander. When he succeeded to the government of Spain he felt that he must move at once if he was going to crush Rome. His own military preparedness was as complete as it was ever likely to be, while Rome was making enemies across the Adriatic and had not yet subjugated Cisalpine Gaul; even a year's delay might prove fatal to his whole enterprise. And so, when the Romans failed to come to Spain in the summer of 218, because he felt that he could not wait he threw overboard a plan that offered him a nicely calculated possibility of success, in that it restricted the war to a single theatre and left both Spain and Africa free to reinforce him, and in its place adopted one that depended upon too many uncertainties. Either he had not thought out, or else he summarily dismissed from his calculations, the consequences to himself and to his city if the Italian confederation did not disintegrate as his plan demanded, following the decisive defeat of the Roman army in the field. He had no alternative plan; he could not even do what a Pyrrhus or a Philip of Macedon could do: cut his losses and return home. The glamour of the Barcids could hardly have survived failure on that scale, and the cross could only have been avoided by a military coup – perhaps even by civil war.

In fact his half-success in detaching the greater part of the 'foot' of Italy from the Italian confederation after Cannae was ultimately as fatal as complete failure would have been. Rome steeled herself to fight the war to a finish and put into the field more legions than ever before. At the same time the Senate took the overall conduct of the war out of the hands of the generals. It attacked his allies and so forced him to disperse his army in garrisons and detachments; and by adhering to the strategy of Fabius, it refused him the opportunity of winning another, and perhaps decisive, Cannae. Thus the initiative passed to the Romans whose supply of fighting men appeared to be inexhaustible, whereas every year saw a diminution, by death in action, by disease and by desertions, of his irreplaceable stock of professional soldiers.

He had not foreseen the effect upon his chances of success of a revolt of only part of Rome's allies; he had not considered the effect of an almost total failure on the part of Spain and Africa to reinforce him. There can be no question but that the elder Scipios, by keeping alive the war in Spain until after the fall of Capua, played as important a part in defeating Hannibal as Fabius. When in 215 Carthage found herself faced by the alternatives of reinforcing Hannibal in Italy and reinforcing Hasdrubal in Spain – and also attempting to recover Sardinia – she chose Spain and Sardinia. Yet it was only where Hannibal was fighting that things went well for her. She made no attempt to challenge Rome's command of the sea or to take advantage of the difficulty that the enemy was experiencing in maintaining his fleets owing to shortage of men and money.

Not until it began to seem to them that the safety, first of Spain, and then of Africa itself demanded that the war in Italy should be revived did the home government actually approve the sending of any substantial forces to the Italian theatre. And it did so then not to reinforce Hannibal but to divert Rome's attention from Africa. The figures speak for themselves. During the course of the war Carthage despatched to Spain, to Sardinia, to Sicily and to Liguria at least 77,800 men and 44 elephants, exclusive of the crews of the fleets that were sent to these theatres and to Italy and Greece. Hannibal received 4,000 men and some elephants after Cannae. But that was not all. The feeling of security engendered in the Carthaginian aristocracy by the knowledge that the defence of Africa and the empire was in the expert keeping of the distant Barcids had bred a generation of men unqualified morally and technically to lead armies and fleets. As a result it did not produce, during the whole course of the war, a single soldier of the calibre of such First War generals as Hamilcar I, Adherbal, or Carthalo. The total inadequacy of her commanders in Spain, Sardinia, and Africa, and of her admirals, contributed largely to Carthage's defeat.

It is clear that there was extensive disaffection in Etruria during the last decade of the war in Italy, bred of a resentment at being exploited – at being drained of food, men and money so that the war in the south could be allowed to drag on. But we have no way of knowing how widespread and, what was more important, how deep-rooted it was. Yet in 210 it was probably only beginning to emerge, and by then it would have required an effort on Carthage's part equal to that made by the Romans to have given her a hope of the ultimate victory. Rome won because of the single-minded steadfastness in the face of disaster of her governing class and because of the dogged courage and tenacity – the *integra atque immobilis virtus* – of the Roman people and their allies. If Hannibal had received from his people the unwavering loyalty and support that Rome's generals received from theirs – if those almost eighty thousand men and forty-four elephants had been sent to him – the war might not have lasted long enough for Rome to produce a soldier of equal genius who was able to bring both him and his city to their knees.

CHAPTER XX

201-149 BC

Second interlude. Rome and the Mediterranean.
Carthage, Masinissa and Rome.

The period between the Second and Third Punic Wars is one of the most momentous in the history of the Roman empire, for during it the foundations of 'world' dominion were laid, while those of the Republic were fatally undermined. First the Senate had to settle its outstanding account with Philip of Macedon. He had played into its hands by entering into a compact with Antiochus the Great of Syria to divide the overseas possessions of the infant Ptolemy v of Egypt. By doing so he upset the precarious balance of power in the Aegean, and gave Rhodes and Pergamum (friends of Rome), and subsequently Athens, who invoked the glamour of her glorious past, grounds for asking Rome for assistance. The Senate browbeat a war-weary people into authorizing war, and by 196 the Romans had defeated Philip and restricted his authority to his own ancestral kingdom and T. Quinctius Flamininus had made his tragic-ironical proclamation of Greek freedom at the Isthmian Games at Corinth. But in that year Antiochus invaded Thrace and the question of the balance of power, which now involved Rome as the guarantor of Greek freedom, was raised again. In the following year the now exiled Hannibal became one of Antiochus' counsellors and by 192 a combination of malice on the part of King Eumenes of Pergamum on the one side and the Aetolians on the other and diplomatic cross-purposes between Antiochus and the Senate, led to the invasion of Greece by Antiochus, summoned by the Aetolians to 'liberate the Greeks' from Roman interference in their national affairs.

Antiochus was beaten out of Greece, followed to Asia and decisively defeated at Magnesia by Lucius Scipio in 190. Two years later, by the Treaty of Apamea, Rome so ordered things in the east that she unavoidably became in time the arbiter of Asiatic as well as of Greek affairs. Unfortunately her attitude towards Greeks and Asiatics now underwent a change for the worse. The phil-Hellenism of the Scipios and of Flamininus was replaced by the anti-Hellenism of Cato, the political heir of Fabius Cunctator. The Senate soon fell out of sympathy with the interminable internecine disputes of the Greeks, on which it was expected to

259

adjudicate so as to satisfy everybody; and began to pay less attention to the merits of each case, preferring to follow the more politic course of supporting Rome's most loyal friends. It began to become apparent that when the Greeks spoke of *eleutheria*, with its classical connotation of 'living as one pleases', they did not mean the same things as the Roman meant when he said '*libertas*', freedom to do such things as are *permissible*; and in their mutual understanding the Romans and Greeks drifted ever further apart.

In 179 Philip died and his son Perseus succeeded him and began to restore Macedonian power and influence in northern Greece. This fresh disturbance of the precarious balance brought Rome's good friend Eumenes to Rome to complain of him. Suspicion reinforced by a preference for the expedient caused Rome to declare war on Perseus in 171, and in 168 the Macedonian kingdom and the phalanx, developed and perfected by Philip II and Alexander, were together crushed at Pydna by L. Aemilius Paullus, the son of the Paullus who fell at Cannae. Perseus' sympathizers in Greece were punished, and in particular the luckless Molossians of Epirus, who were sold into slavery to the number of 150,000.

In the Aegean and in Asia Rome worked by diplomacy and intrigue to prevent the rise of any power that might disturb the peace of the area. Rhodes, an old friend, whose unqualified loyalty had seemed to waver in 168, had a crippling blow directed against her prosperity by the creation of a free port at Delos – a piece of retaliation that was to cost Rome and the *oecumene* dear, for it filled the Mediterranean with pirates. Eumenes, too, had appeared to falter in his loyalty, and if his brother Attalus had been less true to him he would have found himself supplanted. The Romans had evolved and were working to a new principle, that any power or any individual who threatened, in whatever degree, Rome's domination of the eastern no less than of the western Mediterranean must be put down. Rome was coming to believe in the efficacy of deterrent terrorism.

So her old enemy Hannibal, now a refugee at the court of King Prusius of Bithynia, was hunted down and driven to suicide. This was a sad end for one of the greatest soldiers and most glamorous figures in history; yet dying at the age of sixty-four he had lived appreciably longer than any of his fellow 'immortals', Alexander the Great, Caesar or Napoleon. No doubt he might have died peacefully in his bed if he had been content to vegetate in retirement in his castle on the coast between Acholla and Thapsus. Then his later career would not have been unlike that of his conqueror Scipio, who died a year or two before he did, an embittered man living in self-imposed exile from the city that he had served so well and had found so ungrateful. The corruption of Carthaginian society, however, had gone much deeper than that of Roman, and Hannibal, with his 'democratic' family traditions and his estrangement from his own order, felt obliged to rectify abuses. And so, earning the hatred of the magnates, Hannibal destroyed himself, just as, fifty years later, a grandson of Scipio, Tiberius Gracchus, was to destroy himself because he had underestimated the strength and the malignity of the vested interests. Moreover he contributed to the destruction of Carthage, for some of the odium which he incurred at Rome by allying himself with Antiochus attached also to his city, and the very prosperity which he had promoted became an object of Roman fear and suspicion. All in all, it would perhaps have been better for him and for Carthage if he had fallen in the hour of defeat on the field of Zama.

During the time that she was establishing her protectorate over the Greeks Rome was extending and reinforcing her absolute dominion over Liguria, Gallia Cisalpina, the islands and Spain. Until 166 BC Liguria was regularly a consular province, and it was not until the eve of the last Punic War, after several defeats and after transporting forty thousand of these warlike people to Samnium, that Rome could feel that she had pacified the region. By that time, too, Gallia Cisalpina had been so completely subjugated that Polybius could say (albeit incorrectly) that the Celts had been almost wholly expelled from the province. It took some hard fighting to complete the subjugation of Corsica and Sardinia, but it was in Spain that the Romans encountered the longest-lived and bitterest resistance. By 179 Ti. Sempronius Gracchus, whose father had commanded the volones in southern Italy in the war against Hannibal, had reduced the Celtiberi, and by his wise settlement gave Spain a generation's peace. Then, from about 155, disturbances broke out in Lusitania and again among the Celtiberi, and Roman military incompetence and bad faith characterized the operations there during the fifties.

A war on the scale of the Hannibalic War could not fail to have far-reaching – indeed, catastrophic – effects upon Roman and Italian society. During the second century BC, and particularly in the years following the Third Macedonian War, the pattern of Italian agriculture, the economic basis of Italian society, changed as a result of many factors. These included the growth of large estates upon public land, the encroachment of scientific, capitalistic farming for profit upon the essentially 'subsistence' economy of the peasants, the increasing replacement of free labourers by slaves (particularly after 167) and the drift, later swelling to a flood, of country people into the towns and especially into Rome.

There the enormous influx of wealth, public as well as private (the levy of tributum was discontinued after 167), led to extensive building by the state and by individuals; and the rapidly rising standards of living and culture as a result of contact with the Hellenistic world promoted a rapid growth of demand for goods, both manufactured and imported (including luxuries), and for services. The result was that Rome began to offer both the allurements of Hellenistic urban life and the possibility of urban employment. The allies, affected equally by the same economic trends, and increasingly oppressed by a disproportionate share of Rome's military burden, although they were not allowed to share the advantages accruing to Rome from her militarism, were lapsing steadily into the position not of associates but of subjects, and began to voice their indignation over instances of Roman arrogance, stigmatized as 'tyranny'. The number of those – Romans as well as allies – liable for military service on account of their property qualification (*assidui*) fell, and it became increasingly difficult to raise troops for the unpopular campaigns where only hard knocks and little booty were to be had, especially in Spain.

During all this time the governing class, now distinguished as the Senatorial Order, grew further and further away from the business class, the Equestrian Order, and from the mass of the people. The ruling élite, the nobility, enjoyed a virtual monopoly of the consulship, employing bribery now in addition to the traditional methods of manipulating the electorate; and because of the prestige of the ex-consuls in the Senate, they controlled the deliberative machinery while the almost complete subordination of the tribunate to senatorial authority gave them control of the legislative machinery as well. The increasingly extensive manumission of slaves had a significant effect upon the growth and composition of the urban population and upon the political followings of the great houses. 'Parties' rose and fell within the Senate as before. The Scipios were driven out of public life in the eighties, and throughout the period M. Porcius Cato campaigned against the new spirit of luxury and extravagance that had entered the upper classes, bringing with it a decline in public and private morality, an increasing contempt for the state religion and for conventional attitudes and behaviour, and an abandonment of the old rustic simplicity of life – all referable to contact with decadent Hellenism. In his crusade for moral reform, if in nothing else, he had the support of P. Scipio Nasica in the fifties.

Greed, ambition, success, the rise of new families and the weakening of the solidarity of the clan (*gens*) undermined both the morality and the solidarity of the aristocracy as a whole, and Roman foreign policy, which had formerly been characterized in general by a sense of justice, good faith and moderation, was now all too regularly disfigured by expediency, bad faith and oppression. Abandoning a predilection to be allowed to mind her own business and to let others mind theirs, Rome had gradually come to see herself first as the divinely ordained protector of the weak against the tyranny of the great, and then as the only great power, whose supremacy it was tantamount to an act of war to challenge or even to question.

It should however be remembered that by the middle of the century – in the lifetime of men who had fought against Hannibal – Rome had fallen into the rôle, for which there was no precedent, of moderator of the civilized world. Yet to carry out her rôle she had only the political machinery of a third-century Italian city state, and her military resources seemed at times painfully inadequate to the immensity of her task. It is therefore, perhaps, hardly to be wondered at if exasperation not unmingled with anxiety caused her sometimes to have recourse to a 'final solution', and to decree the extirpation of a people whom, rightly or wrongly, she had judged to be incapable of preserving the *pax Romana*.

Although with the loss of her empire Carthage ceased to be a superpower, she was still a great and prosperous city. Masinissa was fully occupied with the tasks of bringing his father's kingdom completely under his authority and of subjugating that of Syphax, whose son Vermina still reigned over a portion of his father's dominions and was accorded peace terms and recognized as king by the Roman Senate. Masinissa, who had been brought up at Carthage and had moved for much of his life among the aristocracy of Carthage, and had recently come in contact with that of Rome, devoted himself to the task that he had inherited from Syphax: that of unifying the Numidians – of creating a single kingdom of Numidia – and of leading them from their primitive pastoral and hunting ways to those of settled agriculture and urban civilization. Syphax had made a start by founding two royal capitals at Siga in the west and at Cirta in the east, striking money embellished with his portrait in the Hellenistic manner, uniting a larger number of tribes under his sway than any of his predecessors and compelling some at least of the Libyphoenician coastal towns to accept his suzerainty. Masinissa continued his predecessor's policy and eventually brought all the northern coastal towns under his sway, even Hippo Regius. Since they were no longer members of a trading association which monopolized the commerce of Spain and the Atlantic coast they had nothing to gain by remaining the loyal allies of Carthage. Indeed they prospered by becoming the outlets and marts of the new Numidia, while at the same time they assisted in the spread of Punic civilization over the hinterland. However much Carthage might deplore this development, she could not complain; her dominion was limited to the area within the Phoenician Trenches.

Although he never gave up his love of horsemanship or the simple habits of a nomadic chieftain Masinissa endeavoured to rule like a Hellenistic monarch from his capital of Cirta. He wore the royal diadem, employed Phoenician as his official language, struck money, encouraged the growth of trade between his kingdom and Carthage to their mutual advantage, sent gifts to Greek cities and gods, and saw one of his sons a Panathenaic victor in the games at Athens. To each of his sons (he had at least ten living at the time of his death, one only four years old) he entrusted an area of ten thousand *plethra* (the *plethron* contained ten thousand square feet) which was to serve as a kind of huge model farm, producing all kinds of crops, so as to prove to the tribesmen – what no one had hitherto believed – that the soil of Numidia could be cultivated. In this way he contributed, as Strabo says, to the process of changing the nomads into community dwellers and agriculturalists. Meanwhile he created and trained a modern national army to take the place of the tribal bands of horsemen, more brigands than soldiers, that had hitherto served the Numidian chiefs.

Deprived of Spanish silver her monopoly of western Mediterranean trade and the tribute and harbour dues of her vanished empire, and saddled with a heavy war indemnity payable to Rome, Carthage's commercial and manufacturing skills and her highly developed methods of intensive farming still gave her the potential for prosperity. Hannibal is said to have played a large part in promoting the cultivation of the olive; and (probably in 196) he put through reforms as suffete, and carried out a thorough review of the nation's resources in conjunction with the popular Assembly, that both restored to the control of the people the Council of 104 judges, which had acquired power over 'the property, reputations and lives of the whole community', and put a stop to the embezzlement and misapplication of the City's revenue by the oligarchs. As a result of Hannibal's policy Carthage was able, by 191, to offer to pay off the whole amount of indemnity still outstanding in a lump sum. But in 195 Hannibal himself had been driven into exile to the court of King Antiochus by an alliance of his inveterate enemies among the nobility and the Romans, on the pretext that he was intriguing with that monarch against Rome.

Becoming one of Antiochus' trusted advisers Hannibal did in fact send an agent, Ariston of Tyre, to Carthage, but he·was detected and forced to leave the city. However Masinissa, taking advantage of Carthage's domestic problems and of the suspicion under which she had inevitably fallen at Rome, now began to encroach upon the areas outside the Phoenician Trenches in which he was permitted, by the treaty of 201, to claim whatever had belonged to his forbears. Carthage complained to Rome; Rome sent a commission to adjudicate on the spot that included Scipio Africanus himself. It set the pattern for the behaviour of future commissions by declining to give a decision, and so leaving Masinissa in possession of whatever gains he had so far made. Scipio and his colleagues had come up against the claim put forward by Masinissa that every inch of Carthaginian territory except for the citadel of Carthage itself, the Byrsa, represented land forcibly acquired by the Carthaginians from 'his ancestors'. And no doubt they were under instructions not to offend an ally whose assistance might be useful to Rome, and at the same time to let the Carthaginians understand that their position was not so secure that they could afford the luxury of indulging in intrigues with Rome's enemies.

During Rome's wars in the east Carthage, whatever may have been her real feelings, behaved like a friend. She offered large quantities of grain to the Roman armies as a gift – the Senate insisted on paying for it – and sent six of her triremes to reinforce the Roman fleet in 191, one of which was lost in the battle of Corycus; and she again supplied the legions with grain at the time of the Third Macedonian War. During these wars, however, Masinissa had also been of assistance to Rome with horsemen and war elephants as well as with supplies; and so in 182, when the Carthaginians again complained that Masinissa had occupied territory which his father had seized and which Syphax had subsequently restored to Carthage, the commission referred the matter to the Senate – and Masinissa was apparently left in possession.

In 172, on the eve of the Third Macedonian War, the Carthaginians complained that Masinissa had seized more than seventy 'towns and forts' in Punic territory and begged the Romans, in short, to come to some final decision on the question of where Carthage's territory ended and Masinissa's began. Masinissa, represented at Rome by his son, the warlike Gulussa, met their charges most adroitly, first by listing the aid which he had already sent (it was by now 171), and then by promising to supply anything further that Rome might require. He went on to accuse the Carthaginians of building warships in order to be in a position to assert their complete independence (the previous year he had accused them of giving secret audience to the envoys of King Perseus). Unfortunately we do not know the outcome of these embassies, but nothing that we do know suggests that the Senate found in favour of Carthage and against Masinissa.

After the battle of Pydna, when an end had been made of the kingdom of Macedon and when a Roman envoy, speaking in the name of the Senate, had ordered King Antiochus IV out of Egypt, Masgaba, Masinissa's son, was one of the host of envoys who came to Rome bearing congratulations on her victory. He rehearsed once more the services that his father had done the Republic, he reminded the Senate that Numidia and everything in it belonged to Rome and that his father was Rome's vassal; and he craved permission for the old man to come to Rome in order to offer a thanksgiving sacrifice to Capitoline Juppiter. He did not labour the point that if the territory of Carthage represented land stolen from the Numidians every fresh acquisition on the part of Masinissa marked the return of Roman property to its rightful owner. Although

Masinissa was not given leave to visit Rome, and a request that a certain Hanno should be included among the Punic hostages held at Rome was turned down, the Senate did come down firmly on the side of the king over the question of the ownership of Emporia. This region was one of the most valuable of Carthage's extra-territorial possessions, and it appears from Livy's account that Masinissa had begun to covet it in the late nineties – although he had recognized Carthage's claim to it not long before. By now he had made himself master of the fertile hinterland with the approval of Rome, but could make no impression on the coastal towns of the Lesser Syrtis, which were well-defended Punic colonies. However in 162 or 161 the Senate ruled in favour of Masinissa in the matter of these towns also, and awarded him five hundred talents in respect of tribute 'owing' to him from the date at which he presented his claim.

There were three factions active in Carthaginian political life by this time. There was the pro-Roman party, which had been in the ascendant since the end of the late war and which still believed that their country's best chance of survival lay in disarming the suspicion and latent hostility of the Romans by friendly acts and prompt obedience to their edicts, however inequitable they might be. A pro-Masinissa party had emerged under the leadership of Hannibal Psar, which took the view that since Carthage was not allowed by the terms of the treaty to beat Masinissa (even if she were able to do so), she would serve her own interests best by joining him. As the industrial, commercial, financial and cultural capital of the new Greater Numidia she could show the Africans the way to become Carthaginians. Lastly there was the old patriotic party, the war party, dormant since Zama, but now reviving and gaining increasing support in the Assembly of the people, the former stronghold of the Barcids. The recrudescence of militarism was encouraged by two considerations. First, that Carthage clearly had nothing to hope for from the Senate's respect for justice, and secondly, that there was no longer any power in the Mediterranean world whose enmity the Romans feared enough to make Carthage worth preserving as an ally, or whose good opinion they valued sufficiently to prevent them from proceeding to extremes against her. Its leaders were Hamilcar the Samnite, whose father or grandfather perhaps campaigned with Hannibal, and Carthalo, the commander of the small mercenary army (boetharch).

Encouraged by Rome's acquiescence in his seizure of Carthage's dependencies Masinissa proceeded to trench upon her territory proper, and it is to be presumed that the senatorial commission of 157 found, as usual, in his favour. Probably in 154, with Rome involved in a serious flare-up in Spain, Carthage for the first time began to hit back. Carthalo was sent to harry Masinissa's settlers on the occupied lands and to stir up their Libyan neighbours against them. In these operations they perhaps had the assistance of a band of Numidians, led by the grandson of Syphax. Masinissa, however, continued to push forward in the valley of the Bagradas and seized the Great Plains and about fifty towns, including Tusca (or Thugga). The Carthaginians complained at Rome, and after a protracted interval another commission was sent to mediate in 153.

The commission included Cato, now over eighty years old. M. Porcius Cato came from Tusculum. He had served in the Hannibalic War, had fought at the Metaurus and had gone to Africa with Scipio as quaestor. He became the political protégé of L. Valerius Flaccus, with whom he held both consulship and censorship, the latter going down in history by reason of its severity. In everything that he said and did Cato showed himself to be an uncompromising champion of tradition: traditional simplicity of life, traditional strictness of morality, traditional moderation and sense of justice, the traditional solidarity of Roman society, of the governing class, of the clan and family. He saw the Greeks and their culture as utterly harmful and corrupting, and would have liked to see Rome disengage herself from close participation in eastern affairs, retaining, in the interest of justice, only her protective rôle. Fair-minded in his attitude towards Macedon and Rhodes, he appears, in his old age at least, to have become obsessed by hatred of Carthage. Maybe it was because he saw that Carthage, by forcing Rome to become a Mediterranean power, had caused her also to abandon her old, simple, rustic ways and embrace the decadence and immorality of the Hellenistic world.

The commission went to the disputed area and asked both parties to submit their respective cases to their adjudication. Masinissa, with past experience to dictate his attitude, at once agreed, but the Carthaginians for the very same reason refused. They said that the matter was not one that admitted of arbitration, involving as it did the simple enforcement of the terms of the treaty. The commission refused to see the matter in this light and returned home. However they took the opportunity of looking carefully about them and noting the visible evidences of prosperity both in the countryside, due to the highly skilled farming methods of the landowners, and in the City itself, where the population had greatly increased since the beginning of the century, as Carthage was no longer able to hive off her surplus citizens onto dependencies. They also observed in the City a great store of shipbuilding material. On his return to Rome Cato commenced his celebrated campaign in the Senate for the destruction of Carthage.

It is not possible to establish with certainty the precise chronology of the next three years, although the order of events seems clear enough. Cato pressed for war on the grounds that Carthage's rearmament threatened Rome's safety. He was opposed by P. Cornelius Scipio Nasica (the grandson of the Gnaeus Scipio who had fought and died in Spain), and as a result another mission was sent to Africa to order Carthage to disarm. It also succeeded in persuading Masinissa to withdraw from at least some part, and very possibly the whole, of the occupied territory. However Prince Gulussa reported to the Senate that Carthage was still recruiting soldiers and building warships, and after Cato and Nasica had again crossed swords over the question of war or peace and after moderate counsels had again prevailed, a fact-finding mission was sent to Carthage. This returned to Rome, accompanied by Carthaginian envoys and Gulussa, probably towards the end of the summer of 152, and reported that Carthage had in fact prepared a fleet and an army. Cato and other leading senators demanded that an army should be sent to Africa at once, but Nasica maintained that Carthage had not yet provided 'a just cause for war'. It was therefore decided that an ultimatum should be sent to Carthage, and that if she disregarded it the next consuls (since 153 the consuls began their term of office on 1 January) should put to the Senate the question of declaring war. Apparently the Carthaginians complied with Rome's demands and war was, for the moment, averted.

However it is clear that Carthage's long patience was at last exhausted. It must have seemed to her, when the Romans compelled Masinissa to give up at least some of his illegal gains, that the tide of senatorial opinion was at length turning in her favour. Then came the demand, at Numidia's insistence, to disarm and, we may be sure, alarming reports of the belligerent attitude of an influential section of the Senate. In 151 Carthage paid the last instalment of her war indemnity and she could now feel truly free and no longer in a sense tributary. The re-emergence of a spirit of national self-reliance – which had, indeed, something of desperation about it – was encouraged by the further circumstance that Masinissa was now eighty-seven years old, and although he still took the field on horseback he could not be expected to last much longer. On his death his kingdom might well disintegrate, and it should not prove beyond Carthaginian diplomacy to sow dissension among his numerous sons and vassals (two of whom did in fact desert him in 150). A violent swing in the political balance at Carthage occurred in favour of the patriotic party; the forty leaders of the pro-Masinissa faction were banished, and the Assembly swore never even to discuss their readmission.

The exiles made their way to Masinissa's court and asked him to reinstate them. The old king sent Micipsa, his eldest son, and Gulussa to Carthage to demand their reinstatement. However the boetharch Hasdrubal refused to admit the princes, and Carthage's bête noire, Gulussa, was attacked on his homeward journey and some of his people were killed. This was a sufficient casus belli for Masinissa, and in the summer of 150 he advanced again into Punic territory and laid siege to the town of Oroscopa.

Although Carthage had been virtually disarmed since 201 she had had some practice recently in raising troops; moreover, as she had now to rely on levies of her own citizens and her Libyan subjects, mobilization was a quicker business than in the days when mercenaries had to be hired overseas. In the autumn of 150 Hasdrubal marched out with 25,000 infantry and 400 knights to relieve Oroscopa, and he was joined by two of Masinissa's cavalry commanders with no fewer than 6,000 of their tribesmen. Masinissa, confident in the hardiness of his Numidians and in their ability to survive and fight on the scantiest rations, retired before him across the frontier into the unfertile regions and camped in a wide plain. Hasdrubal also camped, on higher, defensible ground, his army by now considerably augmented by the number of volunteers who had joined him on his march. However it can scarcely have amounted to the 58,000 men with which Appian credits it – a figure which, if Appian found it in Polybius, may perhaps go back to Masinissa himself.

Hasdrubal had come out to fight – *il faut en finir* was very much the spirit of the Carthaginians in 150 – and when Masinissa offered battle he accepted. The battle lasted all day, with the advantage going to the Numidians, and Hasdrubal retired to his camp. There he learnt that the battle had been witnessed in a spirit of Jovian detachment by a young Roman who had been sent to Masinissa by his commanding officer in Spain, to ask him for elephants. This was P. Cornelius Scipio Aemilianus, son of the Aemilius Paullus who had beaten the Macedonians at Pydna, who had been adopted by Publius Scipio, the son of Africanus. Hasdrubal felt that he had done well enough against Masinissa to convince the old king that it was in the interests of both sides to reach an agreement, and accordingly he asked Scipio to undertake the rôle of peacemaker. The Carthaginians offered, in effect, to make peace on the basis of each party's retaining what it held, recognizing Masinissa's ownership of Emporia and agreeing to pay him an indemnity of a thousand talents. Masinissa, however, demanded in addition the surrender of the deserters, a demand which the dictates of both honour and expediency forbade Hasdrubal to comply with, since he was desperately short of Punic cavalry and had no reason to suppose that Masinissa was to be trusted. Masinissa then threw fieldworks around the hill on which the Carthaginians were camped and set himself to starve the enemy out.

Although his army was in good shape and might very well have effected a successful break-out, Hasdrubal made the fatal error of supposing that his men, with the food that they had brought with them, could outstay Masinissa's tribesmen. Moreover a Roman commission, sent when the news of the outbreak of hostilities reached the city, was on its way. But its instructions were to order a cessation of hostilities only if Masinissa was getting the worst of things. So, with Rome's official encouragement, Masinissa kept the Carthaginian army penned on its hill-top under the remorseless desert sun without shelter and before long without food, until starvation and disease had so wasted its numbers and its strength that further resistance was impossible. The Carthaginians agreed to surrender the deserters, take back into the city the men that they had banished, and pay Masinissa an indemnity of five thousand talents over a period of fifty years. On these terms they laid down their arms – only to be massacred on the orders of Gulussa as they left the camp. So, at least, runs the account that has come down to us in Appian. But in view of the fact that Hasdrubal and certain other magnates escaped, and that we find him, a little later, in possession of an excellent force of cavalry, we may perhaps suspect that he and the 'deserters' broke through Masinissa's cordon after the signing of the agreement, and that Gulussa's 'treachery' was in fact no more than an act of retaliation.

At Carthage a revulsion of opinion followed the news of the disaster. The pro-Roman party recovered their influence; but they realized only too well how desperate the position was. Carthage had broken the treaty of 201, since by the 'close pursuit' of Masinissa across her borders she had made war without Rome's permission; and Rome was legally entitled to declare war upon her in consequence. The Carthaginians at once began to try to disarm Rome's anger. They condemned to death Hasdrubal (who escaped from the City) and Carthalo and other prominent members of the patriotic party, upon whom they threw the whole blame for the war, and they sent envoys to Rome to exculpate themselves and their people. But it was too late. There had been a swing in senatorial opinion at Rome also, and Cato and his friends now commanded a majority in the Senate.

By rearming in contravention of the agreement of 152 and by carrying war across her frontiers – something that went beyond the mere 'repelling of force by force', recognized as the right of every free people by the law of nations, *ius gentium* – Carthage had provided a *casus belli* that even Nasica would have to acknowledge. But by suffering the total loss of her field army and by making submission to Rome she would appear, on the fact of it, to have invalidated the argument employed by Cato, however unrealistic it may appear to us at this distance in time, that she con-stituted a threat to Rome's safety. She had not, in fact, taken up arms against Rome; and the imposition of a heavy indemnity should have been thought sufficient punishment for her offence.

Why then did the Senate fall into line with Cato and his friends and demand her destruction? Commercial rivalry has long since been discre-dited as a motive, nor does it seem that Carthage's territory was an object of desire: it was to be almost thirty years before Rome took any steps to colonize north Africa. We are left with the motives of fear and hatred, and of these there can be no doubt that fear – or, more properly, apprehensiveness – was the predominating factor. Not even Cato can have seriously believed that in 150, even before her defeat by Masinissa, Carthage directly threatened the safety of Rome – even if she was such a close neighbour that Punic figs were still fresh when displayed in the Senate House. Nonetheless she had recently shown a new and disquieting intractability. In 153 she had defied Rome for the first time, over the question of mediation; she had begun to entrust her foreign policy to the militarists; she had started to rearm; and we may be sure that when Cato was in Africa he heard mutterings to the effect that Carthage's patience was exhausted and that she was not going to submit any longer to the encroachments of Rome's favoured ally. She had gone on to offer affront to Masinissa and to break the treaty of 201, and if Masinissa had been defeated and perhaps killed (he was, after all, eighty-eight) and his kingdom thrown into confusion Carthage would certainly have tried to negotiate with Rome from a position of strength.

Another disturbing feature of the situation was that while Rome was experiencing increasing difficulty in finding enough troops to hold down the Spaniards Carthage had raised a force equal at least to a full consular army in a very short time from the population of her own territory, and no senator will have forgotten that it had taken twenty-five legions to contain the menace of Carthage at the height of the Hannibalic War. Masinissa must die soon in any case, and if Carthage succeeded in setting his sons by the ears it was not entirely fanciful to envisage the possibility of the rise of a new Punic empire on the ruins of his kingdom, with the most dire consequences for the future of Rome's position in Spain. Moreover a strong Carthage might still be able to stir up trouble for Rome in Greece and in Asia.

Moderation had been the keynote of Rome's traditional foreign policy, and as a result there was hardly one of her defeated enemies whom she had not been obliged to fight at least a second time. The opinion was gaining ground that Rome had been too generous in the past, and in her treatment of the Epirotes and of the kingdom of Macedon she had already given indications that her patience with treaty-breakers was wearing thin. Carthage had twice already involved her in long and costly wars; it was not to be expected that Rome would give her the chance of doing so a third time.

Yet there was no reason to destroy her. Rome could have established a province of Africa (she had set up no new province for nearly fifty years) and incorporated Carthage in it, stripped of her territory and confined to her peninsula, either as a free city or even as provincial capital. It was, perhaps, some such solution of the problem that Scipio Nasica now favoured. But Carthage was not merely feared: she was also hated. Although there can have been very few senators still alive who had, like Cato, fought against the Barcids, there cannot have been one of them who had not lost a member of his family – in many cases, no doubt, a grandfather or even a father – in that war, and southern Italy still bore the scars of Hannibal's invasion. Scipio Nasica, as steadfast a traditionalist as Cato, might argue that it was actually good for Rome to have a strong Carthage almost on her doorstep, to keep her up to the mark militarily; but the majority of Romans could not discuss Carthage dispassionately. It seemed to them that foreign affairs would be very much simpler, very much less troublesome, if Carthage did not exist. This sentiment was reflected in the wording of Cato's famous dictum as reported by Appian: 'He continually expressed his opinion *that Carthage should not exist.*' Expediency dictated that Rome should take advantage of the crushing defeat inflicted upon her old enemy by Masinissa in order to put it beyond Carthage's power ever to threaten her security again. Hatred, and the desire to settle finally an old score, went one step further and pronounced sentence of destruction.

CHAPTER XXI

149-148 BC

The Third Punic War. Carthage besieged.

Rome's procedure, as F.E. Adcock has said, was Macchiavellian. The Senate had decided upon war but for the time being kept its decision to itself. The Carthaginian envoys, asking how they could make reparation, were told, 'By giving satisfaction to the Roman people.' The Council could make nothing of this reply and sent a further embassy to seek elucidation. The reply was that the Carthaginians 'knew perfectly well' what was required of them. In the meantime Rome began to raise an army, but without disclosing its purpose. It was now 149, and new consuls, L. Marcius Censorinus and Manius Manilius, had entered office. They were political nonentities, Manilius being a 'new man' – a better jurist than soldier – who had suffered defeat in Spain as praetor in 155.

At this juncture, whether or not as the result of secret prompting by the Romans we shall never know, the city of Utica, the 'old town', Carthage's most important but also her most determinedly independent ally, who had, perhaps more out of regard for that independence than from loyalty, resisted all the efforts of the great Africanus to take her at the end of the last century, sent an embassy to Rome and made a formal offer of deditio which was accepted. Utica had never lost her resentment at her eclipse as the leading Phoenician city of north Africa by the upstart 'new town', and once before had offered deditio to Rome, at the height of the Truceless War. To act now as they did the Uticans must have felt very confident that Carthage's days as a territorial power were numbered.

The defection of Utica gave the Romans more than just a first-rate base within thirty miles of Carthage. It gave those senators who had hitherto withheld their open support for Cato's campaign a plausible reason for coming out in favour of it; for now the acquiescence in Rome's African policy of an important African city and ally of Carthage could be adduced at the bar of world opinion to justify Rome's action against her 'enemy'. The Senate now met in solemn conclave on the Capitol and formally voted in favour of war against Carthage.

The Carthaginians had already discussed the advisability of offering deditio, but national pride had made them hesitate in taking so irrevocable a step into the darkness. For they knew as well as anyone that deditio involved 'the voluntary surrender by a State of all its rights and the placing of itself in the power (*potestas* or *dicio*) of another State' (F. E. Adcock). The dediticii – those who had made deditio – were stateless, and the state to which they had made it was bound by no limitation in respect of the action it might take against them. Now the Carthaginians had been deprived by Utica's defection even of the dubious merit of spontaneity in the making of their deditio. But they had no longer any alternative except defiance, and at least Roman custom did not sanction the sack or enslavement of those who had made deditio – although they had departed from this custom in the case of the unhappy Epirotes.

Accordingly the Council, after debating the matter in secret session, sent plenipotentiaries to Rome to do their best for their country. However, the envoys found on arrival that war had been formally declared and that both consuls had sailed for Sicily, Censorinus being in command of the fleet (which included fifty quinqueremes), and Manilius of the army. Appian gives the size of the army as eighty-four thousand men, a figure which, if it has any real significance, can only refer to the size of the expeditionary force as a whole, including naval personnel. In fact it would seem that Manilius had four legions at his disposal – forty to fifty thousand men. The Romans had experienced no difficulty in finding soldiers for what promised to be a short, bloodless and very profitable campaign.

On learning of the army's departure the Carthaginian ambassadors at once offered deditio. The Senate accepted it and promised them 'freedom and autonomy, their whole territory and all their other possessions both public and private' (Polybius): a promise, it should be understood, which represented no more than a statement of intention on the part of the Senate and was in no way legally binding. The legates were further informed that these favours were conditional on their sending to the consuls at Lilybaeum, within thirty days, three hundred hostages, sons of members of the Gerousia (the thirty) and the Council, and obeying the orders of the consuls. The envoys referred these terms to the Council, which accepted them, although with some misgiving on account of the omission of any specific mention in them of the City; for the word rendered above as 'territory' in fact usually connotes countryside as distinct from town.

However it was decided to accept Rome's terms, and three hundred noble hostages were sent to Lilybaeum, amid the grief and despair of their relatives, and from there transferred to the capital, where they were confined in the ship house constructed to accommodate the huge 'sixteen-er' built by Philip v and brought to Rome after Pydna. The Roman army then sailed across to Africa and occupied the Castra Cornelia while the fleet of fifty battleships and many light craft docked at Utica. The Carthaginians, in great perturbation, sent an embassy to the consuls to ask for instructions. Censorinus, who had been fully briefed by the Senate, informed them that they must surrender all their arms and missile weapons. This they agreed to do, although once again with misgiving; for not only did a state of war still exist between themselves and Masinissa but the banished Hasdrubal had collected an army and was camped not far away. The consul replied in language intended to suggest that the protection of Carthage was now Rome's affair and the City handed over its arms, which included no fewer than two hundred thousand complete sets of heavy infantry equipment and two thousand catapults. These were received by two military tribunes, Scipio cousins, and escorted to the Roman camp by the envoys and by a crowd of Carthaginian notables. These were then addressed by Censorinus in the following awful terms: 'Evacuate Carthage and hand it over to us and move your place of habitation inland to any part of your territory that you wish that is [at least] 80 *stades* [that is, ten Roman miles] from the sea; for we have determined to raze the city to the ground' (Appian).

When their first transports of horror and grief had subsided the envoys asked leave to send another embassy to the Senate. Censorinus refused. If we are to believe Appian he told them that it was for their own lasting good that they were being removed both from the sea which tempts nations to crime and so leads them to disaster, and from the City which was the enduring symbol of their former greatness and hence an incitement to revolt. Their temples and their tombs would not be harmed, and they themselves would be much happier as agriculturalists. And as for the argument that a large proportion of their population depended upon the sea for its livelihood, at ten miles' distance they would still be nearer to the sea than Rome.

Censorinus was not peddling heartless sophistries. He was offering a matter-of-fact justification of a policy that he, in common with the majority of senators, had convinced himself was for the ultimate benefit of both parties; while by depriving the populace of the material means of resistance he believed that he had ensured that the destruction of the city could be accomplished without bloodshed on either side. Rome had already employed the transplantation of particularly obstinate adversaries as a humane alternative to wholesale enslavement or slaughter – most recently in Liguria. When the envoys, broken-hearted and despairing, returned to Carthage, the consul brought twenty of his quinqueremes to anchor off the City in the hope of overawing the inhabitants.

When the death-sentence of their City was announced at Carthage the population abandoned themselves to an orgy of despair. Senators of the 'peace party', the envoys, Italian businessmen who had not had the foresight to leave the doomed city, and the gods themselves, were attacked and reviled. A few men kept their heads and closed the city gates and collected heaps of stones upon the walls. When the Council recovered from its initial shock it declared war on Rome and proclaimed the freedom of the slaves whose fate was now bound up with that of the citizens. Hasdrubal, who had already got together an army of between twenty and thirty thousand men, was appointed general in the field, and a message was sent to him asking him to forget bygones in his country's extreme need. A grandson of Masinissa, also a Hasdrubal, was chosen to command inside the City.

A request for a truce, ostensibly in order to enable an embassy to be sent to Rome, was refused; but the consuls, who still hoped that the Carthaginians would realize the hopelessness of their position and surrender the City without fighting, held their hand. They confined their activities to the winning over of certain important east-coast towns, exchanging diplomatic civilities – but no more – with the indignant Masinissa, and taking steps to ensure their food supply. For with Hasdrubal controlling the interior of the country, supplies were more of a problem to the Romans than to the Carthaginians. Now that they had returned to their senses the Carthaginians resolved to die rather than abandon their City, and they took full advantage of the hesitancy of the enemy, turning their temple precincts and other open spaces into workshops and labouring night and day, men and women together, to manufacture arms. The women sacrificed their long, oiled hair to be twisted into ropes to supply the torsion for new catapults.

When it became clear that Carthage was determined to resist, the consuls moved from their base onto the peninsula and assaulted the City. Carthage stood at the eastern end of an isthmus a little less than three miles wide. She was surrounded on three sides by water (today, the bay on the north side is represented by the salt lake of Sebkhet er Riana, while the Lake of Tunis to the south is connected by a ship canal with the sea). On the land side the City was defended by a 'triple wall' running across the isthmus from sea to sea, consisting of a ditch backed by a parapet, with behind them a wall of medium height, and behind that again another, massive wall, forty-five feet high and over thirty feet wide, with battlements above and towers at intervals of two hundred feet. In the thickness of this wall, on two storeys, were stables for 300 war elephants with their fodder rooms below, and, above them, stabling for 4,000 horses and barracks for 24,000 soldiers with store-rooms.

The city wall was single and in at least two places – at the northern and easternmost tips of the city – left a small amount of land unguarded between itself and the water's edge. The weakest part of the whole twenty-two or more miles of fortifications was at the southern tip, at the angle formed by the junction of the 'great' wall and the city wall.

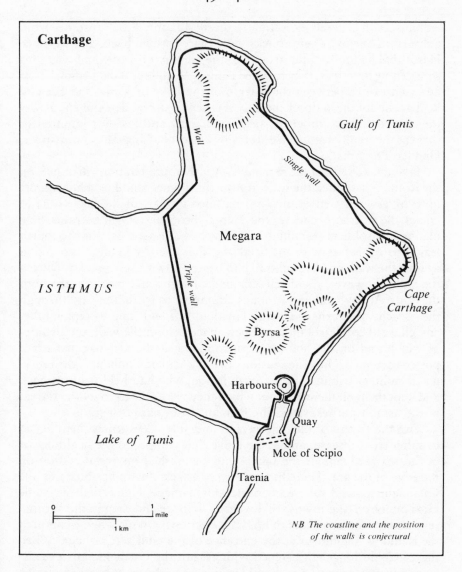

Carthage

Gulf of Tunis

Wall

Single wall

Megara

ISTHMUS

Triple wall

Cape
Carthage

Byrsa

Harbours

Quay

Lake of Tunis

Mole of Scipio

Taenia

0   1
└─────────┘ mile
    1 km

*NB The coastline and the position
of the walls is conjectural*

Here a tongue of land, or rather, a sand-bar (*taenia*), about three hundred
feet wide, even then extended southwards, almost closing off the Lake
of Tunis from the open sea. Clearly the Carthaginians had never envisaged
losing the command of their own coastal waters so completely that an
enemy might be able to attack the walls within catapult-shot of the entrance to their harbour.

It was at this angle that Censorinus directed his attack by land and
sea, while Manilius made a frontal assault on the fortifications of the

isthmus, both generals expecting to meet with only little resistance from a disarmed enemy. Their attacks were twice thrown back, and so, since Hasdrubal had moved his army into the vicinity of Tunis and was thus threatening their rear, they fortified camps, Manilius on the isthmus itself and Censorinus between the margin of the Lake of Tunis and the city wall at the southern tip of the City. He sent a strong detachment across the lake to collect timber for siege appliances and lost five hundred of them as the result of a surprise attack by Hasdrubal's cavalry commander, Himilco Phameas.

Having taken rather more trouble over their preparations than before, the Romans assaulted the walls for the third time. Manilius made almost no progress, but Censorinus, having filled up part of the lake so as to widen the northern end of the taenia, brought two huge rams, one manned by soldiers (Manilius had detached at least a part of the fourth legion to cooperate with the fleet) and the other by sailors, into action against the wall, and by nightfall had beaten down a section of it. During the night, however, the defenders made a sortie and partly burnt both the rams. At daybreak the Romans attempted to storm the City through the breach, which the Carthaginians had not had time to repair fully, and charged recklessly into an open space behind the wall, on all sides of which and on the housetops surrounding it the Carthaginians had posted their men. Only the caution of young Scipio Aemilianus, then serving as military tribune of the fourth legion, who had held his men back and kept them on the wall from which they were able to cover the retreat of the assault parties, saved the Romans from serious loss.

With the advent of the dog-days in mid-July, Censorinus' men began to suffer from disease, and so he moved his camp into the healthier air of the seaward side of the taenia and established his naval station on the edge of the sea. There his ships were attacked with fire-boats by the Carthaginians and suffered considerable damage. He carried out some raids on the coastal towns still loyal to Carthage and then in the autumn returned to Rome in order to hold the elections. On his way he captured the island of Aegimurus at the entrance of the Gulf of Carthage. When they were no longer threatened with assault the Carthaginians became more adventurous and attacked Manilius' camp by night but were driven off by Scipio, who took some horsemen out by the back gate and fell upon the attackers unexpectedly. As a result of this incident Manilius improved the defences of his camp and built a fort on the shore to protect his supply ships. He then led a foraging expedition into the interior, entrusting the raiding parties to the military tribunes; and in this work, too, Scipio distinguished himself by his professionalism. It was noted that he posted his guards and pickets so well that Himilco Phameas never ventured to attack him. After the return of the expedition to the camp the enemy made a night attack upon the waterside fort, and on this occasion Scipio again came to the rescue with his cavalry.

Towards the end of the campaigning season Manilius decided to attack Hasdrubal in his stronghold at Nepheris (Bou-Beker). The Carthaginians were encamped on high ground at the southern end of the triangular, fertile valley that lies some eighteen and a half miles south-east of Tunis. Scipio did not like the look of the place, and when the army reached the steeply banked Wadi-bu-Abid which protected the front of Hasdrubal's position he advised going no further and suggested that, if they had to advance, they should at least fortify a camp on the further side of the river so as to provide a refuge in case of defeat. The feeling of the War Council was against him, however, and Manilius crossed the river. Hasdrubal accepted battle (the Romans were probably superior in numbers) and after some costly fighting withdrew into his strong position; but when he saw the retiring Romans breaking formation in order to effect the difficult crossing of the wadi he attacked them again with devastating effect and only the skill and resolution of Scipio, who covered the crossing with all the horsemen he could collect, prevented a major disaster. As it was four maniples were cut off on the enemy's side of the wadi and were besieged on a hill-top by the Carthaginians.

When the army halted for the night and the loss of these units was discovered it was again Scipio who volunteered to ride back and rescue them; which he succeeded in doing, taking his cavalry around the hills that encompassed the valley and appearing unexpectedly in rear of the enemy, who scattered and made no attempt to interfere with the retirement of the whole body. When he got back to the bivouac he released a prisoner of war and sent him back to Hasdrubal with a request that he would bury the three military tribunes (members of the aristocracy) who had fallen in the fighting by the wadi. The tribulations of the army did not end with their escape from disaster at Wadi-bu-Abid, for Himilco harassed their retreat, and a sortie from the City caused losses among the camp followers as they re-entered their main camp. This was the last military operation of the year, as Manilius now withdrew the legions into winter quarters in Castra Cornelia.

The Romans had been at a disadvantage in the operations in the interior owing to their inferiority to the enemy in cavalry. The Senate therefore decided, after all, to ask Masinissa for aid; but their envoys found him on his deathbed. Having received his kingdom from the hands of Africanus it was to the adoptive grandson of the latter that he turned for advice at the end, and Scipio arrived at Cirta to find that the old man was dead and that he had been appointed his executor. Rome no longer required a strong and centralized Numidia to police Carthage, and Scipio took care to confirm Masinissa's numerous sons, legitimate and illegitimate, in their estates, thus making them in effect vassals of Rome. He divided both the royal power and the royal title between the three eldest surviving legitimate sons. Civil government and the capital, Cirta, were entrusted to Micipsa, the oldest, foreign affairs and the army to Gulussa and the judiciary to Mastanabal, the youngest. Gulussa, no friend of the Carthaginians, at once followed Scipio to the camp with his men, and Scipio and he began to conduct such a diligent and methodical hunt for Himilco's horsemen that Himilco himself put out feelers to discover the nature of his reception at Rome should he decide to change sides.

Manilius, whose imperium had been prorogued, was anxious to have something to show on his return to Rome for his sojourn in Africa other than a defeat, and so he conducted another expedition in the early spring of 148 against Nepheris. This time he did as Scipio had advised and constructed fieldworks that could serve as a refuge, but the only outcome of the operation was the defection to Rome of Himilco together with about 2,200 of his men. On the return of the army to its base, Manilius sent Scipio back to Rome as escort to Himilco and the army gave him an enthusiastic send-off, coupled with good wishes and prayers for his return as general. Himilco was loaded with honours at Rome and returned to Africa to fight against his countrymen.

The year 149, which was also the year of the death of Cato, had ended on a better note for the Carthaginians than they could possibly have hoped for when Censorinus pronounced the doom of their city. Their own patriotic fervour, assisted by the dilatoriness at first and then by the ineffectiveness of the Roman generals, had enabled them to survive the worst period of the siege, while Hasdrubal's success against Manilius in the field left him still master of the open country and able to victual the City without interference during the winter and early spring. Moreover a pretender, Andriscus, had appeared in Macedonia and might be expected to divert some, at all events, of Rome's attention. The consul who came to Africa in the spring of 148, L. Calpurnius Piso Caesoninus, did not seem likely to be a great improvement on Censorinus (his colleague, Sp. Postumius Albinus, remained behind and was active in Gallia Cisalpina). Like Manilius he had suffered defeat in Spain, in 154; nor was he a member of a very distinguished family.

Piso brought with him as commander of the fleet L. Hostilius Mancinus, whether as legate or as propraetor we cannot be certain. The new leaders left both Carthage and Hasdrubal severely alone and confined themselves to attacking her remaining allies and dependencies. A combined assault on Clupea failed, but Neapolis was taken, possibly through treachery, and sacked. They then moved against Hippou Acra (Bizerta), which had been enriching itself in this war by intercepting Roman supply ships bound for Utica and for the camp in front of Carthage. Piso besieged the city, which had been strongly fortified by Agathocles during his campaign in Africa in the late fourth century, but by the end of the summer had failed to take it, having twice had his siege engines burnt in sorties supported by the Carthaginians. He then retired into winter quarters in Castra Cornelia; his campaign having served merely to hearten the enemy, who had been reinforced by a renegade vassal of Gulussa's with eight hundred horsemen.

Indeed at one time the news from Thessaly, where the pretender Andriscus managed to destroy a Roman army, was so encouraging that they sent messages to him, promising him ships and money. Masters of the interior of Libya, they established strongpoints and sought to enlist the support of the natives against the Romans. They also sent embassies to Micipsa and Mastanabal and to the rulers of Mauretania and tried to convince them that they were next on Rome's list for subjugation after Carthage. The Carthaginians had in fact now passed from the depths of despair of the previous year to the opposite extreme of buoyant hopefulness not unmixed with hysteria. For when Hasdrubal, in order to get rid of his namesake who commanded in the City, accused him of planning to betray Carthage to his uncle Gulussa, the councillors fell upon the wretched man and beat him to death with benches.

CHAPTER XXII

147-146 BC

Scipio Aemilianus and the sack of Carthage.

Public disgust at Rome over Piso's lack of enterprise was exploited to the full by the now renascent Scipionic faction. Although Nasica had been defeated in the debate on the future of Carthage he was still highly respected, and was chosen Pontifex Maximus in 150 and sent to Macedonia in an attempt to deal with Andriscus by diplomatic means. Three members of the house had served as military tribunes, and Aemilianus' performance both in Spain, where he won the 'mural' crown, and in Africa had been so outstanding that even Cato – whom, however, he had probably supported politically – had pronounced him, in Homeric language, to be the only sentient person in the army. Full use was made of the praise that the army and the Senate had showered upon him, of the laudatory letters sent by individuals in Africa to influential friends at Rome, and of the fact that he had been awarded the 'siege' crown for his rescue of the beleaguered maniples. His father, Lucius Aemilius Paullus, had been an uncompromising champion of the nobility, but Aemilianus preferred to follow the tradition of his adoptive family and sought to ingratiate himself with the commons. Not surprisingly, therefore, the people, remembering how they had chosen the great Africanus to command in Spain as a private citizen invested with imperium, clamoured for his grandson's appointment to command in Africa. It was widely believed that only a Scipio could take Carthage, and Aemilianus, friend and disciple of the rationalist Polybius, did not neglect to exploit the superstitiousness of his fellow countrymen.

At the elections held in the winter of 148 he was candidate for the curule aedileship, but at the consular elections, which preceded those for the lesser offices, the people – or rather the *centuria praerogativa*, which voted first and by a strange but almost unfailing convention dictated the choice of all the other centuries – insisted on returning Scipio, although he was technically ineligible for election, both because he was too young and because he had not previously held the praetorship. The consul Albinus refused to accept his candidature, and one of the tribunes threatened in return to veto the elections. The people – or in other words the tribunes and those whom they invited to address the meeting –

asserted as a matter of principle that the Roman people had the right
to elect anyone they wished, regardless of laws and regulations. This was,
in fact, a principle that had already been aired – unsuccessfully – this
century, in 184.

Genuine popular enthusiasm allied to the support of the clients and
political allies of two of the most powerful families at Rome lent Scipio
so much political strength that the Senate gave way. It was not prepared
to accept the validity of the disputed principle, but it did agree that the
law (the *lex Villia*) which was the legal stumbling-block should be
suspended for one year. Scipio was duly elected with C. Livius Drusus,
who may have been a kinsman, as his colleague. Drusus would have liked
to cast lots for Africa, but a tribune had the matter referred to the people
and they chose Scipio.

When the great Africanus had threatened to appeal to the people
against the obstructionism of the Senate the tribunes had supported the
Senate. Aemilianus showed how a strong man, enjoying the favour of
the people and backed by the tribunician veto, could defeat senatorial
opposition, even when it had the sanction of the law. It was a lesson
not lost upon his adoptive cousins the Gracchi, nor upon the long line
of demagogues that followed them and paved the way to the principate
of Augustus.

Scipio raised recruits to bring the African legions up to full strength
and received some aid from allied kings and cities to whom he wrote.
He then sailed to Utica. Piso was operating in the interior, but his admiral
Mancinus had observed as he sailed past the city that a part of the wall,
probably in the neighbourhood of Cape Carthage, had been left undefended owing to the natural strength of the position. He improvised
an assault upon it, the enemy, few as they were, made a sortie but were
driven back, and Mancinus with five hundred marines and three thousand
seamen broke into the city through the gate. At nightfall they were in
a strong position but had no food, and no steps had been taken to bring
up reinforcements. Mancinus sent frantic messages to the camp and to
Utica, and about midnight Scipio, who had brought his convoy into land
that same evening, learnt of their plight. He did not waste a moment.
He collected his own forces, sent urgent despatches to Piso recalling him
and released captive Carthaginians, to spread the news in the town that
Scipio was coming. At daybreak the Carthaginians attacked Mancinus'
men and had driven them back onto the wall and were preparing to sweep
them into the sea when Scipio's ships arrived, the decks packed with
soldiers to create the impression of a strong relief force. The Carthaginians were daunted by the spectacle and allowed Mancinus to get his
men away to the safety of the ships.

Mancinus now returned to Rome, and his place as admiral was taken by Sex. (or M.) Atilius Serranus. Scipio moved the army closer to Carthage and the Carthaginians also fortified a camp in front of their walls, so as to keep open their communications with Tunis. Hasdrubal, having got rid of his rival, brought six thousand infantry and one thousand cavalry under Bithyas into this camp and assumed the overall command of the Punic forces. Scipio's first concern was to restore discipline in the legions which had fallen off badly under the lax and ineffectual command of Piso. He scoured the camp of a great mass of camp followers and put the troops back on plain army rations. In this as in all his actions up till now, whether as a subordinate or as a supreme commander, he displayed the same professionalism as his great namesake.

He had not been regarded, like Africanus, as an exceptional young man, but being the heir to the two greatest military reputations of the age he had sedulously schooled himself to be worthy of them. He possessed and cultivated many soldierly virtues: courage, intelligence, organizational ability, prudence and an understanding of the working of the human mind – and of all these he had already given proof. Even if he did not have such a truly noble nature as Africanus he was still one of the outstanding Roman magnates of his time, and for all his phil-Hellenism and his rationalism he respected the traditional virtues of his people as much as Nasica or Cato himself.

Scipio had already made up his mind to lay vigorous siege to Carthage, and as a preliminary to this, as soon as he had restored the fighting efficiency of his army, he determined to remove Hasdrubal from his entrenched position on the isthmus. A frontal assault might have been a long and costly business and Scipio could afford neither failure nor a half-success that could be represented as a failure by his enemies at home. Accordingly he decided to deal with Hasdrubal indirectly. He made a night attack on the Megara, the extensive suburb that lay to the west of the City, mainly occupied by gardens and orchards and crossed by numerous irrigation ditches. It looks as if he skirted the northern angle of the triple line of defences and directed his attack against two sections of the single wall at a part of the circuit where the sea did not come up to its foot. The assault on the fortifications was not pressed home, but by occupying a 'tower' (perhaps a tall house) standing close to the wall, which the enemy had unaccountably neglected to demolish, Scipio succeeded in getting a number of picked men across on planks onto the top of the wall, and these then opened a gate and admitted their general and four thousand men into the City.

No general of Scipio's well-attested caution would have supposed that he could take Carthage with four thousand men; and the fact that Scipio did not have his whole army in position to exploit the break-in at first light shows that the operation had quite another purpose. It was in fact intended to achieve what it did achieve: it created such panic in the City that Hasdrubal abandoned his advanced camp and brought his men inside the walls in order to destroy or at least to repulse the invaders. Scipio did not wait for him, nor did he advance far into the Megara because of the nature of the ground, but withdrew before the enemy should discover the smallness of the assault force, and launch a counter-attack.

Hasdrubal vented his fury on his Roman prisoners, whom he brought out onto the walls and tortured in full view of their comrades. This piece of brutality was not uncalculated, however, for it must have appeared to him that his countrymen's resolution needed stiffening, in view of their panic in the night. Scipio brought the rest of his army up, destroyed Hasdrubal's abandoned camp and at once began digging a trench across the isthmus from sea to sea, only a spear's throw from the outer defences of the City, which was completed in spite of all the efforts of the enemy. Another ditch was then dug parallel to the first, some little way behind it, and the two were connected at each end by cross-ditches. Behind the ditch facing Carthage he built a wall twelve feet high with parapets and towers; the central tower was built tall enough to enable a watch to be kept on what was going on in the City. The other ditches were palisaded and all were filled with sharpened stakes. Thus Carthage was completely cut off from the interior, while the Roman army, camped within the huge rectangle, which had been completed in twenty days and nights of unbroken work, was secure from attack from the direction either of the City or of Nepheris.

Scipio's siege-works sealed the fate of Carthage. Her city population had been greatly swollen by the influx of refugees from the countryside, and the only supplies reaching the City now from the outside world were those brought in by sea, either sent by Bithyas, who had been on a foraging expedition with the cavalry when Scipio walled off the isthmus, or brought in by occasional blockade-runners; for the nature of the coast and the shortcomings of ancient warships prevented the Roman fleet from maintaining a blockade that was totally effective. Hasdrubal, whose treatment of the war prisoners had been denounced in the Council, had reacted by assuming what amounted to a military dictatorship. He initiated a reign of terror, executing some of those who had protested, and he instituted a system of food control by which all supplies brought into the docks were distributed among his thirty thousand soldiers, with the exception – according to his detractors, at least – of such luxuries as he kept back for his own sumptuous dinner parties. Although Carthage must have been able to produce quite a lot of food within the immense circuit of her walls, hunger soon began to make itself felt. Moreover the situation abroad, which had looked deceptively promising early in 147, now offered nothing to inspire hope. Andriscus, the pretender in Macedonia, had been put down, and the rulers of Numidia had made no move to change their allegiance. Nonetheless there was no thought of surrender, and in the secrecy of the circular naval harbour they built triremes from whatever timber they had left.

It became clear to Scipio that enough food was still coming into Carthage by sea to enable the defenders to prolong the siege if not indefinitely at all events well beyond the end of the year; and, since he was not the man to wait on events if he could anticipate them by action, he decided that having walled Carthage off from the land he would wall her off from the sea as well. The port area of Carthage comprised, probably since the end of the fourth century, two interconnected artificial docks: a circular naval dockyard and, to the south of it, a rectangular mercantile dock, today represented by shallow lagoons. The entrance common to both was at the southern end of the commercial dock, facing south, and it was protected on the seaward side by a massive quadrilateral structure whose western side adjoined the city wall and which, projecting well beyond the harbour mouth, served the dual purpose of breakwater and fair-weather commercial quay, providing moorings for merchantmen along its outer face. The naval dockyard was hidden from prying eyes behind a double wall and was surrounded by galley houses and magazines. In the centre of the basin stood a conical, man-made island, also surrounded by ship houses, with the admiralty building at its centre, from which the admiral could issue his orders by trumpet and proclamation and see for himself that they were carried out. Ionic columns stood at each side of the lower end of each ship house, and gave the appearance of continuous colonnades surrounding the dock and the island. The naval harbour provided accommodation for 220 war galleys.

Scipio's plan was to build a mole from the taenia, on which, like Censorinus, he had established his naval station, across the mouth of the harbour to join the south-west face of the great 'quadrilateral'. The mole was constructed of heavy stones, it was ninety-six feet wide at the bottom and twenty-four at the top, and every available man, including the crews of the ships, was put to work on it, labouring day and night in shifts. When the Carthaginians awoke to the realization that this apparently fantastic undertaking was actually going to be successfully completed, they too began to work day and night, women and children as well, to dig out a new entrance to the harbour on the side facing the open sea, beyond the reach of any mole that Scipio could build. They managed to do this without arousing the suspicion of the Romans, and when everything was ready the fleet which they had built in secret sailed out by the new opening, fifty triremes strong, with a swarm of light craft accompanying it. Nothing indeed that the Carthaginians could have done now could have saved them from ultimate destruction, but if their ships had been under the command of a bold and resolute man they could have inflicted a disaster upon the unmanned and helpless Roman fleet that would have delayed their downfall and perhaps even given them the satisfaction of depriving Scipio of his triumphal wreath.

However the Punic admiral was content merely to parade his strength before the enemy and to give his untrained crews a little practice at sea before returning to port. Three days later, having completely forfeited the element of surprise, he came out again, and by this time the Romans were ready for him. The Carthaginians, who had not fought at sea for forty-four years, did well enough against Serranus' larger galleys to have earned a drawn battle, helped as they were by the activities of their small craft; and in the late afternoon they broke off the engagement and retired towards the harbour entrance. Here, however, their lack of training and experience proved disastrous, for the light craft blocked the opening in their undisciplined haste to get inside, and the triremes were forced to take refuge against the outer quay with their bows facing seawards to meet the attacks of the enemy. The quadrilateral had been fortified with a wall during the course of the present war in order to deny it to the Romans, and Serranus' men were met by a fierce resistance from ships, quayside and wall. At last five galleys from Side in Pamphylia (soon to become one of the principal pirate strongholds in the eastern Mediterranean) which had come as a gesture of friendship towards Scipio, showed the Romans how to use their stern anchors to warp themselves back out of reach of the Punic rams when they had delivered their attack, and by nightfall the survivors of the battle were glad to be allowed to retire under cover of darkness into the inner harbour.

Next day Scipio moved rams and other siege engines along the mole and attacked the wall of the quadrilateral where the mole abutted on it, and by nightfall had destroyed part of it. That night a band of Carthaginians waded and swam naked across to the taenia where the engines were parked and set fire to them, producing a panic in the Roman camp that required all Scipio's resoluteness and ruthlessness to allay. The damage to the wall was made good and wooden towers were added to the defences; but the Romans attacked again with new siege engines, set fire to the towers and drove the enemy from the wall, and so gained possession of the whole quadrilateral. They dug a ditch and built a brick wall parallel to the wall of the City and of the same height and this was manned by four thousand men who were able to harass the Carthaginian defenders with missile weapons.

In order to deprive the Carthaginians of their last sources of supplies and also to give his army some active employment during the winter Scipio decided to break the enemy's hold upon the interior. Various detachments were sent out to scour the country while Scipio moved against Nepheris, taking part of his forces across the Lake of Tunis while his legate C. Laelius, son of the Laelius who had served under Africanus, marched by land. Nepheris was now held by Diogenes, presumably a Greek mercenary captain. Scipio fortified a camp in front of Diogenes' position and left Laelius and Gulussa to soften up the enemy, while he returned to supervise the progress of the operations against the capital. When a sufficiently large stretch of the wall of the Punic camp had been destroyed Scipio, who had been backwards and forwards in the meantime, returned and assumed command of the assault. He stationed a thousand picked men in rear of the enemy, and at the height of the frontal attack delivered by successive waves of infantry these broke into the camp from the back. The camp was abandoned amid complete panic, and Gulussa with his elephants and cavalry hunted down those fugitives who did not escape to the town of Nepheris. The siege of this place, conducted under wintry conditions, lasted twenty-two days. Following the destruction of the Carthaginian field army the rest of Libya was easily subjugated, and the City was now wholly deprived of outside aid, since navigation came virtually to a stop during the stormy season. Famine soon made itself felt, and every day numbers of people died or deserted to the enemy. Even before winter had set in Hasdrubal had attempted, through Gulussa, to obtain terms of surrender, but even if Scipio had wished to show mercy, he had his instructions from the Senate; and Hasdrubal, at this stage, still had the spirit to reject an offer of safety limited to himself and his family and the families of ten of his friends.

The consular elections at Rome made no difference to Scipio's position which may, indeed, have been secured by the law which gave him his command, so that it would have required a significant defeat to bring about his recall. His imperium was prorogued and at the beginning of spring, by which time hunger and hopelessness had worn down the resistance of the defenders, he mounted the final assault upon the doomed city.

The attack was directed against the harbour area from the foothold which the Romans had secured, the previous autumn, on the quadrilateral. Among the first men over the wall was the sixteen-year-old Ti. Sempronius Gracchus, a blood-relation and cousin by adoption of the commander-in-chief; Scipio himself entered the City through a gate. In desperation Hasdrubal set fire to the area between the wall and the commercial docks in order to prevent the Romans from advancing, but in the confusion Laelius got some of his men onto the wall that surrounded the naval harbour and the defenders, hungry and dispirited, concluded that the position was taken. But Laelius' achievement acted on the Romans as a spur to yet greater effort. They threw disused rams, balks of timber and scaffold poles into the space between their own wall and the enemy's,

scrambled across, stormed the defences and by nightfall were in possession of the marketplace to the north of the harbour area and the New
City. At first light Scipio brought in four thousand fresh troops, but at
the sight of the temple of Resheph (Apollo) with its treasures of gold,
a thousand talents' weight, their discipline broke down and the advance
against the citadel was held up while the soldiers hacked image and shrine
to pieces with their swords and divided the spoils among them.

Most of the defenders of the City had retreated to the Byrsa, the citadel
hill which rose to the west of the marketplace. Three streets of tall
apartment blocks, up to six storeys high, climbed its lower slopes, and
from their rooftops desperate men were prepared to contest every foot
of the ascent by hurling missiles down onto those below. This was not
the first time that these houses had been used in street fighting: Bomilcar's
followers had been pelted from them when he tried to make himself tyrant
in 308. Now the Romans began to fight their way towards the citadel,
breaking into and clearing the tall buildings one by one, entering those
further up the slope by means of plank bridges laid from the roofs of
those already taken; while in the streets below a bloody hand-to-hand
struggle raged, until the attackers had hacked their way to the foot of
the wall that encircled the Byrsa itself. Then, in order to be able to bring
up all his forces and all the engines that he needed to breach the wall,
Scipio gave the order – which he had not been able to give until then,
with his own men fighting on the rooftops – to clear the whole quarter
between the citadel and the main square by burning the houses and level-
ling the ruins to the ground.

For six days and nights of horror the conflagration raged and the work
of destruction continued. Many of the buildings, not demolished piecemeal but sent crashing down in their entirety, were still occupied, for
the most part by those who are usually the greatest sufferers in all such
disasters, the weakest elements – old men, women and young children
– who fell shrieking into the flames or onto the rubble beneath. Those
who had been told to clear the streets and level the ruins had neither
the time nor, in the general frenzy of activity and fog of war, were they
disposed to listen to the voice of humanity and to distinguish the living
and the half-dead from the dead, but threw the bodies indiscriminately
along with other débris into the holes in the ground as they laboured
to smooth the approaches to the wall. The troops worked in relays; only
the general allowed himself neither rest nor sleep as he hurried on the
terrible work; until at last, quite exhausted, he withdrew to a hill-top,
probably the so-called Hill of Juno, from which he could overlook the
whole operation.

He was found there by suppliants carrying olive branches from the
precinct of Eshmun (Asclepius) who begged merely for the lives of those

beleaguered in the citadel. Scipio granted their request, and fifty thousand men and women came out by a narrow gate in the wall and were put under guard until such time as they could be sold. Now only nine hundred or so Roman deserters, who had (as was customary) been excluded from the agreement, remained behind, together with Hasdrubal and his family; and for a while they resisted all the enemy's attempts to storm the precinct of Eshmun which rose above its flight of sixty steps to crown the summit of the Byrsa.

But not even the courage of utter desperation could hold out indefinitely against hunger, weariness, lack of sleep and odds of more than forty against one. They fled at last to the temple building and crowded onto its roof – all, that is, except Hasdrubal. Not for him the legendary self-immolation of Hamilcar the Magonid in the hour of defeat at Himera, or the hero's death of Hasdrubal Barca by the Metaurus. This Hasdrubal was not cast in the heroic mould. Admittedly there was nothing that he – nothing that even Hannibal – could have done that would have saved Carthage from ultimate destruction once the Romans had made up their minds to destroy her. But he might at least have lived up to his arrogant words uttered the preceding autumn to Scipio, that 'for patriots their fatherland and the flames that consume her are a glorious winding-sheet'.

Now the red-faced, pot-bellied general, who had swaggered like a stage tyrant in full armour and a purple cloak, threw himself at Scipio's knees and begged for his life. The deserters on the roof of the temple shouted to the advancing Romans to hold off and Scipio gave the order to his men. Then in the sudden silence they began to heap the vilest abuse upon Hasdrubal for his cowardice and for having broken his oath not to desert them. The final tragic touch was contributed by his wife, who appeared before the doors of the temple arrayed in her finest garments and embracing her children. Then, after reproaching him for his desertion of them and reviling him for his unmanliness, she turned and plunged with them into the flames which the deserters had kindled and which were already consuming the temple and its occupants.

Carthage was wholly Scipio's now, and he handed it over to his army to be plundered, reserving for the state the gold and silver and all objects dedicated to the gods (the units that had sacked the temple of Resheph were punished by being deprived of military honours and awards). In the magnificent manner of his father Paullus, Scipio took nothing for himself. The Sicilian communities were invited to identify and claim the national treasures looted by the Carthaginians in earlier wars, and among the objects restored was the infamous Bull of Phalaris, in which the tyrant of Acragas used to roast his enemies alive. When the news of the victory reached Rome, the Senate despatched the customary commission of ten to 'advise' (the senatorial euphemism for instruct) the proconsul in his settlement of what became the Roman province of Africa comprising about five thousand square miles of ex-Carthaginian territory.

The City itself was utterly demolished and although the site was not cursed a curse was invoked upon anyone who should build on it. The towns that had supported Carthage to the end were also destroyed, while those that had assisted Rome were rewarded. Utica was particularly well treated, receiving all the land between Hippou Acra and Carthage and becoming, as a free city, the seat of the Roman praetorian administration, and for a while the most prosperous city in Roman Africa. The rest of the former territory of Carthage became Roman public land. The ban on the redevelopment of the site of the City did not prevent the attempt by C. Gracchus, only twenty-three years later, to found the colony of Junonia on suburban soil, although this attempt was utilized by his political enemies to bring about his downfall; and it was also ignored by both Julius Caesar and Augustus. By the second century AD Carthage was again the capital of Africa – of Roman proconsular Africa – and by the third century she was a bastion of Christianity. After that she was successively the capital of a Vandal kingdom and the seat of a Byzantine provincial administration. In 697 she fell to the Saracens and so passed out of the history of the ancient world.

The analogy between the Punic Wars and a grandiose theatrical presentation is a somewhat obvious one: The Fall of Carthage was a tragedy in three acts, fulfilling many of the Aristotelian requirements. The subject undoubtedly has grandeur. The leading characters were of more than ordinary stature; the catastrophe was the logical outcome of the preceding action; and the audience were purged by pity and fear – although, being for the most part Hellenic or Hellenized peoples, they found that their sympathy was divided and hence their emotional response affected by the fact that on an adjacent stage the tragedy of The Sack of Corinth and the Enslavement of Greece was also reaching its dénouement. The analogy holds good in another and historically important respect: namely that the catastrophe was in great measure due to a flaw in the character of the tragic victim. Throughout the entire 118 years of the Punic Wars the Carthaginians never perceived – or never acted on the perception – that a war against Rome could not be won unless they abandoned the thinking habits of the marketplace.

Adherence to these habits had helped them to build up their commercial and maritime empire. They appraised each situation in terms of economic cost, expenditure, profit and loss. These were the considerations that operated in their dealings with barbarians (although by no means xenophobic they were contemptuous of subject and less advanced races, and were bad 'colonial' masters) and their contact with the Greeks, with their interest in trade and their limited resources, encouraged them to believe that this approach was universally valid. The rulers of Carthage identified the interests of the community with their own single-minded pursuit of wealth and comfort, from which the community, and their allies, reaped material benefits. They closed their eyes to the importance of imperial insurance; to the economically unpalatable truth that however 'unproductive' a navy might be it was to their navy, in the final analysis, that they owed their wealth, their power and their security. 'When a strong man armed keepeth his court, the things that he has are at peace; but when a stronger than he cometh upon him ...' The Carthaginian nobles could not enter into the mind of an aristocracy which identified the interest of the community with the pursuit of glory – and carried its people and its allies along with it.

So in 264 Carthage embarked upon a limited war in order to keep the Romans out of a market which for a century and a half she had endeavoured to control; and what had begun as an affair of imperial outposts developed into a conflict of empires because the Romans did not have the habit of counting costs. The rulers of Carthage allowed Hannibal to involve them in what they supposed would be primarily a defensive war for the protection of their economic interests in Spain, with the further possibility of recovering their valuable province of Sardinia. As businessmen their instincts were correct in urging them to concentrate their resources upon the essential task of preserving Spain, as rulers of an empire they failed to realize that he who holds a wolf by the tail should not dissipate his energies in other directions. Even Hannibal, though an uncharacteristic Carthaginian, misjudged the strength of Italian feeling because it was so very different from Libyan and Iberian feeling, and did not see that by striking at the economy of Rome's allies he only welded the majority of them closer to her.

At the end, Carthage made the fatal mistake of failing to gauge the inveteracy of Rome's malevolence towards her. For her own part national animosities were laid aside when she surrendered her empire; she asked for nothing better than amicable, and profitable, relations with Masinissa and with Rome. When at last, goaded beyond further endurance, she defied Rome (trusting perhaps in the protection of the gods to whom, for over six and a half centuries, she had been accustomed to sacrifice the best of her children in the fires of Moloch) she was unaware that she was giving to a mortal enemy the excuse that he had been looking for not simply to punish but to destroy her.

The moral factor in war is to the material in the ratio of three to one: Pericles knew it and Napoleon said it. In Carthage's case the unwillingness of rulers and people alike to make the sacrifices, physical and economic, that would have to be made if an adversary such as Rome was to be defeated meant that she opposed Rome with only a part of her strength as well as with only half a heart. The Barcas alone brought to the struggle a single-mindedness and a will to win that matched Rome's; but neither to Hamilcar nor to Hannibal did Carthage give the support that might have secured him the victory.

Yet it was owing to the Barcas that after 238 Rome's relations with Carthage were what they were. Of course we cannot say that without Hamilcar's militarism and Hannibal's calculated provocation Rome either would or would not have invaded Spain, nor can we say, in either case, what her relations with Macedon and Syria would have been. All that we can say for certain is that things would have happened differently. But it was Hannibal who embarked upon an unlimited war that was beyond Carthage's power to win unless she was prepared to mobilize all the resources of her empire as Rome did. He embarked on it not without consideration of the cost or of the profit that victory would bring, but thinking principally of the glory that would be his and the vengeance that would be his country's. He trusted to his own genius and to the favour of the Ba'als and to so great a moral superiority over the general run of his enemies that only fools and heroes ventured to face him in battle. And it was Hannibal, an exotic portent, closer by far in spirit to Alexander the Great, to Pyrrhus and to Scipio than to the Hannos and Hasdrubal Gisgonises, who by defeating Rome's armies, enticing away her allies and publicly proclaiming his intention of destroying her hegemony of Italy, inflicted such wounds upon her pride that only the utter destruction of the City that had given him birth could in the end assuage the desire for vengeance of the Senate and the people.

Her conqueror wept as he watched the final destruction of the City. He was weeping, as he explained to his friend and mentor Polybius, over the mutability of Fate, the perishability of all earthly things and the fear that one day Rome herself might be destroyed as Carthage was being destroyed. He might perhaps have spared a tear for the needlessness of her destruction. The Romans could well have afforded to leave her in peace on her peninsula, stripped of her territorial possessions, a free city, entering upon the last phase of her life as she had entered upon the first, entrepôt and mass producer of trade goods for the Libyans and eastern Numidians. The Carthaginians were hardly an attractive people. They did not have it in them to be the standard-bearers of a higher civilization. Selfish, parasitic, money-grubbing, corrupt and, when it cost them nothing, oppressive, they could never have provided the means by which all that was best in Hellenic culture, supplemented and reinforced by what was best in their own, could be disseminated over so much of Europe, Asia and Africa itself, providing the foundation for the far loftier moral edifice of Christendom. It was beneficial for humanity that Rome was able to survive the assault of Hannibal, who for all his greatness came only to destroy; and what he would have destroyed was the future of western civilization.

For nearly four hundred years Carthage had dominated the western Mediterranean, yet her disappearance left a far smaller hole in the fabric of Mediterranean civilization than her long history, her political and military strength, and her vast wealth might have led one to expect. It is true that by her colonies and her example she promoted the development of urban civilization in Spain and in north Africa, and that in Africa the Phoenician language and religion persisted long after her fall, and the African towns perpetuated her culture and institutions into Roman imperial times. Yet it was the native princes, not Carthage, that weaned the nomads away from their primitive ways, and the high civilization of both north Africa and Spain was the gift of Rome. If Carthage had not existed, or if she had not become powerful in the sixth century BC, the Greeks would undoubtedly have taken over the western Mediterranean basin, with consequences both for Greece herself and for the history of Europe which can only be conjectured. Indeed, far from deliberately furthering the advance of civilization she did her best to check it, for it suited her purpose better to have backward peoples to trade with than developed ones. Nor was she a contributor, either creatively or as a patron, to the arts and to literature, although her aristocracy was the wealthiest and most leisured in the Mediterranean: the Carthaginians valued such things only for what they would fetch in the marketplace. The conqueror of Carthage carried back to Rome no such profusion of artistic treasures as were looted from Syracuse, Taras and Corinth – only a certain weight of silver and a handbook on farming for profit.

Hannibal is one of history's outstanding characters and it is right that Carthage should today be remembered chiefly as his birthplace. Her philosophy of life was too selfish and too materialistic to have left much room for glory or for regret. Yet there is a grandeur about the refusal of her people at the very end to abandon the City that had given them so much security, so much prosperity and so much comfort. And it was right dramatically that Carthage's valediction should have been pronounced by a woman – who might be described as the queen of the City, since her husband was its tyrant – amid the flames that engulfed the spot where, more than six and a half centuries earlier, Queen Dido had offered sacrifice for the prosperity of the New Town that she had just founded.

APPENDIX

The Roman constitution.

Rome – like Carthage but unlike most Greek cities – did not have a written constitution. By 264 BC the constitution, which had evolved in the course of the Struggle of the Orders between the old hereditary aristocracy (patricians) and the commons (plebeians), was virtually complete, and followed the general pattern of ancient constitutions: magistrates, Council and popular Assembly.

The Magistrates

Executive power, including the initiative in legislation, rested with the consuls, or in default of consuls, with the praetors, annually elected by the whole people, in practice (though not in theory) from the upper classes and normally from the new hereditary aristocracy of office, the nobility (*nobilitas*).

The consuls (two) were heads of state, chairmen of the Senate and commanders-in-chief of the armed forces. The praetors (two, later four) were primarily judges, and later provincial governors. The censors (two) were normally ex-consuls and were elected every four years (in theory), to assign every citizen to his proper social class and group (tribe and century), and to appoint the senators. They also had extensive 'censorial' and financial duties.

A dictator might in an emergency be nominated by a consul on the recommendation of the Senate, in order to concentrate the executive power of the state in one pair of hands. The dictator appointed his master of horse (second-in-command), and their tenure of office was limited to six months.

Lesser magistrates, also annually elective, were (in descending order) the aediles (four), who looked after Rome, the tribunes of the plebs (ten), who were supposed to be the watchdogs of the people's rights, and the quaestors, of whom two administered the treasury at Rome and the others were attached to the consuls and later to provincial governors, to assist them, especially in financial matters.

The Senate

This was nominally composed of three hundred men, 'the best of each order'. In practice, although not in theory, senators held office for life unless they disgraced themselves. In theory the Senate was the advisory body, only, to the magistrates, but in practice it was the government. It virtually controlled both elections and legislation, and in it the influence of the nobility predominated. By the end of the third century the Senatorial Order was recognized as the hereditary ruling class.

The Assemblies

The people (*populus*) was theoretically sovereign. Every full citizen had a vote in at least two, and in most cases three, forms of popular Assembly. However, as the voting in all Assemblies, whether electoral or legislative, was by component groups (tribes or centuries) and not by heads, the aristocracy was usually able to secure the vote that it wanted.

The great Assembly of all citizens, voting by centuries (according to wealth), the centuriate Assembly, was presided over by consuls (or dictator or praetor). It elected the consuls, praetors and censors, and approved or rejected, without power of debate or amendment, important bills (concerned with such matters as war and peace) laid before it after prior consideration and approval by the Senate.

The Assembly of the plebeians by tribes (*concilium plebis*), from which patricians were excluded, was presided over by tribunes. It elected the tribunes and the plebeian aediles (two), and could legislate, without needing the approval of the Senate, for the whole community.

There was also an Assembly of the whole people by tribes, which had legislative power and elected the curule (originally, patrician) aediles (two) and the quaestors. This Assembly and the centuriate Assembly also acted as popular courts. The voting in all the Assemblies was normally influenced by the patron–client relationship that existed between the great families and the common people.

SELECT BIBLIOGRAPHY

ASTIN, A.E. *Scipio Aemilianus* (Clarendon 1967).
BADIAN, E. *Foreign clientelae* (Clarendon 1958).
BRUNT, P.A. *Italian manpower* (Clarendon 1971).
CARSON, R.A.G. *Principal coins of the Romans*, vol. I (British Museum Publications 1978).
DECRET, F. *Carthage, ou l'empire de la mer* (Edn du Seuil, Paris 1977).
DE SANCTIS, G. *La Storia dei Romani* (Turin–Florence, 1907–23, 1953).
HARDEN, D. *The Phoenicians* (Thames & Hudson 1962).
PROCTOR, D. *Hannibal's march in history* (Clarendon 1971).
SCULLARD, H.H. *Scipio Africanus: soldier and politician* (Thames & Hudson 1970).
   Roman politics: 220–150 BC (Clarendon 1951).
   The elephant in the Greek and Roman World (Thames & Hudson 1974).
THIEL, J.H. *A history of Roman seapower* (North Holland Publishing Co., Amsterdam 1946).
   Roman seapower before the Second Punic War (North Holland Publishing Co., Amsterdam 1954).
TOYNBEE, A.J. *Hannibal's legacy* (Oxford University Press 1965).
WALBANK, F.W. *A historical commentary on Polybius* (Clarendon 1957–79).
WARMINGTON, B.H. *Carthage* (Penguin Books 1964).

LAZENBY, J.F. *Hannibal's War* (Aris & Phillips 1978), appeared too late to be consulted in the preparation of this book.

An exhaustive list of articles dealing with the period of the three Punic Wars may be found in the bibliographies of the three volumes of F.W. Walbank's Historical Commentary on Polybius. In particular I should like to mention those by F.E. Adcock, P.A. Brunt, F. Hampl and W. Hoffman.

GLOSSARY

Augur The *augures* were a college of sixteen diviners, who determined whether or not the gods approved of a public act.

Equites A general term for cavalrymen, but also used to designate the aristocracy from whom the cavalry was drawn. At Rome, by the end of the third century BC, the terms *equites* and Equestrian Order were applied to the business and capitalist class, to distinguish it from the Senatorial Order, the hereditary governing class.

Imperium A word for which there is no precise equivalent in English, connoting the power – as distinct from competence or authority – of a dictator, consul, or praetor.

Interrex If, as the result of the deaths or abdication of both consuls, there was no magistrate to hold elections, an *interregnum* was declared by the Senate and a series of senators – *interreges* – were appointed, each for five days, to prepare and hold consular elections.

Legion This term, strictly applicable only to the citizen contingent, is usually applied to the whole body of infantry, at least half of them allies, that formed the basis of the Roman army organization. The normal legion of 8,400 men included 2,400 light-armed skirmishers and to it were attached 1,200 horsemen, 900 of them allies. The heavy infantry were divided into 30 maniples, which were drawn up in three lines – *hastati, principes, triarii* – in chequerboard formation.

Libyphoenician A convenient term that embraces the coastal towns of north Africa – Punic, Afro-Punic and punicized African.

Novus homo New man. One whose family had not previously held the consulship (sometimes held to apply to one whose family had not held any office with imperium).

Proletarii Members of the lowest census class at Rome. In emergencies they might be conscripted and armed by the state – particularly for sea service.

Prorogue Prorogation of imperium was an expedient by which the imperium of a magistrate was extended for one or more years after the expiration of his tenure of office. Prorogued imperium could only be exercised in a specific province. Holders were styled pro-consul, pro-praetor.

GLOSSARY

Quinquereme Or *penteres* (Greek). A 'fiver', the standard battleship of the Hellenistic era, developed from the classical trireme. Larger and more powerful, it had a crew of three hundred (two hundred in a trireme); but there is no firm agreement among historians as to the number of oars or disposition of the rowers.

Socii Allies. Autonomous allied communities. The Italian allies supplied at least half Rome's troops, and the *socii navales* supplied ships, and later seamen, for the navy.

Spolia opima The spoils that a Roman general might offer who had killed the leader of the enemy in single combat. In Marcellus' case they were *spolia prima*, offered to Juppiter Feretrius.

Talent A Greek measure of wealth, containing sixty *minae* and six thousand *drachmae*, used in assessing very large amounts of coin and bullion.

Tributum A direct tax imposed on Roman citizens to meet the cost of a war. Repayable from the spoils or indemnity.

Triumph The triumphal procession, from the Campus Martius through the Forum to the Capitol, granted by the Senate to a Roman general who had defeated a foreign enemy, slain at least five thousand of their men, and brought his army back to Rome.

INDEX

301